The age of internationalism and Belgium, 1880–1930

MANCHESTER
1824

Manchester University Press

The age of internationalism and Belgium, 1880–1930

Peace, progress and prestige

Daniel Laqua

Manchester University Press

Published by Manchester University Press
Altrincham Street, Manchester M1 7JA, UK
www.manchesteruniversitypress.co.uk

British Library Cataloguing-in-Publication Data is available

Library of Congress Cataloging-in-Publication Data is available

ISBN 978 0 7190 9737 9 *paperback*

First published by Manchester University Press in hardback 2013

This paperback edition first published 2015

Printed by Lightning Source

Contents

Acknowledgements

This is a book about cooperation at different levels and about efforts that cut across national borders. It is hardly surprising, then, that fellow historians from different fields and countries have provided feedback on aspects of this study. Special thanks go to Christopher Abel, Charlotte Alston, Julie Carlier, Martin Conway, Stefan Couperus, Sasha Handley, Joseph Hardwick, Axel Körner, Don MacRaild, Boyd Rayward, Amalia Ribi, Bernhard Rieger, Katharina Rietzler, Anne-Isabelle Richard, Nicole Robertson, Pierre-Yves Saunier, Avram Taylor, Wouter Van Acker, Georgios Varouxakis and Christophe Verbruggen. I have also benefited from the support of many archivists and librarians, especially Stéphanie Manfroid and Raphaëlle Cornille of the Mundaneum in Mons. Together with Gita Deneckere and Christophe Verbruggen from the University of Ghent, I have co-edited a special issue of the *Revue belge de philologie et d'histoire/Belgisch tijdschrift voor filologie en geschiedenis*. By the time this book is published, the journal issue will have appeared in print and its contributions will complement the perspective offered by my own work.

I gratefully acknowledge the financial support that has facilitated my research: a doctoral scholarship from the Graduate School of University College London (UCL), a Marie Curie Fellowship at the Rijksuniversiteit Groningen, a grant from the German Historical Institute in Paris, a two-month visiting fellowship at Ghent as well as travel funding from the Royal Historical Society, the UCL History Department and the School of Arts and Social Sciences at Northumbria University.

I am particularly indebted to UCL and Northumbria, the two institutions that supported me on my way towards this book. The fruitful interactions with my students and colleagues have reminded me of the bigger picture and provided a great deal of inspiration.

This study would not have been possible without the support from my friends and family. The collective 'thank you' to them should, however, not obscure the particular gratitude that I owe to two people: my parents. It is to them that this book is dedicated.

Abbreviations

BAPS	Belgian Arbitration and Peace Society
BTNG–RBHC	*Belgisch tijdschrift voor nieuwste geschiedenis – Revue belge d'histoire contemporaine*
BWP	Belgian Workers' Party
CHTP–BEG	Cahiers d'histoire du temps présent – Bijdragen tot de eigentijde geschiedenis
ICIC	International Committee on Intellectual Cooperation
IIB	International Institute of Bibliography
IIIC	International Institute of Intellectual Cooperation
ILO	International Labour Organization
IPB	International Peace Bureau
IPU	Inter-Parliamentary Union
RBPH–BTFG	*Revue belge de philologie et d'histoire – Belgisch tijdschrift voor filologie en geschiedenis*
UDC	Universal Decimal Classification
UIA	Union of International Associations
WILPF	Women's International League for Peace and Freedom

The abbreviations for archival sources feature at the start of the select bibliography.

Introduction

> We have had many congresses this year. We will see even more. Located at the crossroads of races and ideas, Belgium is, par excellence, the chosen land of these cosmopolitan assemblies – for we are speaking here of international congresses, these great gatherings open to all civilisations where, under whatever pretext, eloquence exhausts within eight days more problems than science could resolve in a century, where the most contradictory tendencies collide without crushing each other, where traditional enmities seem ready to disarm forever, to pay homage to universal solidarity.[1]

By 1880 – the year that these hyperbolic lines were written – it was evident that international congresses had become major vehicles for political, cultural and scientific exchange. The increasing number of such events was but one feature of a wider phenomenon: internationalism. The very same period that has often been characterised as an age of nationalism also saw the migration of ideas and people, the foundation of new international associations, and various forms of activism that cut across national borders. As defined in this monograph, internationalism covered diverse efforts that were driven by the impulse to create closer international links. It comprised the efforts of intellectuals, humanitarians, socialists and pacifists, all of whom organised international events or bodies.

This study explores the age of internationalism from the 1880s to the 1930s. It does so by focusing on Belgium – the country which the opening quotation characterises as a 'chosen land' of 'cosmopolitan assemblies'. As Carl Strikwerda has pointed out, Belgium was 'the classic model of an industrial economy in Europe' alongside Britain and Germany: the country may even be viewed as the 'quintessential Western European state'.[2] Because of the presence of the European Commission and the European Parliament, 'Brussels' nowadays serves as shorthand for European integration. Yet already before the First World War, the Belgian capital hosted a great variety of international gatherings, as did the nearby cities of Ghent, Antwerp and Liège. Closely related to this was the great frequency – if not to say enthusiasm – with which Belgians organised world exhibitions. Fittingly, the book cover features a postcard image from the 1910 world's fair in Brussels. The exhibition involved contributions from 27 countries, millions of visitors and a range of international congresses.[3] One American observer commented on its appeal by stating that '[a]ll the world went to Brussels in 1910'.[4] At the time, Belgium was a major site for various international causes, for instance the socialism of the Second International, the peace and arbitration campaigns of the Inter-Parliamentary Union, and the secularism of the International Freethought Federation. Janet Polasky, for instance, has located the Belgian socialist leader Emile Vandervelde 'at the geographical as well as the ideological crossroads of Europe'.[5] Seen from this angle, the Belgian case helps us understand major European developments.

My account of the 'age of internationalism' starts in the 1880s, when new international associations for pacifists, socialists, feminists and scientists were established. Rather than ending with the conflagration of 1914, it traces how internationalism was re-constituted after the First World War. It follows its course until the early 1930s, when international efforts met with a variety of challenges – from the Great Depression to the rise of anti-democratic politics and aggressive nationalisms. Thus, the study explores the enthusiasms of the Belle Époque, the ruptures caused by four years of military conflict, the transnational bonds that survived the war and the new structures created by the League of Nations. The focus is on the practices and ideas of activists, and less so on government policy and diplomacy, which have been examined by Madeleine Herren and Sally Marks in different contexts and admirable depth.[6]

The chapter sequence challenges potential expectations and preconceptions: seemingly 'idealistic' forms of internationalism – socialism, feminism, pacifism and universalism – are only tackled in the second half (chapters 4, 5 and 6). In contrast, the first chapters demonstrate the extent to which internationalists remained wedded to national principles, hierarchies of civilisation and imperial designs, even when they evoked notions of an international community. Chapter 1 examines how Belgian intellectuals constructed narratives about their country as an 'international' nation. It thus illustrates how internationalism nourished notions of national prestige. Chapter 2 traces the connection to King Leopold's imperial project in Africa: it shows that both the supporters and the detractors of the Congo Free State viewed or represented their cases as international. Chapter 3 further considers how internationalism was used by competing groups or movements: freethinkers on the one side and Catholics on the other employed internationalist mechanisms and rhetoric when debating church–state relations. As a whole, the monograph traces the interconnection between causes that often styled themselves as progressive, yet it also acknowledges that internationalism was a site of contestation.

This study is informed by the drive towards transnational history. Given the focus on internationalism in one particular country, this may sound like a contradiction in terms – yet several scholars have successfully combined national and transnational perspectives.[7] Transnational history is not a narrowly defined method, but an approach stimulated by an interest in networks, ideas and connections that range beyond national categories.[8] Although this monograph starts with the national context, it follows the movement of activists and campaigns across borders, placing them in broader European or even global settings. The efforts discussed in this monograph share one feature: the realisation that particular ends – be they political, cultural or scientific – could not be achieved through national action alone.

Internationalism was closely connected to transnational practices. Influenced by Robert Keohane and Joseph Nye's work, scholars have used the term 'transnational' to stress that international organisations and multinational corporations help shape the international system alongside inter-state relations.[9] This approach has influenced research into 'transnational advocacy networks' and transnational protest movements.[10] In line with this understanding of 'transnationalism', scholars in the discipline of international history have examined the role of non-stage actors and the workings of international organisations.[11] Other historians have applied the 'transnational' label to stress the significance of networks and their flows, both when contemplating a transnational history of society and when examining intellectual networks that transcend national boundaries.[12] The linkage between 'transnational action' and 'internationalism' is evident if one considers Akira Iriye's definition of 'internationalism'. For him, the term describes people's awareness 'that they shared certain interests and objectives across national boundaries and they could best solve their many problems by pooling their resources and effecting transnational cooperation'.[13]

Understanding internationalism

Internationalism is an elusive concept. In the field of international history, it is associated with support for the strengthening of international institutions and mechanisms, as captured by terms such as 'liberal internationalism' or, in the American context, 'progressive internationalism'.[14] In contrast, labour historians use it as a label for the transnational reach of socialists. *Geschichtliche Grundbegriffe* – the German landmark work on historical semantics – concentrates on these 'red' connotations.[15] Meanwhile, in the history of science, the term 'scientific internationalism' points to academic collaboration through congresses or research projects.[16] Given these terminological varieties, does it actually make sense to treat internationalism as one phenomenon – to look at it in the singular, rather than the plural? The Belgian case shows that it is indeed possible to do so, as different forms of internationalism were driven by shared ideas, protagonists and practices.

Far too often, studies of internationalism concentrate on individual varieties, be they scholarly cooperation or the campaigns of the left. However, few activists at the time confined their efforts and self-perception to one form of activism. A broader definition of internationalism makes sense if we accept that internationalism could be appropriated by different groups and movements. As this means that internationalism was often diffuse, the focus on a small European state is particularly apt: it allows us to locate overlapping activisms within their national and international contexts.

To contemporaries, internationalism did not simply denote a set of beliefs and practices: it described their perception of a particular historical process. Prior to the First World War, prominent European peace activists argued that history was marked by a development towards global interdependence.[17] They also claimed that the ties between states and their economies would make any future war so terrible as to be of no purpose to anyone.[18] In surveying the increasing number of international bodies in 1911, the American legal scholar Paul Reinsch viewed them as evidence of an increasing movement towards global integration: '[we] are building up cooperation in constantly widening circles, so that it transcends national bounds to become a universal joint effort'.[19] In the midst of the First World War, the British liberal and historian Ramsay Muir reiterated such views, asserting that 'the movement to which we may give the name of Internationalism grew steadily stronger… [for] centuries, until it seemed to be in sight of its triumph with the summons of The Hague conferences in the closing years of the nineteenth century'.[20]

The teleological narratives favoured by many internationalists acted as modes of analysis through which authors and activists made sense of modernity. In an age in which, as Reinhart Koselleck observed, people's 'horizons of expectations' increasingly diverged from their 'spaces of experience',[21] the notion of a purposeful and continuous development towards international community offered a promise of stability. Three examples illustrate this: in 1909, the American journalist Harold Bolce claimed that 'the New Internationalism, rapidly welding the world into an economic unit, is not utopian. It is nothing less than a financial and commercial amalgamation of the nations… [It] makes every nation its brother's keeper'.[22] Three years later, the Belgians Henri La Fontaine and Paul Otlet wrote that 'the internationalism of our period is not only a conception of the spirit; it is based on a totality of realities'.[23] And during the Great War, the Austro-German pacifist Alfred Fried looked back to the pre-war era, stating that 'for a long time, internationalism had ceased to be an idea. It had impacted on the life of states in a perceptible way and presented itself as a clearly recognisable process promising the political adaptation to the natural development of the community of states.'[24] Despite the different backgrounds and persuasions of these authors, all of them understood 'internationalism' as a tangible entity – regardless of whether its essence was primarily defined in economic, social or political terms.

Internationalism was hence a movement, a process and an outlook.[25] It was not antithetical to national categories, despite its recognition of increasing global interdependence. Etymologically and conceptually, the term 'international' – coined by Jeremy Bentham in 1780 – drew upon the 'national'.[26] Significantly, the term 'national*ism*' only appeared in the second half of the nineteenth century and thus at a time when 'nationalism' had already become a distinct feature of political discourse.[27] As stressed throughout this study, particularly in chapter 1, most internationalists conceived of themselves as members of a nation and questioned national sovereignty only to a limited extent.

In this respect, internationalism differed from cosmopolitanism, which had variable meanings and could serve as both an ideal and a term of abuse. To many scholars, the term suggests a detachment from national categories and an embrace of global citizenship.[28] Ulrich Beck and Edgar Grande, for instance, have described cosmopolitanism as 'both *pre*-national and *post*-national'.[29] Nonetheless, clear-cut distinctions between internationalism and cosmopolitanism are difficult to draw: activists who were attacked as unpatriotic 'cosmopolitans' by their political opponents could seem like 'internationalists' in the eyes of their kin. In many respects, the internationalists discussed in this study resembled 'rooted cosmopolitans' as defined by Sidney Tarrow, namely 'individuals and groups who mobilize domestic and international resources and opportunities to advance claims on behalf of external actors, against external opponents, or in favor of goals they hold in common with transnational allies'.[30] While nationhood was an inbuilt feature of many forms of internationalism, so was – in several respects – empire. Certainly, there were alternative internationalisms, constructed by anti-colonial nationalists or other actors who challenged existing power relations and employed transnational means in their quest.[31] However, for many European and American internationalists, the concepts of empire and commonwealth informed their thinking on international organisation and global order.[32] Many efforts studied here can be described as 'reform internationalisms', whose complex relationship to global inequalities has been traced by Susan Zimmermann.[33]

An age of internationalism

Periodisations are open to debate and there is, of course, no fixed start or end date for the 'age of internationalism'. Why, then, begin in the 1880s? Border-crossing exchanges are as old as borders themselves. However, three factors tie internationalism to the nineteenth century. The first of these was the rise of nationalism, which was closely entwined with internationalism. Regardless of scholarly debates about the origins of nations, it is clear that nationalism became a powerful political force during the 'long nineteenth century'. It was boosted by the French Revolution and its emphasis on popular sovereignty, followed by the mobilising impact of the Revolutionary and Napoleonic Wars as well as Napoleon's reforms in different parts of Europe.[34] Nationalism was sustained by the appeal to 'national' pasts, folk traditions and the vernacular. According to Miroslav Hroch's typology, scholarly efforts in this realm were preconditions for the development of broader national movements.[35] By the mid-nineteenth century, the power of national ideas manifested itself in different ways, including the challenges to the empires of the Habsburgs and the Ottomans. The European revolutions of 1848 exemplified the growing interplay between nationalism and internationalism in this period.[36] By the 1880s, nationalism had begun its transformation into a mass movement in many parts of Europe. It had thus created a specific environment for actors who defined their causes internationally.

Secondly, internationalism depended on nineteenth-century developments in terms of transport, communication and economic integration. Major studies by Christopher Bayly and Jürgen Osterhammel have highlighted the intensity of global contacts and circulations in this period.[37] Between 1850 and 1880, the amount of railway track in Europe rose from 14,500 to 101,700 miles.[38] The telegraph network in Europe also expanded: with the opening of the Europe–Asia cable in 1863 and two Atlantic cables in 1886, an 'international system' evolved, allowing news to travel fast across continents.[39] Technological advances sustained economic integration: as Osterhammel has pointed out, the 'quantitative expansion of intercontinental trade' cannot be explained without 'the factor of mass transport'.[40] Fittingly, Robert Gildea has stated that 'it would be fair to say that... a single world market had been created' by 1880.[41] These broader developments influenced the work of international associations: economic contacts provided the context for many international meetings, and railway companies even offered discounts for delegates of international congresses. Karl Deutsch has shown the importance of 'communication' in the construction of national communities – and it has rightly been pointed out that such theories of communication can also apply to the construction of transnational communities.[42]

The rise of voluntary associations was the third factor that linked internationalism to the nineteenth century. Such organisations increasingly gained legal recognition, as exemplified by the French *loi de 1901*, and facilitated middle-class involvement in politics. These changes influenced the course of internationalism because international associations were often composed of, and preceded by, national groups. While voluntary associations in individual countries reflected civil society at the domestic level, the rise of such 'international non-governmental organisations' mirrored this process internationally and, according to scholars such as John Boli and George Thomas, promoted the development of a 'world culture'.[43] By 1914, there were more international associations than at any previous point in history. My monograph has adopted 1880 as a starting point, since the 1880s and 1890s were decades when many of these new actors rose to prominence.

All of this does not diminish the influence of the preceding internationalist efforts, which historians have traced back to 1815 (Lyons), 1848 (Paulmann/ Geyer), 1865 (Herren) or 1870 (Rasmussen).[44] Unlike their accounts, my study follows internationalism beyond the First World War. Evidently, the events of 1914 undermined the optimistic narratives that activists had employed in the Belle Époque. In the interwar years, internationalism continued, but under different and difficult circumstances. Certainly, 'links to the pre-war years are more important for some areas than others'.[45] While the Soviet Union promoted proletarian internationalism through the Communist International (Comintern), liberal internationalism found a new institutional shape in the League of Nations. As Helen McCarthy has argued, the foundation of the League 'created an institutional focus for the work of many existing voluntary associations, and encouraged new transnational endeavours'.[46] Despite being the focus of many hopes, the League was unable to create a genuine system of collective security. In 1937, the British feminist and pacifist Helena Swanwick captured this view in her criticism that 'though the machinery of the League is new, the machine-minders are the same as of yore'.[47] Furthermore, following an earlier wave of 'globalisation', the interwar years were dominated by economic crises and the revival of protectionist policies: Patricia Clavin has spoken of the 'failure of economic diplomacy' and the 'end of economic internationalism' during the Great Depression.[48] The notional terminus of my monograph is 1930. It thus falls within the period that Zara Steiner has described as the 'hinge years' – a point when 'it was becoming clear that the hopes of 1920s internationalism had seen their heyday come and go; national considerations would now dominate'.[49] Nonetheless, where it proves necessary, the study ventures into the early 1930s.

Small states as sites of internationalism

Internationalism developed in many settings. It may be something of a cliché to quote Walter Benjamin's description of Paris as the 'capital of the nineteenth century', to point at Berlin's cultural vitality in the 'Golden Twenties' and to stress London's significance as an 'imperial metropolis'. In order to capture the intensity of cultural and political exchange, it is important to venture beyond these obvious places. As Akira Iriye has suggested, 'the world is created and recreated as much by individuals from "lesser powers" as by the great powers'.[50] Not only Belgium but also countries such as Switzerland and the Netherlands hosted notable international organisations and events. In 1911, a French observer referred to Bern, Brussels and The Hague as 'capitals of these fictional territories created for the greatest good of the States'.[51] In Switzerland, the presence of bodies such as the Universal Postal Union, the International Telegraphic Union and the International Railway Transport Commission preceded the establishment of the League of Nations headquarters by several decades. For most of the period, the International Peace Bureau (IPB) and the Inter-Parliamentary Union (IPU) – two leading associations for peace and arbitration – also maintained secretariats in Swiss cities. Meanwhile, the Netherlands became a centre for international law through the peace conferences at The Hague in 1899 and 1907 and the establishment of a Permanent Court of Arbitration. The creation of the Permanent Court of International Justice in 1922 and an Academy of International Law in 1923 cemented The Hague's centrality for the promotion of international norms.

In 1916, Ramsay Muir described international law as 'the gift of the little states of Europe'.[52] Being relatively weak in military terms and faced with more powerful neighbours, the strengthening of international norms was ultimately a matter of survival. As the Swiss internationalist William Rappard suggested in 1934, 'the nations whose only material bond is a common lack of might are spiritually linked together by a common love of right'.[53] Switzerland and Belgium enjoyed a special status in international law, being recognised as neutral states in 1815 (Switzerland) and 1831–39 (Belgium). In 1867, the Grand Duchy of Luxembourg joined them, having its neutrality enshrined through the Second Treaty of London. While the Great War caused a shift in Belgian approaches to neutrality, Switzerland only acceded to the League of Nations after an official declaration in 1920 that this step would not compromise Swiss neutrality.[54] In the Netherlands, neutrality was a political choice rather than a constitutional necessity. As Michael Riemens has shown, the country's role as a centre for international law was but one example of the Dutch engagement with, and contribution to, an international political culture.[55]

In Scandinavia, governments also opted for policies of neutrality. Fittingly, politicians from Denmark, Sweden and Norway (independent from 1905) made key contributions to internationalist efforts. Prominent examples include the Dane Fredrik Bajer, founding president of the IPB; the Norwegian Christian Lange, secretary-general of the IPU from 1909 to 1933; his compatriot Fridtjof Nansen, the League of Nations' High Commissioner for Refugees; and the Swedish socialist Karl Hjalmar Branting, a leading advocate of international disarmament. Furthermore, as Elisabeth Crawford has argued, the Stockholm-based scientific Nobel Prizes 'were an important creation of the turn-of-the-century movement towards internationalism, both in science and more generally'.[56] Meanwhile, the Nobel Peace Prize in Oslo directly connected to pacifist aspirations: Alfred Nobel's will had stipulated that it be awarded to those who promoted 'fraternity between nations, the abolition or reduction of standing armies, and the holding/promotion of peace congresses'.[57] After the Second World War, transnational ties in the Nordic region translated into institutional settings, notably the Nordic Council, yet it has been suggested that the very concept of 'Norden' was partly constructed within international settings such as the League of Nations.[58]

As sites of internationalism, Switzerland, the Netherlands and Belgium benefited from their geographic location. All three countries were situated between larger states that dominated international politics and academic exchange. Belgium boasted a well-developed railway network, launched in 1834, before any other country in mainland Europe. Over the years, the kingdom's infrastructure became 'the symbol of the progress and prosperity of the new nation'.[59] At the cultural level, the prominence of the French language facilitated the participation in international congresses for both Belgian and Swiss internationalists. Evidently, the Swiss could also forge links with German academics who played an important role in scholarly networks. Alongside such geographic and linguistic assets, these small and neutral states were well-suited compromise sites for international gatherings in periods of great-power rivalry. As Paul Reinsch observed, intergovernmental commissions were often established there because 'jealousy…prevented their location in the territory of more powerful nations'.[60] As my study shows, Belgium provided a fertile soil for international meetings of diplomats and political activists alike.

The Belgian context of internationalism

The overall setting for transnational cooperation in Belgium was by no means static: between 1880 and 1930, the kingdom underwent significant transformations, including pronounced social and cultural tensions, the rise of new political movements and the experience of war and occupation. Reflecting these upheavals, Gita Deneckere has spoken of the 'turbulences of the Belle Époque',[61] and Emmanuel Gerard has described interwar Belgium as 'the theatre of a confrontation between two periods and two generations', namely the 'bourgeois' nineteenth century on the one side and an age of mass politics and state intervention on the other.[62] The Belgian capital was subject to significant change: the population of the 'Greater Brussels' agglomeration rose from 400,000 inhabitants in 1881 to 750,000 in 1913, triggering social unrest and transformations of the urban landscape.[63] According to the Catholic politician and intellectual Henry Carton de Wiart, Brussels in the late nineteenth century was 'a large provincial town which had almost adapted to its role as capital, but not yet raised its ambition to transform itself into the cosmopolitan city it is becoming today'.[64] During this period, Brussels began to assume many features of a European capital city along Parisian lines. Leopold II's ambitions – and profits from his Congo Free State – played a central role, exemplified by the construction of boulevards, the monumental Palais de Justice (1866–83) and the Parc du Cinquantenaire (1880).[65] The Cinquantenaire also hosted the 1897 world exhibition, underlining the links between urban development and internationalism.

Belgium's rise as an international centre was sustained by the 'high degree of internationalisation' of its economy.[66] This aspect partly derived from its early role as the 'bridgehead of industrialization on the continent'.[67] The nineteenth century saw Belgian involvement in a range of business schemes abroad, from railway construction in Latin America to rubber harvesting in the Congo. Such actions generated business elites whose interests – financial or other – stretched beyond their country's boundaries. Marie-Thérèse Bitsch has stressed the significance of economic links and shown how the kingdom's policies in this area differed from its larger neighbours.[68] Furthermore, the Belgian economy attracted many labour migrants, with the capital drawing a high share of well-educated individuals.[69] As Peter Scholliers has stressed, 'foreign workers, capital and ideas were common in Brussels throughout the 19th and 20th centuries'.[70] In the country as a whole, the number of aliens rose from 171,438 to 319,230 between 1890 and 1930.[71] Economic internationalism is not a focus of this study, but it provided the wider context for the campaigns and events that are studied here.

The growth of Belgian internationalism coincided with the period known as the Belle Époque. Internationalism and the notion of a Belle Époque resembled one another in that they were characterised by the convergence of cultural, political and social factors, lending expression to a belief in progress. Internationalism in this period seemingly contradicted the sense of discomfort and decay frequently connoted by the term 'fin de siècle'; instead it evoked prosperity and creativity. Despite mounting criticism of atrocities in the Congo Free State, celebrations of a 'civilising mission' featured prominently in Belgian internationalism, exemplified by the colonial exhibition of 1897 in Tervuren and the Congress of Global Economic Expansion at Mons in 1905. To Madeleine Herren, the years between 1900 and 1909 represented 'the peak of expansionist internationalism' in Belgium.[72] Chapters 1 and 2 in particular draw attention to these aspects.

Many Belgian internationalists operated in a Francophone setting, even though more than half the Belgian population spoke Flemish/Dutch.[73] There were two reasons for this: the first was the predominance of the French language at international congresses and in diplomacy. The second reason was its status in Belgian politics and academia. Until 1873, access to courts was only available in French, which remained the sole official language until 1898. For this reason, Jean Stengers described Belgium before 1898 as a *Belgique de langue française.*[74] At around 1880, the population of Brussels was split between 20–25 per cent French-speakers, 36–39 per cent Dutch-speakers and 30–38 per cent bilinguals.[75] In subsequent decades, this balance shifted towards the French language. Furthermore, even in Dutch-speaking cities such as Ghent and Antwerp, local elites were Francophone. In the late nineteenth century, the Flemish movement combined an affirmation of Flemish culture with campaigns for linguistic equality. It is important to note that 'Flamingantism' did not challenge the authority or cohesion of the Belgian state at this time. Matters became more complicated during the First World War, when the German *Flamenpolitik* sought to appeal to the Flemish population.[76] The interwar years were characterised by increasing disputes regarding the kingdom's language question. The nominal endpoint of this monograph – 1930 – coincides with the year when Ghent University was transformed into a Dutch-speaking institution, fulfilling one demand of the Flemish movement.

These observations point back at a wider issue raised in this monograph, namely the question of unity and conflict. Belgian internationalists often shared a background and language, and also a set of values, experiences and beliefs. Politically, many of them were connected to democratic socialism or progressive liberalism. Els Witte has stressed the absence of a 'clear dividing line' between the two currents. While acknowledging the debates between socialists and progressives, she has noted that '[t]he intellectuals in both camps were very cosy with one another': they were 'chips off the same block'.[77]

In other words, for many of its protagonists, internationalism was part of a wider commitment to progress and reform. This, however, did not preclude considerable Catholic involvement in international ventures. In this monograph, Catholic internationalism is tackled in its secular guise. Evidently, it is equally desirable to trace the transnational movements of pilgrims, priests and missionaries. However, it was Catholic lay activism – for instance social Catholicism, which rose to prominence in the 1890s – that was most clearly linked to the other efforts discussed here. Despite the ideological divisions in Belgium, collaboration between Catholics, liberals and socialists was frequently feasible when it came to international matters. This may illustrate the relatively diffuse nature of internationalism – yet it also underlines the fruitful lines of enquiry that a transnational approach can open up.

The broad chronological perspective adopted in this study does not deny ruptures and changes. As chapter 5 highlights, the First World War demonstrated the limits of internationalism while triggering international activism on behalf of 'poor little Belgium'. After the war, Belgium and Switzerland competed for the League of Nations headquarters. The choice for Geneva was informed by Woodrow Wilson's insistence that the new organisation be hosted by a country unafflicted by the war.[78] The war-related antagonisms affected Belgian involvement in political movements, as illustrated by the discussion of socialist internationalism in chapter 4. Nonetheless, many activists sought to rebuild their ties after the war, and the Belgian government promoted transnational cooperation by granting legal personality to international associations. Yet by the early 1930s, the country had to cope with several domestic crises. The impact of the Great Depression gave rise to social tensions which also manifested itself in a 'xenophobic response' to alien workers.[79] In the 1930s, political instability at home and shifts in the country's foreign policy provided a particularly delicate environment for internationalist efforts, providing further explanation for the book's emphasis on the years between 1880 and 1930. As a whole, however, this study shows that throughout its history, internationalism has been informed by contradictions and challenges that were tied to events at both the national and the international level.

Notes

1 'Revue politique', *L'Indépendance Belge* (5 September 1880).

2 Carl Strikwerda, *A House Divided: Catholics, Socialists, and Flemish Nationalists in Nineteenth-Century Belgium* (Lanham, MD, 1997), p. 14; Strikwerda, 'If all of Europe were Belgium: lessons in politics and globalization from one country', *BTNG–RBHC*, 35 (2005), 503.

3 Brigitte Schroeder-Gudehus and Anne Rasmussen, *Les Fastes du progrès: le guide des expositions universelles 1851–1992* (Paris, 1992), p. 167.

4 William Elliot Griffis, *Belgium: The Land of Art: Its History, Legends, Industry and Modern Expansion* (London, 1912), pp. 292–3.

5 Janet Polasky, *The Democratic Socialism of Emile Vandervelde: Between Reform and Revolution* (Oxford, 1995), p. 4.

6 Sally Marks, *Innocent Abroad: Belgium at the Paris Peace Conference in 1919* (Chapel Hill, 1981); Madeleine Herren, *Hintertüren zur Macht: Internationalismus und mordenisierungsorientierte Außenpolitik in Belgien, der Schweiz und den USA, 1865–1914* (Munich, 2000).

7 Sebastian Conrad and Jürgen Osterhammel (eds), *Das Kaiserreich transnational: Deutschland in der Welt 1871–1914* (Göttingen, 2004); Ian Tyrrell, *Transnational Nation: United States History in Global Perspective since 1789* (London, 2007); Vesna Drapac, *Constructing Yugoslavia: A Transnational History* (Basingstoke, 2010).

8 This broad approach is exemplified by Akira Iriye and Pierre-Yves Saunier (eds), *Palgrave Dictionary of Transnational History: From the Mid-19th Century to the Present Day* (Basingstoke, 2009). See also Ann Curthoys and Marilyn Lake, 'Introduction' in Curthoys and Lake (eds), *Connected Worlds: History in Transnational Perspective* (Canberra, 2005), pp. 6–20.

9 Robert Keohane and Joseph Nye, *Power and Interdependence: World Politics in Transition* (Boston, MA, 1977); Keohane and Nye, 'Transnational relations and world politics: an introduction', *International Organisation*, 25 (1971), 329–49.

10 Margaret Keck and Kathryn Sikkink, *Activists Beyond Borders: Advocacy Networks in International Politics* (Ithaca, NY, 1998); Donatella della Porta and Sidney Tarrow (eds), *Transnational Protest and Global Activism* (Lanham, MD, 2005).

11 Patricia Clavin, 'Defining transnationalism', *Contemporary European History*, 14 (2005), 421–39.

12 Jürgen Osterhammel, 'Transnationale Gesellschaftsgeschichte: Erweiterung oder Alternative?', *Geschichte und Gesellschaft*, 27 (2001), 464–79; Christophe Charle, Jürgen Schriewer and Peter Wagner (eds), *Transnational Intellectual Networks: Forms of Academic Knowledge and the Search for Cultural Identities* (Frankfurt, 2004).

13 Akira Iriye, *Global Community: The Role of International Organizations in the Contemporary World* (Berkeley, CA, 2002), p. 9.

14 Thomas Knock, *To End All Wars: Woodrow Wilson and the Quest for a New World Order* (Oxford, 1992).

15 Peter Friedemann and Lucian Hölscher, 'Internationale, International, Internationalismus' in Otto Brunner (ed.), *Geschichtliche Grundbegriffe*, vol. 3 (Stuttgart, 1982), pp. 367–97.

16 Anne Rasmussen, 'L'Internationale scientifique (1890–1914)' (PhD thesis, EHESS Paris, 1995).

17 Norman Angell, *The Foundations of International Polity* (London, 1914); Jacques Novicow, *Die Föderation Europas: Autorisierte Übersetzung von A.H. Fried* (Berlin, 1901); Alfred Fried, *Das internationale Leben der Gegenwart* (Leipzig, 1908).

18 Jan Bloch, *Is War Now Impossible? Being an Abridgment of 'The Future of War in Its Technical, Economic and Political Relations'* (London, 1899); Norman Angell, *The Great Illusion: A Study of the Relation of Military Power in Nations to Their Economic and Social Advantage* (London, 1910); Yakov Novikov [Jacques Novicow], *War and Its Alleged Benefits. With an Introduction by Norman Angell* (London, 1912).

19 Paul Reinsch, *Public International Unions: Their Work and Organization. A Study in International Administrative Law* (Boston, 1911), pp. 2–3.

20 Ramsay Muir, *Nationalism and Internationalism: The Culmination of Modern History* (London, 1916), p. 34.

21 Reinhart Koselleck, *Vergangene Zukunft: Zur Semantik geschichtlicher Zeiten* (Frankfurt, 1979), pp. 349–75.

22 Harold Bolce, *The New Internationalism* (New York, 1907), pp. 1 and 42.

23 Henri La Fontaine and Paul Otlet, 'La vie internationale et l'effort pour son organisation', *La Vie Internationale*, 1 (1912), 9.

24 Alfred Fried, *Europäische Wiederherstellung* (Zürich, 1915), p. 43.

25 Martin Geyer and Johannes Paulmann, 'Introduction: the mechanics of internationalism', in Geyer and Paulmann (eds), *The Mechanics of Internationalism: Culture, Society, and Politics from the 1840s to the First World War* (Oxford, 2001), p. 23.

26 Jeremy Bentham, *An Introduction to the Principles of Morals and Legislation* (London, 1970 [1780]), p. 296.

27 Friedemann and Hölscher, 'Internationale, International, Internationalismus', pp. 367–8.
28 Steven Vertovec and Robin Cohen, 'Introduction: conceiving cosmopolitanism', in Vertovec and Cohen (eds), *Conceiving Cosmopolitanism: Theory, Context and Practice* (Oxford, 2003), pp. 1–24.
29 Ulrich Beck and Edgar Grande, *Cosmopolitan Europe* (Cambridge, 2007).
30 Sidney Tarrow, *The New Transnational Protest and Global Activism* (Cambridge, 2005), p. 29.
31 Sebastian Conrad and Dominic Sachsenmeier (eds), *Competing Visions of Global Order: Global Movements and Moments, 1880s–1930s* (Basingstoke, 2007); Erez Manela, *The Wilsonian Moment: Self-Determination and the International Origins of Anti-Colonial Nationalism* (Cambridge, MA, 2007); David Featherstone, *Solidarity: Hidden Histories and Geographies of Internationalism* (London, 2012).
32 Mark Mazower, *No Enchanted Palace: The End of Empire and the Ideological Origins of the United Nations* (Princeton, NJ, 2009).
33 Susan Zimmermann, *GrenzÜberschreitungen: Internationale Netzwerke, Organisationen, Bewegungen und die Politik der globalen Ungleichheit vom 17. bis zum 21. Jahrhundert* (Vienna, 2010); Susan Zimmermann, '"Reform"-Internationalismen und globale Ungleichheit im 19. und 20. Jahrhundert: Traditionen und Optionen der Internationalismusforschung' in Karin Fischer and Susan Zimmermann (eds), *Internationalismen: Transformation weltweiter Ungleichheit im 19. und 20. Jahrhundert* (Vienna, 2004), pp. 7–38.
34 Linda Colley, *Britons: Forging the Nation, 1707–1837* (New Haven, CT, 1992); Stuart Woolf, *Napoleon's Integration of Europe* (London, 1991); Biancamaria Fontana, 'The Napoleonic Empire and the Europe of nations', in Anthony Pagden (ed.), *The Idea of Europe: From Antiquity to the European Union* (Cambridge, 2002), pp. 116–28.
35 Miroslav Hroch, *Social Preconditions of National Revival in Europe: A Comparative Analysis of the Social Composition of Patriotic Groups Among the Smaller European Nations* (Cambridge, 1985).
36 Axel Körner (ed.), *1848: A European Revolution? International Ideas and National Memories of 1848* (Basingstoke, 2000).
37 Christopher A. Bayly, *The Birth of the Modern World, 1780–1918: Global Connections and Comparisons* (Oxford, 2004); Jürgen Osterhammel, *Die Verwandlung der Welt: Eine Geschichte des 19. Jahrhunderts* (Munich, 2008).
38 Robert Gildea, *Barricades and Borders: Europe 1800–1914* (2nd edn., Oxford, 1996), p. 150.
39 Bayly, *Birth of the Modern World*, p. 20; Armand Mattelart, *Networking the World, 1794–2000* (Minneapolis, 2000), pp. 7–8.
40 Osterhammel, *Die Verwandlung der Welt*, p. 1036.
41 Gildea, *Barricades and Borders*, p. 150.
42 Geyer and Paulmann, 'Introduction', p. 7. The authors specifically refer to Karl Deutsch, *Nationalism and Social Communication: An Enquiry into the Foundations of Nationality* (Cambridge, MA, 1953).
43 John Boli and George Thomas, 'INGOs and the organization of world culture', in Boli and Thomas (eds), *Constructing World Culture: International Nongovernmental Organizations since 1875* (Stanford, CA, 1999), p. 34.

44 F.S.L. Lyons, *Internationalism in Europe 1815–1914* (Leiden, 1963); Rasmussen, 'L'Internationale scientifique'; Herren, *Hintertüren zur Macht*; Geyer and Paulmann (eds), *The Mechanics of Internationalism*.

45 Patricia Clavin, 'Introduction: conceptualising internationalism between the World Wars', in Daniel Laqua (ed.), *Internationalism Reconfigured: Transnational Ideas and Movements Between the World Wars* (London, 2011), p. 7.

46 Helen McCarthy, 'The lifeblood of the League? Voluntary associations and League of Nations activism in Britain', in Laqua, *Internationalism Reconfigured*, p. 190.

47 Helena Swanwick, *Collective Insecurity* (London, 1937), p. 29.

48 Patricia Clavin, *The Failure of Economic Diplomacy: Britain, Germany, France and the United States, 1931–1936* (Basingstoke, 1996): Robert Boyce, *The Great Interwar Crisis and the Collapse of Globalization* (Basingstoke, 2009), views 1927 as the starting point of a crisis that encompassed politics and the economy.

49 Zara Steiner, *The Lights That Failed: European International History, 1919–1933* (Oxford, 2004), p. 801.

50 Akira Iriye, *Cultural Internationalism and World Order* (Baltimore, 1997), p. 2.

51 Gaëtan Combes de Lestrade, *La Vie internationale* (Paris, 1911), p. 144.

52 Muir, *Nationalism and Internationalism*, p. 147.

53 William Rappard, 'Small states in the League of Nations', *Political Science Quarterly*, 49 (1934), 544–75.

54 Ania Peter, *William E. Rappard und der Völkerbund: Ein Schweizer Pionier der internationalen Verständigung* (Bern, 1973), pp. 50–9.

55 Michael Riemens, *De passie voor vrede: de evolutie van de internationale politieke cultuur in de jaren 1880–1940 en het recipiëren door Nederland* (Amsterdam, 2005).

56 Elisabeth Crawford, *Nationalism and Internationalism in Science, 1880–1939: Four Studies of the Nobel Population* (Cambridge, 1992), p. 7.

57 Irwin Abrams, 'The many meanings of the Nobel Peace Prize', in Karl Holl and Anne Kjelling (eds), *The Nobel Peace Prize and the Laureates: The Meaning and Acceptance of the Nobel Peace Prize in the Prize Winners' Countries* (Frankfurt, 1994), pp. 13–33.

58 Norbert Götz, 'Blue-eyed angels at the League of Nations: the Genevese construction of Norden', in Norbert Götz and Heidi Haggrén (eds), *Regional Cooperation and International Organizations: The Nordic Model in Transnational Alignment* (Abingdon, 2009), pp. 25–46.

59 Els Witte, *La Construction de la Belgique 1828–1847* (Brussels, 2005), pp. 136–7 [in *Nouvelle Histoire de Belgique*, vol. 1].

60 Reinsch, *Public International Unions*, p. 155.

61 Gita Deneckere, *Les turbulences de la Belle Époque (1878–1905)* (Brussels, 2005) [in *Nouvelle Histoire de Belgique*, vol. 1].

62 Emmanuel Gerard, *La démocratie rêvée, bridée et bafouée 1918–1939*, p. 7 (Brussels, 2006) [in *Nouvelle Histoire de Belgique*, vol. 2].

63 Ginette Kurgan-van Hentenryk, 'Économie et transports', in Jean Stengers (ed.), *Bruxelles: croissance d'une capitale* (Brussels, 1979), p. 221.

64 Henry Carton de Wiart, *Souvenirs littéraires* (Brussels, 1938), p. 73.

65 Lianne Ranieri, *Léopold II, Urbaniste* (Brussels, 1972).

66 Ernst Kossmann, *The Low Countries, 1780–1940* (Oxford, 1978), p. 419.
67 Wilhelm Damberg, Claudia Hiepel and Alfredo Canavero, 'The formation of Christian working-class organizations in Belgium, Germany, Italy and the Netherlands (1840s–1920s)', in Lex Heerma van Voss *et al.* (eds), *Between Cross and Class: Comparative Histories of Christian Labour in Europe 1840–2000* (Bern, 2005), p. 56.
68 Marie-Thérèse Bitsch, *La Belgique entre la France et l'Allemagne, 1905–1914* (Paris, 1994). On Belgium's transnational economic links, see Michel Dumoulin and Eddy Stols (eds), *La Belgique et l'étranger aux XIXe et XXe siècles* (Louvain-la-Neuve, 1987).
69 Sophie De Schaepdrijver, *Elites for the Capital: Foreign Migration to Mid-Nineteenth Century Brussels* (Amsterdam, 1990).
70 Peter Scholliers, 'An essay on the internationalisation and representation of Brussels, 1800–2000', in Els Witte and Ann Mares (eds), *19 Keer Brussels* (Brussels, 2001), p. 506.
71 Frank Caestecker, *Alien Policy in Belgium, 1840–1940: The Creation of Guest Workers, Refugees and Illegal Aliens* (New York, 2000), p. xiv.
72 Herren, *Hintertüren zur Macht*, p. 141.
73 'Dutch' is the written standard and official designation in language legislation. The term 'Flemish' comprises different Dutch dialects spoken in Belgium.
74 Jean Stengers and Eliane Gubin, *Le Grand Siècle de la nationalité belge: de 1830 à 1918* (Brussels, 2002), p. 49.
75 Eliane Gubin, 'L'emploi des langues au XIXe siècle: les débuts du mouvement flamand', in Stengers, *Bruxelles: croissance d'une capitale*, p. 238.
76 Ulrich Tiedau, 'De Duitse cultuurpolitiek in België tijdens de Eerste Wereldoorlog', *BEG–CHTP*, 11 (2003), 21–45.
77 Els Witte, 'The expansion of democracy (1885–1918)', in Jan Craeybeckx *et al.*, *Political History of Belgium from 1830 Onwards* (Brussels, 2000), p. 79.
78 William Rappard, 'Woodrow Wilson, la Suisse et Genève', in Centre Européen de la Dotation Carnegie, *Centenaire Woodrow Wilson 1856–1956* (Geneva, 1956), pp. 29–74.
79 Caestecker, *Alien Policy*, p. 155.

1

Nationhood

It might seem counterintuitive to start a book on internationalism by considering nationalism – yet the two phenomena were mutually dependent. Internationalists evoked national arguments to solicit support for their schemes; at the same time, international congresses and associations provided staging grounds for the representation of nationhood. Be it in science, politics or the arts, internationalism depended upon the nation as a central point of reference. In this respect, any discussion of internationalism reveals how, by the late nineteenth century, ideas about 'nationality' and 'nationhood' had become central ways of interpreting the world. Activists were at pains to stress that 'nationalism' and 'internationalism' were not conflicting ideologies. The sociologist Adolphe Quetelet offers a case in point. As organiser of the first International Statistical Congress in Brussels (1853), he made an early contribution to internationalism in Belgium.[1] However, in his work *Du Système social et des lois qui le régissent*, Quetelet sounded a cautious note. He recognised the advantages of a 'federation between a great number of small states', yet regarded such an organisation as unlikely, unless its members closely resembled each other or were forcefully unified.[2] Despite his confidence in international law, Quetelet rejected the 'cosmopolitanism preached by some writers' which would 'destroy any kind of national spirit'. To him, it risked 'stifling man's self-love … that sense of personal dignity that raises him above himself and makes him capable of the finest actions'.[3]

In a similar vein, one of the intellectual fathers of the League of Nations, the French politician Léon Bourgeois, asserted in 1910 that the 'cause of peace through [international] law… has nothing in common with the cause of the naysayers and detractors of the idea of the fatherland'.[4] After the First World War, the architecture of the League of Nations signposted nationhood in both organisational and conceptual terms. In this context, the historian Glenda Sluga has drawn attention to the 'enthusiastic embrace of nationality in the name of a more democratic world order'.[5] The affirmation of the nation was not confined to overtly political projects. George Sarton – the Belgian founder of *Isis*, the leading international journal in the history of science – echoed the claims of Quetelet and Bourgeois when stressing that 'the internationalism of *Isis* is very different from, and indeed hostile to that childish cosmopolitan spirit, which would ignore and despise racial and national peculiarities'.[6]

Nationalism and internationalism bore underlying resemblances. For instance, intellectuals played an active part in shaping ideas about the nation, on the one hand, and visions of international fraternity, on the other.[7] Furthermore, the belief in the existence of nations resulted from communicative acts that were linked to the social and economic transformations of modernity.[8] Internationalism provided a mirror image of this process: advances in transport and communication facilitated international exchanges, with international congresses being communicative events par excellence. It is also worthwhile recalling that some scholars view nationalism as a form of politics that particular groups appropriated in the pursuit of power.[9] Similar observations apply to internationalism: appeals to an 'international community' could be political tools, both for groups within individual states and for competing transnational actors.

If nationalism and internationalism were intertwined, how did these connections play out in the national arena? The Belgian case sheds a great deal of light on this question. The nature and force of Belgian nationalism have long been subjects of debate. Some people have questioned the extent to which Belgians truly experienced 'nationhood' and have pointed to rival identities based on language, class and religion.[10] In contrast, the late historian Jean Stengers emphasised the strength of national sentiment as expressed in the Belgian Revolution of 1830.[11] Further studies have traced a common sense of identity back to earlier historical episodes, for instance the Brabant Revolution of 1789–90.[12] While independent statehood provided a focus for national feelings, divisions along cultural and linguistic lines were already apparent before the First World War. During the interwar years, the dominance of the French language in politics and education was a source of increasing tensions, as highlighted by the electoral performance of the radical Vlaamsch Nationaal Verbond (Flemish National Alliance) in 1936. However, these conflicts did not tear the country into two, as they were mediated by other dividing lines, notably the social question and the tensions between Catholics and liberals. Indeed, even in the period when language-based antagonism gained traction, socialists such as Hendrik de Man and Louis Piérard suggested that the underlying tensions were of a social, rather than national, nature; they pointed at divisions between the Flemish population and French-speaking elites in Antwerp and Ghent to support such arguments.[13] This chapter shows how intellectuals redefined a potential source of instability – namely a population comprised of two major cultural groups – as an asset, engendering the notion of Belgians as a particularly 'international' people.

The Belgians: an international people?

The Belgian example reveals a form of nationalism that was couched in international terms. The prominence accorded to different images of Belgian nationhood changed according to period and purpose. The monarchy played an important part, as highlighted by the veneration of Albert I, the *roi chevalier* who seemed to embody the national cause during the First World War.[14] A study of Belgian coins and stamps has drawn attention to the frequent depictions of economic and industrial progress; such representations celebrated the country's early industrialisation, its factories and railways.[15] In other contexts, affirmations of localism and regional traditions were noteworthy. Alongside these representations, the idea of Belgium as a European junction was an underlying thread – both because of its location and its composition. As Jo Tollebeek has shown, the image of Belgium as a meeting ground of different cultures or civilisations began to take shape in the nineteenth century. Such discourse portrayed the country as shaped by 'the hyphen of national culture'.[16]

One way of tracing the development of these representations is through historiography: after all, national histories formed a cornerstone of nation-building, and Belgium was no exception.[17] Owing to Belgium's short history of independent statehood, such endeavours performed a legitimising role, seeking to demonstrate that Belgian statehood was more than a historical accident. In 1900, the doyen of Belgian historians, Henri Pirenne, published the first volume of his *Histoire de Belgique*. Its narrative began in medieval Europe; the Ghent historian thus sought to trace the emergence of a distinct 'Belgian civilisation' whose character derived from the unity of its social life. To Pirenne, 'this Belgium, divided ethnographically between the Roman race and the Germanic race, in the same way as it is politically located between France and Germany', appeared as a Western European 'microccosm'.[18] The country had emerged as a particularly suitable place for international encounters as the Belgians themselves combined 'the spirit of two races':

> The basins of the river Scheldt and the river Meuse have not only served as a battlefield of Europe: it is also through them that the trade in ideas between the Latin world and the Germanic world, which touch each other on [... Belgian] territory, has taken place; it is these ports which, for centuries, have served as entrepots for goods from North and South.[19]

Although Pirenne's views on Belgium's international features were affected by the Great War, he restated his view of Belgium as a 'syncretism' in the final volume of his magnum opus, published in 1932: 'The Belgian environment is truly a syncretism of the most diverse civilisations, comparable to ancient Syria, similarly located at the contact point of great empires and, similarly, in constant relations with them through its trade and industry.'[20] Again, Pirenne asserted that his country had remained the 'common soil of all nations' because of its openness to external influences. In this context, the country's domestic tensions appeared as a 'manifestation of the two contradictory tendencies that characterised European civilisation at the time: nationalism and internationalism'.[21]

While Pirenne worked on his *Histoire de Belgique*, Edmond Picard – one of Belgium's most prominent intellectuals – outlined his own position on Belgian identity.[22] Picard asserted that his nation was united by a 'Belgian soul'.[23] Such characterisation complemented fin-de-siècle notions 'that national differences were the products of psychological processes and characteristics', which led to nations being represented as psychological entities.[24] Despite notable differences with Pirenne's analysis, Picard echoed the historian's comments on the country's role in overcoming 'ethnic' divisions. To Picard, a United States of Europe had two natural precursors, namely Switzerland and Belgium: 'this Belgium, prodigiously peopled, remarkably prosperous, diverse in its elements, harmonious despite what one could call its mechanisms…, doesn't it offer a foretaste of the future United States of Europe? Aren't our national qualities what one would hope for from such an entity?'[25]

His views enjoyed 'enormous resonance', partly because of Picard's role in Belgian politics and culture.[26] As a driving force behind the periodicals *L'Art Moderne* (1881–1914), *Revue Moderne* (1882–83) and *La Société Nouvelle* (1884), Picard was at the centre of the artistic and literary networks of the Belle Époque.[27] Yet the arts were merely one field of action for him: he joined the bar at the Belgian Court of Cassation in 1881 and soon made his mark as a public speaker and editor of a compendium of Belgian laws and jurisprudence. Having unsuccessfully run for parliament as a liberal candidate, Picard joined the Belgian Workers' Party in 1884 and served as senator between 1894 and 1908. The Catholic politician and writer Henry Carton de Wiart later described him as 'the master of us all', and the socialist Louis Piérard called him 'one of the most engrossing personalities of independent Belgium'.[28]

Picard was no internationalist: he was well known for his anti-Semitism and his embrace of imperialist visions, showing little interest in pacifism or socialist internationalism.[29] However, his ideas on the 'Belgian soul' were attractive to Belgian intellectuals involved in transnational activities. Picard's influence was, for instance, acknowledged by Emile Cammaerts, an author and literary critic who went into British exile after the German attack on Belgium in 1914 and soon became an Anglo-Belgian cultural mediator. In 1932, he succeeded with his proposal that the Belgian government fund a professorial Chair of Belgian Studies at the University of London, which he held until 1948.[30] During the interwar years, Cammaerts explained the kingdom's 'land and people' as well as its 'art and literature' to an English audience. In this context, he suggested that Picard had realised that Belgium's 'position at the cross-roads of Western Europe gave her an essentially European character derived from Latin and Germanic influences. He also understood the true character of patriotism at a time when the notion was not so popular as it is to-day.'[31]

Internationalists and the Belgian nation

The notion of Belgians as peaceful and adept at managing internationalism offered a solution to the country's perceived shortcomings, namely its short history of independent statehood, its limited military power and apparent lack of international prestige. It could even appear as a national vocation. Louis Piérard suggested that the country had a 'great mission to fulfil':

> [Belgium] can be a bond between the great Latin, Germanic and Anglo-Saxon civilisations. It is better placed than any other country to work for cooperation, for the mutual understanding of the peoples, for international rapprochement, for the demobilisation of spirits. Look at the map of the world: Belgium is a corridor for the transit of values.[32]

Belgian advocates of internationalism could appeal to such a sense of mission: they thus forestalled suspicions of being 'cosmopolitan', 'de-national' or 'anti-national'. Seen from one angle, their activism complemented the country's foreign-policy interests – which, evidently, favoured strong provisions for international law. Yet, at another level, pacifist activity nourished the discourse about the country's international mission. This became evident at the Universal Peace Congress of 1894, held in Antwerp. Patrons of the event included distinguished representatives of all political parties, and King Leopold II even welcomed a delegation to Ostend. Belgian support for the congress exemplified the phenomenon that the historian Sandi Cooper has described as 'patriotic pacifism'.[33] This became evident in the closing speech by Baron de Moreau d'Andoy, a former Belgian Minister of Agriculture and (briefly) of Foreign Affairs: 'You love the fatherland, it is holding on to you with all the fibres of your soul, and you understand this noble élan of patriotism and military value!'[34] The statesman acknowledged Belgian support for the pacifists:

> Belgium, glad about its neutrality as it is about its independence and its freedom, understands more and more the importance of your work … It does not have the ambition to play the role of a great power, … it will always know to respect others and the treaties which have made it independent and free.[35]

In other words: peace congresses in Belgium provided an occasion to assert patriotic credentials. One episode at Antwerp showed the interplay of national and international ideas related in the field of education. The Belgian president of the congress, Auguste Houzeau de Lehaie, took the opportunity to praise the *Histoire du peuple belge et de sa civilisation*, a textbook written by a Belgian schoolmaster:

> It is the history of the progress and civilisation of Belgium. Here the accounts of battles, which play such a great role in other books of the same genre, are relegated to the second tier. Military events, which still need to be included in such a history, as they are events that one cannot ignore, do not constitute the most important part of this work.[36]

Houzeau de Lehaie mentioned this particular work as a Belgian government committee had adopted it as a school textbook. The Universal Peace Congress welcomed this step and sent its congratulations to the author. Thus, an international forum – the Universal Peace Congress – became a stage for promoting a particular form of national history-writing.

The Belgian lawyer and women's rights campaigner Louis Frank was a delegate at the 1894 congress. A decade later, he argued in his book *Les Belges et la paix* that the Belgians' experience of foreign domination and the kingdom's neutrality after independence had rendered them particularly peace-loving.[37] According to Frank, the Belgians, 'more than any other people in this world, have worked through all means for the supreme good of Humanity, to facilitate and develop international peaceful relations'. In this context, he referred to Pirenne's comments on the distinct nature of 'Belgian civilisation' and presented his country's geographic location as part of its destiny.[38]

Frank reiterated his belief in Belgium's pacifist mission in his essay 'La Paix et le District Fédéral du Monde', suggesting to turn Belgium into the 'Federal District of the World'. He complained that The Hague's hosting of the widely celebrated Peace Conference of 1899 was 'an error or diplomatic injustice'.[39] Frank's proposal often features in accounts about Belgian internationalism, but few historians have commented on the extravagant nature of his arguments. Frank suggested that Belgians – alongside the English and the Americans – had formulated 'the first pacifist utopias', that the country's geology was unique and that its soil contained traces of human settlement and trade preceding pre-historical remnants elsewhere.[40] His arguments were characterised by their circularity: the Federal District of the World had to be 'a microcosm, that means a small world, the summary and miniature version of the universe'; it had to benefit from a 'unique topographical situation and be the closest neighbour of the world's principal races'. These qualifying criteria evidently chimed with Frank's description of his own country: 'located at the intersection of the three great human races which share hegemony of the earth, Belgium represents their conjunction zone'. Accordingly, Belgium did not merely have the 'honour and privilege' of becoming the future Federal District: 'it has the right'.[41]

The essay on the Federal District of the World appeared in a lavish book, *La Belgique illustrée*, which addressed a French audience and provided a guide to Belgian history and cities. Frank had been charged with editing this tome in time for the Brussels world's fair of 1910, but the main part was authored by another intellectual: Louis Dumont-Wilden, co-founder of the weekly *Pourquoi Pas?* and a highly prolific journalist.[42] Dumont-Wilden referred to Pirenne's work, echoed his language in describing Belgium as being 'the frontier of two civilisations' and sought to demonstrate the country's multiethnic character. He praised Picard for having provided resonance for Pirenne's ideas 'in both speech and pen'.[43]

Dumont-Wilden was particularly interested in the role of the Belgian capital. In *La Belgique illustrée*, he described how a visitor from Paris would at first get the impression that Brussels was a 'little Paris', before discovering that the city had a spirit of its own.

> Brussels, ancient crossroads of the European peoples, old hostel of princes in exile, is uniquely welcoming… but you must have frequented it for a long time before you know it well. To welcome foreigners, it dresses *à la française*, or, more exactly, it wears this cosmopolitan uniform which one today sees in most of the great European cities. But in its heart, it remains very *brabançonne*, very *bruxelloise*.[44]

La Belgique illustrée was not the first publication in which Dumont-Wilden described Brussels in such terms: in an earlier article, he had praised it as 'an international crossroads', a city that was 'in the process of becoming a great cosmopolitan capital', with a cultural life that belonged to 'the great fatherland of universal intellectualism'.[45] The city, according to Dumont-Wilden, was 'marvellously prepared' to play the 'role of a European capital, that is to say, a city of exchange'. In these comments, the city's 'cosmopolitan' features did not seem problematic, as they were tempered by the continuing existence of local and regional peculiarities.

Both before and after the First World War, Dumont-Wilden discussed the 'European spirit' in his writings.[46] If one views Europeanism as a form of internationalism, it is hardly surprising that Europeanists embraced the notion of Belgium at the 'crossroads of Europe'. For instance, a travelogue by Paul Colin, founder of the cultural review *Europe*, was entitled *Carrefour de l'Occident*.[47] The book portrayed Belgium as a nation that had endured foreign dominance and military conflict, while praising the cultural riches that this central location had brought to its towns and regions. The suitability of such imagery for Europeanists became evident at the First Pan-European Congress, held in Vienna in 1926. In his speech, the Belgian delegate Irenée Van der Ghinst picked up tropes of Belgian nationalism: Belgium, he claimed, was a 'country of workers' which had long been a 'battlefield of Europe'. Yet because of these experiences, Belgians had become peace-loving: 'We are more proud of our artistic, literary and cultural glory than of our success on the battlefield.'[48]

Exceptional case or discourse of exceptionalism?

We must not take the exceptionalist narratives of Belgian intellectuals at face value. An 'international crossroads' can be located in various places, depending on the roads on which one travels. Belgian intellectuals acknowledged that their country shared features with other states. Louis Piérard saw Belgium as one of several 'great small countries', listing Switzerland, Norway and Holland as further examples. According to the Walloon socialist, these countries were 'detached from imperialist aims, passionately attached to the cause of international understanding, and the best artisans of peaceful civilisation'.[49] Jo Tollebeek has pointed out that even representations of Flemish distinctness *within* the Belgian nation resembled the country's discourse at large: intellectuals such as Auguste Vermeylen saw the Flemings as mediators between the Germanic and Latin cultures.[50]

The idea of internationalism as a national characteristic, or even destiny, was not uniquely Belgian. In the Netherlands, historians such as Johan Huizinga portrayed their country in a way that resembled Pirenne's representation of Belgium.[51] The construction of a Dutch mission was encapsulated by ideas of being a *gidsland* – a 'guiding country' with moral leadership in international affairs and a pioneering role in international law. Such notions gained in prominence in the decade after the Hague Peace Conference of 1899, becoming part of the discourse on Dutch nationhood.[52] Ideas about the country's distinct role in international relations were particularly associated with Cornelis van Vollenhoven, a leading expert in international law.[53]

The idea of internationalism as a national mission also found resonance in Switzerland, another small country with different linguistic communities and powerful neighbours. The writings of the leading Swiss internationalist William Rappard are a case in point. His negotiating skills had helped to ensure Geneva's designation as seat of the League of Nations, and he subsequently headed the League's Mandates section. An ardent supporter of international organisation, he also co-founded the Graduate Institute of International Studies in Geneva. Rappard combined his commitment to internationalism with a language that stressed the distinct features of Geneva and of Switzerland as a whole. He claimed that the city's 'historical traditions, her neutral status, and her geographical position, near the watershed of three great European civilisations, have given her a peculiar international outlook and have, in the course of the nineteenth century, made of her the centre of various international activities'.[54]

Such reflections on neutrality, geography and civilisational encounters recall the language which Belgian intellectuals adopted for their own nation. To Rappard, the Swiss Confederation's history was 'the history of 657 years of collective security'; in that sense, 'the Alpine league of cantons bears far more resemblance than most other states to the world League of Nations'.[55] These comments recall Picard's description of Belgium as the precursor of a 'United States of Europe'. Yet there were further similarities between Swiss and Belgian discourse, for instance in the celebration of local traditions: the conservative Swiss author Gonzague de Reynold (a member of the League of Nations' Committee on Intellectual Cooperation) described his country as a product of its surroundings, a 'civilisation of cities' and even 'the most ancient western civilisation'.[56]

Did Belgium offer a model for other countries? Dumont-Wilden liked to think so, claiming that its history was 'an object of admiration and emulation to the small peoples, and an object of respect to the great nations'.[57] In some instances, speakers from other countries did indeed refer to the country's exemplary features – although their statements might be interpreted as a form of flattery. At the Antwerp peace congress of 1894, for instance, the Danish peace leader and IPB president, Fredrik Bajer, favourably compared Belgium and Switzerland to his own country. He pointed out that Switzerland and Belgium were neutral in international law and recommended that Denmark follow suit because of its strategic location between the Baltic and the North Sea. Moreover, Bajer appreciated the way in which Switzerland and Belgium balanced different national or ethnic groups; he hoped that Denmark and Germany would learn from the apparent success of these countries.[58] A second example is provided by the Czechoslovakian ambassador to Belgium, who made the following comments on the occasion of the 1935 world's fair:

> Belgium and Czechoslovakia resemble each other in an astonishing manner. Located at the crossroads of several civilisations, at the meeting point of the great currents of ideas, historical developments have subjected them to an identical treatment and fashioned their inhabitants with a mentality that is particularly receptive to the ideas of others, which has rendered them particularly adept at international cooperation. Their geographical location, at the great thoroughfares of travel, made them develop their trade and industry early on, and... [they have] thus reached a result that has much exceeded the possibilities of their own territory.[59]

Such comments can be read in different ways: on the one hand, they show how Czechs and Slovaks reasoned about their heterogeneous, newly formed state and its potentially threatening neighbours. Czechoslovakian statesmen and intellectuals focused on their central role in Europe as a solution to this potential problem.[60] Yet, on the other hand, the quotation also says something about Belgium – namely that the image of the Belgian 'crossroads' was sufficiently prominent to be noted by foreign observers.

Two Belgian internationalists and their idea of the nation

With the basic parameters of the discourse on 'international Belgium' firmly established, it is worthwhile to examine projects and activities that expressed such notions. How did Belgian intellectuals combine nationalism and internationalism in theory and practice? The writings of the pacifist Henri La Fontaine and the bibliographer Paul Otlet shed light on this question. Both individuals are usually viewed as idealists who played a central role in Belgian internationalism. In 1913, the presentation speech for La Fontaine's Nobel Peace Prize praised him as 'the true leader of the popular peace movement in Europe' and estimated that '[t]here is no one who has contributed more to the organization of peaceful internationalism'.[61] The author of the pioneering study of Otlet has described the latter as 'something of a visionary whose ideas were at least fifty years ahead of his time'.[62] The idealism of these two activists found its most tangible expression in the opening of a world palace (the *Palais Mondial*) in Brussels after the First World War. Even more ambitious was their scheme for a 'world capital city', the *Cité Mondiale*. The universalist dimensions of these schemes are discussed in chapter 6. However, a closer look at La Fontaine and Otlet's writings over three decades reveals that nations in general, and the Belgian nation in particular, were essential to their conceptualisation of an international community. To them, nations represented a form of social collaboration of which internationalism was the logical extension.[63] Even on a visual and organisational scale, internationalism was the extension of nationhood: when the two Belgians opened an 'international museum', national sections made up a large part, with states themselves providing the exhibits.

During the First World War, the two Belgian internationalists recognised the important and potentially explosive role of nationhood in international relations. La Fontaine acknowledged that 'the principle of nationalities dominated the whole history of the last century and of the beginning of the next one', arguing that any future world order would have to take this into account.[64] Otlet regarded the nationality question as a key factor in causing the conflict.[65] In his blueprint for the post-war order, he therefore stressed that a world organisation would need to 'guarantee the primordial rights of man, of nationalities, races, religions, associations, social categories, states'.[66] La Fontaine also promoted stipulations on the rights of nations and national minorities, both in his proposal for an international peace treaty and his discussions with European pacifists.[67]

Both internationalists supported national movements during the war. Otlet drafted a declaration on the rights of nations.[68] He argued that one of the problems of international law was that it had ignored stateless nations: 'If nationalities are misjudged and oppressed by the State to which they are arbitrarily attached, there is no other resort for them but revolt and violent secession.'[69] Meanwhile, La Fontaine hoped for Belgian leadership in addressing 'the legitimate complaints of all oppressed nations', and expressed his disappointment in the Belgian prime minister Charles de Broqueville for not having taken up the cause of oppressed nationalities.[70] La Fontaine hoped that the USA would initiate a conference of neutral countries to address Europe's 'national question'.[71]

Underling such concerns, La Fontaine served as a patron of the Central Office of Nationalities. The French journalist Jean Pelissier had founded this body in 1912 to collect information on nations and help oppressed peoples gain autonomy.[72] The first congress initiated by Pelissier was covered in La Fontaine and Otlet's periodical *La Vie Internationale*.[73] One of the event's keynote speakers was the French historian Charles Seignobos, who had influenced the Office's creation and was 'an advocate of oppressed nationality, and of a view of history oriented around evolutionary determinism and the indivisibility and inevitability of France as a nation-state'.[74] Mirroring La Fontaine's association with Pelissier's office, Otlet presided over a Congress of Nationalities which Pelissier organised in Lausanne in 1916. Such examples demonstrate the centrality of the nation to internationalist discussions during the First World War. Similarly, Glenda Sluga has observed that the Congress of Oppressed Nationalities in Rome (1918) was 'indicative of the ways in which the principle of nationality had become a self-fulfilling discourse'.[75]

The support for specific national causes was evident in La Fontaine's involvement in the Executive Council of the Ligue Internationale Philarménienne. This Geneva-based organisation also counted William Rappard, the anti-slavery activist John Harris and the historian Arnold J. Toynbee among its members. In 1922 and 1923, the Ligue lobbied the Conference of Lausanne, which had been convened to address the international implications of the end of the Ottoman Empire. La Fontaine provided the Ligue with access to transnational pacifist networks. When the organisation's secretary asked the IPB to circulate a pro-Armenian appeal, he stressed that La Fontaine had 'taken part in all of our deliberations in September and is a member of our Executive Council'.[76] On behalf of the IPB, La Fontaine subsequently drafted a message to the diplomats gathered in Lausanne. The document urged Turkey to accept the principle of national self-determination and to respect national minority rights.[77]

Despite his dependence on national categories, Otlet did not treat nations as perennial phenomena, but as outcomes of specific historical processes. As a consequence, the nation-state appeared as a historical stage that could be overcome. Otlet envisaged an era that exceeded the nation-state, marked by the 'advent of universal and global life'.[78] While he had referred to a 'Republic of Nations' during the First World War, by the mid-1930s, he evoked a 'United States of the World' or a 'Global Republic' (*République Mondiale*).[79]

Membership of this organisation was to be universal, compulsory and permanent. Unlike an 'Association of Governments', this system was not premised on national sovereignty and unanimity.[80] Such shifts suggest that Otlet's position towards the nation was subject to conceptual, strategic and rhetorical changes.

What was the role of the Belgian nation in this context? La Fontaine referred to the 'mission which Belgium must fulfil' and portrayed the establishment of their *Palais Mondial* as a first step towards this aim.[81] In promoting this 'Belgian mission', his friend Otlet relied on national stock images: Belgium appeared as 'an ancient country where all civilisations of the past have left their traces in the cities, in the monuments and institutions'.[82] Moreover, its capital Brussels was 'the centre of the great quadrangle linking up London, Amsterdam, Cologne and Paris'; it was 'situated in a country having the densest population in the world and in proportion to its surface it is endowed with a maximum of inheritance of Civilisation'.[83] This notion of being at the heart of an imaginary quadrangle frequently featured in Otlet's writings. To him, it was due to its geographic location that Brussels had become a 'cosmopolitan city'.[84] Such writings echoed Picard and Pirenne in referring to the confluence of the 'Germanic tide' and 'Gallo-Roman civilisation' on Belgian soil.[85]

These quotes stem from the period after the First World War, demonstrating the durability of the image of Belgium as an international nation. This is not to say, however, that the war itself was without consequence for the two Belgians' views. As early as August 1914, La Fontaine argued that his country had 'definitely merited through its bravery and self-discipline to become the *Cité Internationale*. It is in Brussels where the peace must be concluded, one hundred years after the Treaty of Ghent.'[86] The peace activist later expressed the conviction that Belgium 'must become the chosen land of the cordial entente between the peoples. She has, in fact, already become it a long time ago'.[87] In this context, he reiterated notions of the kingdom as a European 'microcosm', its past as a 'crossroads of the nations' and the Belgians' historic 'love of freedom'. Meanwhile, in his discussion of *La Fin de la Guerre*, Otlet emphasised that Belgium would have to play a central role in a future League of Nations. He later regretted that Geneva had been chosen as site for the League's headquarters 'in defiance of all moral rights and all advantages of Belgium',[88] and in spite of Belgium's 'martyrdom'.[89] In this respect, campaigns for a world capital city on Belgian soil sought to redress this perceived injustice. Yet by 1923, La Fontaine had come to regard these endeavours as futile, as he revealed in a letter to the Belgian ambassador to the USA:

> In all cases that paralyse our work, it is primarily in Belgium that the damage has been inflicted. It is nearly certain that it won't become the International Centre for which we sought to lay the basis. I have but one regret, namely to have had illusions in this regard and to have sacrificed years in vain.[90]

Otlet seemed less perturbed. He continued to promote his *Cité Mondiale* throughout the 1920s and 1930s – although he also explored Geneva as a non-Belgian site. To attract support from Belgian officials, Otlet adopted a national line of argument: the German attack had demonstrated that the country had a tangible interest in international stability. In a note to the Belgian government and parliament in 1931, he suggested that a Belgian *Cité Mondiale* would become the kingdom's 'moral shield of defence'.[91] The same year, Otlet spoke at the Universal Peace Congress in Brussels, claiming that only a comprehensive world organisation would guarantee Belgium's safety and that the country should therefore establish a 'Centre for all exchanges, for all cooperation'.[92] He reiterated this view in 1935, when he argued that the 'organisation of Europe, of the world' would 'protect Belgium, Flanders and Wallonia'.[93]

Beyond its potential for serving the cause of Belgian security, the *Cité Mondiale* offered another national advantage, namely the alleviation of domestic tensions. Like other European states, Belgium experienced a period of great instability in the 1930s, reflected in fiscal and economic crises, frequent changes of government and the growth of radical political movements. Otlet recognised these divisions and in 1935 expressed his concern about

> Linguistic struggles, tending to divide public life, going until administrative division, the hegemony of one race of the other, amongst some extremists going until separation... Intense political and social struggles that complicate each problem through a triple cut Walloon-Flemish, Catholic-liberal, conservative-reformist.[94]

According to Otlet, the construction of a *Cité Mondiale* would soften tensions between the 'Belgian races'.[95] In this respect, it might even reverberate beyond the kingdom's borders by demonstrating the 'possibilities on the road to an international synthetic polyculture'.[96]

As support from Brussels was not forthcoming, Otlet shifted his attention to the city of Antwerp as a potential site for his 'world capital'. To make his case, he appealed to Flemish sentiment, praising Flemings as 'the first workers of the world' and comparing them favourably to the Walloons and the *Bruxellois*.[97] He repeated these views in a paper which described the Flemish as 'diligent and intelligent' and referred to the region's splendid past.[98] Yet Flemish consciousness was not supposed to preclude an international spirit: the *Cité Mondiale* was to ensure that the Flemish 'reach a national consciousness that is henceforth accompanied by a global consciousness'. To Otlet, the Flemings would be 'great, because their place will be determined not only in Belgium, but in the world.' Flemish nationalism was thus conceived as one of several attachments: 'Flanders, Belgium, Europe, the world'.[99] In line with this view, Otlet warned against a narrow-minded, aggressive nationalism: 'Auguste Vermeylen has written: "We need to be Flemish to be European"… it would be one of the greatest ills if nationalism, triumphant today, establishes itself between Flanders and the Enlightenment of the World.'[100]

Such statements demonstrate Otlet's attachment to both international community and national unity, which he did not want to see challenged by the Flemish movement. In the 1930s, Otlet therefore conceived the idea of a national knowledge centre, the *Belganeum*, which was meant to gather the 'total knowledge of the country' and thus reconcile competing interests and factions.[101] Thus, the proposal expressed the idea that unity and community had to be imposed at multiple levels, from the local to the global. A related scheme by Otlet was the so-called *Urbaneum*, his plan for a new centre for intellectual life in Brussels.[102] Alongside its local function, the *Urbaneum* would ensure the 'permanent collaboration between Flanders and Wallonia' and 'secure for itself the capital centres of international life', allowing Belgium 'to benefit from the great currents of international economic, social and intellectual life'.[103] In a way, then, such proposals were both national and international undertakings – and this multiplicity was characteristic of many forms of internationalism.

Arguments that affirmed the national benefits of a *Cité Mondiale*, a *Belganeum* or an *Urbaneum* can also be read in a different way: in order to maximise the likelihood of official support, it made sense to frame internationalist ventures in national terms. Already in 1910, La Fontaine and Otlet drew up a 'confidential note' to the Belgian government, aiming to convey the national significance of their activities. The document suggested that Belgium's eminence as an international centre was threatened by efforts elsewhere: the Netherlands, for instance, was '[i]nformed about everything that has been done in Belgium' and had started to 'use the ideas implemented by us'.[104] Switzerland was 'also a rival of Belgium in the international realm': given the 'intellectual limitations' of the city of Bern, 'great efforts are underway to attract new institutions to Geneva'. Further competition came from France: for instance, due to actions of French diplomats, 'Belgium, which had anterior rights, had lost the seat of the great international office of hygiene'.[105] While these alarmist comments express national concerns, the note's concluding sections revealed the instrumentalism of such arguments. To fight off the Dutch, Swiss and French rivals, La Fontaine and Otlet recommend measures that would have benefited their own ventures: financial support, designated contacts in the Ministry for Foreign Affairs and an official legal recognition of international organisations, including official status for their own Central Office of International Institutions.[106]

Staging Belgian internationalism

Images of 'international Belgium' were not only a matter for intellectuals and politicians: they were broadcast to national and international audiences. The Belgian world's fairs shed light on the practical applications of this discourse. Between 1885 and 1935, Belgium hosted more world's fairs than any other European country. Such events were more than government affairs: they were often launched by business circles, although they relied on official patronage for organisational and financial support, for instance through state-sponsored lotteries.[107]

The world's fairs were characterised by both international and national features. Paul Greenhalgh has stressed the way in which world's fairs were 'a product of the European and American sense of being involved in a mighty global enterprise'.[108] The organisers of the Brussels exhibition of 1910 claimed that 'international expositions admirably serve the cause of universal peace, towards which all people reach out in general, and the Belgian people in particular', with one observer describing such events as 'miniature international societies'.[109] While the 1910 exposition attracted a range of foreign exhibitors, the Ligue pour Attirer les Étrangers en Belgique also used the event to promote tourism.[110] King Albert I expressed his pride in these visits: 'Is foreign participation not the most striking of the sentiments of esteem and friendship which diligent and peaceful Belgium inspires in other nations?'[111] The holding of such events facilitated the representation of Belgium as an international meeting place. Commenting on the 1913 exhibition in Ghent, the British town planner Patrick Geddes observed that

> internationally, it [the exhibition] is keenly conscious of the immense importance and growing significance of Belgium as a 'Key-stone State' whose very material and military weakness, in the midst of great armed Powers, gives her an advantage of common appeal to them all – an appeal impossible to any one of these, through their respective jealousies.[112]

Beyond their intrinsic international features, world's fairs had practical links to the 'mechanics of internationalism' and have even been interpreted as 'the epitomes of nineteenth-century internationalism'.[113] From 1908, an international federation brought together representatives of national organising committees, and in 1928 an international convention established the Bureau International des Expositions. Furthermore, exhibitions were accompanied by a many international congresses: officially, over 90 for the Brussels fair of 1910 and over 200 for 1935.[114] Since exhibition events were supposed to be 'apolitical' affairs, the actual number of congresses in the host city that year was even higher.[115]

These international ramifications notwithstanding, world's fairs evidently performed a national role. National competition for greater and better displays was one aspect, as evidenced by the French, German and British contributions in Brussels in 1910.[116] Furthermore, the Belgian world's fairs of 1905 and 1930 marked national jubilees. On the former occasion, the civil servant and internationalist Cyrille Van Overbergh stressed that 'it is essential to display under the eyes of the nation and the world what this small country has produced for sixty-five years in all scientific areas'.[117] While such events showcased the country's scientific and technological accomplishments, they did not imply a rupture with the past. The 1894 world exhibition in Antwerp has been interpreted as an 'ambiguous spectacle of modernity', as reflected in its underlying quest for authenticity.[118] At this event, displays of modern technology and colonial expansion coexisted with an 'Old Antwerp' section. Such reconstructed city quarters also featured at subsequent Belgian fairs, from 'Bruxelles Kermesse' in 1897 and 'Old Liège' in 1905 to 'Old Brussels' in 1935. The Ghent world exhibition of 1913 illustrates this balancing act between tradition and modernity: the city promoted itself as an industrial centre, a 'city of flowers' and as the heir to a glorious past. Its 'Old Flanders' section was described as an 'audacious attempt to simultaneously resurrect the era of Guicciardini and the era of Anton Sander'.[119] 'Old city quarters' were not unique to Belgium: the 1889 exhibition in Paris boasted a resurrected version of the Bastille area, the 1893 Chicago exhibition a 'German village' and the Parisian world's fair of 1900 both a 'Vieux Paris' and a Swiss village.[120]

The Belgian exhibitions show that world's fairs were not subject to a simple dualism between nationalism and internationalism: they also expressed regional identities. The historian Eric Storm has noted the pioneering function of old city quarters at Belgian events as regionalist architecture began to feature more prominently at exhibitions in other countries in the 1920s and 1930s.[121] In representations of Belgian nationhood, the tradition of its cities and provinces was a key feature. Whereas international exhibitions in Britain and France mostly took place in London and Paris, several Belgian cities hosted major events: Antwerp, Brussels, Liège and Ghent. In addition, Charleroi staged an international industrial exhibition in 1911. This multiplicity was partly due to the competition between Belgian cities.[122] On the occasion of the Brussels exhibition of 1910, Dumont-Wilden poked fun at the extent to which such events – despite their organisational shortcomings – became matters of local or regional pride:

> There isn't a single Brussels resident,... not a single flower vendor or newspaper boy, who does not expect something from this exposition and who does not believe he has a stake in its success. At Liège in 1905, the phenomenon was striking and this enthusiasm, this unconscious bluff stretched across all of Wallonia. It would not have gone down well at a club in the Ardennes to say that the Liège exhibition was not the most beautiful exhibition that had ever taken place. For their own international forum, the *Bruxellois* have a similar tenderness and they regard those who criticise it as fools... as bad patriots who betray the prosperity of Brussels.[123]

The Ghent organisers of 1913 estimated that the world's fair would allow their city to raise its profile and attract 'universal attention'.[124] They alleged that the 'law of progress' dictated that their municipality would 'take its seat amongst the great international family, and to make itself better known and more appreciated'.[125] Such competition was complicated by the country's growing linguistic tensions after the First World War. The 1930 exhibition was initially planned for Brussels and Antwerp. However, complaints from Wallonia led to the conclusion 'that it was impossible to organise an exhibition on Flemish land, to commemorate the Centenary, without according the same honour and the same rights to a Walloon city'.[126] As a result, Antwerp and Liège served as joint hosts.

Beyond internationalism, nationalism and regionalism, world's fairs related to a fourth current: colonialism. The interplay of these forces was already apparent at the London Great Exhibition of 1851, the prototype for subsequent world's fairs.[127] In the wake of the 'new imperialism' of the late nineteenth century, colonial aspects became even more pronounced. The Chicago world's fair of 1883 initiated a tradition of colonial sideshows.[128] Even before Belgium annexed the Congo Free State in 1908, it showcased King Leopold's colonial venture. The Antwerp world's fair of 1894, for instance, included an African exhibition with 'products and curiosities from the Congo'.[129] Three years later, a colonial exhibition accompanied the Brussels world's fair and attracted nearly 1.2 million people. Located in the park of Tervuren, a 'Congolese village' – inhabited by 267 Africans – proved to be a particularly popular, albeit problematic event.[130] Such 'living exhibits' had already featured on a smaller scale during the Belgian world's fairs of 1885 and 1894. In France, similar presentations had accompanied the 1877 Paris exposition, while in Germany, the animal dealer Carl Hagenbeck organised ethnographical shows with Africans and Pacific Islanders from the 1870s.[131]

Belgian world exhibitions continued to feature African displays after the annexation of the Congo. As an official guide to the exhibition of 1910 noted, the event allowed Belgium to 'affirm itself as a colonial power'.[132] Once again, Tervuren had its colonial sideshow, coupled with the inauguration of a permanent Congo Museum. It has been argued that the Brussels fair celebrated the 'new imperial Belgium' and that the Congo pavilions at Belgian world's fairs between 1910 and 1935 were central features of the country's representation as a modern nation.[133] Indeed, three years after the event in Brussels, the Ghent exhibition featured a Congo Palace which aimed to project 'force, power and prosperity'.[134] The Flemish city also hosted so-called 'Colonial Days' as well as congresses on the 'improvement of colonial material' and on 'colonial science'.[135] Such projects evidently connected to the internationalism of conferences and knowledge exchange.

The staging of colonialism added further layers to narratives about 'international Belgium'. Internationalism, nationalism and colonialism converged in the concept of 'Belgian expansion' – the plan to overcome national limitations through concerted efforts in the colonial, economic and intellectual spheres. To Edmond Picard, 'expansion' was compatible with Belgium's 'national character', namely 'work, modesty and peacefulness'; it was a way of avoiding the 'decadence' that he associated with contemporary France.[136] The historian Madeleine Herren has drawn attention to a striking manifestation of these efforts: the Congress of Global Economic Expansion (Congrès d'Expansion Économique Mondiale), held in Mons in 1905.[137] It was a landmark event in the history of state-sponsored internationalism, shaped by the interactions of intellectuals, civil servants and the monarchy. The Mons congress enabled Belgian elites to stage their country as a colonial and economic power, but also as a centre for internationalism, with around 2,000 delegates from more than 30 countries attending this 'congress of congresses'.[138] Chaired by Auguste Beernaert, the elder statesman and IPU president, the event covered topics from economic theory to international cooperation and bibliography. According to Herren, the Mons congress sought to present 'scientifically legitimised visions of conquest through a combination of economics and civilisational aspirations'.[139] The liberal newspaper *L'Indépendance Belge* praised it as the start of a new 'epoch', forming part of a drive towards 'global action' that was shaped by the 'internationalisation of economic interests'.[140]

The Mons congress had evident national features: it coincided with the Liège world's fair and the seventy-fifth anniversary of the Belgian Revolution – hence taking place at a time which, according to Jean Stengers, marked a peak in public affirmations of national pride.[141] The national dimension of this event was reflected in a reception at the Brussels Stock Exchange. On this occasion, King Leopold II stressed that 'Little Belgium increasingly wants to be the capital of a notable intellectual, artistic, civilising and economic movement, be a modest, but useful member of the great family of nations, and to contribute a small part to the services to humanity'.[142]

Although the congress produced over 400 reports, proponents of Belgian expansion deplored that 'contrary to what one had hoped, the great expansionist demonstration of 1905 was not the start of a truly new era, of a concerted movement – coherent and cohesive and irresistible – of a true renovation of our methods and manners'.[143] To rectify this state of affairs, businessmen, intellectuals and politicians launched the periodical *L'Expansion Belge* in 1908. One year later, the journal's circle gave birth to the Société Belge d'Expansion Nationale, counting among its members the industrialist and philanthropist Ernest Solvay and the former minister Gustave Francotte, chair of the committee that prepared Belgian participation in international exhibitions.[144] After the First World War, the bulletin of another group, the Société Belge d'Études et d'Expansion, carried contributions from figures such as Adrien de Burch, president of the Comité Belge des Expositions et des Foires.[145]

Even beyond its links to world exhibitions, 'Belgian expansion' had internationalist dimensions. The Union of International Associations – discussed in greater detail in chapter 6 – had its roots in the Mons congress, as La Fontaine, Otlet and Cyrille Van Overbergh founded a Central Office of International Institutions in response to one of the Mons resolutions. The 'confidential note' through which the Belgian internationalists sought to ensure official support for their venture quoted Leopold II's speech at the Brussels Stock Exchange and praised the events of 1905 for having effected a 'rapprochement' between the Belgian protagonists of different international organisations.[146] Furthermore, in the first issue of *L'Expansion Belge*, Otlet outlined his country's role as an international centre, citing the presence of around 40 major international associations as evidence. In addition to the kingdom's geographic location, its neutrality and tradition of liberty, Otlet attributed this status to the Belgians themselves who had 'a particular aptitude to understand different forms of civilisation and to assimilate them, which derives from the fact that our race is an aggregate of neighbouring races and that the usage of two national languages renders our relation with French, English and German culture more familiar and intimate.'[147]

Otlet emphasised that 'expansion' did not threaten the Belgian nation. Expansion meant 'to organise a system of collective life that permits the Belgians to remain Belgian, to remain attached by spirit and sentiment to the corner of land that supports their nationality and their fatherland'.[148] In October 1908, an anonymous article in *L'Expansion Belge* reiterated these points: describing Brussels as a site for international congresses, it praised the benefits for the Belgian nation – foreign visitors to international gatherings in Belgium would return to their countries, speak about Belgium and thus become 'active agents of expansion'.[149]

Conclusion

The Belgian case reveals how internationalism formed part of a national discourse. Being a nationalist, an internationalist and an imperialist were not mutually exclusive categories; in Belgium, they intersected in a narrative that stressed the country's inherent international features. This construct allowed intellectuals to make sense of their country's bilingual features and its relatively short history of independent statehood. In such narratives, even the battles and wars fought on Belgian soil seemed to prove Belgium's location at a 'European crossroads'. For proponents of closer international cooperation, the discourse about 'international Belgium' had evident advantages: it allowed them to frame their demands in a way that enhanced their chances of domestic support.

Colonial expansion in Africa could form part of this discourse: it reinforced the notion of a people who had to look beyond their own borders. Yet expansionist notions seemed to contradict another element that featured prominently in images of Belgium: namely the idea of Belgian modesty and of the Belgians' rootedness in local and regional settings. A figure such as Louis Piérard, who subscribed to the idea of Belgium's international mission, admitted that most Belgians were hardly 'citizens of the world' and remained attached to their immediate environment.[150] Seen from this angle, groups such as the circle around *L'Expansion Belge* did not so much express a consensus but appropriated ideas about 'international Belgium' to push for their own aims. The complex relationship between internationalism and King Leopold's colonial venture is discussed further in chapter 2.

Ideas about the Belgian nation were not static or clear-cut: national discourse is a matter of contestation, and Belgium was hardly an exception.[151] As subsequent chapters will show, notions about Belgium's international features did not mean that internationalist efforts always met with unequivocal support. Moreover, domestic tensions or international events could lead intellectuals to change their position. For instance, Henri Pirenne, whose account of Belgium as a 'microcosm' proved so influential, was in many respects an internationalist who cooperated with historians from other countries and was active in the International Committee of the Historical Sciences.[152] Yet after the First World War, he was reluctant to work with German academics and in 1923 opposed German involvement in an international historical congress at Brussels. His overall stance in the interwar years has even been interpreted as 'abortive internationalism'.[153] It is important to bear in mind that as far as individual actors were concerned, both nationalism and internationalism were subject to shifts and uncertainties.

Notes

1 *Compte rendu des travaux du Congrès général de Statistique, réuni à Bruxelles, le 19, 20, 21 et 22 Septembre* (Brussels, 1853).

2 Adolphe Quetelet, *Du Système social et des lois qui le régissent* (Paris, 1848), pp. 156–7. Cf. Nico Randeraad, 'The International Statistical Congress (1853–1876): knowledge transfers and their limits', *European History Quarterly*, 41 (2011), 50–65.

3 *Ibid.*, pp. 222–3.

4 Léon Bourgeois, *Pour la Société des Nations* (Paris, 1910), p. 26.

5 Glenda Sluga, *The Nation, Psychology, and International Politics, 1870–1919* (Basingstoke, 2006), pp. 3 and 5.

6 George Sarton, *War and Civilization* (Brussels, 1919), p. 4.

7 The role of intellectuals in national movements features prominently in Elie Kedourie, *Nationalism* (3rd edn., London, 1966) and Hroch, *Social Preconditions*. On transnationalism and intellectual activity, see Gisèle Sapiro (ed.), *L'Espace intellectuel en Europe: de la formation des États-nations à la mondialisation, 19–20e siècle* (Paris, 2009) and, regarding the interwar years, Daniel Laqua, 'Transnational intellectual cooperation, the League of Nations, and the problem of order', *Journal of Global History*, 6 (2011), 223–47.

8 Ernest Gellner, *Nations and Nationalism* (Oxford, 1983).

9 John Breuilly, *Nationalism and the State* (2nd edn., Manchester, 1993).

10 Such attempts were exemplified by the Flemish nationalist Hendrik Elias and his *Geschiedenis van de Vlaamse gedachte* (2nd edn., Antwerp, 1970). For a survey of Flemish nationalism, also discussing Elias's role therein, see Lode Wils, *Van de belgische naar de Vlaamse natie: een geschiedenis van de Vlaamse beweging* (Leuven, 2009).

11 Jean Stengers, *Les Racines de la Belgique* (Brussels, 2000), the first part of the author's two-volume *Histoire du sentiment nationale en Belgique des origines à 1918*.

12 Johannes Koll, 'Revolution und Nation. Zur Entstehung von belgischem Nationalbewusstsein im späten 18. Jahrhundert', in Koll (ed.), *Nationale Bewegungen in Belgien: Ein historischer Überblick* (Münster, 2005), pp. 15–40; Koll, *'Die belgische Nation': Patriotismus und Nationalbewusstsein in den Südlichen Niederlanden im späten 18. Jahrhundert* (Münster, 2003). For a different perspective, see Geert van den Bossche, *Enlightened Innovation and the Ancient Constitution: The Intellectual Justifications of Revolution in Brabant (1787–1790)* (Brussels, 2001).

13 Louis Piérard, *Wallons et Flamands* (Brussels, 1929); Hendrik de Man, *Nationalisme en socialisme* (Brussels, 1931).

14 Laurence van Ypersele, *Le Roi Albert, histoire d'un mythe* (Ottignies, 1995).

15 Alexis Schwarzenbach, *Portraits of the Nation: Stamps, Coins and Banknotes in Belgium and Switzerland, 1880–1945* (Bern, 1999). For other perspectives on Belgian nationhood, see Louis Vos and Kas Deprez (eds), *Nationalism in Belgium: Shifting Identities, 1780–1945* (Basingstoke, 1995); Lode Wils, *Van Clovis tot Di Rupo: de lange weg van de naties in de Lage Landen* (Antwerp, 2005).

16 Jo Tollebeek, 'The hyphen of national culture: the paradox of national distinctiveness in Belgium and the Netherlands, 1860–1918', *European Review*, 18 (2010), 207–25.

17 Stefan Berger, Mark Donovan and Kevin Passmore (eds), *Writing National Histories: Western Europe since 1800* (London, 1999); Stefan Berger and Chris Lorentz, *Nationalizing the Past: Historians as Nation Builders in Modern Europe* (Basingstoke, 2010).

18 Henri Pirenne, *Histoire de Belgique*, vol. 1: *Des origines au commencement du XIVe siècle* (5th edn., Brussels, 1929 [1900]), p. x. Cf. Jo Tollebeek, 'At the crossroads of nationalism: Huizinga, Pirenne and the Low Countries in Europe', *European Review of History*, 17 (2010), 187–215.

19 Pirenne, *Histoire de Belgique*, 1, pp. xii–xiii. Cf. Pirenne, *La Nation belge* (Brussels, 1900).

20 Pirenne, *Histoire de Belgique*, vol. 7: *De la révolution de 1830 à la guerre de 1914* (Brussels, 1932), p. 393. Pointing to changed circumstances, Tollebeek has argued that '[t]o call Belgium a "syncretism" no longer sounded convincing': Tollebeek, 'The hyphen of national culture', p. 222.
21 Pirenne, *Histoire de Belgique*, 7, pp. 391–3.
22 Marc Quaghebeur and Madéleine Rebérioux, 'Intellectuels en Belgique et en France: "Pilliers", citoyenneté, Etat', *Le Mouvement Social*, 178 (1997), 110–2.
23 Edmond Picard, *Essai d'une psychologie de la nation belge: suivi de l'idée du droit en Belgique* (Brussels, 1906). Picard had previously expressed these ideas in the *Revue encyclopédique Larousse* (24 July 1897).
24 Sluga, *The Nation, Psychology, and International Politics*, p. 61.
25 Cited in Geneviève Duchenne, *Visions et projets belges pour l'Europe: de la Belle Époque aux Traités de Rome* (Brussels, 2001), p. 28.
26 Stengers and Gubin, *Le Grand Siècle*, p. 122.
27 Paul Aron, *Les Écrivains belges et le socialisme (1880–1913)* (Brussels, 1985); Nathalie Aubert *et al.* (eds), *La Belgique entre deux siècles: laboratoire de la modernité, 1880–1914* (Bern, 2007); Christophe Verbruggen, *Schrijverschap in het Belgische belle époque: een sociaal-culturele geschiedenis* (Ghent, 2009).
28 Carton de Wiart, *Souvenirs littéraires*, p. 89; Louis Piérard, *Regards sur la Belgique* (Grenoble, 1945), p. 273.
29 Edmond Picard, *Synthèse de l'Antisémitisme* (Brussels, 1892) and *Nécessité et conditions de l'Expansion belge au dehors* (Brussels, 1906).
30 Jeanne Lindley, *Seeking and Finding: The Life of Emile Cammaerts* (London, 1962), p. 143.
31 Emile Cammaerts, *The Treasure House of Belgium: Her Land and People. Her Art and Literature* (London, 1924), p. 110.
32 Piérard, *Wallons et Flamands*, p. 33.
33 Sandi Cooper, *Patriotic Pacifism: Waging War on War in Europe, 1815–1914* (New York, 1991).
34 Henri La Fontaine (ed.), *Bulletin officiel du VIme Congrès international de la Paix, tenu à Anvers (Belgique) du 29 août au 1 septembre 1894* (Antwerp, 1895), pp. 92–3.
35 *Ibid.*, pp. 93–4.
36 *Ibid.*, p. 86.
37 Louis Frank, *Les Belges et la paix* (Brussels, 1905), p. 178.
38 *Ibid.*, pp. 1–3.
39 Louis Frank, 'La Paix et le District Fédéral du Monde', in Louis Dumont-Wilden, *La Belgique illustrée* (Paris, 1911), p. 285. A discussion of Frank's scheme features in Roel De Groof 'Promoting Brussels as a political world capital: from the national jubilee of 1905 to the Expo 58', in De Groof (ed.), *Brussels and Europe – Bruxelles et l'Europe* (Brussels, 2008), pp. 104–7.
40 *Ibid.*, pp. 286–8.
41 Frank, 'La Paix et le District Fédéral du Monde', p. 288.
42 On the wider context of this newspaper, see Pierre Van den Dungen, *Milieux des presse et journalistes en Belgique (1828–1914)* (Brussels, 2005).
43 Dumont-Wilden, *La Belgique illustrée*, pp. 8–9.

44 *Ibid.*, p. 18.
45 Louis Dumont-Wilden, 'Un carrefour international', *Le Matin* (27 March 1908).
46 Geneviève Duchenne, *Esquisses d'une Europe nouvelle: l'européisme dans la Belgique de l'entre-deux-guerres (1919–1939)* (Brussels, 2008), pp. 110–1 and 127–8.
47 Paul Colin, *Belgique. Carrefour de l'occident* (Paris, 1933). Demonstrating his cultural internationalism, Colin signed Romain Rolland's *Déclaration d'indépendance de l'Esprit* in 1919. He founded the revue *L'Art libre* (1919–1923) before editing *Europe*. During the Second World War, however, he became a proponent of the 'New European Order' and collaborated with the Germans.
48 MS GEHEC, folder II, no. 2: Irénée Van der Ghinst, 'Allocution au Premier Congrès Paneuropéen de Vienne, le 3 octobre 1926'.
49 Piérard, *Régards sur la Belgique*, p. 207.
50 Tollebeek, 'The hyphen of national culture', pp. 215–20.
51 Tollebeek, 'At the crossroads of nationalism', esp. pp. 196–8; Tollebeek, 'The hyphen of national culture', pp. 220–1. Cf. Anne-Isabelle Richard, 'Huizinga, intellectual cooperation and the spirit of Europe, 1933–1945', in Mark Hewitson and Matthew d'Auria (eds), *Europe in Crisis: Intellectuals and the European Idea, 1917–1957* (New York, 2012), pp. 243–56.
52 Pepijn Corduwener, 'Risee van de wereld of land van Grotius? De synthese tussen nationalisme en internationalisme in het Nederlandse fin de siècle', *Tijdschrift voor Geschiedenis*, 125 (2012), 205–15.
53 Riemens, *De passie voor vrede*, pp. 82–6. Cf. Peter Malcontent and Floribert Baudet, 'The Dutchman's Burden? Nederland en de internationaale rechtsorde in de twintigste eeuw', in Bob de Graaf, Hellena Duco and Bert van der Zwan (eds), *De Nederlandse buitenlandse politiek in de 20e eeuw* (Amsterdam, 2003), pp. 69–100; Remco van Diepen, *Voor volkenbond en vrede: Nederland en het streven naar een nieuwe wereldorde 1919–1946* (Amsterdam, 1999).
54 William Rappard, *International Relations as Viewed from Geneva* (New York, 1925), p. 2.
55 Rappard, *Collective Security in Swiss Experience 1291–1948* (London, 1948), pp. xi–xiii.
56 Gonzague de Reynold, *Grandeur de la Suisse* (Neuchâtel, 1940), pp. 166–7.
57 Dumont-Wilden, *La Belgique illustrée*, p. iv.
58 La Fontaine, *Bulletin officiel du VIme Congrès international de la Paix*, p. 41.
59 *1935: Section tchécoslovaque à l'Exposition universelle et internationale de Bruxelles*, p. 13.
60 Andrea Orzoff, *Battle for the Castle: The Myth of Czechoslovakia in Europe, 1914–1948* (Oxford, 2009).
61 Ragnvald Moe, secretary to the Nobel Committee, as cited in Frederick Haberman (ed.), *Nobel Lectures: Peace 1901–1925* (new edn., Singapore, 1999), p. 270.
62 W. Boyd Rayward. *The Universe of Information: The Work of Paul Otlet for Documentation and International Organisation* (Moscow, 1975), p. 3.
63 Paul Otlet, *La Loi de l'ampliation et l'internationalisme* (Brussels, 1908).
64 Henri La Fontaine, *The Great Solution: Magnissima Carta* (Boston, 1916), p. 18.

65 Otlet, *La Fin de la guerre: traité de paix générale basé sur une Charte Mondiale déclarant les droits de l'humanité et organisant la confédération des états* (Brussels, 1914), pp. 64–6.
66 *Ibid.*, p. 13.
67 La Fontaine, *The Great Solution*, p. 100; Cooper, *Patriotic Pacifism*, p. 196.
68 Rayward, *Universe of Information*, p. 204.
69 Otlet, *Constitution mondiale de la Société des Nations: le nouveau droit des gens* (Geneva, 1917), p. 9.
70 MS HLF 066: La Fontaine to Emile Vandervelde, 12 December 1916 and 18 March 1918.
71 *Ibid.*, La Fontaine to Vandervelde, 12 December 1916 and 30 December 1916.
72 MS HLF 139: leaflet 'Office central des Nationalités' and press clipping 'Un Syndicat de Nationalités', *La Petite Republique* (13 February 1912). On the organization, see D.R. Watson, 'Jean Pelissier and the Office Central des Nationalités, 1912– 1919', *English Historical Review*, 110 (1995), 1191–206.
73 UAI, *La Vie Internationale*, 1 (1912), 125–6.
74 Sluga, *The Nation, Psychology, and International Politics*, p. 24.
75 *Ibid.*, p. 59.
76 MS IPB 317.2: Ligue Internationale Philarménienne to Henri Golay, 1 November 1922.
77 *Ibid.*, La Fontaine to Golay, 5 November 1922 and 'Botschaft des Internationalen Friedensbureau an die Delegierten der Lausanner-Konferenz'.
78 *Ibid.*, p. 446 (appendix).
79 Otlet, *Constitution mondiale*, p. 49; Otlet, *Plan Belgique: essai d'un plan national général, économique, social, culturel* (Brussels, 1935), p. 140; Otlet, *Monde: essai d'universalisme* (Brussels, 1935), p. 209.
80 *Ibid.*, pp. 223–4.
81 MS HLF 066: La Fontaine to Edmond Picard, 9 May 1921.
82 Otlet, *Sur la création d'une Université internationale: rapport présenté à l'Union des Associations internationales* (Brussels, 1920), p. 24.
83 MS APM, 'Cité Mondiale. UAI 15/I': 'Note N° 6372. 22 May 1931. Application submitted to the Belgian government and parliament with regard to the World City' in 'Munda. Textes en anglais'.
84 *Ibid.*, Otlet, 'Le Quadrilatere' in 'La Cité Mondiale. Doc. 4557 (Brussels, 1931)'.
85 Otlet, *Plan Belgique*, p. 21
86 MS HLF 064: La Fontaine to Fried, 6 August 1914.
87 MS HLF 097: La Fontaine, 'La reconstruction de la Belgique', p. 23.
88 Otlet, *L'Exposition Universelle de 1930 en Belgique et l'établissement d'une Cité Mondiale* (Brussels, 1930), p. 6.
89 Otlet, *Monde*, pp. 459–61.
90 MS HLF 139: La Fontaine to the Belgian ambassador in Washington, 5 March 1923.
91 MS APM, 'Cité Mondiale. UAI 15/1': Application submitted to the Belgian government and parliament with regard to the World City ('Munda: textes en anglais').
92 Otlet, *Monde*, p. 459.

93 Otlet, *Plan Belgique*, p. 139.
94 *Ibid.*, p. 27.
95 MS APM, 'Cité Mondiale. UAI 15/1': Otlet, 'La Cité Mondiale à Anvers', *Encyclopaedia Universalis Mundaneum*, doc. 8429 (Brussels, 1937).
96 Otlet, *Plan Belgique*, p. 25
97 MS APM, 'Cité Mondiale. UAI 15/I': Otlet, 'Les Flamands et le Palais Mondial', in 'Mundaneum et les Flamands'.
98 Otlet, 'De wereldstad en de Vlamingen', *Ibid.*
99 *Ibid.*
100 Otlet, 'Les Flamands et le Palais Mondial'.
101 'Par quels moyens réaliser le nationaeum ?' in 'Etterbeek-oneum', as well as Otlet, *Plan Belgique*, p. 155.
102 Otlet, 'L'Urbaneum – Bruxelles, Cité Mondiale. Bruxelles, Grande Ville. Bruxelles, Capitale de la Belgique', *La Cité*, 9 (1931), 128–9.
103 *Ibid.*, 122.
104 MS UIA: 'Note confidentielle sur la participation de la Belgique au mouvement international et sur les moyens de maintenir et de développer la situation qu'elle a acquise en ce domaine' (17 March 1910), p. 5, in 'La Belgique et l'internationalisme'. I am grateful to Pierre-Yves Saunier for sharing this document.
105 *Ibid.*, p. 6.
106 *Ibid.*, p. 7.
107 Ray Nist, 'Comment on fait une exposition', *L'Exposition de Gand (Editions Illustrés du Soir), Avril-Novembre 1913* (Brussels, 1913); 'Comment est financée l'exposition de 1935', *1935: Bulletin officiel de l'Exposition universelle et internationale de Bruxelles* (15 November 1935).
108 Paul Greenhalgh, *Ephemeral Vistas: The Expositions Universelles, Great Exhibitions and World's Fairs, 1851–1939* (Manchester, 1988), p. 17. Cf. Eckhardt Fuchs, *Weltausstellungen im 19. Jahrhundert* (Leipzig, 2000).
109 D'Arsac, 'Les expositions: leur origine, leur utilité', *Bruxelles-Exposition* (22 March 1908), p. 3 and Louis Dumont-Wilden, 'Comment on fait une exposition', *ibid.*, p. 13.
110 That said, of 29,000 exhibitors, 6,500 were Belgian and 10,000 French – Schroeder-Gudehus and Rassmussen, *Les Fastes du progrès*, pp. 163–4; 'Le pavillon de la Ligue pour attirer les étrangers en Belgique', *L'Exposition de Bruxelles: Organe Officiel de l'Exposition Universelle 1910*, 2 (1910), 182.
111 'Discours de Sa Majesté le Roi', *L'Exposition de Bruxelles: Organe Officiel de l'Exposition Universelle*, 2 (1910), p. 6.
112 Patrick Geddes, *Two Steps in Civics: 'Cities and Town Planning Exhibition' and the 'International Congress of Cities', Ghent International Exhibition, 1913* (Liverpool, 1913), p. 1.
113 Geyer and Paulmann, 'Introduction', p. 6.
114 *Revue des Congrès et Conférences* (22 April 1910); 'Les congrès qui se tiendront à Bruxelles en 1910', *L'Expansion Belge*, 9 (1908), p. 386; *1935: Bulletin officiel* (3 May 1935), p. 368; *Exposition universelle et internationale de Bruxelles 1935: Programme des Fêtes et Congrès. Avril–October 1935.*

115 For instance, article 3 of the *Règlement Général des Congrès, Conférences et Concours* of the 1935 world exhibition prohibited 'political or religious discussions'. On congresses at world's fairs, see Schroeder-Gudehus and Rasmussen, *Les Fastes du progrès*, p. 18. For examples of international activism during the Paris exhibition of 1900, see Jay Winter, *Dreams of Peace and Freedom: Utopian Moments in the Twentieth Century* (New Haven, CT, 2006), pp. 11–37.

116 Bitsch, *La Belgique entre la France et l'Allemagne*, pp. 297–308; Céline Préaux, 'Les présences nationales à l'Exposition universelle et internationale de Bruxelles 1910', in Serge Jaumain and Wanda Balcers (eds), *Bruxelles 1910: de l'Exposition universelle à l'Université* (Brussels, 2010), p. 160.

117 Cyrille Van Overbergh, *Le Mouvement scientifique en Belgique 1830–1905* (Brussels, 1905).

118 Bram Van Oostveldt and Stijn Bussels, 'De Antwerpse wereldtentoonstelling van 1894 als ambigu spektakel van de moderniteit', *Tijdschrift voor Geschiedenis*, 125 (2012), 4–19.

119 Victor Fris, *La Vieille Flandre: Exposition Universelle et Internationale de Gand 1913* (Brussels, 1913), p. 3.

120 Martin Wörner, *Vergnügung und Belehrung: Volkskultur auf den Weltausstellungen 1851–1900* (Münster, 1999), pp. 49–144.

121 Eric Storm, *The Culture of Regionalism: Art, Architecture and International Exhibitions in France, Germany and Spain, 1890–1939* (Manchester, 2011), p. 201.

122 Schroeder-Gudehus and Rasmussen, *Les Fastes du progrès*, p. 15.

123 Dumont-Wilden, 'La vie à Bruxelles', *La Vie intellectuelle* (15 March 1910).

124 'Les bienfaits d'une exposition', *Gent Wereldtentonstelling: Gand-Expositio* (10 November 1912), 258.

125 *Gent Wereldtentoonstelling* (March 1911), 1.

126 'Interview de Comte Adrien Van der Bursch, Commissaire général du gouvernement auprès du Comité eventuel de l'Exposition de 1935', *1935: Bulletin officiel* (15 August 1935), 12.

127 Jeffrey Auerbach, *The Great Exhibition of 1851: A Nation on Display* (New Haven, CT, 1999), pp. 158–89.

128 Burton Benedict, 'Rituals of representation: ethnic stereotypes and colonized peoples', in Robert Rydell and Nancy Gwinn (eds), *Fair Representations: World's Fairs and the Modern World* (Amsterdam, 1994), pp. 28–61; Raymond Corbey, 'Ethnographic showcases, 1870–1930', *Cultural Anthropology*, 8 (1993), 338–69; Sylviane Leprun, *Le Théâtre des colonies: scénographie, acteurs et discours de l'imaginaire dans les expositions 1855–1937* (Paris, 1986).

129 *Exposition Universelle Anvers 1894: La Belgique à Table* (Brussels, 1894), p. 10.

130 Maurits Wynants, *Des Ducs de Brabant aux villages Congolais: Tervuren et l'Exposition Coloniale de 1897* (Tervuren, 1997), pp. 125–7; Maarten Couttenier, *Congo tentoongesteld: een geschiedenis van de Belgische antropologie en het museum van Tervuren (1882–1925)* (Leuven, 2005), pp. 143–65. Several Congolese died in Tervuren, and the organisers found it difficult to cope with the high number of visitors to the exhibition.

131 Robert Rydell, 'Wissenschaft im Dienste von Macht, Macht im Dienste von Wissenschaft', *Weltausstellungen im 19. Jahrhundert*, p. 132; Stefan

Arnold, 'Propaganda mit Menschen aus Übersee: Kolonialausstellungen in Deutschland, 1896 bis 1940', in Robert Debusman and Janosz Riesz (eds), *Kolonialausstellungen – Begegnung mit Afrika?* (Frankfurt, 1995), pp. 9–10.

132 'Inauguration officielle de l'exposition' in *L'Exposition de Bruxelles: Organe Officiel de l'Exposition Universelle 1910*, 2 (1910), 3.

133 Préaux, 'Les présences nationales', p. 153; Kurt Goldentops, 'Congo als clou van het modern België: de kolonie op de Belgische Wereldtentoonstellingen (1910–1935), in Vincent Viaene *et al.* (eds), *Congo in België: Koloniale cultuur in de metropol* (Leuven, 2009), p. 93.

134 'Exposition Universelle de Gand. Les Floralies', *L'Indépendance Belge* (1 March 1913).

135 Exposition universelle et internationale de Gand 1913, *IIIe Congrès International Colonial sous le haut patronage du roi: compte rendu* (Ghent, 1922).

136 Picard, *Nécessité et conditions de l'Expansion belge au dehors*, pp. 9, 43 and 18 respectively.

137 Herren, *Hintertüren zur Macht*, pp. 165–85.

138 Van Overbergh, *Mouvement scientifique*, p. xiv.

139 Madeleine Herren, 'Modernisierung, Außenpolitik und Integration im Jahrhundert des Internationalismus', *Historische Mitteilungen*, 7 (1994), 37.

140 Roland de Marès, 'L'Expansion Mondiale', *L'Indépendance Belge* (27 September 1905).

141 Stengers and Gubin, *Le Grand Siècle*, p. 119.

142 Cited in Comité de Gérance, 'Le Cercle de L'Expansion belge: son programme', *L'Expansion Belge*, 1 (1908), 1.

143 *Ibid.*, 2.

144 *L'Expansion Belge*, 2, 4 (1909).

145 Adrien Van der Burch, 'A propos du Centenaire de l'Indépendance de la Belgique', *Bulletin périodique – Société Belge d'Etudes et d'Expansion*, no. 74 (1930). Van der Buch was also the commissioner for the 1935 world's fair. On the Société, see Marc Mayné, 'Les lieux de rencontre des milieux économiques, politiques et universitaires. La Société belge d'économie politique, la Société d'études et d'expansion, la Société royal belge des ingénieurs et industriels', in Ginette Kurgan-van Hentenryk (ed.), *Laboratoires et réseaux de diffusions des idées en Belgique (XIXe-XXe siècle)* (Brussels, 1994), pp. 119–33.

146 'Note confidentielle', p. 1.

147 Otlet, 'L'Expansion intellectuelle de la Belgique', *L'Expansion Belge*, 1 (1908), 15.

148 *Ibid.*, p. 13.

149 'Les Congrès internationaux qui se tiendront à Bruxelles en 1910', *L'Expansion Belge*, 1 (1908), 386.

150 Piérard, *Regards sur la Belgique*, p. 1

151 Marnix Beyen and Benoit Majerus, 'Weak and strong nations in the Low Countries: national historiography and its "others" in Belgium, Luxembourg, and the Netherlands in the nineteenth and twentieth centuries', in Stefan Berger and Chris Lorentz (eds), *The Contested Nation: Ethnicity, Class, Religion and Gender in National Histories* (Basingstoke, 2009), pp. 283–310.

152 Karl Dietrich Erdmann, *Die Ökumene der Historiker: Geschichte der Internationalen Historikerkongresse und des Comité International des Sciences Historiques* (Göttingen, 1987); Lewis Pyenson and Christophe Verbruggen, 'Elements of the modernist creed in Henri Pirenne and George Sarton', *History of Science*, 49 (2011), 377–94.

153 Tollebeek, 'At the crossroads of nationalism', pp. 194–6.

2

Empire

Empire and internationalism interacted in complex and conflicting ways. They bore underlying resemblances in that their practices frequently contradicted their rhetoric about progress and idealism. Similar to internationalism, empires used and created transnational networks; they drew upon expertise that had been gained within the contexts of scientific and cultural exchange, working with missionaries, explorers and scholars. While the unequal power relations at the heart of empire are self-evident, internationalism was not always based on egalitarian principles either. International law – which played such a major role in internationalist discourse – was sustained by notions of civilisational difference, which it could even reinforce.[1] Seen in this way, imperialism may appear as a form of 'hegemonic internationalism'.[2]

Few aspects of Belgian history have generated as much controversy as the country's imperial past. Leopold II's personal rule in the Congo – terminated by Belgium's annexation of the Congo Free State in 1908 – was characterised by exploitation, violence and a death toll whose sheer extent remains difficult to comprehend. In the 1990s and 2000s, the contentious legacy of imperialism in the Congo became evident in the responses to Adam Hochschild's best-seller *King Leopold's Ghost* and the overhaul of the permanent exhibition at the Royal Central Africa Museum in Tervuren.[3] The debate, however, stretches back to the late nineteenth and early twentieth centuries: at the time, 'Congo atrocities' and 'red rubber' were bywords for imperialism's dark underbelly.

As the first part of this chapter shows, Leopold and his supporters used the language of humanitarian internationalism and promoted the Congo venture through a series of international initiatives. However, internationalism also provided the means to challenge and question imperial designs. As the second half highlights, the attack upon colonial practices made use of international conferences, associations and communication channels: missionaries provided evidence for the atrocities in the Congo Free State, and British campaigners fostered links with activists in mainland Europe and America. Thus, the history of Belgian expansion reveals the Janus-faced nature of internationalism.

Internationalism and the making of King Leopold's Congo

Internationalism played a major role in the creation of King Leopold's Congo Free State. Geographers – whose discipline exemplified the rise of scientific internationalism in the 1870s – helped shape the colonial thinking surrounding the Congo project.[4] The Belgian network that supported Leopold's imperial ambitions in the 1870s included internationalists such as Emile de Laveleye, a Belgian scholar and peace activist who corresponded with John Stuart Mill, William Gladstone and William Stead on social and political questions.[5] In 1873, he was among the co-founders of the Institute of International Law, a body whose important role for legal internationalism is discussed in chapter 5. De Laveleye also participated in the international event that initiated the colonisation of the Congo: the Geographical Conference of 1876. Convened by Leopold II, this event brought explorers, scholars, humanitarians and military leaders to the Belgian capital.

Seen from one angle, the Geographical Conference exemplified the age of internationalism. It evoked principles of scientific collaboration and also adopted a humanitarian discourse. African slavery was one issue that was raised in this context. The participants did not target the transatlantic slave trade, which had come to all but an end; instead, they expressed their concern about the inner and East African slave trade. As the key actors in this trade were not European, the cause was suitable for professions of a 'civilising mission'. The prominent Belgian diplomat Emile Banning, for instance, claimed that it was 'high time that the civilised nations come together in a generous and powerful effort to put an end to such abominable injustices. Without the absolute suppression of the slave trade, any attempt to penetrate African civilisation would be... fruitless.'[6] He staunchly supported Leopold's plans for Belgian expansion in Africa, which was the principal motivation behind the Geographical Conference. As Banning argued, 'there are no small states; there are only small spirits'.[7] Cardinal Lavigerie – Archbishop of Algiers and Carthage and an abolitionist campaigner – later echoed such language: he claimed that in 1876, 'the European kingdom which, in terms of its territory, is the smallest, appeared... as the greatest because of the initiative of its king'.[8] The conference professed humanitarian intentions by creating the Association Internationale pour Réprimer la Traite et Ouvrir l'Afrique Centrale (International Association to Repress the Slave Trade and Open Up Central Africa). In practice, however, this body did not carry out anti-slavery efforts. Instead, it prepared the exploration of Africa and laid the ground for the International Congo Association, the body that led Leopold II's expansionist drive.

The ill-defined status of the International Congo Association triggered the second major conference in the history of King Leopold's Congo: the Berlin

Africa Conference of 1884–85, which brought together diplomats from fourteen countries. Although the Berlin General Act did not formally create the Congo Free State, it provided the wider context for its recognition.[9] Today, the Berlin Conference is mostly remembered for its links to the 'scramble for Africa'. As Ronald Robinson argued, the event 'surely began the wholesale carving of Central Africa into spheres of influence', linked to 'the interdependence of the bilateral and multilateral agreements involved in setting up the Congo state'.[10] However, the event was also an episode in the history of internationalism. The Berlin General Act made the Congo a free-trade area – and despite the evident economic interests that underpinned this measure, it was compatible with the demands of many internationalists.[11] Furthermore, the 'open door' in the Congo was also portrayed in humanitarian terms, as notions of 'free and legitimate trade' featured prominently in anti-slavery discourse.[12] Indeed, British humanitarians used the Berlin Conference as a forum to demand international provisions against the African slave trade. In this respect, the negotiations at Berlin were the latest attempts to address the slave trade at diplomatic conferences. With very limited success, the topic had previously featured at the Congress of Vienna (1814–15) and the Congress of Verona (1822) and had been the focus of negotiations for the largely unapplied Quintuple Treaty of 1841. Although the General Act did contain clauses on the slave trade, they were of 'little real value'.[13]

The Brussels Anti-Slavery Conference

Accounts of European imperialism invariably mention the Berlin Africa Conference. The Brussels Conference of 1889–90 is less well known – yet it was charged with 'completing the work of the Berlin Congress' in the realm of anti-slavery.[14] Convened by Leopold II, it brought together diplomats from seventeen countries and further illustrates the relationship between internationalism and imperialism. Its connection with the age of internationalism was noted by an Australian observer who stated that international conferences had 'now become such an established mode of settling, or attempting to settle, the affairs of all the world that the existence of the Anti-Slavery Convention at Brussels is readily accounted for'.[15]

The involvement of internationalist milieus is illustrated by three prominent delegates at the Brussels Conference: August Lambermont, Fyodor Martens and Edouard Descamps. All three were members of the Institute of International Law and tackled international questions beyond the Brussels Conference. As an experienced Belgian diplomat and confidant of King Leopold, Lambermont presided over the Brussels Conference. Yet his career also included the arbitration of several international disputes, for instance between Switzerland and Italy in 1889, between Germany and Britain in

1899, and between Britain and France in 1902. The Russian delegate Martens also served as an arbitrator at various points in his life. He later contributed to The Hague Peace Conference of 1899 and to the peace negotiations between Russia and Japan in 1905. Before becoming a diplomat, Martens had held a professorship in international law. This was a position that Descamps – an associate delegate for the Congo Free State – still occupied at the time of the Brussels Conference, holding a chair at the University of Louvain. Later, Descamps's internationalist commitment was reflected by his membership of the IPU and his work as secretary-general of the Institute of International Law (1900–06). In 1892, he became a senator for the Catholic Party, and in 1908, he was appointed Minister of Science and the Arts. Descamps's presence at the Brussels Conference was not only linked to his legal expertise. For over two decades – from the 1880s to the 1900s – he promoted his vision of a 'New Africa' based on 'the uplifting of the African race, the civilisation of a continent'.[16] In 1888, he co-founded a Belgian anti-slavery association, the Société Antiesclavagiste, whose ambivalent features are discussed later in this chapter.

The General Act of the Brussels Conference entered into force in April 1892 and introduced a range of anti-slavery measures. For a designated region, the signatory powers allowed mutual checks of the papers of ships. In mainland Africa, fugitive slaves were to be granted asylum in all territories where the legal status of slavery had been abolished. Meanwhile, countries that had not yet outlawed slavery committed themselves to ending the import, export and transit of slaves. In addition, the import of arms and spirits into African territory became subject to restrictions. Finally, in order to monitor the implementation of these measures, the conference established two offices: the Special Bureau Against the Slave Trade in Brussels and the Bureau on the Maritime Slave Trade in Zanzibar.[17] The creation of these new institutions resembled other 'public international unions' that were set up in the 1880s and 1890s.[18] Yet the General Act also had inherent limitations: it only addressed the slave trade and not the continued existence of slavery as such. The 'slow death for slavery' in many parts of Africa as well as the readiness with which European powers used forced labour undermine optimistic assessments about its outcome.[19]

Humanitarians showed considerable enthusiasm for the Brussels General Act. The British anti-slavery activist Charles Allen praised Lambermont for his 'calm judgement, conciliatory manner and unrivalled experience' and expressed his confidence about 'the dawning of a new and brighter era in the history of Africa'.[20] Carmel Brincat, Titular Bishop at the See of Hadrumetum, described the agreement as 'the century's most important diplomatic act, which will undeniably remain the greatest honour of the Powers that have accomplished it'.[21] Banning, who had been a member of the Belgian delegation, viewed the General Act as reflective of an era in which Africa became a

'European patrimony' whose residents would 'participate in the work of civilisation'.[22] Commentators praised Belgium's role in the international anti-slavery struggle: the Catholic politician Emile Keller, president of a French anti-slavery committee, lauded 'this Belgium, small in size, but always great in its heart and its generosity'.[23] The Belgian anti-slavery periodical *Le Mouvement Antiesclavagiste* echoed this sentiment: 'Who would have thought that this Belgium, so small in territory, would one day play such a great role in the history of civilisation?'[24] The view of the General Act as a Belgian accomplishment was reiterated in the Belgian Chamber of Representatives:

> For several centuries, Belgium has been the battleground of nations and its soil had absorbed its fair amount of blood. A purer kind of glory is reserved for her today. In her capital, she has witnessed the gathering of the International [Anti-Slavery] Conference, for a work of peace, of civilisation, of humanity – inspired by her sovereign and chaired by one of our most eminent citizens.[25]

Even though the Brussels Conference ostensibly dealt with a humanitarian issue, it 'was also an incident in the scramble for the [African] continent', as Suzanne Miers has observed.[26] This dimension became evident at various levels: Portuguese diplomats, for instance, were determined to fight off any limitations to their country's colonial expansion.[27] Indeed, when contentious details of the negotiations appeared in the French and Belgian press, participants such as Banning suspected the Portuguese delegation of having leaked the information.[28] Furthermore, the French Chamber of Deputies nearly blocked the General Act's ratification: it opposed provisions that allowed foreign powers to search vessels carrying the French flag.[29] A third controversy centred on the status of the Congo basin as a free-trade area. In line with Leopold II's wishes, the delegates of Belgium and the Congo Free State succeeded in adding provisions for limited import duties to the Brussels General Act – allegedly to raise funds for anti-slavery measures in the Congo.[30] This arrangement met with resistance from the Netherlands, where the Nieuwe Afrikaansche Handels Vernootschap (New African Trading Association) feared detrimental effects for its commercial activities.[31]

Between the Dutch refusal to sign the General Act in July 1890 and the Netherlands' ultimate compliance on 31 December 1890, the Belgian and Dutch protagonists sought to influence public opinion at home and abroad. A publication by 'a Dutch negotiator' argued that 'he who volunteers for a duty has to calculate in advance if he can accomplish it'.[32] Banning responded with an anonymous pamphlet which attacked the Dutch government for refusing to 'make its share of sacrifices for the repression of the slave trade'.[33] Similarly, the German *National-Zeitung* dismissed the Dutch objections as self-serving.[34] Britain was a key venue for this controversy. In November 1890, the London Chamber of Commerce hosted a debate at which the director of the Nieuwe

Afrikaansche Handels Vernootschap argued that Congo duties 'would infringe the great principle of freedom of commerce which was the very basis of the programme of the Berlin Conference'.[35] John Holt of the Liverpool Chamber of Commerce backed his views, proclaiming that 'the humanitarians should put their hands in their pockets and assist the Government to carry it out'.[36] Another participant echoed his position: 'if this Congo Free State is doing great philanthropic work, philanthropists should pay for it, and not the merchants.'[37] Other participants questioned whether the struggle against the slave trade was the true reason behind the measure. Rather presciently, Francis William Fox – a British peace and anti-slavery activist – predicted that the Congo Free State would spend its funds on weapons and trigger local conflicts. He argued that the slave trade 'ought to be suppressed by judicious efforts, by the extension of legitimate commerce, by fair consideration for the natives, by being just to the Arabs and enlisting their sympathy, and not by exterminating the natives or the Arabs by a series of wars'.[38] Two representatives of the Anglo-Belgian Chamber of Commerce participated in the London debate, yet could not persuade the merchants, who voted to oppose the duties. In contrast to this stance, British anti-slavery activists sought to lobby their Dutch contacts and urged Lord Salisbury to exercise diplomatic pressure on the Dutch government.[39] These examples reveal the interrelated issues that formed the context of Brussels Conference: humanitarian concerns, economic interests, colonial policy and the extension of international law.

Internationalism and Belgian anti-slavery

Despite its nature as a diplomatic event, the Brussels Conference interacted with the transnational efforts of humanitarians. In 1888, Cardinal Lavigerie had launched an 'international anti-slavery crusade', inspiring the foundation of several – largely Catholic – committees in mainland Europe.[40] The Belgian Société Antiesclavagiste was founded after the French clergyman had visited Brussels in August 1888 during a tour which also saw him address audiences in Britain, France and Italy. Speaking at Saint-Gudule Cathedral, the church leader discussed 'l'Afrique belge' and appealed to the Belgians' 'religious sentiment, Christian mercy and patriotism'.[41] Lavigerie praised Leopold II for his African endeavour and reprimanded the Belgian Catholics for their insufficient support for their king: 'You have been…asleep, Belgian Catholics! You have not given…to the fight against barbarism all the assistance which was your duty…I say with sadness that you have not done enough.'[42] In one respect, this observation was not entirely unfounded: at the time the Congo venture did indeed attract only lukewarm backing in Belgium: 'Empire without enthusiasm'.[43]

By January 1889, the Société Antiesclavagiste counted 700 members and 300,000 francs in subscriptions.[44] Theoretically, the association was open to

'Catholics, Protestants and Israelites, conservatives and liberals'.[45] In practice, however, it was closely connected to the Catholic church: Cardinal Goossens, the Archbishop of Mechelen (Malines), acted as its patron, and the Vatican provided 50,000 francs in funds. At a public meeting in Liège, the industrialist Baron Sadoine – former director of the Cockerill Company – was joined by prominent Catholic academics such as Descamps and the historian Godefroid Kurth.[46] Vincent Viaene has viewed 1895 as the 'key date in the crystallization of the Belgian *parti colonial*'.[47] At the time, several organisations backed Leopold's imperial visions, covering a broad political and cultural spectrum – albeit with limited success. Seen in this context, the Société Antiesclavagiste formed part of the early history of colonial agitation in Belgium, as it sought to invest the Congo project with moral and religious meaning. For instance, in 1890, the society organised a reception for Henry Morton Stanley after his return from the Emin Pasha Relief Expedition.[48] In 1894, it displayed the alleged benefits of the Congo venture at the Antwerp world's fair.[49] In its activities, the association typified the 'age of imperial humanitarianism'. As Michael Barnett has put it, humanitarian 'discourses of human equality...existed alongside discourses of Christianity, colonialism, and commerce that deemed the "civilized" peoples superior to the backward populations'.[50] If 'civilising missions' were a key component of imperial expansion, the Société Antiesclavagiste helped construct its Belgian variety.[51] The role of anti-slavery in colonial discourse proved remarkably persistent: the Antwerp world's fair of 1930, for instance, contained a section on 'slavery in the Congo'.[52]

Despite the national and imperial dimensions of their endeavours, Belgian activists networked across national borders. In doing so, they drew on the transnational links of Catholicism, which chapter 3 examines in further detail. As early as October 1888, Descamps visited an anti-slavery congress of German Catholics in Cologne.[53] Meanwhile, Louis Delmer, editor of *Le Mouvement Antiesclavagiste*, described the scope of his publication as 'in some way international'.[54] Indeed, members of the British and Foreign Anti-Slavery Society supplied the Belgian periodical with reports.[55] Such collaboration was not entirely self-evident: unlike the Belgian movement, British anti-slavery was driven by religious Nonconformists and liberal radicals, many of whom were also involved in the British peace movement.[56] Despite such different backgrounds, the Belgo-British connection was significant in several ways. In 1889, British campaigners urged their government to take steps for an international conference on the African slave trade. Taking up the cause, British diplomats proposed Belgium as a host country, stressing the positive Belgian reception to Cardinal Lavigerie's anti-slavery campaign.[57] In these respects, the diplomatic event in Brussels was connected to a new wave of anti-slavery activism from different countries and constituencies.

Anti-slavery activists, particularly from Britain, sought to influence the course of the Brussels Conference. They did so although the negotiations were not held in public – allegedly to prevent newspapers from inflaming 'public feeling *pro* or *con*' on controversial issues.[58] In January 1890, campaigners organised large-scale meetings in Birmingham and London. Activists from the British Isles were also responsible for 150 of the 155 petitions that are preserved at the Belgian Foreign Ministry Archives. Most of them were submitted in the winter of 1889–90 and forwarded to the Belgian ministry by Lord Vivian, the British minister-plenipotentiary in Belgium.[59] On two occasions, representatives of the British and Foreign Anti-Slavery Society travelled to Belgium. They considered themselves 'well-received' by Lord Vivian and were granted an audience with King Leopold, who had 'graciously expressed his wish that they should be presented to him'.[60] During their first visit, the British activists also met with Bishop Brincat, Hippolyte d'Ursel of the Belgian Société Antiesclavagiste, Dutch and Italian diplomats, as well as the Mayor of Brussels, Charles Buls.[61] On their second trip, they were again received by King Leopold whom they presented with a memorandum.[62] In October 1890, after the conference had ended, the society's secretary Charles Allen visited the king in Ostend; he returned, alongside Buxton, in March 1891 to discuss diplomatic obstacles to the international ratification of the Brussels General Act.[63]

In the meantime, activists affirmed their transnational links through an international congress in Paris in October 1890. As the Brussels General Act had not been signed by the Dutch and Ottoman representatives at this stage, the event served as a demonstration in favour of the General Act.[64] The Paris gathering was chaired by Cardinal Lavigerie and attracted campaigners from seven countries, including d'Ursel and Descamps from Belgium. Six months later, the Belgian Société Antiesclavagiste staged a series of 'international lectures' at the Academy Palace in Brussels. Speakers came from Belgium, Britain, France, Italy, Switzerland and the Netherlands, and the audience comprised various ambassadors and luminaries such as Auguste Lambermont. Despite being invited, the two British anti-slavery societies did not send any delegates: initially, their refusal was linked to the belief that the series would be an exclusively Catholic affair, highlighting the underlying differences between British and continental activism.[65] Anti-slavery groups maintained their links through congresses in Paris (1900) and Rome (1907), both of them with Belgian participants.[66]

Anti-slavery was merely one example of the relationship between diplomacy, humanitarianism and internationalism. The history of an organisation such as the Woman's Christian Temperance Union, for instance, highlights how humanitarian concerns, religious beliefs and women's activism intersected.[67] As a moral and political cause, temperance also related to anti-slavery:

alcoholism could appear as another form of captivity that prevented the continent's civilisation. Both at the Berlin Conference and the Brussels Conference, activists raised the issue of the African liquor trade.[68] In fact, each of the documented petitions to Brussels asked delegates to adopt measures on this issue. As nearly all of them originated in Britain, Lord Vivian initiated the creation of a committee on the liquor trade. In contrast to the Berlin Conference, the Brussels General Act introduced concrete measures: it prohibited the import of alcoholic drinks in some areas and introduced a levy in others.[69] The Special Bureau Against the Slave Trade, established in Brussels through the General Act, collected information on the liquor traffic. This issue remained on the agenda for governments and campaigners beyond the Brussels Conference: the Belgian capital hosted follow-up conferences in 1899, 1906 and 1912, attracting letters, petitions and visits from temperance campaigners.[70] These diplomatic conferences were evidently connected to economic and imperial agendas, as their subject related to the issue of import duties in the Congo.[71]

The sub-texts of Belgian anti-slavery internationalism

Humanitarian and imperial concerns were not the only interests at stake in the transnational debates surrounding slavery and the Congo. For instance, the embrace of the anti-slavery cause could help validate the African endeavours of missionaries, who maintained close links with the new anti-slavery associations. Cardinal Lavigerie had previously founded the missionary society of the White Fathers, which collaborated with the French anti-slavery committee from 1888.[72] In Belgium, *Le Mouvement Antiesclavagiste* praised missionary works from the start and merged with the bulletin of the *Œuvre des Missions Catholiques au Congo* in 1899. Announcing this step, Hippolyte d'Ursel argued that 'now that all African territories have their responsible masters, independent anti-slavery action focuses on the development of missions'.[73] In subsequent years, the periodical increasingly featured missionary and ethnographical accounts rather than reports on slavery. This shift became even more evident in 1903, as the periodical was renamed *Le Mouvement des Missions Catholiques au Congo*. Ten years later, d'Ursel became president of a new association, the Ligue pour la Protection et l'Evangélisation des Noirs.

The link to missionary campaigns does not mean that anti-slavery was simply a smokescreen for colonial expansion. Historians such as Andrew Porter have warned against underestimating the religious – as opposed to imperial – dimension of missionary activity.[74] Indeed, imperial and religious motivations clashed on various occasions. For instance, although Lavigerie corresponded with Leopold II and praised his efforts, he questioned the king's policies when they seemed to conflict with missionary works.[75] Furthermore, the Congo Free State experienced competition between the White Fathers, Belgian

Catholic missionaries as well as Protestant missionaries from Britain and the USA, challenging the notion of a coherent 'missionary interest'. The Swiss anti-slavery society – mostly driven by conservative Protestants – was critical of Lavigerie's campaign and soon broke with both Leopold and Lavigerie.[76] Meanwhile, the king's supporters had reservations about Lavigerie: Banning described the cardinal's plan for an 'anti-slavery crusade' as having 'some chimerical or dangerous sides', despite its 'elevated sentiments'.[77]

These caveats notwithstanding, the discourse of the Société Antiesclavagiste was compatible with Belgian expansion. Alongside their evocation of a civilising mission in Africa – as previously discussed – activists denounced 'Arab' slave-raiders and slave-traders, a term by which they meant African Muslims from the continent's East Coast.[78] Their discourse, which conflated ethnic and religious categories, exemplified growing European fears about the 'Moslem Menace'.[79] Contemporary representations evidently ignored the variety of Muslims' views on freedom and captivity.[80] They also downplayed Europe's slave-trading past and glossed over the inconsistent implementation of anti-slavery policies. This 'orientalisation' of slave-trade representations was not a Belgian peculiarity: it featured prominently in Lavigerie's 'anti-slavery crusade' and was adopted by the European groups founded in its wake.[81]

Anti-slavery activists conveyed their message through speeches, reports and literary efforts. Such accounts contrasted the European role in 'civilising Africa' with the wrongdoings of 'Arab slave-traders'. Two prominent members of the Belgian Société Antiesclavagiste even published anti-slavery plays: Louis Delmer – who, besides editing *Le Mouvement Antiesclavagiste*, headed an anti-slavery committee in Brussels – in 1890, and Edouard Descamps in 1893.[82] *Le Mouvement Antiesclavagiste* complimented the latter for the way in which he had portrayed the conflict between 'Negro barbarism, Muslim villainy and Christian civilisation... in breath-taking fashion'.[83] This description echoed the introduction to the published version of Descamps's drama: 'Three worlds meet on African soil: the barbarian world, the Muslim world, the Christian world. The antagonism between these three worlds manifests itself, in poignant and formidable manner, in the question of the slave trade.'[84]

Both authors sought to reach a national audience and had their French-language plays translated into Dutch. Yet their literary efforts also stood in the context of anti-slavery internationalism. For instance, Descamps and Delmer corresponded with the British and Foreign Anti-Slavery Society to prepare English translations of their plays.[85] Descamps even won a literary competition which the Parisian anti-slavery congress of 1890 had launched.[86] By 1894, his piece was also available in German and Italian, and Stanley had lauded it as a 'moving drama'.[87]

Alongside its religious connotations, the Belgian anti-slavery discourse had military dimensions. *Le Mouvement Antiesclavagiste* portrayed colonial conflicts in Africa as anti-slavery wars and 'struggles against Arab domination'.[88] Early on, the Société Antiesclavagiste cooperated with colonial troops, raised funds for expeditions to Africa and hosted receptions for colonial officers.[89] The Belgian captain Jacques (later Baron Jacques de Dixmude) praised these measures: 'although the Brussels General Act has emitted beautiful theories about the slave trade, the Société Antiesclavagiste has done more'.[90] At the 1900 international congress of anti-slavery societies, he recounted an expedition he had conducted on behalf of the Société Antiesclavagiste ten years earlier. He stressed the initial intention to support missionaries in the region, yet also described violent clashes with 'Arabs'. Thus, he portrayed his actions as a precursor to subsequent colonial wars.[91] In similar fashion, a 1909 book on Belgium's 'struggle against the horrible plague' of slavery cited the efforts of colonial soldiers alongside the Brussels Conference and the Société Antiesclavagiste.[92] Underlining the willingness to combine anti-Arab or anti-Islam discourse with support for military action, the Belgian activist d'Ursel applauded Italy's occupation of Tripoli in 1911, describing 'the suppression of Muslim power between Tunisia and Egypt… [as] a good deed from a humanitarian point of view'.[93] The Belgian activists' support for military action was mirrored by the French and German anti-slavery societies. In contrast, the British Foreign and Anti-Slavery Society opposed such policies.[94] Tellingly, the sole British speaker at the 1891 anti-slavery lectures series in Brussels was the explorer Verney Lovett Cameron, whom other British campaigners criticised for his support of military action.[95]

Alongside the sub-texts of religion and warfare, there was a third element to the Belgian anti-slavery discourse: knowledge. *Le Mouvement Antiesclavagiste* in Belgium as well as French and German anti-slavery periodicals constructed knowledge about colonial subjects and maintained links to the nascent field of colonial science. In 1894, a congress in Brussels created the International Colonial Institute, which aimed to 'facilitate and disseminate the comparative study of colonial administration and legislation'.[96] Based in Paris, this body brought together colonial administrators, academics and politicians, including prominent figures such as Descamps. Nearly four decades later, League of Nations officials noted that the institute attracted 'colonial figures of the first order and of all main countries'.[97] Before the war, further colonial congresses took place in Brussels in 1897 and 1898. On the latter occasion, the former Belgian prime minister Auguste Beernaert stressed that it was 'just and Christian to see the civilised nations, having arrived on the mountain summit, extend a helping hand to the populations that vegetate in the marshes of the plain'.[98] Furthermore, after the Mons Congress of Economic Expansion – discussed in chapter 1 – the Catholic civil servant and internationalist Cyrille Van Overbergh founded an International Bureau of Ethnography in Brussels. Another internationalist, Henri Rolin, wrote for the *Bulletin de colonisation comparée* – over a decade before becoming a leading Belgian advocate of the League of Nations, as discussed in chapter 5. Internationalism, in its different guises, hence provided means to legitimise colonial rule.

Congo atrocities

During the Brussels Anti-Slavery Conference, the image of Leopold II as a monarch adamant to civilise Africa still prevailed. Yet at the time, the Congo Free State already used forced labour: in 1890, the American Baptist minister George Washington Williams witnessed how 'volunteers' were recruited via slave-traders, both for porter services and for the Force Publique, the Congo's military and police force. The same year, the British and Foreign Anti-Slavery Society questioned Lambermont about slave labour in the Congo.[99] The appointment of Tippo-Tip, an infamous slave-trader, as governor in the Upper Congo region in 1887 also sat at odds with the proclaimed anti-slavery sentiments of the Belgian sovereign. In support of this policy, *Le Mouvement Antiesclavagiste* approvingly cited the German explorer Hermann Wissmann: 'It is sometimes deft to use the devil against the devil, or one demon against other demons'.[100]

The 'Stokes Affair' of 1895 – the first widely known scandal in the Congo – demonstrated the interplay between anti-slavery rhetoric and colonial rule. In January 1895, the British ivory trader Charles Stokes was sentenced to death by a Belgian officer in the Force Publique, Major Hubert-Joseph Lothaire. He claimed that Stokes had sold ammunition to 'Arab slave-raiders' and had him strung up on the same day – without informing the accused of the possibility to appeal.[101] Especially from summer 1895, British newspapers voiced suspicions that the firearms charges had been trumped up so as to eliminate a commercial competitor.[102] By October, the *Pall Mall Gazette* denounced Lothaire's actions as 'murder'.[103] In contrast, Belgian publications defended Lothaire. *Le Mouvement Antiesclavagiste* suggested that the 'civilising undertaking' in this instance 'was not threatened by métis of Arabs and Negroes, but by Europeans' such as Stokes.[104] It praised Lothaire as executing 'the will of the twenty signatory powers of the Brussels General Act' who fought the 'gangs of enslavers on the Black Continent'. The controversy illustrated the ambiguous relationship between Belgium and the Congo Free State. After a court in Borma had acquitted Lothaire, a second trial was held in Brussels, even though the Congo Free State was not a Belgian colony. Belgian critics of imperialism noted this contradiction and cited British reports on the case. The affair had significant financial implications because of subsequent compensation payments, yet it also undermined the philanthropic narrative that King Leopold and his supporters had constructed.[105]

The most horrific abuses in the Congo set in with the rubber boom of the 1890s. The Congolese were forced to fulfil quotas in the harvesting of wild rubber; failure to do so triggered violent reprisals.[106] Exploited by private companies and the King of the Belgians, the African population faced indiscriminate violence by the Force Publique. From the mid-1890s, Congo atrocities became subject to increased public scrutiny. The image of severed hands was particularly infamous: soldiers cut off hands to 'prove' that they had not used their ammunition for hunting. Photographic evidence was an important campaigning tool in this respect, as highlighted by the 'lantern lectures' of British activists.[107] In Britain, the Aborigines' Protection Society – an important anti-slavery association which had previously offered honorary membership to King Leopold – played a key part in mobilising popular opinion. The most renowned campaigner, however, was the journalist E. D. Morel: in 1904, he co-founded the Congo Reform Association with Roger Casement, a British consul who in 1903 had travelled to the Congo and published a widely noted report.[108] Meanwhile, Catholic and Protestant missionaries responded in an ambivalent manner. Some, such as John Murphy and John Harris, provided vital information on the atrocities; yet many others refrained from criticism of the atrocities as long as their own interests remained unaffected. In the early years of the campaign, the Congo administration used these silences against its critics.[109]

Congo critics evoked the international agreements of 1885 and 1890. For instance, the secretary of the Aborigines' Protection Society and leading Congo campaigner, H. R. Fox Bourne, argued that the Congo Free State 'shamelessly disregarded and grossly violated' the Berlin and Brussels General Acts.[110] The British Foreign Office even compiled a dossier on Leopold's violation of the 'spirit of the Berlin Act'.[111] Yet the attack on Congo atrocities went beyond legal issues: as the historian Frederick Cooper has noted, it contained 'echoes of nineteenth-century anti-slavery'.[112] Many humanitarians portrayed forced labour as a 'new slavery' and their own activism as a continuation of abolitionist traditions.[113] Morel explicitly labelled the Congo Free State a 'slave state'.[114] Adopting a similar language, a Swiss campaigner claimed that 'each native – man, woman or child – only counts as a labour machine' and deplored the fate of 'twenty million slaves' in the Congo.[115] Leopold II, who had previously been styled as a philanthropic liberator, now appeared as a slave master.

The Congo controversy extended beyond the circles of British humanitarians and Belgian imperialists. The Congo reformers were supported by internationalists such as the American pacifist Edwin Mead and the jurist Paul Reinsch. The Universal Peace Congresses of 1898 and 1900, held in Turin and Paris respectively, featured general resolutions on the 'treatment of natives' and the 'injustices inflicted on weak peoples by strong peoples'. In 1904, Morel raised the issue at the Universal Peace Congress in Boston. In response, the Belgian pacifist Henri La Fontaine proclaimed that 'as a Republican and a Socialist' he did 'not care one whit for King Leopold'. Nonetheless, he objected to pronouncements that would single out the Congo and described attacks on the Free State as 'exaggerated'.[116] La Fontaine's reference to 'territories that are without a master and without population' indicates his underlying acceptance of the *terra nullius* notions that underpinned European imperialism.[117] Two years later, the Universal Peace Congress at Milan attacked the 'murder, violence, theft, injustice and unnameable atrocities' committed in African colonies. By that stage, official enquiries had acknowledged abuses in both the Congo Free State and the French Congo; the delegates therefore proposed a successor event to the Berlin Africa Conference.[118] This attempt to combat colonial crimes through the tools of internationalism continued in subsequent years: in 1907, pacifists demanded that the provisions for international arbitration be extended to the Congo.[119]

Such instances highlight the interactions between humanitarians and peace activists. Morel himself subsequently embarked on a trajectory towards pacifism: this, it has been argued, was influenced by his experiences with the British Foreign Office, triggering a 'crusade' that covered imperial policies and opposition to war.[120] As co-founder of the Union of Democratic Control in 1914, he became a leading critic of British foreign policy, famously defeating Winston Churchill in the Dundee by-election of 1922.[121] Meanwhile, a former French Congo campaigner, Félicien Challaye, emerged as a spokesman for 'absolute pacifism' in interwar France.[122]

The use of international congresses was but one aspect of the transnational campaign against 'Red Rubber'. In the USA, an American branch supported the work of the Congo Reform Association.[123] Furthermore, in 1908, French campaigners launched the Ligue Internationale pour la Défense des Indigènes dans le Bassin Conventionnel du Congo 'to impose the respect of the Berlin Act'.[124] This association was run by Challaye, his compatriot Pierre Mille and the Swiss activist René Claparède. Its board of patrons illustrates the organisation's international ambitions: it listed, inter alia, E. D. Morel, Stanley Hall of the American Congo Reform Association, the Swiss literary scholar Philippe Godet, the French historian Charles Seignobos, the Italian anthropologist Giuseppe Sergi, and, as honorary president, the Norwegian author and Nobel Prize laureate Bjørnstjerne Bjørnson. Alongside this organisation, Challaye led the Ligue Française pour la Défense des Indigènes dans le Bassin Conventionnel du Congo, which also attacked abuses in the French Congo.[125] Half a year after the foundation of the international league, Claparède established a Swiss section which gained around 400 members in its first year and, like its French counterpart, campaigned against atrocities in both the Congo Free State and the French Congo.[126]

Activists in mainland Europe cooperated with the Congo Reform Association, which applauded the Franco-Swiss initiative.[127] From the start, Challaye looked towards the British campaigners for support.[128] Meanwhile, Claparède acknowledged the inspiration he took from Morel: 'after God, it is your example that supports me.'[129] Morel contributed an essay to his organisation's inaugural bulletin; in this context, he distinguished between Belgian colonial practices on the one side, and British and French on the other.[130] In February 1909, the leaders of the international league organised lecture events with Morel in Paris and four Swiss towns.[131] The same year, the league was transformed into a committee whose national branches maintained their 'absolute independence of action', illustrating limits to the organisation's transnationalism.[132]

Belgian responses

The campaign against Congo atrocities met with widespread hostility in Belgium. Morel was subjected to frequent counter-attacks – the historian Jean Stengers concluded that 'the root of the problem lay in the Belgians themselves, who understood Morel even less than he understood them'.[133] Strikingly, the Belgian Société Antiesclavagiste sided with its king, portraying the activism of the Congo reformers as anti-Catholic propaganda or a smokescreen for the interests of 'Liverpool merchants'. Its periodical claimed that it was the British who degraded indigenous populations: 'The born enemy of inferior races, that's the Anglo-Saxon, who destroys by all means, through famine, alcohol, mass prescriptions and strychnine'.[134] This counter-attack was reinforced by special organisations and publications that represented the Congo Free State's standpoint.[135] One Belgium-funded periodical, *The Truth on the Congo*, even ran a section denouncing the 'Beauties of British Colonialism'.[136] In Britain, Leopold's supporters drew on Catholic networks. They defended him in the pages of *The Tablet* and of the *Catholic Herald*, whose editor attacked Morel's alleged 'anti-Congo conspiracy'.[137] The Brussels correspondents of *The Times* and *Kölnische Zeitung* also swung behind Leopold – 'thanks to hard cash', as Stengers pointed out.[138]

Defending King Leopold, *Le Mouvement Antiesclavagiste* reproached British campaigners with presenting 'certain isolated acts as characteristic of the conduct of all Belgians'.[139] Previously, the periodical had compared the Congo Free State favourably with other European colonies:

> In this time of decadence…and boundless greed, if one had to draw up the balance sheet of injustices and cruelties committed in different countries, one will see that the Congo, in this respect, has stayed behind other colonies.

> Everywhere, there is systematic destruction of inferior races. At no point are the crimes against Indians or Negroes reprimanded, the Free State alone has decreed penalties and considered the life of blacks as having some value.[140]

Similarly, in his book *New Africa*, Descamps praised the achievements in the Congo. Prior to the arrival of King Leopold's troops, '[c]annibalism, human sacrifices, man-hunting and slave trading, with their accompanying nameless cruelties and endless suffering, were the features of the ferocious tribal anarchy which alternated with the incursions of men of prey, in search of plunder and of captives for far-off slave-markets'.[141]

Descamps justified forced labour as a form of 'taxation' by which Africans would pay back the expenses incurred in 'civilising' the Congo: 'Everybody knows that, in tropical countries, the dislike of the natives to work is... the greatest obstacle to their civilisation.'[142] In 1905, Descamps was responsible for a section on 'civilising expansion towards new countries' at the Congress of Global Economic Expansion in Mons.[143] At the event, he reiterated his praise for King Leopold's efforts 'for the development of his people and for the good of humanity as a whole'.[144] As Martti Koskenniemi has pointed out, Belgium's international law community – of which Descamps was a key member – steered clear of direct criticism of the situation in the Congo. Félicien Cattier, a law professor at the Free University of Brussels, was an exception to the rule; his 1906 study of the Congo acknowledged the scale of the atrocities.[145]

Criticism in Belgium came from a small group of individuals, notably the liberal politician Georges Lorand and the socialist leader Emile Vandervelde. Both were actively involved in other forms of internationalism: Lorand as vice-president of the International Freethought Federation (discussed in chapter 3) and Vandervelde as president of the Second International (discussed in chapter 4). Furthermore, they were among the patrons of the Ligue Internationale pour la Défense des Indigènes dans le Bassin Conventionnel du Congo, as was the Belgian sociologist and socialist Hector Denis. Vandervelde maintained strong links with the British campaigners – his London-born wife Lalla later noted that Morel 'was constantly with us'.[146] Yet these links met with hostility at home: 'In Belgium my husband and M. Lorand were insulted in Parliament and in the Press. They were openly accused of being traitors to their country.'[147] His biographer Janet Polasky has even described Vandervelde's 'struggle to rescue the people of the Congo from Leopold's rule' as 'the loneliest of his political life'.[148]

Vandervelde was backed by his wife, who felt 'keenly on the subject of the present administration of the Congo State' and deemed Morel's 'energy and tenacity in documenting its abuses' as 'really admirable'.[149] She maintained her own correspondence with Morel, inviting him to Belgium on various occasions.[150] In the letters to her compatriot, she vented her frustration about Belgian attitudes: 'The Belgians care only about eating & drinking…I can't tell you how I hate & despise them. I could tell you things that would make your blood boil – as they do mine. But I don't think you have a very much better opinion of them than I have. The way they treat you is too abominable.'[151] Lalla Vandervelde deplored the indifference of Belgian socialists: 'The Socialist party…won't have anything to do with the Congo. They want better wages, i.e. more food & more drink.' As the historian Guy Vanthemsche has shown, the socialist position was indeed far from consistent, and for considerable time periods, there was limited socialist engagement with events in the Congo.[152] The ambivalent stance was also evident at the international congresses of the Second International, which initially allowed national parties to determine their attitude towards colonies.[153]

Matters were complicated by the fact that Belgian critics differed as to the measures that might end the atrocities. Emile Vandervelde favoured turning the Congo into a Belgian colony – one of the few Belgian socialists to do so, although he cited Henri La Fontaine and Modeste Terwagne as supporters.[154] This 'Belgian solution' was endorsed by the British Foreign Secretary Edward Grey; in June 1905, the Congo Reform Association had adopted this policy, which was eyed critically by Morel and Casement.[155] Yet when Vandervelde proposed annexation in a draft report for the Second International, his party blocked it.[156] The prominent socialist and anti-Congo critic Louis Bertrand believed that it would result in a heavy financial burden for the Belgian state and, ultimately, the Belgian people.[157] He argued that King Leopold had deceived the Belgian public in the past and was likely to keep all profits for himself. As an alternative, the socialist senator Hector Denis suggested turning the Congo into an international protectorate. Vandervelde deemed this proposal unrealistic: 'Certainly, the internationalisation of colonies by the United States of Europe is an ideal, but it is a distant ideal which will only be realised in a Europe that is entirely different from the Europe of today.'[158]

Among progressive liberals, Lorand was particularly outspoken in his opposition to annexation. As he explained to Morel, he opposed it because he deemed it 'dangerous for the interests of Belgium and inefficient for ending the abuses'.[159] He predicted a problematic outcome: 'You will be cheated, *Messieurs les Anglais*: [in the end] you will have imposed on us the takeover, which Belgium does not want, and the king will continue to rule the Congo in his fashion. In reality, you will have done his business and we will have taken on a ruinous task which we will accomplish poorly.'[160] Lorand criticised the stances of Vandervelde and the liberal politician Paul Hymans as opportunistic: 'The attitude of Hymans and Vandervelde is very severely judged by their best friends. Personally, it does not astonish me…Among our aspiring ministers, there is a prejudice that one cannot desire power unless one has voted for the takeover. Only [the progressive liberal Paul] Janson understands that this is idiotic.'[161]

Annexation and its aftermath

Despite the objections of some activists, the Belgian parliament voted to annex the Congo in 1908. Whereas Roger Casement's report of 1903 had been brushed off as British propaganda, the situation changed after a Belgian commission of enquiry had acknowledged widespread abuses in 1905.[162] The Congo Reform Association disseminated the enquiry's findings in Belgium and criticised those who had attacked the Congo reformers 'under the cover of Belgian patriotism'. It argued that 'the worst enemies of Belgium' were those 'who have striven by all means possible to conceal from the Belgian public the sad realities of the Congo regime'.[163] With atrocities in the Congo being officially recognised, even erstwhile defenders of King Leopold shifted their position: *Le Mouvement pour les Missions Catholiques en Congo* – the successor of *Le Mouvement Antiesclavagiste* – maintained that Catholic missionaries had been unable to witness the atrocities as they were hardly represented in the affected areas.[164] The revelations about the Congo, it has been argued, triggered a Belgian 'identity crisis', with the takeover of 1908 being staged in relatively low-key fashion.[165] In subsequent years, however, the Belgian state showcased its colonial activities to national and international audiences – and, as mentioned in chapter 1, the world's fair of 1910 was an early example of the renewed confidence of Belgian advocates of empire.

This is not to say that debates on the Congo ended immediately. Was Belgium actually fit to run the colony? British officials concluded that it would be wise to accept the annexation and thus draw the country towards the *Entente*.[166] Lorand continued to doubt the benefits of annexation: 'So this is the triumphant Belgian solution, and the King has fooled us all. I fear that nothing good will come out of this – neither for us, nor for the Negroes.'[167] The case of William Sheppard, an African American Presbyterian missionary, also undermined claims of a departure from Leopoldian practices: in 1908, shortly before the Belgian takeover, Sheppard had published an article about the violent ways in which the Kasai Rubber Company had treated the local population. The article resulted in Sheppard and his editor William M. Morrison being called before a tribunal in Leopoldville.[168] Legal proceedings continued beyond the annexation, and in July 1909, the American branch of the Congo Reform Association followed suggestions from Swiss activists when asking US president William Taft to intervene.[169] The same year, Vandervelde successfully took on Sheppard's defence in a libel suit brought by the Kasai Company. The fact that the secularist and socialist Vandervelde offered his legal service for free reveals the unlikely alliances triggered by the Congo question.[170]

Arthur Conan Doyle's *The Crime of the Congo* added fuel to the post-annexation debates. The famous creator of Sherlock Holmes suggested that the Congo be divided up between Germany and France, deeming Belgium too discredited to govern its new colony.[171] In a letter to his fellow activist Claparède, Morel estimated that this book would 'undoubtedly make a profound impression upon the mass of the public here. Conan Doyle has got the ear of the public as very few living Englishmen have.[172] Morel's stance towards Conan Doyle was somewhat ambivalent: 'I shall not endorse, but I have done nothing to prevent it, because it is perhaps just as well that I should appear more moderate than he is, and also because it is my belief that such a demand coming from him will be instrumental in rousing the British Government to the seriousness which the position is assuming'.[173] Vandervelde was 'very much upset' about *The Crime of the Congo*, as his wife noted:

> My husband who, in spite of being an internationalist, has a warm love in his heart for his native country, will not admit that the Belgian people should be rendered responsible for what has happened & is happening in the Congo. I told him that it enrages people like Conan Doyle to think that the state of affairs we all know of, has been going on for years & there has been no... movement of public indignation in Belgium. I feel the same – personally – but then, of course, I am not Belgian. [174]

Lalla Vandervelde explained that her spouse was 'not at all angry' with Morel, but 'only with Conan Doyle & his partisans': he was 'very angry when he thinks that people in England are agitating for the Congo to be taken away from Belgium'.[175] Indeed, after the annexation, a series of public meetings in Britain called upon the British government 'to send Belgium an ultimatum' to improve matters in the Congo.[176] In December 1909, prominent Belgians – including Auguste Beernaert, Cardinal Mercier and the industrialist Ernest Solvay – appealed to foreign critics, asking them to accept the Kingdom's willingness to improve matters.[177]

King Leopold's death on 17 December 1909 meant that the main target of the attacks disappeared. In subsequent representations of Belgian colonialism, for instance at the Ghent world's fair of 1913, organisers stressed the advances since King Leopold's rule.[178] In Britain, many activists concluded that his successor, Albert I, had better intentions.[179] By 1910, Morel regarded it as 'a great joy to think that the treatment of the natives is very different from what it was', even if there might well be 'general chaos out there'.[180] Two years later, he forwarded a note by the French explorer Auguste Chevalier, who, having returned from a trip to Central Africa, was 'full of admiration for the works accomplished since the Belgian annexation. The old regime had come to an end, and this country, like the rest of Africa, is on the path towards civilisation.'[181] Morel still preferred to take colonial policy out of the hands of Belgian officials, as he explained in a letter to Lalla Vandervelde:

> Of course there is only one man who will do any good at the Belgian Colonial Office, and that is your husband… [I]f King Albert and the Belgians who are capable of thinking had any sense, they would remove the Colonial Office from Belgian Party Politics while leaving full freedom to the Belgian Colonial Minister to carry on his own political career apart from his work at the Belgian Colonial Office, and put your husband in.[182]

Meanwhile, other British campaigners continued to adopt a critical stance towards the Belgian Congo.[183] Despite continuing problems in Africa, the Congo Reform Association dissolved in 1913. Public attention in Britain was on the wane and Morel had reached the conclusion that 'he was fighting for a losing cause'.[184]

Institutional legacies

The Congo atrocities make it easy to be cynical about the humanitarian rhetoric attached to Belgian expansion. Yet even at the peak of the scandal, diplomats and activists evoked the Brussels General Act. The clearest manifestation of these continuities was the Special Bureau Against the Slave Trade in Brussels. British representatives had initially proposed to endow it with supervisory powers, yet it was merely charged with collecting and publishing information on different aspects of the Brussels Act. Operative from July 1892, the Special Bureau was based at the Belgian Ministry of Foreign Affairs, with the ministry's chief archivist coordinating its work. It was jointly funded by all signatory powers, with a reduced share for Sweden-Norway and Denmark.[185] Between 1892 and 1914, its budget was so small that its fluctuations merely reflected changes in printing costs. Surprisingly, in 1923, long after the Bureau's dissolution, the German Foreign Office remembered that fees for 1913 had not yet been paid and sought to rectify this – a suggestion which the German Minister of Finance rejected in light of the French and Belgian occupation of the Ruhr.[186]

Between 1892 and 1914, the Brussels bureau published 22 volumes of its annual *Documents relatifs à la répression de la traite des esclaves*, containing information on the trade in spirits and firearms as well as the slave trade itself.[187] The bureau adopted a proactive approach, asking governments for new information and taking note of new stipulations.[188] Its publications also included information provided by the Zanzibar Bureau on the Maritime Slave Trade. The Zanzibar office first met in November 1892, became fully operative in January 1894, and comprised representatives from Germany, France,

Britain, Italy, Portugal and Russia, but not Belgium. With more determined supervision of the African east coast, the illegal trade via Zanzibar decreased and thus limited the bureau's importance. In 1904, the German ambassador claimed that the primary concern of its members was the appointment of the bureau's secretary – a position with no workload, but monthly remuneration.[189] Similarly barbed comments followed in subsequent years: the German representative described the annual subsidy as a 'waste of money' and proposed to close the Zanzibar office because of its 'total insignificance'.[190] However, it was only after the First World War that the work of the Brussels and Zanzibar bureaus officially ended, as a new convention, negotiated at Saint-Germain-en-Laye in 1919, abrogated the provisions of the Brussels General Act.

In one respect, the Special Bureau in Brussels continued its work beyond the Great War: in January 1922, the League of Nations Council 'entrusted [the Bureau] with the task contemplated by the St. Germain Convention... insofar as the liquor traffic is concerned'.[191] The convention had declared Central Africa to be a prohibition zone for 'trade spirits' and defined duties for the import of pure alcohol. The Belgian government lobbied to retain its Special Bureau Against the African Spirits Trade and, in February 1922, formally took on the task of supervising the convention's alcohol-related provisions.[192] Costs for the office were shared between Belgium, Britain, France, Japan and Portugal. Thus, staff at the Ministry of Foreign Affairs in Brussels continued to collect official communications regarding the spirits trade, forwarding this information to the League's Section for International Bureaux and, from 1928, to its Mandates Section. Yet a League of Nations official noted in 1930 that only Britain complied with the St. Germain Convention by sending annual reports to Brussels. Other governments occasionally submitted statistics and ordinances.[193] Neither the Brussels bureau nor the League secretariat published this material.

The spirits trade was not the only way in which the League of Nations perpetuated the efforts of the Brussels Conference. Article 23 of the League Covenant demanded 'fair and humane conditions of labour for men, women and children', and the St. Germain Convention asked for the 'complete suppression of slavery in all its forms'. In 1922, New Zealand's delegate to the General Assembly of the League of Nations raised the resurgence of slavery in parts of Africa.[194] This initiative ultimately triggered the establishment of the Temporary Slavery Commission, which compiled information on the persistence of slavery in Africa and Asia.[195] The Temporary Slavery Commission contributed to the Slavery Convention of 1926, a legal instrument with limited impact. Comprised of government representatives with a background in colonial administration, this committee and its successors (the Committee of Experts on Slavery and the Advisory Committee of Experts on Slavery) hesitated to address further-reaching questions about colonial practices. Suzanne Miers has therefore asserted that the commission's members 'played the anti-slavery card to further national interests' – not unlike government representatives in the 1880s and 1890s.[196]

That said, the League of Nations clearly offered a new target authority for humanitarian campaigners. In theory, the Mandates affirmed notions of international 'trusteeship', as states administered territories on behalf of the international community.[197] Humanitarians addressed the Mandates section in order to hold mandatory powers to account, exemplified by the efforts of John Harris, anti-slavery activist and former Congo campaigner.[198] Meanwhile, the pre-war efforts of René Claparède had given rise to the International Bureau for the Protection of Native Races. Headed first by Claparède and later by Henri Junod, it was conceived as an international umbrella organisation for anti-slavery societies. Despite inconsistent backing from their British associates, the office published reports, held international congresses, and lobbied governments and the League of Nations.[199] Its causes also encompassed the African spirits trade: in 1929, Junod asked to view the information compiled by the Brussels bureau, yet both Belgian and League of Nations officials declined this request.[200] Nonetheless, Junod's association published a memorandum on the unsatisfactory impact of the St. Germain Convention. In attacking the liquor traffic, the documentation evoked civilisational categories: 'Is it not a mission of civilisation and regeneration to fulfil with regard to these weaker races? Is not Africa a "sacred trust" given to Europe that she may preserve her from destroying influences and develop her resources for the good of humanity at large?'[201] Internal correspondence suggests that League staff looked favourably upon this activism but had limited leeway to initiate official responses.[202]

What was Belgium's role in interwar debates on slavery? Congo atrocities had ceased to be in the focus of international attention. Four years of military conflict had arguably played their part in changing perceptions of Belgium. During the war, German soldiers were reported to have chopped off the hands of Belgian civilians, with John Horne and Alan Kramer describing 'children's "severed hands" [as] the key Allied myth in 1914'.[203] Such imagery evidently recalled the 'severed hands' of the Congolese – only this time with Belgians as the victims. Furthermore, when the German government deported Belgians for labour purposes in 1916, speakers at a large-scale protest meeting in Boston 'compared the opposition to the enslavement of Belgians to the anti-slavery struggle'.[204] Belgium now appeared as victim rather than as perpetrator. While the government initially aimed to preserve the neutrality of the Belgian Congo, the colony subsequently joined the allied war effort, leading to gains in Central Africa.[205] After the war, Belgium was entrusted with the League of Nations Mandate of Ruanda-Urundi, formerly German East Africa. This arrangement was the outcome of diplomatic proceedings that overcame

British scepticism and the Belgian record in Africa.[206] Belgium even came to have a role in the League's anti-slavery activities: Albrecht Gohr, Director-General of the Belgian Ministry of the Colonies and formerly an official of the Congo Free State, chaired the League of Nations' Temporary Slavery Commission and later the Advisory Committee on Slavery.

During the 1920s, Gohr was also involved in the International Colonial Institute, as was Descamps and a key Belgian protagonist of interwar internationalism, Henri Rolin. In 1929, the Belgian Senate hosted the institute's twentieth congress. At this event, several delegates criticised plans for firmer international regulations against forced labour.[207] Forced labour was indeed an ongoing concern, with conditions in the Belgian Congo being a case in point.[208] During the interwar years, Vandervelde pointed out that its population was still subject to exploitation.[209] In 1928, an assembly of bishops, prefects and missionaries at Stanleyville also condemned the 'exaggerated recruitment' of workers in the Congo.[210] The same year, the Brussels congress of the Labour and Socialist International declared that all forced labour, including that under pretexts of 'education' or 'military purposes', should be ended.[211] Yet definitions of forced labour were contested. A Belgian submission to the Temporary Slavery Commission, for instance, described it as 'conceivable… that labour could be made compulsory not only for public works but for purposes of education and social welfare'. In similar terms, Portuguese diplomats asserted that '[i]n an organised society it is an obligation upon all citizens to work for the advancement of civilisation and the continuance of progress'.[212]

In 1930, the International Labour Organization (ILO) overcame political obstacles and produced a Forced Labour Convention which, according to Frederick Cooper, was 'in its own way, a radical document'.[213] Belgium was slow to ratify this agreement: a scheduled debate during the parliamentary session of 1935–36 was postponed. While asserting their opposition to forced labour, officials re-stated their 'civilising mission':

> In order to ensure that education was not frustrated by the laziness, the unmindful passivity of those who should benefit from it, it has made the practice of 'taught labour' obligatory, anticipating that the habit becomes implanted. The provisional regime… deserves to continue until the education of natives has had durable effects.[214]

In March 1936, King Leopold III announced that Belgium would accept the convention, provided that it allowed for 'works of public interest, as determined by competent authorities'.[215] However, it was only during the Second World War that the Belgian government-in-exile ratified the agreement. This measure was portrayed as an 'act of sovereignty' and at the same time 'an anticipation of the promises included in the Atlantic Charter, to which Belgium has signed up'. This step allowed Belgian exile politicians to perpetuate a narrative which stressed both the 'civilising' nature of the Congo venture and their country's 'international-mindedness':

> In adopting the Convention, the Belgian government methodologically pursues the social policy which it has always practiced since Belgium annexed the Belgian Congo... The Forced Labour Convention is the 33rd international convention ratified by our country. Of all industrialised countries, Belgium has ratified the highest number of them. [216]

Conclusion

Internationalism sustained the construction of a Belgian civilising mission, the country's imperial expansion as well as the attack on its colonial practices. The period in which internationalism took shape through associations, congresses and campaigns coincided with the 'new imperialism'. Rather than being an invariably benign force in international politics, it could reinforce colonial hierarchies. These inherent tensions became evident at the Brussels Anti-Slavery Conference of 1889–90. Characterised by the interaction of diplomats, experts and activists, the event provided an example of transnational cooperation in the age of internationalism. The outcome of the conference expanded international law on a significant humanitarian issue, leading Hippolyte d'Ursel, president of the Belgian Société Antiesclavagiste, to praise the Brussels General Act as 'le Code de la Civilisation'.[217] Such language fed into notions of a Belgian 'civilising mission' and could thus be used in defence of Leopold's imperial policies.

Not everyone bought into the portrayal of a humanitarian Belgian endeavour in Central Africa. Protagonists of internationalism – both its pacifist and socialist varieties – joined the attack against Congo atrocities. In doing so, they clashed with Belgians such as Descamps who promoted international arbitration and peaceful cooperation but defended King Leopold. Whereas Belgium had previously appeared as a champion of international norms, the situation in the colonial sphere gave the opposite impression. These divisions cut straight through Belgian internationalism. Belgian socialists took a great variety of stances when it came to the Congo question. Taken together, 'humanitarian internationalism' and the Congo case force us to retain a critical perspective when considering Belgian internationalism and its protagonists.

Notes

1 Martti Koskenniemi, *The Gentle Civilizer of Nations: The Rise and Fall of International Law 1870–1960* (Cambridge, 2002); Antony Anghien, *Imperialism, Sovereignty and the Making of International Law* (Cambridge, 2004).

2 Fred Halliday, 'Three concepts of internationalism', *International Affairs*, 64 (1988), 187–98.

3 Adam Hochschild, *King Leopold's Ghost: A Story of Greed, Horror and Heroism in Colonial Africa* (New York, 1995). A response features in the Tervuren exhibition's catalogue: Philippe Marechal, 'La controverse sur Léopold II et le Congo dans la littérature et les médias: réflexions critiques', in Jean-Luc Vellut (ed.), *La Mémoire du Congo: le temps colonial* (Tervuren, 2005), pp. 43–50. Cf. Jan-Bart Gewald, 'More than Red Rubber and figures alone: a critical appraisal of the memory of the Congo exhibition at the Royal Museum for Central Africa, Tervuren, Belgium', *International Journal of African Historical Studies*, 39 (2006), 471–86.

4 Jan Vandersmissen, *Koningen van de Wereld: Leopold II en de aardijkskundige beweging* (Leuven, 2009); Vandersmissen, 'The king's most eloquent campaigner: Emile de Laveleye, Leopold II and the creation of the Congo Free State', *BTNG–RBHC*, 41 (2011), 7–57.

5 Marcel Bots (ed.), *Lettres adressées à Emile de Laveleye* (Ghent, 1992). The contact with Stead is noteworthy as the British journalist later became a vociferous critic of the Congo Free State.

6 Emile Banning, *L'Afrique et la Conférence géographique de Bruxelles* (Brussels, 1877), p. 81.

7 Emile Banning, *Réflexions morales et politiques* (Brussels, 1899), p. 101.

8 Charles Lavigerie, *L'Esclavage africain: conférence sur l'esclavage dans le Haut Congo, faite à Sainte-Gudule de Bruxelles* (Brussels, 1888), p. 5.

9 Stengers, 'Les cinq légendes de l'Acte de Berlin', in Stengers, *Congo: mythes et réalités* (Brussels, 2005), pp. 87–98; Wm. Roger Louis, 'The Berlin Congo Conference and the (non-) partition of Africa, 1884–85', in Louis, *Ends of British Imperialism: The Scramble for Empire, Suez and Decolonization* (London, 2006), pp. 75–126.

10 Ronald Robinson, 'The conference and the future of Africa' in Stig Förster *et al.* (eds), *Bismarck, Europe and Africa: The Berlin Africa Conference and the Onset of Partition* (New York, 1988), p. 25. One should, however, heed the advice to 'be careful with such concepts as scramble and partition': Henk Wesseling, 'The Berlin conference and the expansion of Europe: a conclusion', in *ibid.*, p. 535.

11 On the wider context of free trade, see Sidney Pollard, 'Free trade, protectionism and the world economy' in Geyer and Paulmann, *The Mechanics of Internationalism*, pp. 27–54.

12 Zimmermann, *GrenzÜberschreitungen*, pp. 31, 50 and 57.

13 Suzanne Miers, *Britain and the Ending of the Slave Trade* (London, 1975), p. 173. See also Miers, 'Humanitarianism at Berlin: myth of reality?', in Förster *et al.*, *Bismarck, Europe and Africa*, pp. 333–45.

14 Léon Béthune, 'Les puissances européennes et la traite des nègres depuis le Congrès de Berlin', *Le Mouvement Antiesclavagiste*, 1 (August 1889), 267.

15 MS Bxl. FO, P299: 'Pétitions': newspaper report cited in a letter from the Belgian Consulate in Melbourne to the Belgian Ministry of Foreign Affairs, 23 January 1890.

16 Edouard Descamps, *La Part de la Belgique dans le mouvement Africain* (Louvain, 1889).
17 *General Act of the Brussels Conference, 1889–1890, with Annexed Declaration* (London, 1890).
18 Reinsch, *Public International Unions*, p. 64.
19 This often-cited phrase is from Paul Lovejoy and Jan Hogendorn, *Slow Death for Slavery: The Course of Abolition in Northern Nigeria, 1897–1936* (Cambridge, 1993). Cf. Suzanne Miers, 'Slavery and the slave trade as international issues 1890–1939', *Slavery and Abolition*, 19 (1998), 16–37; David Seddon, 'Unfinished business: slavery in Saharan Africa' and Suzanne Miers, 'Slavery to freedom in Sub-Saharan Africa: expectations and reality', both in Howard Temperley (ed.), *After Slavery: Emancipation and Its Discontents* (London, 2000); Frederick Cooper *et al.*, 'Introduction', in Cooper *et al.* (eds), *Beyond Slavery: Explorations of Race, Labor, and Citizenship in Postemancipation Societies* (Chapel Hill, 2000), pp. 1–32.
20 'The Brussels Conference', *Anti-Slavery Reporter*, 10 (September–October 1890), 194.
21 Société Antiesclavagiste de Belgique, *Les Conférences antiesclavagistes libres données au Palais des Académies de Bruxelles les 28, 29 et 30 avril 1891* (Brussels, 1892), p. 16.
22 Emile Banning, *La Conférence de Bruxelles: son origine et ses actes. Communication faite à l'Académie Royale dans la séance du 13 octobre 1890* (Brussels, 1890), pp. 25–6.
23 'Séance d'ouverture du Congrès libre Antiesclavagiste', *Le Mouvement Antiesclavagiste*, 2 (November 1890), 414.
24 'Les Conférences antiesclavagistes libres de Bruxelles', *Le Mouvement Antiesclavagiste*, 3 (May 1891), 162.
25 'L'Acte Général de la Conférence antiesclavagiste de Bruxelles devant la Chambre des Représentants de Belgique: son approbation', *Le Mouvement Antiesclavagiste*, 3 (March 1891), 114.
26 Miers, *Britain and the Ending of the Slave Trade*, p. 315.
27 MS Bxl. FO, P299: letters from the Belgian ambassador in Lisbon, 22 November 1889 (in doss. 364, vol. 2, 'Préliminaires) and 19 December 1889 (doss. 365, vol. 3, 'Lieux de capture; Routes des caravanes. 1889–1890').
28 Emile Banning, *Mémoires politiques et diplomatiques: comment fut fondé le Congo Belge* (Paris, 1927), pp. 80, 100–1 and 112. Cf. Miers, *Britain and the Ending of the Slave Trade*, p. 276.
29 'L'Acte Général de la Conférence de Bruxelles à la Chambre des Deputés', *Bulletin de la Société Antiesclavagiste de France*, 3 (April–June 1891), 55–8.
30 MS Bxl. FO, P401: doss. 369, vol. 7 ('Droits d'entrée. 1889–1890'): 'Propositions relatives à l'établissement d'un droit d'entrée dans le bassin conventionnel du Congo. Très confidentiel. 6 mai 1890'.
31 Miers, *Britain and the Ending of the Slave Trade*, pp. 286–91. For the diplomatic discussions, see *La Conférence de Bruxelles et la question de l'établissement de droits d'entrée dans le bassin conventionnel du Congo: extrait des protocoles* (Brussels, 1890).

32 Anon., *La Conférence anti-esclavagiste et les droits d'entrée dans l'État du Congo: par un négociant hollandais* (Rotterdam, 1890), p. 9.
33 Anon., *La Conférence de Bruxelles et les Pays-Bas: par un ami de la vérité* (Anvers, 1890). Cf. Banning, *Mémoires*, pp. 179–87.
34 MS Bxl. FO, P. 302: doss. 372, vol. 12, 'Question douanière': translated article (9 July 1890) in letter from Greindl, Belgian Legation in Berlin, to the Prince de Chimai, 10 July 1890.
35 MS Bxl. FO, P. 304: doss. 372, vols 15–17, 'Question douanière (suite)': *Report of the Proceedings of the Conference of African Merchants on the Congo Free State and Import Duties. Held at the Rooms of the London Chamber of Commerce, 4th November, 1890*, p. 11.
36 *Ibid.*, pp. 21–2.
37 *Ibid.*, p. 29.
38 *Ibid.*, p. 27.
39 MS Brit. Emp. 20, *Minute Book 6* (E2/11): Notes 287 (1 August 1890), 292 (5 September 1890), 304 (7 November 1890), 306 (5 December 1890), 324 (2 January 1891).
40 Daniel Laqua, 'The tensions of internationalism: transnational anti-slavery in the 1880s and 1890s', *International History Review*, 33 (2011), 705–26. Cf. François Renault, *Lavigerie, l'esclavage africain et l'Europe, 1868–1892* (Paris, 1971); Gianni La Belle, 'Leo XIII and the anti-slavery campaign', in Vincent Viaene (ed.), *The Papacy and the New World Order: Vatican Diplomacy, Catholic Opinion and International Politics at the Time of Leo XIII* (Brussels, 2005), pp. 381–94.
41 Lavigerie, *L'esclavage africain*, p. 2.
42 *Ibid.*, p. 5.
43 Matthew Stanard, 'Learning to love Leopold: Belgian popular imperialism, 1830–1960', in John MacKenzie (ed.), *European Empires and the People: Popular Responses to Imperialism in France, Britain, the Netherlands, Belgium, Germany and Italy* (Manchester, 2011), p. 127; cf. Guy Vanthemsche, *La Belgique et le Congo: empreintes d'une colonie 1885–1980* (Brussels, 2007). Stanard has drawn attention to the great extent of pro-imperial propaganda and its effectiveness in some areas, especially after 1908: Matthew Stanard, *Selling the Congo: A History of European Pro-Empire Propaganda and the Making of Belgian Imperialism* (Lincoln, NE, 2012), pp. 56–7.
44 'La Belgique et l'œuvre antiesclavagiste', *Le Mouvement Antiesclavagiste*, 1 (January 1889), 49.
45 'Le mouvement antiesclavagiste en Belgique', *Le Mouvement Antiesclavagiste*, 1 (November 1889), 388.
46 'Meeting antiesclavagiste de Liège', *Le Mouvement Antiesclavagiste*, 1 (January 1889), 61–3.
47 Vincent Viaene, 'King Leopold's imperialism and the origins of the Belgian Colonial Party, 1860–1905', *Journal of Modern History*, 80 (2008), 764.
48 'Stanley à Bruxelles: sa réception à la Société antiesclavagiste de Belgique', *Le Mouvement Antiesclavagiste*, 2 (April 1890), 130.

49 'La Société antiesclavagiste à l'Exposition universelle d'Anvers', *Le Mouvement Antiesclavagiste*, 6 (July/August 1894), 291; Van Oostveldt and Bussels, 'De Antwerpse wereldtentoonstelling', 11.
50 Michael Barnett, *Empire of Humanity: A History of Humanitarianism* (Ithaca, 2011), p. 55.
51 Jürgen Osterhammel, '"The Great Work of Uplifting Mankind": Ziviliserungsmission und Moderne', in Boris Barth and Jürgen Osterhammel (eds), *Zivilisierungsmissionen: Imperiale Weltverbesserung seit dem 18. Jahrhundert* (Konstanz, 2005), pp. 363–425.
52 Stanard, *Selling the Congo*, pp. 56–7.
53 Edouard Descamps-David, 'Les grands initiatives dans la lutte contre l'esclavage', *Le Mouvement Antiesclavagiste*, 1 (1888), 10.
54 MS Brit. Emp. 18, Misc. I, C155: Louis Delmer to Charles Allen, 10 November 1888.
55 'Lettre de Londres', *Le Mouvement Antiesclavagiste*, 1 (December 1888), 26.
56 On links between these movements, see Martin Ceadel, *Semi-Detached Idealists: The British Peace Movement and International Relations, 1854–1914* (Oxford, 2000), p. 20; Paul Laity, *The British Peace Movement, 1870–1914* (Oxford, 2001), pp. 2–3.
57 MS Bxl. FO, P298: doss. 364, vol. 1, 'Préliminaires': letter by Lord Vivian of 26 September 1888.
58 MS Brit. Emp. 20, *Minute Book 6* (E2/11): note 272 (2 May 1890).
59 MS Bxl. FO, P304 and 304: doss. 372–73, 'Pétitions'. Cf. Miers, *Britain and the Ending of the Slave Trade*, p. 276.
60 *Quarterly Paper of the United Committee for the Prevention of the Demoralization of Native Races by the Liquor Traffic* (December 1889), p. 7.
61 MS Brit. Emp. 20, *Minute Book 6* (E2/11): note 246 (6 December 1889).
62 *Ibid.*, note 272 (2 May 1890).
63 *Ibid.*, notes 304 (7 November 1890) and 324 (3 April 1891).
64 'Lettre de S.E. le Cardinal Lavigerie aux Comités nationaux de la Société antiesclavagiste', *Le Mouvement Antiesclavagiste*, 2 (August 1890), 281. Cf. Laqua, 'The tensions of internationalism', pp. 709–10.
65 MS Brit. Emp. 18, C56 (correspondence Charles Allen): Louis Delmer to Charles Allen, 27 November 1890 and 19 December 1890; Hippolyte d'Ursel to Charles Allen, 29 March 1891.
66 On these congresses, see Amalia Ribi, 'Humanitarianism imperialism: the politics of anti-slavery activism in the interwar years' (DPhil thesis, Oxford, 2008), pp. 62–7.
67 Ian Tyrell, *Woman's World/Woman's Empire: The Woman's Christian Temperance Union in International Perspective 1880–1930* (Ann Arbor, MI, 1991).
68 Miers, 'Humanitarianism at Berlin', pp. 338–43.
69 Justin Willis, 'Indigenous peoples and the liquor traffic controversy', in Jack Blocker, David Fahey and Ian Tyrell (eds), *Alcohol and Temperance in Modern History: An International Encyclopaedia*, vol. i (Oxford, 2003), p. 311. Cf. Willis, 'Brussels Act and Convention, 1890–1912', in *ibid.*, pp. 118–19; Laqua, 'The tensions of internationalism', pp. 712–13.

70 MS Bxl. FO. Conférence des Spiritueux 1899: 'Pétitions' in Renseignements statistiques/Notes et renseignements divers. See also MS Bxl. FO Conférence des spiritueux 1912/IX. 'Protocole n°2. Séance du 6 janvier 1912' in Protocoles signés.

71 Herren, *Hintertüren zur Macht*, p. 456.

72 Philippe Delisle, 'La campagne antiesclavagiste de Lavigerie et Léon XIII devant "l'opinion missionnaire" française', in Viaene, *The Papacy and the New World Order*, pp. 395–412.

73 Hippolyte d'Ursel, 'A nos lecteurs', *Le Mouvement Antiesclavagiste*, 11 (April 1899), 3.

74 Andrew Porter, *Religion versus Empire? British Protestant Missionaries and Overseas Expansion, 1700–1914* (Manchester, 2004), Porter, 'Evangelical visions and colonial realities', *Journal of Imperial and Commonwealth History*, 38 (2010), 145–55.

75 Ruth Kinet, *'Licht in die Finsternis': Kolonisation und Mission im Kongo, 1876–1908: Kolonialer Staat und nationale Mission zwischen Kooperation und Konfrontation* (Münster, 2005), pp. 29–30.

76 Thomas David and Janick Marina Schaufelbuehl, 'Swiss conservatives and the struggle for the abolition of slavery at the end of the nineteenth century', *Itinerario*, 34 (2010), 87–103.

77 Banning, *Mémoires*, p. 84.

78 'L'Islam et l'Afrique centrale', *Le Mouvement Antiesclavagiste*, 9 (April 1897), 81.

79 Porter, *Religion versus Empire?*, p. 295.

80 Regarding Muslim perspectives on slavery, see William Gervase Clarence-Smith, *Islam and the Abolition of Slavery* (Oxford, 2006).

81 Lavigerie, *Conférence sur l'esclavage*, pp. 6–7; cf. Laqua, 'The tensions of internationalism', pp. 716–19.

82 Louis Delmer, *L'Esclave: drame antiesclavagiste et national. Pièce en quatre actes* (Brussels and Paris, 1890); Edouard Descamps, *Africa: drame en cinq actes* (Paris, 1893).

83 'La représentation d'Africa au Théâtre flamand', *Le Mouvement Antiesclavagiste*, 7 (February 1895), 59.

84 Descamps, *Africa*, p. 7.

85 MS Brit. Emp. S18, C56 (correspondence Charles Allen): Delmer to Allen, 25 June 1889; Descamps to Allen, 26 June 1893 and 22 February 1894.

86 'Le meilleur ouvrage sur l'esclavage africain', *Le Mouvement Antiesclavagiste*, 5 (December 1892/January 1893), 89.

87 'Chronique antiesclavagiste', *Le Mouvement Antiesclavagiste*, 6 (March 1894), 143.

88 'La lutte contre la domination arabe', *Le Mouvement Antiesclavagiste*, 6 (January 1894), 49.

89 'La Belgique et l'œuvre antiesclavagiste', *Le Mouvement Antiesclavagiste*, 1 (January 1889), 48; *L'Indépendance belge*, 5 July 1894.

90 Letter of 23 October 1892 in Hippolyte d'Ursel (ed.), *La Campagne antiesclavagiste belge racontée par les lettres de Jacques de Dixmude* (Brussels, 1929), p. 37.

91 Société Antiesclavagiste de France, *Congrès international antiesclavagiste tenu à Paris le 6, 7, 8 août 1900: Compte rendu des séances* (Paris, 1900), pp. 71–8.

92 Armand Winandy, *La Répression de la traite et de l'esclavage* (Brussels, 1909), p. 49.

93 'La question Tripolitaine', *Le Mouvement des Missions Catholiques au Congo*, 23 (June 1911), 187.

94 Miers, 'Slavery to freedom in Sub-Saharan Africa', p. 245.

95 'Commander Cameron and the Anti-Slavery Society', *Anti-Slavery Reporter*, 9 (1889), 32.

96 MS IIIC, D.IV. 89: note '20e session, à Bruxelles sous la présidence du Prince Léopold' (1929).

97 MS LON, 6A/5167/758 (R2326), 'Correspondance avec l'Institut Colonial International': Catastini to Drummond, 1 May 1931.

98 Fernand Van Ortroy, *Congrès colonial international de Bruxelles: extrait de la Revue des questions scientifiques, avril 1898* (Brussels, 1898), p. 33. The 1897 congress coincided with the world's fair in Brussels: *Exposition international de Bruxelles 1897: XVIme Section. Congrès International Colonial sous le haut patronage de S.M. le Roi des Belges* (Brussels, 1897).

99 MS Brit. Emp. 20, *Minute Book 6* (E2/11): note 281 (4 July 1890).

100 'Stanley à Bruxelles', *Le Mouvement Antiesclavagiste*, 2 (April 1890), 130.

101 MS Bxl. FO, doss. 363, 'Incident Stokes'. See also Wm. Roger Louis, 'Great Britain and the Stokes case', *Uganda Journal*, 28 (1964), 135–49; Daniel Vangroenweghe, *Voor rubber en ivoor: Leopold II en de ophanging van Stokes* (Leuven, 2005).

102 *The Times* (17 August 1895), *Pall Mall Gazette* (28 August 1895). See also MS Bxl. FO, doss. 363, letter from the Belgian ambassador in London, 17 August 1895.

103 *Pall Mall Gazette* (14 October 1895).

104 'L'Affaire Stokes: le procès d'un juge', *Le Mouvement Antiesclavagiste*, 8 (February 1896), 53.

105 Vangroenweghe, *Voor rubber en ivoor*, p. 10. Cf. Wm. Roger Louis, 'The Stokes affair and the origins of the anti-Congo campaign, 1895–1896', *RBPH–BTFG*, 43 (1965), 572–84.

106 Neal Ascherson, *The King Incorporated: Leopold the Second and the Congo* (new edn., Cambridge, 2001); Daniel Vangroenweghe, *Rood rubber: Leopold II en zijn Kongo* (Brussels, 1985).

107 Kevin Grant, 'Christian critics of empire: missionaries, lantern lectures, and the Congo reform campaign in Britain', *Journal of Imperial and Commonwealth History*, 29 (2001), 27–58.

108 Jules Marchal, *E.D. Morel contre Léopold II: L'histoire du Congo 1900–1910* (Paris, 1996); Wm. Roger Louis, 'Roger Casement and the Congo' and 'E. D. Morel and the triumph of the Congo Reform Association', in Louis, *Ends of British Imperialism*, pp. 127–82.

109 Kevin Grant, *A Civilised Savagery: Britain and the New Slaveries in Africa, 1884–1926* (New York, 2005), pp. 47–9. Cf. William Phipps, *William Sheppard: Congo's African American Livingstone* (Louisville, KY, 2002), p. 149.

110 MS Brit. Emp. 22, APS, G261 CFS (Congo): H.R. Fox Bourne to *Daily News*, 20 March 1903.

111 Louis, 'Berlin Congo Conference', p. 124.

112 Cooper, 'Conditions analogous to slavery: imperialism and free labor ideology in Africa', in Cooper *et al.*, *Beyond Slavery*, p. 130.

113 Grant, *A Civilised Savagery*, pp. 36–7. Pavlakis locates the origins of the movement in the 'humanitarian tradition'; compared to Grant, he stresses the role of Morel, the Congo Reform Association and the British Foreign Office during 'waves of agitation' in the first decade of the twentieth century: Dean Pavlakis, 'The development of British overseas humanitarianism and the Congo reform campaign', *Journal of Colonialism and Colonial History*, 11 (2010) [online via *Project MUSE*, http://muse.jhu.edu].

114 E.D. Morel, *The Congo Slave State: A Protest against the New African Slavery; and an Appeal to the Public of Great Britain, of the United States, and of the Continent of Europe* (Liverpool, 1903).

115 Hermann Christ-Socin, *Les Missions évangéliques et l'État du Congo : l'affaire Morrison-Sheppard* (Saint-Blaise, 1909), p. 20.

116 William Rose (ed.), *Official Report of the Thirteenth Universal Peace Congress held at Boston, Massachusetts, USA, October 3rd to 8th, 1904* (Boston, 1904), pp. 275–7.

117 On this issue, see Jörg Fisch 'Africa as *terra nullius*: the Berlin conference and international law', in Förster *et al.*, *Bismarck, Europe and Africa*, pp. 347–76.

118 MS IPB 199/13: Résolution du XVe Congrès universel de la Paix (Milan, 15–22 septembre 1906).

119 MS IPB 209/16: document 'Comité de protection et de défense des indigènes: Voeux adoptés par le Comité dans sa réunion du 13 juin 1907'; leaflet 'Fourth National Peace Congress of Great Britain and Ireland, Scarborough, 1907'.

120 Catherine Ann Cline, 'E.D. Morel and the crusade against the Foreign Office', *Journal of Modern History*, 39 (1967), 126–37.

121 Sheldon Spear, 'Pacifist radicalism in the post-war British Labour Party: the case of E. D. Morel, 1919–1924', *International Review of Social History*, 23 (1978), 193–223.

122 Norman Ingram, *The Politics of Dissent: Pacifism in France 1919–1939* (Oxford, 1991), pp. 70–5.

123 Michael Patrick Cullinane, 'Transatlantic dimensions of the anti-imperialist movement, 1899–1909', *Journal of Transatlantic Studies*, 4 (2010), 301–14.

124 'Extrait des Statuts', *Bulletin Trimestriel: Ligue Internationale pour la défense des Indigènes dans le Bassin Conventionnel du Congo*, 2 (May–August 1908), 26.

125 Félicien Challaye, 'Les Réformes nécessaires au Congo français', *Bulletin Trimestriel*, 1 (1908), 12–14; 'Au Congo français', *Bulletin Trimestriel*, 4 (1909), 32–5; Pierre Mille, 'La question du Congo Français', *Bulletin Trimestriel*, 5 (1909), 2–11.

126 'La campagne antiléopoldienne en Suisse', *Bulletin Trimestriel*, 1 (1908), 20; 'La Ligue Suisse pour la défense des Indigènes dans le bassin conventionnel du Congo', *Bulletin trimestriel*, 2 (1908), 41–3; 'Ligue Suisse pour la défense des indigènes dans le bassin du Congo: Rapport présenté à l'Assemblée générale le 22 Juin 1909 par M. René Claparède', *Bulletin Trimestriel*, 5 (1909), 12–18.

127 MS Morel F8/27 (Félicien Challaye): Challaye to Morel, 16 September 1908.
128 *Ibid.*, Challaye to Morel, 17 May 1908.
129 MS Morel F8/131 (René Claparède): Claparède to Morel, 7 June 1908.
130 Morel, 'Les indigènes du Congo Belge et du Congo Français: un appel à la France', *Bulletin Trimestriel*, 1 (1908), 8–11.
131 'E. D. Morel en France' and 'E. D. Morel en Suisse', *Bulletin Trimestriel*, 4 (1909), 35–40.
132 'Comité International pour la défense des Indigènes du Congo', *Bulletin Trimestriel*, 4 (1909), ii.
133 Jean Stengers, 'Morel and Belgium' in W. Roger Louis and Jean Stengers (eds), *E. D. Morel's History of the Congo Reform Movement* (Oxford, 1968), p. 221.
134 'De la supériorité de la race anglo-saxonne', *Le Mouvement Antiesclavagiste*, 10 (May 1898), 109.
135 See e.g. 'Une conférence en faveur du Congo à Washington (Etats-Unis)', *Le Mouvement des Missions Catholiques au Congo*, 17 (January 1905), 9.
136 Stengers, 'Morel and Belgium', p. 228.
137 Marchal, *E.D. Morel contre Léopold II*, pp. 292–4.
138 Stengers, 'Morel and Belgium', pp. 22–8.
139 'The Aborigines Protection Society', *Le Mouvement Antiesclavagiste*, 14 (May 1902), 128.
140 'Les atrocités dans les colonies', *Le Mouvement Antiesclavagiste*, 12 (June 1900), 104. Cf. Jean Stengers, 'Les accusations anglaises contre le Congo: E.D. Morel, le fondateur de la Congo Reform Association, et la Belgique', in Stengers, *Congo: mythes et réalités*, pp. 129–58.
141 Edouard Descamps, *New Africa: An Essay on Government Civilization in New Countries and on the Foundation, Organization and Administration of the Congo Free State* (London, 1903), p. 6.
142 *Ibid.*, p. 89.
143 MP IPB, 209/11: pamphlet *Congrès International d'Expansion Économique Mondiale, septembre 1905 (Bruxelles, le 7 mars 1905)*, p. 8.
144 'Le Congrès d'Expansion Mondiale', *L'Indépendance Belge*, 4 October 1905.
145 Koskenniemi, *Gentle Civilizer of Nations*, pp. 159–64. Félicien Cattier, *Étude sur la Situation de l'Etat indépendant du Congo* (Brussels, 1906).
146 Lalla Vandervelde, *Monarchs and Millionaires* (New York, 1925), p. 39.
147 *Ibid.*
148 Polasky, *The Democratic Socialism of Emile Vandervelde*, p. 55.
149 MS Morel F8/139 (Emile Vandervelde): Lalla Vandervelde to Morel, 6 November 1906.
150 *Ibid.*, e.g. Lalla Vandervelde to Morel on 8 March, 15 March and 14 June 1911.
151 *Ibid.*, Lalla Vandervelde to Morel, 20 September 1909.
152 Guy Vanthemsche, 'De belgische socialisten en Congo 1895–1960', *Brood en Rozen*, 2 (1999), 31–65.
153 Polasky, *The Democratic Socialism of Emile Vandervelde*, pp. 70–1.
154 'La reprise: discours de Vandervelde devant la Commission des XVII', *Bulletin Trimestriel*, 1 (January–April 1908), p. 6. Edmond Picard supported

annexation, yet his stance was shaped by imperialist views, rather than sympathy for Congo reform.

155 Wm. Roger Louis, 'Morel and the Congo Reform Association 1904–1913', *History of the Congo Reform Movement*, pp. 189–91.
156 Polasky, *The Democratic Socialism of Emile Vandervelde*, p. 68.
157 Louis Bertrand, *Le Scandale congolais* (Brussels, 1908).
158 'La reprise', p. 6.
159 MS Morel F8/104 (Georges Lorand): Lorand to Morel, 1 December 1906.
160 *Ibid.*, Lorand to Morel, 1 April 1908.
161 *Ibid.*
162 Jean Stengers, 'Le rôle de la commission d'enquête de 1904–1905 au Congo', in Stengers, *Congo: Mythes et réalités*, pp. 159–79; Louis, 'E. D. Morel and the triumph of the Congo Reform Association', pp. 162–3. Cattier's *Etude sur la situation de l'Etat internationale du Congo* also affected public opinion in Belgium.
163 E.D. Morel, 'Preface', in Congo Reform Association, *Témoignage devant la Commission d'Enquête au Congo: evènements qui se sont déroulés au Congo depuis le retour de la Commission* (Liverpool, 1905), p. 9.
164 'Pourquoi les Missionnaires catholiques n'ont ils pas parlé', *Le Mouvement des Missions Catholiques au Congo*, 18 (February 1906), 48. See also Catherine Ann Cline, 'The church and the movement for Congo reform', *Church History*, 32 (1963), 46–56.
165 Viaene, 'Reprise-remise: de Congolese identiteitscrisis van België rond 1908' in Viaene, *Congo in Belgë*, pp. 44–5.
166 Mary Elizabeth Thomas, 'Anglo-Belgian military relations and the Congo question, 1911–1913', *Journal of Modern History*, 25 (1953), 157–65.
167 MS Morel F8/104: Lorand to Morel, undated letter.
168 Morrison had been drawing attention to conditions in the Congo since 1899: Marchal, *E.D. Morel contre Léopold II*, i. 75–91.
169 Christ-Socin, *Les Missions évangéliques*, p. 63.
170 Phipps, *William Sheppard*, p. 167; Emile Vandervelde, *Souvenirs d'un militant socialiste* (Paris, 1939), pp. 90–2.
171 Arthur Conan Doyle, *The Crime of the Congo* (London, 1909).
172 MS Morel F8/131: Morel to Claparède, 17 September 1909.
173 *Ibid.*
174 MS Morel F8/139: Lalla Vandervelde to Morel, 22 October 1909.
175 *Ibid.*
176 MS Morel F8/131: Morel to Claparède, 17 September 1909.
177 'Un manifeste national de protestation contre l'agitation congophobe en Angleterre', *Le Mouvement des Missions Catholiques au Congo*, 21 (1909), 145–6.
178 Stanard, 'Learning to love Leopold', p. 134.
179 MS Brit. Emp. 22, G262, 'Various Congo Letters': Congo Reform Association to Edmond Grey, 30 May 1910.
180 MS Morel F8/139: Morel to Lalla Vandervelde, 17 October 1910.
181 *Ibid.*, Morel to Emile Vandervelde, 30 September 1912, containing note dated 12 August 1912.

182 *Ibid.*, Morel to Lalla Vandervelde, 17 October 1910. Similar comments in Morel to Emile Vandervelde, 9 February 1910.
183 *Ibid.*, Travers Buxton to Morel, 2 November 1912.
184 Louis, 'Morel and the Congo Reform Association', p. 200.
185 MS BA, R1001/7409 (Sklavensachen 11): letter from Greindl, 25 January 1895.
186 *Ibid.*, docs. 85–92.
187 *Documents relatifs à la répression de la traite des esclaves publiés en exécution des articles 81 et suivants de l'Acte Général de Bruxelles* (Brussels, 1892–1914).
188 MS BA, R1001/7413 (Sklavensachen 11): letters of 14 December 1901 and 8 February 1907.
189 MS BA, R1001/7407 (Sklavensachen 9): letter to von Bülow, 7 February 1904.
190 *Ibid.*, letter from Zanzibar, 3 January 1907.
191 MS LON, 6B/17172/1864: E. de Haller to George Maxwell, 22 March 1935.
192 *Ibid.*, note on 'International Bureaux Dealing with the Slave Traffic', *c.* 1935.
193 MS LON, 6A/4479/758: note by Vito Catastini, secretary of the League's Mandates section, *c.* May 1930. See also MS LON, 5A/783/783: 'Liquor Traffic in Africa. Information Communicated to the Secretariat 1928'.
194 MS LON, 6B/17172/1864: 'Memorandum du Secrétariat au sujet des Commissions temporaires de l'Esclavage de 1924/5 et de 1932 et de la Commission Consultative d'Experts en matière d'esclavage. Geneva, 30 August 1935 et 4 March 1935'.
195 *Ibid.*, 'Note on the International Bureaux Dealing with the African Slave Trade', 22 March 1935.
196 Miers, 'Slavery and the slave trade as international issues', p. 25. Cf. Miers, *Slavery in the Twentieth Century: The Evolution of a Global Problem* (Lanham, MD, 2002), p. 110.
197 Susan Pedersen, 'The meaning of the Mandates system: an argument', *Geschichte und Gesellschaft*, 32 (2006), 560–82; Michael Callahan, *Mandates and Empire: The League of Nations and Africa, 1914–1931* (Portland, OR, 1999); Callahan, *A Sacred Trust: The League of Nations and Africa, 1929–1946* (Brighton, 2004).
198 Amalia Ribi, '"The breath of a new life"? British anti-slavery activism and the League of Nations', in Laqua, *Internationalism Reconfigured*, esp. pp. 96 and 106–7.
199 *Ibid.*, pp. 99–102. See e.g. '2me assemblée générale de la Ligue internationale pour la défense des indigènes', *Journal de Genève*, 4 September 1925.
200 MS LON, 6A/4479/758: letters of 17 October 1929 and 9 November 1929 as well as internal note from *c.* April 1930.
201 *Ibid.*, 'Alcoholism in Africa and the Convention of Saint-Germain-en-Laye: Memorial presented by the International Bureau for the Protection of the Native Races to the Governments which have ratified the Convention of Saint-Germain-en-Laye relating to the Liquor Traffic in Africa'.
202 *Ibid.*, exchange between Catastini and Drummond, 4 June 1930.
203 John Horne and Alan Kramer, *German Atrocities, 1914: A History of Denial* (New Haven, CT, 2005), p. 204.

204 Michaël Amara, 'La propagande belge et l'image de la Belgique aux Etats-Unis pendant la Première Guerre mondiale', *BTNG–RBHC*, 30 (2000), 188.

205 Jonathan Helmreich, *Belgium and Europe: A Study in Small Power Diplomacy* (The Hague, 1976), pp. 177–84; Ingeborg Vijgen, *Tussen mandaat en kolonie: Rwanda, Burundi en het Belgische bestuur in opdracht van de Volkenbond (1916–1932)* (Leuven, 2005), pp. 49–85.

206 Jeannick Vangansbeke, '"Comrades in arms?" Het diplomatieke streekspsiel tussen België en het Britse "Empire" tijdens de Groote Oorlog, *BTNG–RBHC*, 38 (2008), 131–58.

207 *Le Vingtième Siècle*, 25 and 26 June 1929.

208 Julia Seibert, 'Travail Libre ou Travail Forcé? Die "Arbeiterfrage" im belgischen Kongo 1908–1930', *Journal of Modern European History*, 7 (2009), 93–108.

209 MS Brit. Emp. 20, *Minute Book 11* (E2/16): note 4735 (7 July 1932). Cf. Vanthemsche, 'De belgische socialisten en Congo', p. 35.

210 'Forced labour in the Congo: modern substitute for slavery', *Catholic Times* (8 February 1929); 'Belgian Congo', *The Tablet* (9 February 1929).

211 Secrétariat de l'Internationale Ouvrière Socialiste, *Le Problème colonial: matériaux présentés au IIIe Congrès de l'Internationale Ouvrière Socialiste à Bruxelles août 1928* (Zurich, 1928), pp. 179–82.

212 *Publications of the League of Nations:* VI.B. Slavery.1926.1–7: A.10.1926.VI: Geneva, Draft Convention on Slavery. Replies from Governments (22 July 1926 and 31 August 1926).

213 Cooper, 'Conditions analogous to slavery', pp. 132–3. Susan Zimmermann has argued that in doing so, the ILO took up the anti-slavery mantle but sacrificed some of its earlier commitment to addressing other forms of non-metropolitan labour: Zimmermann, 'Sonderumstände in Genf: Die ILO und die Welt der nicht-metropolitanen Arbeit in der Zwischenkriegszeit', in Fischer and Zimmermann, *Internationalismen*, pp. 147–69.

214 MS Bxl. FO, direction P: Convention sur l'Esclavage. Ratifications et Adhésions, no. 11.152/I. 'Chambre des Représentants, Session de 1935–6. Séance du 7 avril 1936'.

215 *Ibid.*, Leopold III on 23 March 1936.

216 MS Bxl. FO, Affaires Coloniales, Direction P, 'Dossier N°11.152/I: Convention Travail forcé': 'Radiodiffusion National Belges (Londres): Ratification de la Convention sur le Travail Forcé', 6 August 1943.

217 d'Ursel, *La Campagne antiesclavagiste belge*, p. 2.

3

Church and state

In the second half of the nineteenth century, Europe experienced intense antagonism between secular and ecclesiastical forces. In Germany, these conflicts peaked with the *Kulturkampf* of the 1870s; in Italy, they were exemplified by the 'Rome question' and the Papacy's hostility towards the liberal state.[1] In France, the legitimacy of the Third Republic was initially contested by an alliance of monarchists and Catholics. Spurred on by Cardinal Lavigerie in 1890, some French Catholics adopted a policy of accommodation, but the 1905 law on the separation of church and state testified to ongoing tensions. Indeed, the legacies of the European culture wars lasted well into the twentieth century, as exemplified by the rise of political Catholicism: parties and associations sought to defend religion against the – perceived or real – onslaught of secular forces.[2] Particular subsets of political Catholicism, namely social Catholicism and Christian trade unionism, received a boost from Pope Leo XIII's encyclical *Rerum Novarum* (1891) which 'provided an intellectual platform that valorized serious Catholic labour movements across Europe'.[3] Consequently, Catholics developed distinct responses to the social ills of modernity through trade unions and mutual-help societies.

Universalism is intrinsic to many belief systems, and churches developed manifold cross-border links that involved clergymen and laypeople. Nonetheless, new forms of activism in the secular sphere – from lay associations to large-scale congresses – make it possible to trace the rise of a distinct 'religious internationalism' in the late nineteenth century. In this context, it has been argued that Catholic internationalism experienced its 'phase of consolidation' between 1878 and 1914.[4] After the First World War, it was boosted further by bodies such as the International Federation of Christian Trade Unions and specialised Catholic organisations on international relations, science and film. Protestants established their own international bodies, starting with the Evangelical Alliance (1846) and the World's Christian Endeavor Union (1895) and culminating with the World Council of Churches (1937). The age of internationalism also heralded opportunities for inter-faith dialogue, most famously with the World Parliament of Religions during the Chicago World Columbian Exposition of 1893.[5]

Religious internationalism had a secular counterpart: the International Freethought Federation (Fédération Internationale de la Libre Pensée). Founded in 1880, it represented groups and individuals who described themselves as 'freethinkers' (*libres-penseurs*) or 'rationalists' (*rationalistes*).[6] The constituency and underlying principles of this 'Freethinkers' International' were described in various ways: in Britain, the term 'secularism' was coined by G. H. Hoyoake and associated with the campaigns of the liberal MP Charles Bradlaugh.[7] In France, the term 'laïcisme' referred to the agenda of politicians such as Léon Gambetta and bodies such as the League for the Separation of State and Church (founded in 1882).[8] There were significant overlaps between such appellations: freethinkers, laïcists and secularists contested the worldly power of churches – be they Roman Catholic or Anglican – but distanced themselves from 'infidels' or 'atheists'.[9] The Freethinkers' International involved individuals who believed in the primacy of science over belief, but it also drew support from liberals, radicals and socialists for whom anticlericalism was a motivating factor. At the 1904 congress of the International Freethought Federation, held in Rome, the French radical Ferdinand Buisson provided a definition which covered the movement's different bases: he described freethought as a 'method' characterised by the rejection of dogma.[10]

Freethinkers and Catholics in Belgium

The relationship between church and state was a particularly divisive issue in Belgium. As Vincent Viaene has put it, 'Belgium was not only the most liberal state in Europe, but also the most Catholic country north of the Alps'.[11] Political Catholicism had a significant Belgian support base, sustained by a rich associational life and a period of uninterrupted Catholic rule between 1884 and the First World War. Martin Conway has even suggested that Belgium has 'a good claim to have been the birthplace of modern forms of political Catholicism'.[12] Yet at the same time, a coalition of different forces waged a long-lasting campaign against the role of the Catholic church in schooling and other areas of public life. This alliance comprised a strong Masonic movement that was organised in the Grand Orient de Belgique; liberal politicians who sought to limit Catholic control over education; and a confident labour movement which partly defined itself in anticlerical terms.

The divide surrounding questions of church power was not always as severe as the conflicts of the Belle Époque suggest: Belgian independence had been achieved through the combined efforts of Catholics and liberals. Although some liberal and Catholic politicians continued to cooperate in the national interest, the era of 'unionism' ended in the 1840s and tensions became manifest at several levels. The Vatican's denunciation of freemasonry had particular implications in Belgium, given the strength of the country's Masonic movement.[13] The growing connection between freemasonry, freethought and liberalism was not a Belgian peculiarity: similar convergences existed in France and in Latin American countries such as Mexico, Colombia and Brazil. Germany was a different case: there, freethinkers criticised freemasonry's secrecy, its rituals and the notion of a 'Great Architect' to which German and British lodges adhered.[14] Yet it was not only freemasonry that caused domestic tensions: another complicating factor was the prominence of Ultramontanism among Belgian Catholics. From 1859, the country played 'a major role as a centre of Catholic mobilisation for the Pope' as well as constituting a 'battleground' between liberal Catholics and Ultramontanes.[15] While ultimately referring to the primacy of Rome, the label 'Ultramontanism' summarised a variety of stances and was often used polemically.[16] Its underlying features resulted in clashes with secular forces: Manuel Borutta has pointed out that liberals and Ultramontanes were akin to each other in their pursuit of 'universalising missionary agendas', characterised by antagonistic views on lifestyles, education and order.[17]

Yet even after the 1850s, there was no clear-cut dichotomy in Belgium's political life: liberal Catholics and Ultramontanes adopted different levels of intransigence vis-à-vis the state and could enter into unlikely alliances with secular liberals.[18] Similarly, Belgian freethought was far from unified. The associations L'Affranchissement and Les Solidaires, founded in 1854 and 1857 respectively, maintained strong links with the labour movement, exemplified by the participation of socialists such as Désiré Brismée and César De Paepe.[19] In contrast, the Libre Pensée de Bruxelles, founded in 1863, was connected to Belgian freemasonry and liberalism. It was only in 1885 – partly inspired by the foundation of the International Freethought Federation – that liberal and socialist freethinkers set up a joint national federation. Furthermore, freethought in Flanders proved weaker than in the Belgian capital and the industrial regions of Wallonia; a 'Vlaamse Vrijdenkersfederatie' was not established until 1895.[20]

The polarisation of Belgian politics and culture was epitomised by the so-called 'School War', which started when a liberal government passed the Organic Law of 1879. The law obliged each municipality to establish secular schools and prohibited religious instruction in schools. The law was dismantled after the election of a Catholic government in 1884. That year, Belgium appeared to be a 'country in crisis', with some historians describing the post-election atmosphere in the capital as like a 'civil war'.[21] The Catholic Party's period of undivided rule only ended with the formation of a national unity government during the First World War. In the Belle Époque, Catholic school policies under the politicians Franz Schollaert and Prosper Poullet ensured that the relationship between education and religion remained a hotly contested issue.

Complementing the Catholics' efforts in government, activists committed themselves to broadening their field of action. Under the influence of Joris Helleputte and Arthur Verhaegen, Catholics founded lay organisations such as the Boerenbond (1890) and the Belgische Volksbond/Ligue Démocratique Belge (1891). These bodies extended the associational life of Belgian Catholicism to farmers and workers. Their initiatives proved particularly successful in Flanders, which had a higher church-going population than the industrial areas in the south. In Ghent, these groups responded to the rise of socialist associations and cooperatives.[22] Christian trade unionism remained 'a marginal phenomenon' until around 1900.[23] In the subsequent years, their growth was encouraged by Désiré-Joseph Mercier, who became Archbishop of Mechelen (Malines) in 1906 and Cardinal one year later. This development differed from the situation in other European countries, where Christian trade unions experienced a crisis in the early twentieth century.[24] On the eve of the First World War, Christian trade unions in Belgium claimed a share of 41.8 per cent of total trade union membership in the country. Although the post-war proportion was lower, numbers had climbed back to 28.8 per cent by 1930.[25] Protagonists of Catholic labour tended to portray themselves as 'Christian Democrats',[26] but such terms need to be used cautiously: as late as the 1920s and 1930s, many politicians who evoked 'Christian democracy' did not lend wholehearted support to parliamentary democracy. As a whole, Christian democracy was characterised by a 'great plurality of political ideas and aims'.[27]

At a time when Catholic activists built new associations, freethinkers consolidated their ties. Soon after its foundation in 1885, their national federation claimed around 25,000 members – a size that matched each of the two major freethought associations in France.[28] It has been estimated that between 1854 and 1914, there were around 300 different freethought groups in Belgium.[29] Furthermore, the reformist agenda of Belgian socialists meant that secularist campaigning could bridge the divide between liberalism and socialism. Emile Vandervelde was a case in point: while emerging as a leading figure in the Belgian Workers' Party (BWP), he remained a member of the 'bourgeois' Libre Pensée de Bruxelles. Although Belgian socialists officially adhered to the notion of religion as a private matter, their involvement in anticlerical agitation meant that freethought maintained relations with a range of mass organisations.

As Hugh McLeod has pointed out, polarisation is only one potential relationship between religious and secular forces.[30] Rather than living in a state of permanent conflict, many Catholics, socialists and liberals organised their own spheres, developing separate 'pillars' based on ideology, culture and belief.[31] The model of 'pillarisation' features prominently in studies of Belgian society, although its limitations and grey areas have been widely acknowledged. The historians Els Witte and Jeffrey Tyssens, for instance, have argued that freethought and freemasonry did not constitute pillars in themselves.[32] However, by providing a forum for particular sociabilities and accompanying the life cycle – for instance, through the provision of secular funerals – freethought associations contributed to the socialist or liberal pillars. As an analytical tool, pillarisation has the advantage of explaining how Belgian society managed conflict: the existence of separate associational structures allowed for negotiation and compromise at the elite level, that is, between the leaders of associations, movements or parties.

After the First World War, divisions according to class and language gained in prominence, overshadowing the agitation surrounding church–state relations.[33] In this period, the freethinkers' and the Catholics' camps experienced internal fragmentation. For instance, Emile Vandervelde resigned his membership of the Libre Pensée de Bruxelles in 1922, and several socialist freethinkers left Vandervelde's party because it began to accept members of Catholic workers groups. Meanwhile, the Liberal Party toned down its anticlericalism, to the disappointment of activists who continued to view freethought as a key element of liberal politics.[34] Among Catholics, efforts to achieve greater unity had limited effect: from 1921, the Catholic Union (Union Catholique Belge/Katholiek Verbond van België) combined four strands of Catholic life: organisations for workers, farmers and the middle classes as well as political representation. Emmanuel Gerard has noted that the interwar years remained a period of 'permanent reform' for political Catholicism.[35] No longer holding an absolute majority in parliament, the Catholic Party nonetheless performed strongly at the polls and participated in coalition governments.

How did Belgium's domestic disputes regarding secular and religious issues relate to internationalism? The connection was twofold: first, national groups and associations were connected to international movements, be they Catholic or secularist. Examples ranged from the Freethinkers' International to the European links of Christian trade unions. It has also been argued that Ultramontanism had its own internationalising qualities.[36] Secondly, many varieties of internationalism – pacifism, socialism, feminism – attracted a constituency that regarded itself as 'progressive' and overlapped with freethought. Two Belgian protagonists of the International Workingman's Association – César De Paepe and Eugène Hins – helped develop the transnational links of the Freethinkers' International: De Paepe co-founded the International Freethought Federation and Hins later became its secretary. Georges Lorand – the progressive liberal who had been such a vociferous critic of King Leopold's Congo – was a vice-president of the federation. Furthermore, one of Belgium's most prominent feminist campaigners, Isabelle Gatti de Gamond, was associated with international freethought beyond her death: a posthumous collection of her writings was edited by the leaders of the International Freethought Federation, and at the 1913 freethinkers' congress in Lisbon, her Rationalist Orphanage in Forest/Vorst was praised as a model of secular education.[37] Seen from this angle, an understanding of freethought internationalism provides us with a clearer picture of the reformist environment in which protagonists of Belgian internationalism operated.

Catholic internationalism versus freethought internationalism

Vincent Viaene has found an apt description for Belgium's significance for international Catholicism: having initially been a 'litmus test' for the Catholic church, Belgium turned into a 'laboratory' where the church developed and tested its responses to modernity.[38] It is, therefore, hardly surprising that internationalism was a prominent feature of Belgian Catholicism. For instance, the Catholic congresses at Mechelen in 1863, 1864 and 1867 had been inspired by the example of the German *Katholikentage*.[39] Highlighting the links to the internationalism discussed in chapter 2, another congress at Mechelen, held in 1891, featured anti-slavery speeches by Edouard Descamps and Hippolyte d'Ursel.[40]

Through the Confrérie de Saint-Michel (founded in 1875), Belgians were connected to the 'Black International', a network sustained by the Comité de Défense Catholique in Geneva at the height of the European culture wars.[41] While these bodies involved limited numbers of activists, they offered new mechanisms for lay participation. Another initiative explicitly appealed to mass audiences: in 1881, the first International Eucharistic Congress took place in Lille.[42] Belgian Catholics soon embraced these events, hosting congresses in Liège (1883), Antwerp (1890), Brussels (1898), Namur (1902) and Tournai (1906). On the one hand, the Eucharistic Congresses were national occasions aimed at Belgian Catholics who received indulgences for participation.[43] On the other hand, the Vatican's blessing and the participation of church dignitaries from abroad stressed the internationalism of these events: at the Eucharistic Congress of Antwerp, for instance, the Archbishops of New York and Cagliari as well as the Bishops of Arras, Constance, Luxembourg and Salford were involved.[44]

The Eucharistic Congresses were but one type of large-scale Catholic event in the age of internationalism. For instance, in 1895, Joris Helleputte, co-founder of the Boerenbond, was invited to a congress through which Portuguese Catholics marked the 700th birthday of St Anthony of Padua, the patron saint of Lisbon. The event covered science as well as political questions such as the response to socialism and anarchism.[45] The Belgian experience held important lessons in this respect: in Flanders, Helleputte had helped broaden the appeal of political Catholicism. Sebastiano Nicotra, the Apostolic Nuncio to Portugal insisted that Helleputte 'must go to Lisbon. It is the first

Congress in Portugal, [a country] in the process of religious awakening.'[46] A subsequent telegram was more explicit: 'Your absence would be a disaster'. Yet the Belgian politician did not make it, citing an important vote in the Chamber of Representatives. Instead, he expressed his 'great sympathy for the congress' by telegram.[47] Alongside speakers from France, Italy and Spain, the organisers received many written messages of support, inter alia from bishops in Spain, Italy and the Netherlands, and from individual groups such as a Catholic anti-slavery committee in the Italian city of Monza and representatives of the German *Katholikentage*. Belgian greetings included a Catholic workers group from Tournai and an organisation of Catholic scholars, the Société Scientifique de Bruxelles.[48] Episodes such as the Lisbon congress formed part of a wider endeavour. As the Portuguese organisers stressed, their aspirations 'correspond[ed] not only to one of the necessities of the moment, but also to the wishes of the Holy Father Leo XIII who recommends the urgent constitution of Catholic congresses of which the advantages for Religion and Science are evident'.[49] Thus, the efforts of Catholic activists formed part of an international drive that was supported by the Vatican.

Meanwhile, freethinkers developed their own transnational structures, with Belgian activists playing a leading part. Having proposed closer links between European freethinkers, César De Paepe initiated contacts with the British activists of the National Secular Society and the British Secular Union.[50] These efforts provided the impetus for an international congress which took place in Brussels from 30 August to 1 September 1880, shortly after the city had hosted an international congress for secular education.[51] It brought together 200 delegates from Britain, France, Germany, Austria-Hungary, Spain, Italy, the Netherlands and Belgium. *La Bombe* – a satirical and anticlerical periodical published between 1878 and 1884 – portrayed the occasion as 'genuine anticlerical fireworks'.[52] The liberal *L'Indépendance Belge* covered the event with a delay of nearly one week and stressed its scientific character. The newspaper thus responded to the Catholic *Courrier de Bruxelles*, which had claimed that the initial silence was due to the presence of 'sinister doctrines' at the congress, which had shed 'compromising light on liberalism'.[53] After the foundation of the International Freethought Federation, activists sought to organise regular congresses. Initial obstacles became apparent when the second international congress, held in London in 1881, met with a competing gathering in Paris.[54] The latter, despite being labelled 'international', was only attended by French freethinkers and a handful of Belgian activists. The federation subsequently achieved a greater degree of stability: between 1880 and the outbreak of the First World War, it held altogether sixteen international congresses. International freethought returned to Belgium twice before the war: to Antwerp in 1885 and to Brussels in 1910. On these occasions, Catholic newspapers renewed their attacks, describing the Antwerp meeting as a 'congress of madmen'.[55] The Antwerp event had initially been planned for 1884. However, the electoral struggles of that year had 'focused all the thinking of progressives on the question of saving public education' during a 'period of unprecedented political agitation'.[56]

In the federation's early years, French freethinkers tended to dominate proceedings. Prior to the 1900 congress in Paris, the German socialist Ida Altmann argued that the 'temper and current national conditions' of French freethinkers meant that they were ill-equipped for organising the congress.[57] She later reported that the French had formed the largest delegation, having mobilised anticlerical forces from freemasons to socialists.[58] Similarly, at the 1904 congress in Rome, French delegates were only outnumbered by the hosts.[59] When, one year later, another international congress in Paris took place with an overwhelming number of French participants, it triggered misgivings among British secularists.[60] In light of these tensions, Brussels became a convenient site for the federation's headquarters: Belgians benefited from their proximity to France but raised fewer suspicions of wanting to dominate the organisation. From 1900, the Council of the International Freethought Federation – with two representatives per country – operated alongside a Permanent Bureau solely comprised of Belgian members. The latter was conceived as an 'information and documentation office, an intermediary between different national organisations, a centre of guidance, impulsion and propaganda, an initiator and organiser of protests, of demonstrations, of celebrations and of commemoration'.[61] Altmann approved the installation of a more permanent structure in Brussels, praising the city's location, the country's relatively liberal system and the organising skills of the 'sober, practically-minded Belgians'.[62]

The Brussels secretariat was led by Léon Furnémont, a socialist member of parliament. He had a history of cooperation with freethinkers from other countries, for instance during preparations for the 1892 congress in Madrid.[63] As secretary, he provided organisational and moral support to the federation's affiliates. Before the Rome congress of 1904, for instance, he addressed nine local meetings in Italy.[64] Two years later, Furnémont and his compatriot Georges Lorand returned to Italy: they visited the congress of the Italian federation, whose foundation had been sparked by the Rome congress.[65] In 1908, Furnémont lectured in Budapest, working towards the creation of a Hungarian association.[66] The Hungarian freethinker Joseph Diner-Dénes had previously expressed his hope that freethought internationalism could help invigorate the Hungarian freethought movement.[67] Besides such organisational work, the Brussels secretariat launched an international bulletin in 1904, and in 1908 and 1909 it published almanacs with biographical sketches and reports from across the world. Between 1911 and 1914, Eugène Hins issued annual reports on the federation's activities.[68] These activities remained intertwined with those of the national

Belgian federation: both organisations published information in the Belgian periodical *La Pensée*, also edited by Hins. Belgium's leading role within the federation was rarely challenged, except for a 1910 proposal by Italian free-thinkers that the federation's headquarters be transferred to Rome.[69]

The federation was more than a Belgian undertaking: in 1910, for instance, Belgian, German, Dutch, Swiss and Polish affiliates all paid full membership fees, with British, French and Bohemian branches making partial contributions.[70] These national organisations represented significant constituencies: British freethinkers attracted thousands of people to their events in the mid-1880s, and by 1908, the federation's German affiliates boasted around 70,000 members.[71] Furthermore, many international congresses were large-scale affairs. At the 1892 congress in Madrid, 4,000 people listened to speeches at the Prince Alphonso Theatre.[72] The 1904 congress in Rome received 20,000 adhesions, and attracted more than 3,500 delegates from 34 nations, including 650 from France, 150 from Spain, 110 from Belgium and 50 from Germany.[73] The event also involved a large-scale public march to the Porta Pia, where Italian troops had entered papal Rome in 1870. The procession was led by a musical group comprised of former 'Garibaldinis'.[74] Processions were, of course, also part of the Catholic repertoire. The Catholic Congress of Lisbon in 1896, for instance, was combined with a procession in honour of St Anthony, followed by a boat procession on the river Tagus.[75] Such public events were potential sites of conflict: it has been noted that the Lisbon festivities 'ended in fiasco when anticlericals broke up the main procession'.[76]

The popular dimension of international congresses was accompanied by political networking. When hosted by municipalities under liberal or socialist control, delegates relied on official backing. Even though the scale of international freethought events decreased during the interwar years, the links with politicians continued. For instance, in 1930, when the International Freethought Federation celebrated its fiftieth anniversary, the mayor of Brussels, Adolphe Max, welcomed delegates to the city hall. In seeking access to political leaders, freethinkers hardly differed from Catholic activists. In 1894, for instance, an international congress for Catholic scholars in Brussels attracted Catholic politicians such as Auguste Bernaert and Charles Woeste.

In the interwar years, protagonists of political Catholicism went one step further by developing transnational bonds between their parties. In 1925, a conference in Paris led to the foundation of the International Secretariat of Democratic Parties of Christian Inspiration, with Luigi Sturzo, the exiled leader of the Partito Popolare Italiano, playing an important part. As Guido Müller has suggested, the organisation was a 'suitable go-between for a Franco-German rapprochement',[77] whose overall significance was 'on the level of personal exchange between a small group of individual politicians, who repeatedly took part in international meetings'.[78] Leading Belgian contributors to the International Secretariat were Hendrik Heyman (Union Catholique Belge/Ligue des Travailleurs Chrétiennes) and the Dominican father and Catholic senator Georges-Ceslas Rutten, who had emerged as 'the prime organizer of the Belgian Christian trade unions, moulding the loose trade union federations into an effective trade union apparatus'.[79] Belgian involvement in the Secretariat meant that its second conference was held in Brussels in 1926. Sturzo acknowledged that some 'fairly good statements were made' at this event.[80] Four years later, the International Secretariat returned to Belgium with a conference in Antwerp. By that point, however, the limitations of the organisation had become evident: it remained tacit in its political pronouncements, only involved a limited number of activists and ceased operations in 1932.

The limited success of the International Secretariat seems exemplary of a period in which, as Martin Conway has argued, national frontiers appeared to be 'more defined and less permeable'.[81] Nonetheless, Catholic internationalism survived and developed in a variety of guises. At the level of church diplomacy, Cardinal Mercier initiated a dialogue with the Church of England: between 1921 and 1928, his 'Malines Conversations' brought Catholic clergymen together with figures such as the Bishop of Truro and Lord Halifax, the British Conservative who later became Viceroy of India (1926–31) and Foreign Secretary (1938–40). Meanwhile, new international organisations for Catholics were founded after the end of the First World War, ranging from the Catholic Union of International Studies in Fribourg to the International Federation of Christian Trade Unions in The Hague. In Rome, an International Office of Catholic Organisations collected information on such initiatives. Modern technology provided further impetus for international efforts, reflected in the foundation of separate international Catholic offices for cinema (OCIC) and radio (BCIR) in 1928. On the one hand, these bodies were meant to counter secularising forces. On the other hand, they also showed that the church could use such media, exemplified by Catholic radio stations such as the Katholieke Vlaamsche Radio-Omroep in Belgium (from 1924) and Vatican Radio in Rome (from 1931).[82] The Belgian Dominican priest Felix Morlion – later a collaborator of both the American secret service and the film director Roberto Rossellini – was associated with OCIC and launched a cinematic press service in 1931.[83] In 1934, the priest Jean Bernard – Luxembourg-born, but a former Louvain student – became OCIC's secretary-general and coordinated the organisation's affairs from Brussels. Between 1933 and 1947, a Belgian canon, Abel Brohée, served as the organisation's president.

Brohée had already been a significant activist prior to his involvement in OCIC: Cardinal Mercier made him secretary-general of the Oeuvre Apologétique in Louvain in 1909 and he played a key role in Catholic youth work, including the foundation of the Catholic Association of Belgian Youth

(Association Catholique de la Jeunesse Belge, ACJB) in 1921.[84] ACJB formed part of an international movement in its own right – Catholic Action – which was promoted by Pope Pius XI. Targeting laypeople, Catholic Action presented itself as apolitical and operated with a hierarchical structure. In Belgium, such efforts stood in potential conflict with the more class-based approach of social Catholicism. These tensions became apparent in the relationship between the ACJB and the Catholic Workers' Youth. The latter organisation, founded by the abbot Joseph Cardijn in 1926, had counterparts in France (Jeunesse Ouvrière Chrétienne) and Germany (Christliche Arbeiterjugend).[85] The subsequent compromise with the church hierarchy meant that Cardijn's organisation 'had one leg in the Christian workers' movement and the other in Catholic Action'.[86]

Such examples illustrate the dynamic nature of Catholic internationalism and its Belgian hubs beyond the First World War. Meanwhile, freethought internationalism faced various challenges. The international congress of 1915 was cancelled in the face of the German occupation, and by the 1920s, Belgian freethought had lost many of its leaders who had been involved in the International Freethought Federation. Both the federation's president Hector Denis and its treasurer Jean Dons died in 1913, its vice-president Georges Lorand in 1918, the secretary-general Eugène Hins in 1923 and Denis's successor Guillaume De Greef in 1924. Of the pre-war leadership, only Modeste Terwagne continued to play a pronounced role, serving as the Federation's president from 1924. Between 1920 and 1938, freethinkers nonetheless managed to organise eight congresses, with the 1930 congress in Brussels marking the organisation's half-centenary.

Internationalism between science and politics

Freethinkers presented their movement as part of the onward march of science and reason, underlined by their self-identification as 'rationalists'. They juxtaposed religious universalism with the 'internationalism of freedom, of science, of law'.[87] At their 1885 congress in Antwerp, for instance, delegates demanded the translation of major scientific works to 'liberate the minds from dogma', listing Darwin but also Marx, Quetelet and Comte.[88] The latter names testify to the influence of the social sciences on international freethought. As the British secularist John Robertson claimed, 'The basal proposition of Sociology is that all social like all cosmic change is to be viewed as "natural", not supernatural'.[89] Comtean positivism and sociology had a significant following in Belgium.[90] The Free University of Brussels – founded by liberals and freemasons in 1834 as a counterweight to the Catholic University of Louvain – provided a potential setting for Belgian sociology, although it was not until 1901 that it launched its first course in the discipline.[91] From 1892 to

1894, the sociologist Hector Denis served as its rector. Denis – who became a BWP senator in 1894 – presided over the International Freethought Federation until his death in 1913. In this position, he was succeeded by another Belgian sociologist, Guillaume De Greef, founding rector of the New University (Université Nouvelle), an institution which is discussed further in chapter 4. At events such as the international congress of 1905, Denis presented the project of a universal *Nouvelle Encyclopédie* which was to combine his scientific and secularist aspirations. This was only one instance of the celebration of science in the transnational encounters of freethinkers. For instance, when Belgian delegates attended a congress in London in 1887, they visited the headquarters of the National Secular Society in Britain, named 'Temple of Science'. Inspired by this experience, freethinkers from Charleroi decided to erect a similar building and founded a cooperative society. As a result, Charleroi's 'Temple de Science' hosted the headquarters of the region's Rationalist Federation from 1893 to 1908.[92]

From the start, the International Freethought Federation stressed its links to international science, listing the British sociologist Herbert Spencer, the French philosopher Charles Renouvier, the Dutch physiologist Jacob Moleschott and the German biologist Ernst Haeckel among its founding members. The chemist Marcelin Berthelot served as an honorary president of the 1904 congress in Rome. He played an important role for French *libres-penseurs*, exemplified by a widely reported banquet speech at Saint-Mandé in 1895. Although he did not appear in person, Berthelot addressed the Rome delegates in an extended letter.[93] In contrast, another honorary president, namely Haeckel, did travel to the Italian capital where he was celebrated as the 'anti-Pope' of international freethought.[94] The freethinkers' praise for Haeckel indicates the inspiration that Darwinian science offered to many activists. For instance, the academic and politician Ludwig Büchner was one of the leading German members of the Freethinkers' International. His main work *Kraft und Stoff* helped popularise Darwinism in Germany, Italy and France.[95] Büchner stressed the universal qualities of science and reason – not only at international congresses but also at the inauguration of a monument to Diderot in Paris in 1886 and in publications such as the British periodical *Truth Seeker*.[96] In discussing the German popularisers of Darwin, including the likes of Büchner, Alfred Kelly has argued that 'internationalism was firmly entrenched in the institutions of the free-thought movement'.[97] Darwin was a corresponding member of the Royal Academy of Belgium, but initially, Belgian engagement with Darwinian thought mostly occurred via the reception of Haeckel.[98]

James Hocart, a Brussels-based Unitarian pastor, offered a critical assessment of the Rome congress of 1904. As a representative of a religious minority in Belgium, Hocart hardly sided with the Catholic church, but he also rejected anticlerical rhetoric. Instead of going to Italy, he had travelled to Amsterdam where he attended a congress of 'religious freethinkers' with 900 delegates from 13 countries – including Unitarians, Reformed Christians, Lutherans, United Evangelists and Mennonites. In his subsequent account, Hocart argued that religion was far from incompatible with freethought.[99] He urged freethinkers not to exclude religion from their debates, as this would be antithetical to a genuinely free spirit of enquiry. Hocart pointed at a potentially fruitful relationship between freethinking and faith: 'My free-thinking brethren, who call yourselves anti-religious: you believe that you are the latter, but you are not. You are opposed to certain ceremonies, to certain superstitions, to certain so-called religious dogmas; but you are not opposed to the essence of religion.'[100]

The pastor conceded that religious freethinkers did 'not have scholars of renown as universal as Berthelot and Haeckel, Maudsley and Lombroso'.[101] At the same time, he criticised the likes of Hector Denis for regarding science as a source of morality. A similar line of argument was adopted by the Catholic opponents of freethought. In 1910, for example, the Maison d'Action Catholique in Belgium discussed whether science had made religion redundant. It praised Augustine of Hippo and Gregory of Nazianzus as the first 'evolutionists' (albeit not in a Darwinian sense) and argued that modern science was unable to explain the existence of the human soul.[102] Two years later, in his pastoral letter for Lent, Cardinal Mercier discussed the relationship between 'atheist freethought' and 'public morality'. Stressing the universal features of religion, he suggested that 'the most eminent anthropologists regard atheism as an aberration, that is, what in scientific language one calls a monstrosity'.[103]

While being a hub for freethinkers' international debates on science and religion, Belgium was also at the heart of a major development in Catholic scholarship, namely the neo-scholastic appraisal of the teachings of Thomas Aquinas. 'Neo-Thomism' became the dominant current in Catholic philosophy after Leo XIII had validated it through his encyclical *Aeterni Patris* (1879). This 'project of Christian rationalism', it has been argued, informed the Church's engagement with nineteenth-century developments, but also 'traced its limits'.[104] Belgian theologians had contributed to these debates: as Carl Strikwerda has put it, Louvain was 'both a center for Thomistic studies and the intellectual capital of the Belgian church'.[105] In recognition of its importance, the Vatican established an Institute of Philosophy in the city in 1891, initially led by Mercier. According to Emmanuel Gerard and Kaat Wils, Neo-Thomism provided Mercier with 'a context in which to develop a Catholic philosophy that would match positivism'.[106] He challenged secularist interpretations of sociology and, in doing so, developed Louvain as a site for Catholic sociology, establishing a chair in the History of Social Theory in 1903. The university was keen to avoid direct interference by the Vatican and, from 1899, also offered a course in the critical history of the Old Testament.[107]

Sociology was merely one way in which Catholics countered the identification of freethought with science. The scientific congresses for Catholics were another initiative in this vein. In 1894, after similar events in France, Brussels was the venue of the Third International Scientific Congress of Catholics, a Vatican-endorsed event.[108] The local organiser – Ferdinand Lefebvre, former Dean of the Faculty of Medicine at Louvain – cited the Vatican Council to stress the event's aims: 'there can never be any real disagreement between faith and reason.'[109] This motto had previously been adopted by the Société Scientifique de Bruxelles, founded in 1875 to 'expand interest in science in Catholic circles'.[110] The Société published the *Revue des questions scientifiques*, which displayed a degree of openness to evolutionist ideas and maintained contacts with Catholic scholars in France. Both the Franco-Belgian links and the question of Catholicism's engagement with evolutionism featured at a regional Catholic congress in Rouen in 1885 and the first two International Scientific Congresses of Catholics, held in Paris (1888 and 1891).[111] The organisers of the Brussels event acknowledged difficulties in recruiting participants from abroad, yet were pleased with their resonance in Belgium.[112] Their congress covered history, 'religious science', philosophy, law, philology, mathematics and natural sciences, anthropology, and Christian art. The Liège historian Godefroid Kurth played an active role, and Mercier sat on the organising committee. The question of Catholic science preoccupied many observers: a subsequent article in the Belgian *Revue néo-thomiste* appreciated the delegates' rebuttal of positivism and Kantian idealism, but urged them to go further: 'We can barely wait to reach this new phase of philosophy, [that is] the adaptation of scholastic theories to the principles of modern science'.[113] Darwinian concepts featured in the debates: Giovanni Giovannozzi, a Piarist father from Florence, used the congress to argue that Catholics should study the role of evolution. Such statements highlight the relative 'climate of freedom', despite critical responses from the adherents of religious orthodoxy.[114] The protagonists of a Catholic rationalism encountered a setback with the encyclical *Providentissimus Deus* (1893), and after further events in Fribourg (1888) and Munich (1900), the International Scientific Congresses of Catholics reached their end. However, their example highlights the key role that science played in the international efforts of both freethinkers and Catholics – and Belgium's role as a staging ground for these debates.

Campaigns and controversies

The conflict between state and church became manifest not only in general terms, but also in specific incidents and controversies. The Dreyfus Affair was one such case: in France, the Dreyfusards saw the Catholic church as being in cahoots with reactionary forces and thus partly responsible for the ordeal of Alfred Dreyfus. In his 'letter to France' – which was published in January 1898, shortly before his more famous *J'accuse* – Emile Zola expressed this view very clearly:

> And do you know where else you're headed, France? To the Church. You're going back to the past, the past filled with intolerance and theocracy that your most illustrious children wrestled with and thought they had slain by sacrificing their intelligence and their blood.[115]

Such analysis may have partly been informed by the Catholic nationalism of some of Dreyfus's detractors, notably Maurice Barrès.[116] To both Georges Clemenceau in France and Georges Lorand in Belgium, the sentencing of Dreyfus appeared as a 'clerical crime'.[117] Many of Dreyfus's supporters were freethinkers and promoters of *laïcité*: Ferdinand Buisson, for instance, was both a protagonist of the Freethinkers' International and a key figure in the Ligue des Droits de l'Homme et du Citoyen, the republican organisation that brought together many French Dreyfusards. Inspired by the French example, Eugène Monseur, a professor at the Free University of Brussels, established the league's Belgian counterpart in 1901. Freethinkers' links played a key role in this organisation, exemplified by Modeste Terwagne's leadership of its Antwerp branch.[118] Such examples testify to the freethinkers' interest in the case. In Germany, the periodical *Der Freidenker* praised Emile Zola's *J'accuse* and likened it to Voltaire's defence of the Protestant merchant Jean Calas.[119]

Paul Aron and Jean-Philippe Schreiber have concluded that, with the exception of France, Belgium was the country 'where the Affair most profoundly impacted on public opinion, but [that] this influence was mediated by various factors, in particular the ideological divisions within Belgian society'.[120] To Jean Stengers, the Belgian left – as an alliance of liberals and socialists – became 'a psychological reality' during the campaign.[121] One of the earliest documents of the pro-Dreyfus campaign, Bernard Lazare's *Une erreur judiciaire, la vérité sur l'Affaire Dreyfus* was published in Brussels, placing it beyond the reach of the French authorities.[122] Stengers has pointed out that Belgium was the site of further 'premieres' in the affair: a newspaper article on 12 October 1897, which was the first piece that hinted at the Affair without naming individuals, and on 31 October 1897 an article that proclaimed 'The Innocence of Captain Dreyfus'.[123] In contrast, Belgium's Catholic press evoked the spectre of a 'Jewish-Masonic plot'.[124]

Belgian responses did not, however, present a simple dichotomy between Catholics and the left. Edmond Picard promoted anti-Semitic ideas despite being a senator for the BWP and a key figure in artistic and reformist circles. In the newspaper *Le Peuple*, Jules Destrée – socialist, freethinker and freemason – publicly refused to align himself with the Dreyfusards. His gesture has been interpreted as an expression of his underlying anti-Semitism, which contrasted with the attitudes of comrades such as Emile Vandervelde.[125] And while Catholic newspapers in Belgium were anti-Dreyfusard, many Catholic politicians did not take sides publicly. Having visited Belgium and spoken to Auguste Beernaert, a French abbot concluded that 'they are all Dreyfusards in this country'.[126] For the historian Gita Deneckere, the blurred lines but also fears that became evident during the Dreyfus Affair exemplified the 'duality and tensions of the Belle Époque' in Belgium.[127]

In 1903, Georges Lorand took the reins of the Ligue Belge des Droits de l'Homme et du Citoyen. Two years later, the organisation mobilised on behalf of the Antwerp anarchist Edward Joris, who had been involved in an assassination attempt on the Ottoman Sultan. Having been threatened with execution, the subsequent activism on his behalf has been interpreted as a 'mini-Dreyfus Affair'.[128] It provided a foretaste of a much larger solidarity campaign in which both the Ligue Belge and the International Freethought Federation were active participants. In October 1909, the Catalan anarchist and educator Francisco Ferrer was executed for his alleged involvement in Barcelona's 'Tragic Week', a period of violent unrest triggered by the call-up for military service in Morocco. As the Spanish authorities acknowledged, Ferrer had spent most of this time outside Barcelona; nonetheless, he was one of over 1,700 people indicted.[129] The background to these charges lay in Ferrer's past: in 1886, he was linked to the Republican coup attempt of General Villacampa and had spent thirteen years in exile. In 1906, he was charged with, but cleared of, involvement in the assassination attempt on King Alfonso XIII – with the extent of his actual contribution a matter of controversy.[130]

What was Ferrer's appeal to freethinkers in Belgium and elsewhere? Rather than his anarchism, his secularism was the key. During his exile, he established links with French freemasons and freethinkers. In 1901, two years after his return to Barcelona, he founded the *Escuela Moderna* (the 'modern school') as a model for secular education. Ferrer published widely in Spanish and French, outlining his educational vision and authoring textbooks for secular schooling. He collaborated with freethinkers, for instance participating in their international congresses of 1889 and 1904.[131] After the 1906 attempt on King Alfonso, freethinkers portrayed Ferrer's imprisonment as a punishment for his secularist efforts and rejoiced in 1907 when he was released due to a lack of evidence. At the Prague congress of 1908, Ferrer thanked the delegates for their support.[132] As most of his European backers stemmed from liberal or socialist milieus, it was significant that Ferrer, since the start of his pedagogical work, had promoted anarchism less overtly. The contacts established during the 1906 campaign proved helpful in launching the periodical *L'Ecole Rénovée*, first published in Brussels (eight issues in 1908) and then in Paris (weekly, from 1909), with contributors such as the Dutch socialist Domela Nieuwenhuis and the French libertarian pedagogue Paul Robin.

In early 1908, Ferrer also created an international association, the Ligue Internationale pour l'Education Rationelle de l'Enfance, with Anatole France as president and Ernst Haeckel and Giuseppe Serpi among its supporters. While the league only counted 442 members by October 1908 – 58 of them Belgian – it attracted secularists, political activists from different left-wing factions as well as scientists without clear political affiliation.[133]

A study of the Ferrer campaign has concluded that 'Belgium and Italy were the countries which most closely approached or even rivaled France in the number and scale of protests against Ferrer's persecution'.[134] Two members of the International Freethought International emerged as 'the dominant figures in Belgian Ferrism':[135] Lorand – who later acted as executor of Ferrer's will – and Furnémont. Local groups of freethinkers and socialists drafted resolutions and participated in protest marches both before and after Ferrer's execution. The Belgian embrace of Ferrer contrasted with an initial report of *L'Indépendance Belge* on 18 September 1909: the newspaper's Spanish correspondent referred to 'evidence' that during the Tragic Week, anarchists had been assisted by 'numerous centres and so-called "modern" schools that were created and organised by the famous anarchist Francisco Ferrer'. The author suggested that Ferrer was 'not an ordinary anarchist', but a 'man of action, intelligent, audacious, fanatical about his subversive ideas', and also questioned the Catalan's 1907 acquittal.[136]

Over the subsequent weeks, however, the liberal and socialist press in Belgium swung behind the Ferrer campaign. Meanwhile, Catholic newspapers such as *Het Volk* and *Le Bien Public* remained more critical of Ferrer.[137] After his death, a Belgian pamphlet originating in Catholic circles defended the execution.[138] In response, an anonymous group of freethinkers publicly demanded Cardinal Mercier to distance himself from this publication which, it claimed, had libelled Ferrer.[139] As Mercier did not respond, Lucien Anspach – Professor of Mechanical Engineering in Brussels – reiterated the request in an open letter. In a private response, Mercier suggested that the polemics of anonymous freethinkers should not be dignified with a response. Anspach's subsequent published this correspondence. Thus, the episode illustrates how the Ferrer affair allowed anticlerical activists to target church authorities for their involvement in an alleged authoritarian-clerical plot. Anspach himself had previously published a pamphlet on the 'clerical peril and the Dreyfus Affair'.[140]

Anspach was the vice-president of the Comité international de l'Œuvre Francisco Ferrer, established in Brussels five days after Ferrer's death, on 18 October 1909. Among the leaders of Belgian freethought, it also included the pacifist Henri La Fontaine and the 'religious freethinker' James Hocart. The committee raised funds for a Ferrer monument, having obtained the authorisation of a Ferrer statute from the liberal-dominated municipal council of Brussels. The involvement of the International Freethought Federation in the committee's initial meeting and its support for the call for subscriptions underline the interplay between Belgian and international freethought.[141] On 13 October 1911 – exactly two years after Ferrer's death – the monument was inaugurated at the Place Sainte-Catherine. The event brought together an international cast of activists, including French anarchists and British, Dutch and Swiss secularists.[142]

The inauguration of the Ferrer monument was not the first international Ferrer event in the Belgian capital: on the eve of the international freethought congress of 1910, an estimated 25,000 people, including foreign delegates, congregated on the Grand-Place of Brussels for a commemorative 'Ferrer demonstration'. On this occasion, the Flemish socialist Emile Vinck invoked the cases of the Count of Egmont and the Count of Hoorn, who had been beheaded in the same location in 1568 after opposing the Inquisition's introduction to the Spanish Netherlands:

> Three illustrious victims of sacerdotal intolerance, Egmont and Hoorn, Ferrer: how different and yet how similar by the greatness of the cause that their sacrifice symbolises. This ceremony, here at the Grand'Place of Brussels, in the same location where the scaffold was erected! What memories! What similarities!... With an interval of three centuries, it is the same crime.[143]

Such statements portrayed history as an ongoing struggle between freethought and the Catholic church. The campaign reverberated beyond the Great War: after the war, Belgian freethinkers created a committee for the resurrection of the Brussels Ferrer monument, which had been removed during the German occupation.[144] In the same period, they raised funds for a Francisco Ferrer house in Masarrochos near Valencia.[145] The example of the Ferrer campaign shows that the communication fostered by international congresses and groupings interacted with campaigns at a national level. One pamphlet, published anonymously in Belgium, argued that Ferrer 'belonged to humanity' rather than being a Spanish figure.[146] A similar discourse had been evident during the Dreyfus Affair: noting the role of the 'international intellectual world', the Belgian liberal Paul Hymans stated that it acted 'to form and awaken universal public conscience, without distinction of race or nationality'.[147]

Internationalism and the nation among freethinkers and Catholics

The Belgian socialist César De Paepe described freethought as 'the solidarity between men and fraternity between peoples'.[148] In practice, however, freethinkers and Catholics alike wrestled with their rapport with national categories. Attacks on the Catholic church often represented the latter as an 'anti-national' force. This was a prominent charge in Bismarck's *Kulturkampf* and in the rhetoric associated with the Italian *Risorgimento*. With regard to France, the historian René Rémond described anticlericalism as 'partly... a defensive reaction of national sentiment against a foreign influence, a reflex against action that had become international'.[149] Such portrayals were also frequent in Belgium, where Ultramontanes met with accusations that their ultimate loyalty lay with Rome rather than the nation.[150] Yet the socialists themselves faced charges of being insufficiently patriotic. Catholic workers' organisations, for instance, reproached the socialist movement for its internationalism.[151]

In many instances, Catholic activists and freethinkers celebrated their internationalism *and* their attachment to the nation. At their international congress of 1907, freethinkers debated 'patriotism and freethought' and affirmed that their convictions did not threaten the nation: 'Freethought, just like science, is international; like science, it recognises the right of everyone to an individual life, [and] it recognises the same right for the political formations and natural moralities which are the nationalities'.[152] In the interwar years, Renaud Strivay – an activist from Liège – expressed the intertwined nature of internationalist principles and national peculiarities: 'An international congress is always interesting. There, one sees friends again; . . . one hears very curious opinions, both with regard to form and content, in which one senses the particular qualities of each nation despite their common base of [shared] principles.'[153]

Accepting nationhood as an element of internationalism, freethinkers measured national greatness through a nation's contribution to their cause rather than in military might – and this made it possible for smaller states to make a contribution on a par with larger ones. At the 1910 congress in Brussels, for instance, Georges Lorand praised Belgium as a land of liberty and freedom of conscience.[154] This ambiguity of celebrating transnational ideals in national settings became evident when international freethought congresses coincided with world exhibitions (for instance, Antwerp in 1885 and Brussels in 1910) or national anniversaries (Brussels in 1880 and 1910). The choice of such dates was mirrored by Belgian Catholics who held an International Eucharistic Congress in the same year that their country celebrated the sixtieth anniversary of its revolution.

The interplay between national and international attachments also manifested itself in musical terms. Among freethinkers, the *Internationale* proved a particularly popular tune.[155] Renaud Strivay even composed an anthem for the Freethinkers' International, the *Chant des libres-penseurs*, which referenced pacifist ideas and past struggles such as the Ferrer campaign:

> And we desire only that peace
> May rule on this earth rather soon
> We will have neither rest nor truce
> Until, with superb élan,
> Our sons will live the dream
> For which Ferrer gave his blood.[156]

Alongside such explicitly international anthems, freethinkers used songs that were invested with both national and transnational meanings. The most prominent example was the popularity of the *Marseillaise*: beyond France, freethinkers and socialists sang it to stress their identification with the principles of the French Revolution.[157] International freethought congresses also featured other national anthems whose interpretation could be tied to past freedom struggles, notably the Italian *Inno di Garibaldi*, the Spanish *Himno de Riego* and the Belgian *Brabançonne*.[158]

This dualism was not a secular prerogative. Among Catholics, the *Te Deum* was a prominent case: for instance, Leo XIII's Golden Jubilee as a priest in December 1887 triggered a number of 'relay events' in other countries, with the Belgian bishops marking the occasion with a *Te Deum*.[159] The very same hymn also had national connotations, as it featured prominently in the annual celebrations of national independence on 21 July. In 1880, during the conflict surrounding the liberal school laws, the staging of the *Te Deum* became an indication of tensions between the liberal government and the episcopate.[160] Recounting the final national celebration of the *Te Deum* before the First World War, Brand Whitlock, former US ambassador to Belgium, noted that 'the whole city was *en fête*' and that the Belgian flag 'was flying everywhere'.[161] Indeed, national flags also featured at the international congresses, evoking an international community viewed through the lens of nationhood. At the Third International Scientific Congress of Catholics, for instance, the ground of the conference hall 'disappeared under beams of coloured flags of all nations'.[162]

Beyond a purely symbolic level, the tension between national and transnational allegiances became evident with the outbreak of the First World War. Catholics and freethinkers alike rallied to the defence of their country, with Cardinal Mercier becoming 'a symbol of the patriotic resistance against the German invader'.[163] He addressed German bishops about the Belgians' plight, but also adopted pacifist ideas towards the end of the war.[164] One of the most infamous war atrocities occurred at the heart of Catholic learning in Belgium: in Louvain, German reprisals against alleged 'snipers' resulted in the deaths of thousands of civilians and the burning of Louvain library, including 250,000–300,000 of its books. Tracing the 'dynamic of destruction' during the Great War, the historian Alan Kramer has viewed this event as a 'symbol for warfare that…targeted the culture of the enemy'.[165] At the same time, he has argued that German actions were informed by 'anti-Catholic phobias in the German army and Louvain's status as the intellectual centre of Belgian Catholicism'.[166] Meanwhile, for the Spanish activist Fernando Lozano, it was the German attack on freethinking Belgium that caused him to express his solidarity in a *Manifeste de la Libre Pensée internationale (section d'Espagne, du Portugal et de l'Amérique)*, juxtaposing German bellicosity with Belgian internationalism:

> Belgium is the fatherland of cosmopolitanism and the asylum of internationalism. It is in Belgium that both Freethought, which prepares a new civilisation, and free labour, which will create a new humanity, had their natural capital…Brussels had become the capital of internationalism where international Freethought and international Socialism held their meetings – that is to say that it was Brussels that protected the Tabernacle of the liberated Humanity of the future.[167]

The Great War ruptured the transnational bonds among freethinkers and Catholic activists alike. Nonetheless, as we have seen, internationalism was soon rebuilt in various ways. With regard to political Catholicism, Emmanuel Gerard has even suggested that 'transnational communication in Europe became more intense as a result of the war', pointing at the international coverage of Catholic journals in interwar Europe.[168] The national question posed new challenges for the Catholic Party: before the war, it had sought links with the Flemish movement, and politicians such as Frans Van Cauwelaert built on this tradition in the interwar years. However, given the Flemish Frontpartij's electoral gains and the politicisation of the Flemish movement, Flemish nationalists increasingly appeared to challenge political Catholicism, leading the Belgian bishops to denounce Flemish nationalism in 1925.

Another tension became manifest in the broader context of the international movement of Catholic Action: despite its allegedly apolitical nature, many of its protagonists favoured corporatist models of society. It is also worth noting that Pius XI sought to ensure that the movement would avoid clashes with the fascist authorities in Italy. In Belgium, the student organisation associated with Catholic Action adopted nationalist rhetoric.[169] Furthermore, in the 1930s, Léon Degrelle's 'Rexist' movement merged nationalism, fascist ideas and Catholicism. Underlined by the name of Degrelle's publishing house (Christus Rex), the party's name alluded to the Cult of Christ the King, which was also promoted by the Catholic Action movement.[170] The Rexists celebrated their key success in 1936, when twenty-one of their candidates were elected to the Chamber and twelve to the Senate. One year later, Mercier's successor, Cardinal Van Roey, denounced Rex, and the movement soon lost electoral support. For freethinkers, the movement illustrated the authoritarian dangers of Catholicism, and groups such as the Libre Pensée de Schaerbeek organised meetings on this issue.[171]

The social question

Alongside tensions linked to national principles and persuasions, political Catholicism and freethought experienced internal divisions on the social question. Initial Catholic responses to the social problems of the industrial age were characterised by paternalist or corporatist notions. Such attitudes featured at the Social Work Congresses of Liège in 1886, 1887 and 1890, which also attracted German and Austrian participants.[172] At the international level, the Comité de Défense Catholique in Geneva was succeeded by a body with a specific social mission, the Union Catholique d'Études Sociales et Économiques, also known as the 'Fribourg Union', whose stance has been described as 'economic antiliberalism'.[173] As a Belgian partner in these networks, the Confrériere de Saint-Michel increasingly discussed the social question, too.[174] Although these efforts differed from subsequent 'Christian democratic' initiatives, they fed into *Rerum Novarum* which in turn influenced these new movements. John Boyer, for instance, has spoken of 'the international cause empowered by the encyclical'.[175] In 1895, the Belgian bishops followed suit and made their support for Catholic workers organisations explicit. This, however, does not mean that the nature of such action was undisputed. At the political level, there was a wide gap between Catholic trade unions and conservative politicians such as Charles Woeste. Adolf Daens – the Flemish priest who favoured an alliance of workers and farmers and founded a separate Christene Volkspartij in 1891 – was opposed by the church hierarchy.[176] In France, Marc Sangnier's social-Catholic Sillon movement was condemned by Pius X in 1910.

Other actions proved more durable: in 1904, the French 'Semaines Sociales' started 'as a kind of summer school for social Catholic militants'.[177] They have been described as seeking 'to foster a new vision of Christian economic life that eschewed both positivism and neo-scholasticism'.[178] This initiative was soon emulated in other countries, including Belgium, leading to the creation of the Union International d'Études Sociales in Mechelen in 1920. This organisation was supported by Mercier and involved Rutten.[179] Furthermore, from the mid-1920s, Brussels hosted the secretariat of the Catholic International Union of Social Service. This association had been founded in 1925 to 'develop social service based on Catholic doctrine and Christian duty'; it maintained a network of Catholic institutions that taught or performed social work.[180] The organisation was supported by Mercier's successor Van Roey and prominent Christian democrats; its secretariat was headed by Maria Baers, founder of the General Secretariat of Christian Women's Trade Associations (1912) and the Catholic Women's College of Social Work (1920).

Despite varying views on social activism, Catholics shared an understanding of society that lay at odds with Marxist concepts. As Patrick Pasture has put it, 'The rejection of the class struggle and the ideal of a "harmonious society" was perhaps the essential ideological component all Christian organization shared'.[181] Even Catholic trade unions pursued the goal of 'class reconciliation'.[182] This consensus did not preclude internal tensions: in the interwar years, Catholic Action opposed the political activism of Catholic workers.[183] In Belgium, the protagonists of Catholic Action criticised the existence of separate Catholic labour organisations such as the Algemeen Christelijk Werkersverbond/Ligue Nationale des Travailleurs Chrétiens (founded in 1923). In the context of his own efforts for Catholic young workers, Joseph Cardijn made the case for the ongoing relevance of separate institutions as 'milieu organizations within Catholic Action'.[184] At the same time, the corporatist notions that were associated with Catholic Action met with resistance from Catholic trade unions who lobbied the Vatican to 'criticise authoritarian versions of Catholic corporatism'.[185] While seemingly favouring corporatist ideas, Pius XI's encyclical *Quadragesimo Anno* (1931) was sufficiently broad to find support among both camps.

Tensions surrounding the social question were also apparent among freethinkers. As early as 1892, the Belgian freethinkers of L'Affranchissement complained that only the 1881 international congress at Paris had considered the relationship between freethought and the social question.[186] Delegates had proposed that future events be labelled as 'Universal Congresses of Socialist Freethinkers' – but without consequence, as the Paris event was not recognised as an official congress of the International Freethought Federation.[187] With the exception of Georges Lorand, the federation's Belgian leaders were linked to the BWP, and many of them described freethought and socialism as interrelated phenomena. Modeste Terwagne, the socialist deputy who presided over the International Freethought Federation during the interwar years, acknowledged César De Paepe's influence in this context: 'the fact that De Paepe fought for freethought made him recruit people for socialism.[188] Leon Furnémont even served as a Belgian representative on the International Socialist Bureau in 1908 and 1910–12. In 1902, he had already addressed an international freethought congress on the social question, and the topic also featured at the 1910 congress in Brussels.[189] At the federation's final congress before the First World War, Guillaume De Greef affirmed the connection between the principles of 'freethought' and 'equality': 'freedom of thought…is impossible in profoundly unequal societies…the bases of Freethought are social and notably economic'.[190] However, many freethinkers were wary about alienating liberal supporters and refrained from more specific pronouncements.

The federation's secretary Eugène Hins, embodied this ambivalent stance vis-à-vis socialism. He had worked in Brazil in 1863–64, where he supported the abolition of slavery, and taught in Russia from 1872 to 1880. In between these two sojourns, he served as secretary of the Belgian section of the International Workingmen's Association, was an outspoken advocate of syndicalism at the First International's Basel congress (1869) and edited the periodical *L'Internationale*.[191] His connection to the Belgian labour movement extended to his private life: in 1868, he married Jeanne Brismée, daughter of Désiré Brismée and sister-in-law of César De Paepe. His commitment to freethought was as pronounced as his socialism. A member of the Libre

Pensée de Bruxelles and freemason, he became 'one of the great figures of the laïcist movement' and was the founding editor of *La Pensée*.[192] However, within the International Freethought Federation, Hins recommended that freethinkers confine themselves to questions on which all 'democratic forces' could agree: 'If all rationalist groups do everything, especially politics, who then will do the free-thinking and rationalist propaganda?'[193]

The cautious attitudes surrounding social issues had divisive consequences for German freethinkers, whose main organisation was torn apart by this question in 1908.[194] After the Great War, this split affected the International Freethought Federation, as socialist freethinkers in Germany created their own international committee in 1922. This group contemplated joining the International Freethought Federation, but refrained from doing so since the Brussels-based federation did not commit itself exclusively to socialist values.[195] Instead, it established a 'Proletarian Freethinkers' International', albeit with limited results. Apart from the leftist German groups, it represented associations from Austria, Czechoslovakia, Lithuania, Denmark and the Soviet Union. The presence of the Soviet League of Atheists meant that the Proletarian Freethinkers' International soon became subject to struggles between socialists and communists, reflecting the Comintern's 'Third Period' policies of 1928. This conflict resulted in the formation of a third international faction, which comprised communist freethinkers. Alongside its Soviet members, this group included the Union Fédérale de Libres Penseurs Révolutionnaires de France (after 1932: Associations des Travailleurs sans Dieu), Czechoslovakian activists and the Ligue Matérialiste Belge. The Belgian affiliate criticised the International Freethought Federation for its perceived failure to represent the working classes and noted that the older federation had lost much of its membership.[196] However, the Belgian 'materialists' only had a small following themselves: given the Comintern's condemnation of freemasonry in 1922, communist freethinkers constituted something of an oddity in countries such as France and Belgium, where 'freethought' and 'freemasonry' had a long relationship.[197] Another Belgian group which competed with the Ligue Matérialiste Belge on the left – the Action Rationaliste – has been described as 'equally insignificant'.[198]

The rise of fascist groups necessitated cooperation between freethinkers: as early as 1925, an international freethought congress was prohibited by the authorities in Rome.[199] In light of the rising tide of authoritarianism, socialist freethinkers joined forces with the International Freethought Federation at an international congress in Berlin in 1931. The two groups agreed on a resolution that expressed solidarity with the struggle against fascism.[200] After the Comintern had adopted its Popular Front strategy, the communist freethinkers also joined the federation. In 1936, 'a congress of unity' in Prague adopted the name 'World Union of Freethinkers' to reflect the merger.[201] A joint Declaration of Principles emphasised anti-fascism and workers' emancipation as international objectives.[202] As one speaker put it, fascism was not only as an ideology, but another form of misguided belief:

> The Catholics promise heaven to those chosen by God; the Nazis promise the Third Reich to the chosen ones, who are of pure race. The Catholics are burdened with the original sin, and the Nazis are burdened with the hereditary sins of a non-Aryan grandmother. The Catholics pray to their Saviour, and the inhabitants of the German Empire pray to their dictator.[203]

Conclusion

The histories of Catholic and freethought internationalism in their Belgian setting show how the culture wars and their legacies were shaped by transnational factors. The protagonists of these conflicts built alliances across national borders. In doing so, they consciously presented their causes as transnational. Internationalism was also a strategy. It has been argued that 'internationalism was despised as being politically "red", that is to say, communist or socialist in the sense of the "left international"'.[204] If viewed as a tool and practice, however, internationalism was rather useful for Catholics: it allowed for an engagement with the culture and politics of modernity. Vincent Viaene has made the case for a rapprochement between religious history and international history: he views religious internationalism as 'a more specific category of analysis to denote an essential aspect of the interaction of all major religions – universal or not – with modernity'.[205] Meanwhile, liberals and socialists temporarily bridged their ideological gaps when participating at international freethought congresses or joining forces in campaigns such as the solidarity movement for Ferrer. Put differently, internationalism allowed religious and secularist actors to engage with an era of mass politics and combine the latter with high-level networking.

A study of the competing internationalisms illustrates that neither Catholicism nor freethought were coherent phenomena, but characterised by numerous internal divisions. International debates on 'Catholic science' proved controversial among the patrons of orthodoxy, and Catholic conservatives showed little enthusiasm for Christian trade unionism, which internationalised itself in this period. In their turn, while freethinkers could be united in their hostility to church power, the responses to the social question could vary significantly. The next chapter further discusses the 'red' varieties of internationalism by considering the theme of 'Equality'.

Notes

1 Christopher Clark and Wolfram Kaiser (eds), *Culture Wars: Secular-Catholic Conflict in Nineteenth-Century Europe* (Cambridge, 2003). On Germany and France, see e.g. Olaf Blaschke (ed.), *Konfessionen im Konflikt: Deutschland*

zwischen 1800 und 1970 – ein zweites konfessionelles Zeitalter (Göttingen, 2002); René Rémond, *L'Anticléricalisme en France: de 1815 à nos jours* (3rd edn., Paris, 1999); Jacqueline Lalouette, *La République anticléricale: XIXe – XXe siècles* (Paris, 2002).

2 Martin Conway, 'Introduction', in Martin Conway and Tom Buchanan (eds), *Political Catholicism in Europe, 1918–1965* (Oxford, 1996), p. 2.

3 John Boyer, 'Catholics, Christians and the challenges of democracy: the heritage of the nineteenth century', in Wolfang Kaiser and Helmut Wohnout (eds), *Political Catholicism in Europe 1918–45* (London, 2004), p. 25.

4 Vincent Viaene, 'International history, religious history, Catholic history: perspectives for cross-fertilization (1830–1945)', *European History Quarterly*, 38 (2008), 596.

5 Bayly, *Birth of the Modern World*, pp. 240–2.

6 Daniel Laqua, '"Laïque, démocratique et sociale"? Socialism and the Freethinkers' International', *Labour History Review*, 74 (2009), 257–73. On French *libres-penseurs*, see Jacqueline Lalouette, *La Libre Pensée en France, 1848 à 1940* (Paris, 1997).

7 Edward Royle has shown the fluid boundaries between 'secularism' and 'freethought': Royle, *Radicals, Secularists and Republicans: Popular Freethought in Britain, 1866–1915* (Manchester, 1980). On the controversy triggered by Bradlaugh's initial refusal to swear the House of Commons' oath of allegiance, see Walter Arnstein, *The Bradlaugh Case: A Study in Late Victorian Opinion and Politics* (Oxford, 1965).

8 Jean Baubérot, *Histoire de la laïcité française* (Paris, 2000); Baubérot, *Laïcité 1905–2005, entre passion et raison* (Paris, 2004); Jacqueline Lalouette, *La Séparation des églises et de l'état: genèse et développement d'une idée, 1789–1905* (Paris, 2005).

9 Lucian Hölscher, 'Semantic structures of religious change in modern Germany', in Hugh McLeod and Werner Ustorf (eds), *The Decline of Christendom in Western Europe, 1750–2000* (Cambridge, 2003), pp. 194–6.

10 Fédération Internationale de la Libre Pensée, *Congrès de Rome: XX Septembre 1904. Compte-Rendu Officiel* (Ghent, 1905), pp. 183–96.

11 Vincent Viaene, *Belgium and the Holy See from Gregory XVI to Pius X, 1831–1859: Catholic Revival, Society and Politics in 19th-Century Europe* (Brussels, 2001), p. 7.

12 Martin Conway, 'Belgium', in Conway and Buchanan, *Political Catholicism in Europe*, p. 190.

13 John Bartier, 'La franc-maçonnerie et les associations laïques en Belgique', in Hervé Hasquin (ed.), *Histoire de la laïcité en Belgique* (Brussels, 1994), pp. 203–21; John Bartier, *Laïcité et franc-maçonnerie: études rassemblées et publiées par Guy Gambier* (Brussels, 1981).

14 The Belgian 'Grand Orient' removed the notion of the 'Grand Architecte de l'Universe' from its statutes in 1871: Hubert Derthier, 'Libre pensée, franc-maçonnerie et mouvements laïques', in Liliane Voyé *et al.* (eds), *La Belgique et ses dieux: Eglises, mouvements, religieux et laïques* (Louvain-la-Neuve, 1985), p. 40. Freethinkers observed that 'German freemasons were neither generally nor

necessarily freethinkers': *Almanach-annuaire illustré de la Libre-Pensée Internationale* (Brussels, 1908), p. 60.

15 Viaene, *Belgium and the Holy See*, p. 540.

16 Gisela Fleckenstein and Jochen Schmiedl, 'Ultramontanismus in der Diskussion: Zur Neupositionierung eines Forschungsbegriffs', in Fleckenstein and Schmiedl (eds), *Ultramontanismus: Tendenzen der Forschung* (Paderborn, 2005), esp. pp. 11–13.

17 Manuel Borutta, *Antikatholizismus: Deutschland und Italien im Zeitalter der europäischen Kulturkämpfe* (Göttingen, 2009), p. 392.

18 The complex nature of stances adopted by Belgian Catholics is the theme of Viaene's *Belgium and the Holy See.*

19 In 1875, L'Affranchissement initiated a federation of freethought groups in Brussels: L'Affranchissement, *Historique des Sociétés rationalistes de la Belgique* (Brussels, 1879), p. 22.

20 Jeffrey Tyssens and Els Witte, *De vrijzinnige traditie in België: van getolereerde tegencultuur tot erkende levensbeschouwing* (2nd edn., Brussels, 1996).

21 These two quotes are respectively from Jacques Lory, 'Introduction' and Luc Keunings, 'Le maintien de l'ordre en 1884: les manifestations d'août et de septembre à Bruxelles', both in Emiel Lamberts and Jacques Lory (eds), *1884: un tournant politique en Belgique/de machtswisseling van 1884 in België* (Brussels, 1986), pp. 1 and 99.

22 Strikwerda, *A House Divided*; Jan De Maeyer, *De rode baron: Arthur Verhaegen, 1847–1917* (Leuven, 1994).

23 Patrick Pasture, *Histoire du syndicalisme chrétien internationale: la difficile recherche d'une troisième voie* (Paris, 1999), p. 44.

24 Damberg *et al.*, 'The formation of Christian working-class organizations', p. 69.

25 Patrick Pasture, 'Introduction: between cross and class. Christian labour in Europe 1840–2000', in Heerma van Voss *et al.*, *Between Cross and Class*, p. 18.

26 Emmanuel Gerard, 'Religion, class and language: the Catholic Party in Belgium', in Kaiser and Wohnout, *Political Catholicism in Europe*, p. 98.

27 Kaiser and Wohnout, 'Introduction', p. 2.

28 Jacqueline Lalouette, 'Approche comparative de la Libre Pensée belge et de la Libre Pensée française', 1848–1914', in Marc Quaghebeur and Nicole Savy (eds), *France – Belgique (1848–1914): affinités – ambiguités* (Brussels, 1997), pp. 67–86.

29 Tyssens and Witte, *De vrijzinnige traditie en België*, p. 37.

30 McLeod distinguishes between societies that are 'religiously polarised', 'pillarised', 'pluralist' or 'dominated by nationalism': Hugh McLeod, 'The religious crisis of the 1960s', *Journal of Modern European History* 3 (2005), 211.

31 Hans Righart, *De katholieke zuil in Europa: het ontstaan van verzuiling onder katholieken in Oostenrijk, Zwisterland, België en Nederland* (Meppel, 1986); Staf Hellemans, *Strijd om de moderniteit: sociale bewegingen en verzuiling in Europa sinds 1800* (Leuven, 1990).

32 Tyssens and Witte, *De vrijzinnige traditie en België*, p. 59; Regarding post-war Belgium, see Jeffrey Tyssens, *Guerre et Paix Scolaire 1950–1958* (Brussels, 1997), pp. 15–16.

33 Gerard, 'Religion, class and language', in Kaiser and Wohnout, *Political Catholicism in Europe*, p. 99.
34 Tyssens and Witte, *De vrijzinnige traditie en België*, pp. 89–90.
35 Emmanuel Gerard, *De katholieke partij in crisis: partijpolitiek leven in België 1918–1940* (Leuven, 1985), p. 5.
36 Margaret Anderson, 'The limits of secularization: on the problem of the Catholic revival in nineteenth-century Germany', *Historical Journal*, 38 (1995), 647–70.
37 Isabelle Gatti de Gamond, *Education – Fémin*isme, ed. by Hector Denis and Eugène Hins (Brussels, 1907); Marie Mulle, *L'Education Rationaliste: telle qu'elle est donnée à l'Orphelinat de Forest (Bruxelles). Rapport présenté au Congrès de Lisbonne* (Brussels, 1913).
38 Viaene, *Belgium and the Holy See*, p. 601.
39 Emiel Lamberts, 'Catholic congresses as amplifiers of international Catholic opinion', in Viaene, *The Papacy and the New World Order*, p. 215.
40 Edouard Descamps-David, 'L'avenir de la civilisation en Afrique', *Le Mouvement Antiesclavagiste*, 3 (1891), 331; Hippolyte d'Ursel, 'Rapport sur l'œuvre antiesclavagiste de Belgique, présenté au Congrès de Malines le 10 août 1891', *Le Mouvement Antiesclavagiste*, 3 (1891), 351–64.
41 Jan de Maeyer, 'La Belgique: un élève modèle de l'école ultramontaine', in Emiel Lamberts (ed.), *The Black International 1870–1878: The Holy See and Militant Catholicism in Europe* (Brussels, 2002), pp. 367–8.
42 Lamberts, 'Catholic congresses', p. 221. See also Jean Vaudon, *L'œuvre des congrès eucharistiques* (Paris, 1910).
43 See e.g. *Congrès Eucharistique de 1880, tenu à Anvers du 16 au 21 août* (Antwerp, 1890), pp. 3–4.
44 *Ibid.*, p. 111.
45 MS Bxl. Royaume, Fonds Schollaert/Helleputte (201), microfilm 2071 (74+): letter to Joris Helleputte, 24 April 1895.
46 *Ibid.*, letter to Helleputte, 8 June 1895. See also letters of 26 May and 23 June 1895.
47 'Congreso Catholico de Lisboa', *Correio Nacional* (25 June 1895).
48 For the adhesions and messages, see 'Adhesoes' and 'Congreso Catholico de Lisboa', *Correio Nacional* (25 and 26 June 1895); 'A Arte no centenario Antonio', *O Seculo* (30 June 1895).
49 Letter to Joris Helleputte, 24 April 1895 (as cited in note 45). In 1886, Leo XIII had addressed Portuguese Catholics 'to unite to regain the liberties of the church': R. A. H. Robinson, 'The religious question and the Catholic revival in Portugal', *Journal of Contemporary History*, 12 (1977), 347.
50 Fédération des Sociétés Rationalistes de la Belgique, *Compte-rendu du VIII Congrès Rationaliste, Bruxelles, 28 et 29 mars 1880* (Brussels, 1880).
51 'Congrès international de l'Enseignement', *L'Indépendance Belge* (4 August 1880).
52 'Congrès international de la Libre-Pensée', *La Bombe* (4 September 1880).
53 *L'Indépendance Belge* (7 September 1880).
54 MS IRELP, L. Lacassagne 1: *Compte-rendu du Congrès International de la Libre-Pensée du 18 au 22 septembre 1881 à Paris* (Nice, 1882).
55 'Un Congrès des Délirants', *Courrier de Bruxelles* (25 September 1885).

56 *Congrès International d'Anvers en 1885: Compte-Rendu Officiel* (Brussels, 1887), pp. 24–5.
57 Ida Altmann, 'Der internationale Freidenker-Kongress in Paris: Vorbericht', *Der Freidenker*, 8 (1900), 153.
58 Altmann, 'Der internationale Freidenkerkongreß in Paris', *Der Freidenker*, 9 (1901), 71.
59 *Congrès de Rome*, pp. liv-lxi, listing over 750 French delegates. It is, however, likely that most of them submitted written adhesions, rather than travelling to Rome.
60 *Congrès de Paris: 3, 4, 5, 6, 7 septembre 1905 au Palais du Trocadéro* (Paris, 1905), p. 221.
61 Raphaël Rens, 'Rapport au Bureau International par le Secrétaire du Bureau Permanent', in *Annuaire Illustré de la Libre Pensée Internationale 1909* (Brussels, 1909), p. 12.
62 Altmann, 'Der international Freidenker-Kongress in Paris: Vorbericht', p. 154.
63 MS IEV, Léon Furnémont LF/I/13: Odón de Buen to Furnémont, 7 March 1892.
64 'Léon Furnémont en Italie', in *Congrès de Rome: XX Septembre 1904. Compte-Rendu Officiel* (Ghent, 1905), pp. xvi–xxxiv.
65 *Almananch-annuaire illustré*, p. 169.
66 Rens, 'Rapport au Bureau International', pp. 6 and 13.
67 *Congrès de Paris*, p. 91
68 Eugène Hins, *La Libre Pensée internationale en 1910* (Brussels, 1911), *La Libre Pensée internationale en 1911* (Brussels, 1912), *La Libre Pensée internationale en 1912* (Brussels, 1913) and *La Libre Pensée internationale en 1913* (Brussels, 1914).
69 Gastone Cavalieri, *Pour la construction d'une siège internationale de la libre-pensée à Rome* (Rome, 1910).
70 Bibliothèque de La Pensée, *Le Congrès de Bruxelles et la Manifestation Ferrer 20–24 août 1910* (Brussels, 1910), p. 43.
71 For these numbers, see Royle, *Radicals, Secularists and Republicans*, pp. 23–35; *Almanach-annuaire illustré*, p. 60.
72 Fédération Nationale des Sociétés de Libres-Penseurs, *Guide illustré dédié aux Libres-Penseurs qui assisteront au Congrès International et Universel de Bruxelles* (Brussels, 1910), p. 26.
73 *Ibid.*, p. 34. French freethinkers counted 900 participants and 50,000 moral adhesions from their country: MS IFF 5: Libre Pensée, 'Après le congrès de Rome'.
74 Fédération Nationale, *Guide Illustré*, p. 36.
75 'Congrese Catholico de Lisboa', *Correio Nacional* (26 June 1895).
76 Robinson, 'The religious question and the Catholic revival in Portugal', p. 347.
77 Guido Müller, 'Anticipated exile of Catholic democrats: the Secrétariat International des Partis Démocratiques d'Inspiration Chrétienne', in Kaiser and Wohnout, *Political Catholicism in Europe*, pp. 255–6.
78 *Ibid.*, p. 252.
79 Pasture, 'Introduction', p. 24.
80 Roberto Papini, *The Christian Democrat International* (Lanham, MD, 1997), p. 25.

81 Martin Conway, 'Catholic politics or Christian democracy? The evolution of inter-war political Catholicism', in Kaiser and Wohnout, *Political Catholicism in Europe*, p. 237.

82 Guido Convents, 'OCIC/Unda: The First International Activities', available via www.signits.net (accessed 28/12/2011). The Belgian labour movement had its own radio service, the Socialistische Arbeiders Omroep van Vlaanderen (SAROV).

83 David Alvarez, 'A few bits of information: American intelligence and the Vatican, 1939–45', in David B. Wooner and Richard G. Kurial, *FDR, the Vatican and the Roman Catholic Church in America, 1933–1945* (New York, 2003), pp. 253–68.

84 Gerard, *De katholieke partij in crisis*, p. 361.

85 Oscar Arnal, 'Towards a lay apostolate of the workers: three decades of conflict for the French Jeunessse Ouvrière Chrétienne', *Catholic Historical Review*, 73 (1987), 211–27; Louis Vos, 'La Jeunesse Ouvrière Chrétienne' in Emmanuel Gerard and Paul Wynants (eds), *Histoire du mouvement ouvrier chrétien en Belgique*, 2 vols (Leuven, 1994), pp. 425–99; Françoise Rosart and Thierry Scaillet (eds), *Entre jeux et enjeux: mouvements de jeunesse catholiques en Belgique 1910–1940* (Louvain-la-Neuve, 2002).

86 Jan De Maeyer, 'The formation of a Christian workers' culture in pillarized societies: Belgium, Germany and the Netherlands, *c.* 1850–1950', in Heerma van Voss *et al.*, *Between Cross and Class*, p. 100.

87 MS IFF 5: *Bulletin*, 15 August 1904, p. 1.

88 *Congrès international de Anvers*, p. 7.

89 John Mackinnon Robertson, *A Short History of Freethought*, 2 vols, vol. 1 (London, 1936), p. 339.

90 Kaat Wils, *De omweg van de wetenschap: Het positivisme en de Belgische en Nederlandsche intellectuelle cultuur, 1845–1914* (Amsterdam, 2005).

91 André Uyttebrouck, 'L'Université libre de Bruxelles et l'enseignement privé non confessionnel', in Hasquin, *Histoire de la laïcité en Belgique*, pp. 212–16.

92 *Fédération rationaliste de Charleroi. XXXVIIe anniversaire* (Gand, 1913), pp. 9–10.

93 *Congrès de Rome*, pp. 21–4. On the 'Berthelot banquet', see Lalouette, *La République anticléricale*, pp. 262–84.

94 Erika Kraußе, *Ernst Haeckel* (Leipzig, 1987), p. 113.

95 On Büchner's impact in France, see *Der Freidenker*, 7 (1899), 71; on Italy, see Guido Verucci, *L'Italia laica prima e dopo l'unità 1848–1876: Anticlericalismo, libero pensiero e ateismo nelle società italiana* (Rome, 1981), e.g. pp. 171, 177 and 183–4. Büchner's brother was the famous author Georg Büchner.

96 Frederick Gregory, *Scientific Materialism in Nineteenth Century Germany* (Dordrecht, 1977), pp. 119–20; Büchner, 'Der Glaube des Freidenkers', *Der Freidenker*, 5, 11 (1897).

97 Alfred Kelly, *The Descent of Darwin: The Popularization of Darwinism in Germany* (Chapel Hill, NC, 1981), p. 118.

98 Raf de Bont, '"Foggy and contradictory": evolutionary theory in Belgium, 1859–1945', in Eve-Marie Engels and Thomas F. Glick (eds), *The Reception of Charles Darwin in Europe*, vol. 1 (London, 2008), pp. 191 and 193.

99 James Hocart, *Le Congrès de la Libre-Pensée à Rome* (Brussels, 1905), p. 11.

100 *Ibid.*, p. 26.
101 Hocart, *Le Congrès de la Libre-Pensée à Rome*, p. 7.
102 Léon Roelandts [Maison d'Action Catholique], *Catholique ou Libre Penseur?* (Brussels, 1910), p. 3.
103 Cardinal Désiré-Joseph Mercier, *La 'Libre Pensée' athée et la moralité publique: lettre pastorale pour le carême de 1912* (Brussels, 1912).
104 Vincent Viaene, 'Introduction: reality and image in the Pontificate of Leo XIII', in Viaene, *The Papacy and the New World Order*, p. 20.
105 Strikwerda, *A House Divided*, p. 216.
106 Emmanuel Gerard and Kaat Wils, 'Catholics and sociology in Leuven from Désiré Mercier to Jacques Leclerq: a process of appropriation', in Liliane Voyé and Jaak Billiet (eds), *Sociology and Religions: An Ambiguous Relationship* (Leuven, 1999), p. 40.
107 Jean Remy et Liliane Voyé, 'L'Eglise catholique de Belgique et la transaction avec la modernité', in Voyé *et al*, *La Belgique et ses dieux*, p. 15.
108 Letter of Cardinal Rampolla to Dr Lefebvre, 11 February 1894, as cited in *Compte rendu du Troisième Congrès Scientifique international des Catholiques, tenu à Bruxelles du 5 au 8 septembre 1894* (Brussels, 1895), p. 1.
109 Letter of Ferdinand Lefebvre to Leo XIII, as cited in *ibid.*, p. 5. The quote refers to chapter 4 of the Decrees of the First Vatican Council (1870).
110 de Bont, 'Foggy and contradictory', p. 194.
111 Francesco Beretta, 'Les Congrès scientifiques internationaux des catholiques (1888–1900) et la production d'orthodoxie dans l'espace intellectuel catholique', pp. 4–7 and 10–16, http://hal.inria.fr/docs/00/45/32/94/PDF/Beretta_Congres.pdf [accessed 05/01/2012], first published in Claude Langlois and Christian Sorrel, *Le Catholicisme en congrès (XIXe – XXe siècles)* (Paris, 2009).
112 'Introduction historique', in *Compte rendu du Troisième Congrès*, p. 11.
113 J. Homans, 'La Philosophie au Congrès Scientifique International des Catholiques', *Revue neo-scholastique*, 3 (1896), 90.
114 Beretta, 'Les Congrès scientifiques', p. 16. On the resistance to such notions, see Paul Misner, 'Catholic anti-modernism: the ecclesial setting', in Darrell Jodock (ed.), *Catholicism Contending with Modernity: Roman Catholic Modernism and Anti-Modernism in Historical Context* (Cambridge, 2000), pp. 56–87.
115 Emile Zola, *The Dreyfus Affair. 'J'accuse' and Other Writings*, ed. Alain Pagès (New Haven, CT, 1996), p. 39.
116 Charles Maurras, founder of the anti-Dreyfusard *Action française*, was a 'self-declared agnostic' but 'nurtured the idea of an alliance between Positivists and Catholics': Michael Sutton, *Nationalism, Positivism and Catholicism: The Politics of Charles Maurras and French Catholics, 1890–1914* (Cambridge, 1982), pp. 1–2.
117 Jean Stengers, 'La Belgique, un foyer de dreyfusime', *RBPH–BTFG*, 82 (2004), 361.
118 Verbruggen, *Schrijverschap in het Belgische belle époque*, pp. 159–61.
119 Dr. Fr. Maier, 'Hoch Zola!', *Der Freidenker*, 6 (1898), 17–18.
120 Paul Aron and Jean-Philippe Schreiber, 'La réception de l'Affaire en Belgique', in Michel Drouin (ed.), *L'Affaire Dreyfus* (Paris, 1994), p. 547.

121 Stengers, 'La Belgique, un foyer de dreyfusisme', p. 360.
122 Ruth Harris, *Dreyfus: Politics, Emotion, and the Scandal of the Century* (New York, 2010), p. 56.
123 Stengers, 'La Belgique, un foyer de dreyfusisme', p. 360. The articles in question are 'Un pétard monstre', *Le Soir* (12 October 1897), and 'L'innocence du capitaine Dreyfus', *La Réforme* (31 October 1897).
124 Aron and Schreiber, 'La reception de l'Affaire en Belgique', p. 543.
125 *Le Peuple* (29 January 1898); see also Marcel Liebman, *Les Socialistes belges, 1885–1914: La révolte et l'organisation* (Brussels, 1979), pp. 214–15.
126 Stengers, 'La Belgique, un foyer de dreyfusisme', p. 371.
127 Deneckere, *Les Turbulences de la Belle Époque*, p. 200.
128 Verbruggen, *Schrijverschap in het Belgische belle époque*, p. 166. Cf. Jan Moulaert, *Rood en zwart: de anarchistische beweging in België 1880–1914* (Leuven, 1995), p. 376.
129 Murray Bookchin, *The Spanish Anarchists: The Heroic Years 1868–1936* (Edinburgh, 1998), p. 137.
130 Joaquín Romero Maura, 'Terrorism in Barcelona and its impact on Spanish politics, 1904–1909', *Past and Present*, 41 (1968), 130–84.
131 *Congrès de Rome*, p. xliii.
132 Eugène Hins, *Le Congrès de Prague: 8 au 12 septembre 1907* (Brussels, 1908), p. 9.
133 Maurice De Vroede, 'Francisco Ferrer et la Ligue internationale pour l'éducation rationelle de l'enfance', *Paedagogica Historica*, 19 (1979), 278–95.
134 T. Peter Park, 'The European Reaction to the Execution of Francisco Ferrer' (PhD dissertation, University of Virginia, 1970), p. 298. See also Moulaert, *Rood en zwart*, pp. 362–6. On Belgian responses to and memories of Ferrer, see Jacques Lemaire, 'La reception de Francisco Ferrer en Belgique' in Anne Morelli and Jacques Lemaire (eds), *Francisco Ferrer: cent ans après son exécution. Les avatars d'une image* (Brussels, 2010), pp. 263–6.
135 Park, 'The European Reaction', p. 299.
136 'Lettre d'Espagne: le mouvement révolutionnaire et anarchiste en Espagne', *L'Indépendance Belge* (18 September 1909).
137 Park, 'The European Reaction', p. 323.
138 Anon., *Francisco Ferrer, sa vie – Ses oeuvres* (Iseghem, 1909).
139 Œuvre Francisco Ferrer, *Le Cardinal Mercier et l'Affaire Ferrer: un crime clérical* (Brussels, 1910).
140 Lucien Anspach, *Le Péril clérical et l'affaire Dreyfus* (Brussels, 1899).
141 Park, 'The European Reaction', p. 325.
142 *Ibid.*, p. 21. French groups planned a similar statue for Paris which, however, never materialised – see Lalouette, *La Libre Pensée en France*, p. 299.
143 Bibliothèque de la Pensée, *Le Congrès de Bruxelles*, p. 6.
144 MS HLF 123: 'Comité Belge et International pour la remise, en son état primitif, du Monument Ferrer' (1924). See Jeffrey Tyssens, 'Le monument Ferrer à Bruxelles ou l'histoire d'une statue mal aimée', in Morelli and Lemaire, *Francisco Ferrer*, pp. 199–222.

145 Jeffrey Tyssens, 'Les associations de libre pensée pendant l'entre-deux-guerres', in Centre d'Action Laïque, *1789–1989: 200 ans de Libre Pensée en Belgique* (Charleroi, 1989), p. 45.

146 Un témoin oculaire, *La Vérité sur Francisco Ferrer et les événements de Barcelone* (Brussels, 1909), p. 38.

147 Paul Hymans in *La Meuse* (12–13 February 1898) as cited in Stengers, 'La Belgique, foyer du Dreyfusisme', p. 290.

148 *Congrès universel des Libres Penseurs tenu à Paris, du 15 au 20 septembre 1889: Compte-rendu officiel de la Commission du Congrès* (Paris, 1890), p. 155.

149 Rémond, *L'Anticléricalisme en France*, p. 56.

150 Fleckenstein and Schmiedl, 'Ultramontanismus in der Diskussion', p. 8.

151 Pasture, *Histoire du syndicalisme chrétien internationale*, pp. 56–8.

152 Hins, *Le Congrès de Prague*, pp. 38–40 and 53.

153 Renaud Strivay, *Union Mondiale des Libres Penseurs: Bruxelles 1880 – Prague 1936* (Brussels, 1936), pp. 31–2.

154 Bibliothèque de La Pensée, *Le Congrès de Bruxelles*, p. 38.

155 See e.g. *Congrès de Paris*, p. 93. On its popularity among French freethinkers, see Lalouette, *La République anticléricale*, pp. 406–7.

156 Strivay, *Union mondiale des Libres Penseurs*, pp. 141–2.

157 Spanish freethinkers also used the Marseillaise, see e.g. *Almanach-annuaire illustré*, p. 117. On the Marseillaise's use by French and German socialists, see Axel Körner, *Das Lied von einer anderen Welt: Kulturelle Praxis im deutschen und französischen Arbeitermilieu* (Frankfurt, 1997), pp. 237–40. The song even retained its transnational revolutionary connotations after French socialists had started to view the song more critically: Frédéric Robert, *La Marseillaise* (Paris, 1989), pp. 72–5 and 98. In 1880, Belgian socialists sang the Marseillaise at protests in favour of universal suffrage: Deneckere, *Les Turbulences de la Belle Époque*, p. 8.

158 'Le Congrès de la Libre Pensée', *Courrier de La Plata* (21 September 1906).

159 Jean-Marc Ticchi, 'Le Jubilé pontifical de 1888: un exemple de l'interaction entre Question romaine, diplomatie vaticane et dévotion de masse au pape', in *The Papacy and the New World Order*, p. 232.

160 Deneckere, *Les Turbulences de la Belle Époque*, p. 8. On the *Te Deum* during the anniversaries of 1880 and 1905, see Jeroen Janssens, *De belgische natie viert: de Belgische nationale feesten 1830–1914* (Louvain, 2001), pp. 114–15 and 179–81.

161 Brand Whitlock, *Belgium: A Personal Narrative* (New York, 1919), p. 21.

162 *Troisième Congrès Scientifique International des Catholiques*, p. 7.

163 Gerard, 'Religion, class and language', p. 98.

164 Henri Haag, 'Le Cardinal Mercier devant la guerre et la paix', *Revue d'histoire ecclésiastique*, 79 (1984), 709–83.

165 Alan Kramer, *Dynamic of Destruction: Culture and Mass Killing in the First World War* (Oxford, 2007), p. 1. Cf. Wolfgang Schivelbusch, *Eine Ruine im Krieg der Geister: Die Bibliothek von Löwen, August 1914 bis Mai 1940* (Frankfurt, 1993).

166 Kramer, *Dynamic of Destruction*, p. 20.

167 MS IEV, Léon Furnémont, LF/III/26: *Manifeste de la Libre Pensée internationale (section d'Espagne, du Portugal et de l'Amérique).*

168 Gerard, 'Religion, class and language', p. 110.

169 Gerard, 'De katholieke partij in crisis', p. 362.

170 Martin Conway, 'Building the Christian city: Catholics and politics in interwar Francophone Belgium', *Past and Present*, 128 (1990), 117–51.

171 Philippe Cullus, 'La Libre Pensée de Schaerbeek' in Andrée Despy-Meyer and Hervé Hasquin: *Libre Pensée et pensée libre (eds) Combats et débats. Hommage à André Uyttebrouck* (Brussels, 1996), p. 42.

172 Damberg *et al.*, 'The formation of Christian working-class organizations', p. 52.

173 Emiel Lamberts, 'L'Internationale noire: une organisation secrète au service du Saint-Siège', in Lamberts, *The Black International*, p. 98. Cf. Lamberts, 'Catholic congresses', p. 219.

174 De Maeyer, 'La Belgique: un élève modèle', p. 368.

175 Boyer, 'Catholics, Christians and the challenges of democracy', in Kaiser and Wohnout, *Political Catholicism in Europe*, p. 25. See also Paul Furlong and David Curtis (eds), *The Church Faces the Modern World: Rerum Novarum and Its Impact* (Hull, 1994).

176 Lode Wils, *Het Daenisme* (Leuven, 1969).

177 James Macmillan, 'France', in Conway and Buchanan, *Political Catholicism in Europe*, p. 34.

178 Peter Bernardi, 'Social modernism: the case of the *Semaines Sociales*', in Jodock, *Catholicism Contending with Modernity*, p. 278.

179 Emmanuel Gerard, 'L'épanouissement du mouvement ouvrier chrétien (1904–1921)', in Gerard and Wynants, *Histoire du mouvement ouvrier chrétien*, vol. 1, p. 136. Cf. Emiel Lamberts, 'Les Semaines Sociales en Belgique', in Jean-Dominique Durand (ed.), *Les Semaines Sociales de France: Cent ans d'engagement social des catholiques français, 1904–2004* (Paris, 2006), p. 349.

180 MSS WILPF, reel 57: 'Union Catholique Internationale de Service Social: bulletin d'Information', May 1937.

181 Pasture, 'Introduction', p. 41.

182 Carl Strikwerda, '"L'organisation, clé du succès !" European Christian labor movements in comparative perspective', in Heerma van Voss *et al.*, *Between Cross and Class*, p. 362.

183 Pasture, 'Introduction', p. 35.

184 Paul Misner, 'The Roman Catholic hierarchy and the Christian labor movement: autonomy and pluralism', in Heerma van Voss *et al.*, *Between Cross and Class*, p. 114.

185 William Patch, 'Fascism, Catholic corporatism, and the Christian trade unions of Germany, Austria and France', in *ibid.*, p. 173.

186 L'Affranchissement, *Guerre aux préjugés!*, pp. 20–1.

187 MS IRELP, L. Lacassagne 1: *Compte-rendu du Congrès International de la Libre-Pensée du 18 au 22 septembre 1881 à Paris* (Nice, 1882), p. 56.

188 MS IEV, Louis Bertrand, LB/I/464: Terwagne to Bertrand, 9 July 1909.

189 MS IIF 2-4: 'Programme. Congrès Génève, 14–15 Septembre 1902'. On the Brussels debates, see Bibliothèque de La Pensée, *Le Congrès de Bruxelles*, pp. 38–41.

190 Guillaume De Greef, *L'Internationalisation de la pensée*: *Congrès international de la Libre Pensée à Lisbonne (Octobre 1913). Discours du président* (Brussels, 1913), pp. 7–8.
191 MS IEV, Archives Rationalistes, LP/3.5: Jean Robin, 'Discours aux funérailles d'Eugène Hins'. See also MS AMSAB, Hins (205): Eugène Hins to Stephney Cowell, 21 January 1880.
192 Marc Mayné, *Eugène Hins: une grande figure de la Première Internationale en Belgique* (Brussels, 1994), p. 219.
193 Lucien Vertongen, *Le Congrès de Lisbonne (4 au 8 Octobre 1913)* (Brussels, 1913), p. 6.
194 Cf. contributions by Gustav Tschirn and Ida Altmann in the *Almanach-annuaire* of 1909, discussing the split at the German freethinkers' Frankfurt congress and a socialist freethought congress in Eisenach.
195 Jochen-Christoph Kaiser, *Arbeiterbewegung und organisierte Religionskritik: Proletarische Freidenkerverbände im Kaiserreich und der Weimarer Republik* (Stuttgart, 1981), pp. 188–90.
196 Emile Chapelier, *La Libre-Pensée prolétarienne contre la Libre Pensée bourgeoise* (Brussels, 1929), p. 24.
197 On communist freethought in France, see Lalouette, *La Libre Pensée en France*, pp. 74–5.
198 Tyssens and Witte, *De vrijzinnige traditie en België*, p. 94.
199 Strivay, *Union Mondiale des Libres Penseurs*, pp. 22–3.
200 Renaud Strivay, *Libre-Pensée universelle: documents généraux indispensables à tout esprit libre* (2nd edn., Liège, *c.* 1931), pp. 36–7.
201 Between 1931 and 1936, the International Freethought Federation was known as 'Union Internationale des Cercles de Libre-Pensée'.
202 Strivay, *Union Mondiale des Libres Penseurs*, pp. 9–10.
203 *Ibid.*, p. 62.
204 Müller, 'Anticipated exile of Christian democrats', p. 259.
205 Viaene, 'International history, religious history, Catholic history', 594.

4

Equality

In their contribution to a Belgian tourist guide, Alexandre Dumas and Victor Hugo praised the Belgian constitution as 'the most liberal one in Europe'.[1] The flexibility of the country's political framework became evident during the upheavals of 1848, when the government pre-empted unrest by extending the franchise.[2] Dumas and Hugo were but two activists who moved to Belgium after the rise of Louis Napoleon in France; others included Pierre-Joseph Proudhon, Jean Baptiste Clément, François-Vincent Raspail and Edgar Quinet. Even prior to 1848, Brussels hosted a range of radicals, including Giuseppe Mazzini, Mikhail Bakunin, Karl Marx and Friedrich Engels. Refugee communities could be breeding cells for transnational political activity: Marx contributed to the *Deutsche Brüsseler Zeitung*, was vice-president of Alliance Démocratique of Brussels and first published the *Communist Manifesto* in the Belgian capital.[3] In this respect, there were similarities between Brussels and London, as the British capital also provided a fertile environment for exile activism.[4] This shared tradition later became evident when the Second Congress of the Russian Social Democratic Labour Party (1903) started in Brussels and, following expulsion by the local authorities, continued in London.

Claims about Belgian tolerance must be approached with caution. In May 1871, the authorities expelled Victor Hugo from Brussels: he had publicly protested against the Belgian government's refusal to welcome French activists after the defeat of the Paris Commune and offered them personal asylum at his temporary residence.[5] Although former Communards and anarchists settled in Belgium during the 1870s and 1880s, there were obstacles to their political activism: they lived under the watchful eyes of the police and intelligence service, facing potential recriminations for political activity.[6] Furthermore, as Jean Stengers noted, the prominence of Belgium-based exiles tends to obscure the fact that their overall number remained relatively small.[7] In this respect, notions of Belgium as a *terre d'asile* formed part of the self-fashioning of 'international Belgium' that has been discussed in chapter 1.[8] These caveats notwithstanding, Belgium undeniably constituted a key site for transnational political movements in the late nineteenth and early twentieth centuries.

Early industrialisation had created precarious labour and living conditions, captured by Karl Marx's critique of Belgium as 'the snug, well-hedged, little paradise of the landlord, the capitalist, and the priest'.[9] Indeed, liberal politicians were slow to tackle the country's emerging social question: Carl Strikwerda, for instance, has noted that 'Belgium has been seen, rightly for the most part, as having been behind other Western European countries in terms of social legislation'.[10] In the face of major inequalities, social unrest was widespread and frequent in nineteenth-century Belgium.[11] The country's social tensions laid the foundations for a strong and well-organised labour movement which made prominent contributions to international socialism. This chapter focuses on socialist internationalism in Belgium and discusses its rapport with other leftist or reformist movements. In this context, it is worth bearing in mind that 'Early Marxist-socialist and liberal internationalism had far more in common than is generally acknowledged'.[12]

Socialist internationalism

To many people, the term 'internationalism' is primarily associated with the labour movement, exemplified by the slogan 'workers of the world, unite!' and the practices of the First and Second Internationals. According to James Joll, internationalism was 'deeply rooted in the socialist tradition' and Georges Haupt has viewed it as one of the movement's strengths.[13] The International Workingmen's Association – or First International – was founded in London (1864) and held its first congress in Geneva (1866), yet one of its precursors had been a Brussels-based organisation, the Association Fédérative Universelle (1863).[14] Marcel van der Linden has suggested that the period between 1848 and the 1870s was characterised by 'sub-national internationalism', as the transnational structures of socialists preceded the existence of strong national organisations in many countries.[15] The Belgian case confirms this view, as the First International influenced organisational consolidation at the national level. According to Els Witte, the International 'opened a new era in the Belgian labour movement'.[16]

Belgian activists such as César De Paepe and Eugène Hins were prominently involved in the First International and organised its 1868 congress in Brussels. In the dispute between the followers of Karl Marx and Mikhail Bakunin, they maintained links with both camps. Hins, for instance, defended Bakunin against some of Marx's charges.[17] At the 1872 congress in The Hague, which marked Bakunin's expulsion, Belgian delegates sided with the anarchist view of rejecting involvement in the political system. This stance was particularly widespread among activists in Verviers, a city which hosted the 1877 congress of Bakunin's competing 'anti-authoritarian international'.[18] The same year, a socialist congress in Ghent aimed to reconstitute the First

International by uniting different political factions. The delegates included Wilhelm Liebknecht, Tito Zanardelli and Peter Kropotkin, and a majority approved political means in the conquest of power – a view that also came to prevail among Belgian socialists.[19] While the event did not resurrect the International Workingmen's Association, it put its host city on the map of the international left, reflected in Liebknecht's praise for Ghent as 'the strongest citadel of socialism'.[20]

Over the subsequent decade, socialists organised themselves nationally. In 1885, they founded the Belgian Workers' Party (BWP), whose first deputies were elected to parliament in 1894. From the outset, Belgian socialists combined extra-parliamentary action – exemplified by the general strikes of 1893, 1902 and 1913 – with an involvement in parliamentary politics. Adopting a strategy of 'revolutionary reformism', the BWP favoured mass action to achieve universal male suffrage.[21] While the party and many of its founding figures were rooted in workers' culture, some of its emerging leaders, notably Emile Vandervelde, stemmed from bourgeois backgrounds and had entered socialism via progressive liberalism. Janet Polasky has drawn attention to the underlying tensions of Vandervelde's 'democratic socialism', pointing out how he sought to reconcile his self-perception as a Marxist theorist with his commitment to gradual change.[22]

Belgian socialists participated in the two socialist congresses that took place in Paris during the world's fair of 1889 and laid the foundations for the Second International. In this period, national parties and trade unions began to consolidate themselves and experience success at several levels: seven socialist deputies were elected to the French parliament in 1889, and 35 German social democrats made it into the Reichstag in the following year.[23] In line with wider changes since the demise of the International Workingmen's Association, the Second International was based on delegates sent by national affiliates. Moira Donald has therefore described it as 'a prototype of an international organisation and one which benefited from and made the most of the very latest in communication and technology'.[24]

With initial divides between 'Possibilists' and Marxists evident in 1889, the Belgian socialists took the initiative towards another international congress, held in Brussels in 1891. The socialist leader – and head of the BWP's foreign section – Jean Volders later described it as 'the most important of the socialist congresses since the end of the International Workingmen's Association'.[25] The event bridged ideological, but also national boundaries: statements by the German socialist Wilhelm Liebknecht and his French comrade Édouard Vaillant demonstrated their willingness to overcome Franco-German antagonism. In this context, Liebknecht stressed that 'The enemy of the German worker is not the French citizen, but the German bourgeois'.[26] The congress report reinterpreted the notion of Belgium as an international crossroads in a socialist sense: it located the country 'at the confluence of different industrial races and European socialists'.[27]

The mediating role of Belgian socialists contributed to the choice for Brussels as the site for the International Socialist Bureau in 1900. Georges Haupt has viewed this institutionalisation as the Second International's true starting point.[28] The new structure included the bureau itself, comprised of two delegates per country, and a secretariat run by Belgian socialists. Vandervelde – by then the BWP's dominant figure – headed this bureau. As Polasky has noted, the Belgian socialist 'travelled, climbed mountains, dined, and corresponded with German, French, British, Dutch, and Russian Socialist leaders, most of whom were at least a decade his senior'.[29] However, it was only with the appointment of Camille Huysmans as secretary in 1905 that the Brussels secretariat became fully effective.[30] Brussels emerged as the heart of the Second International at a point when the BWP experienced significant success at home: in 1900, it attracted 22.5 per cent of the popular vote in the general election.

The consolidation of the Second International was merely one manifestation of labour internationalism: trade unionists – who had participated in the Second International's congresses – developed their own links. From the 1890s, International Trade Secretariats fostered inter-union collaboration within particular sectors. Furthermore, in 1901, British, German and Belgian representatives attended a Scandinavian workers' congress, helping to launch the International Trade Union Secretariat. By 1913, eighteen centres with altogether seven million workers had become affiliated to this information office, and a proposal was passed to transform it in into an International Federation of Trade Unions.[31] Having fallen victim to war, the organisation was revived in 1919, with the Belgian trade unionist Corneel Mertens as vice-president.[32]

In light of the broader developments of international socialism and labour, James Joll has described the Basel Congress of 1912 as 'the high point of the International's optimistic self-confidence'.[33] However, such internationalism was subject to intrinsic tensions. One major dispute centred on the question of participation in 'bourgeois' governments, triggered by the entry of the French socialist Alexandre Millerand into Pierre Waldeck-Rousseau's cabinet in 1899. Reflecting the attitude of the German Social Democratic Party, the International rejected such cooperation. This, to some extent, posed a dilemma for the BWP, some of whose members – for instance, Edouard Anseele and Louis Bertrand – favoured cooperation with progressive liberals in the quest for franchise extension. However, given their hosting of the International Socialist Bureau, the BWP's leaders had little inclination to defy the resolutions of international socialist congresses.[34]

Another tension related to the question of nationhood. Socialists stressed the overriding importance of class solidarity. During the national anniversary celebrations of 1905, the Belgian socialists Louis Bertrand, Louis de Brouckère and Camille Huysmans sounded a critical note about 'seventy-five years of bourgeois domination'.[35] Emile Vandervelde argued that socialists had no reasons 'to celebrate a regime and to glorify a dynasty'; and when Leopold II visited Antwerp that year, the BWP responded with an antimilitarist demonstration.[36] Nonetheless, Belgian attitudes were not clear-cut. For instance, Maarten Van Ginderachter has shown how tensions based on language, culture and community already affected Belgian socialists before the First World War.[37] At a different level, he has noted that 'Radical-internationalist ideas went together with patriotic convictions about [being] the cradle of the coming world revolution'.[38]

Such observations point at the interaction between national and international allegiances. At international socialist congresses, delegates were wont to push national agendas or – as was famously the case with the German social democrats – promote their own interpretation of Marxism. In the multinational empire of the Habsburgs, social democrats organised themselves according to national groups from 1911. Indeed, relatively few socialists – Gustave Hervé and Rosa Luxemburg, for instance – openly rejected 'nationality' as an organisational principle. Having examined the international labour movement in connection with French syndicalism, Susan Milner concluded that 'on a practical level . . . national priorities and interests were paramount'.[39] Even the anarchist movement, with its evident transnational ambitions, 'lived in close and symbiotic relationship to both nationalism and the nation-state', as Carl Levy has pointed out.[40] The overall picture therefore seems to validate the label 'national internationalism' for the period from the 1890s.[41]

Socialist debates on war and peace reflected the ambiguous relationship between socialist internationalism and national ideas. At the 1891 international congress in Brussels, a debate on militarism concluded that a socialist order would guarantee peace, while a more concrete resolution, which envisaged a strike in the event of war, was only supported by French, British and Dutch delegates.[42] Subsequent congresses – most prominently at Stuttgart in 1907 – denounced armies as instruments of bourgeois domination and called for anti-war efforts without specifying concrete responses to military conflict.[43] Nonetheless, Kevin Callahan has argued that by 1914, 'European socialists had become adept practitioners of a form of peace activism that not only helped further the cause of peace but also equally importantly unified the disparate international movement itself'.[44] In partial contrast, Nicholas Stargardt has argued that the German social democrats' 'pacifist policy... [after 1908] was not based on a fundamental conscientious objection' and it 'retained all its earlier qualifications about the duty of nations to defend themselves'.[45]

The ambivalent stances on nationhood and war were key factors in the collapse of international solidarity in 1914. Even when socialist leaders adopted antimilitarist stances, their outlook was not necessarily shared by intellectuals or the grass roots.[46] During the July Crisis, the International Socialist Bureau held an emergency meeting in Brussels, yet 'nothing positive' came out of it, as Bertrand later commented.[47] On 29 July, a socialist peace gathering took place at the Cirque Royal in Brussels, with foreign speakers including the German social democrat Hugo Haase and the French socialist leader Jean Jaurès, who was assassinated two days later. After the start of military actions, many socialists backed their government, claiming that their country was engaged in a defensive war. While this interpretation was open to question in many countries, it could hardly be disputed in Belgium. Belgian socialists reacted with 'rage and anger' when they found out that their German comrades had approved the Kaiser's war credits.[48] As later parts of this chapter will show, the war clearly affected their involvement in socialist internationalism – with Vandervelde joining the government and the International's secretariat moving to the Netherlands after the German attack.

Beyond the Belgian Workers' Party

It is impossible to discuss socialist internationalism by focusing exclusively on the BWP. One of the key features of the Belgian labour movement was the prominence of cooperatives, for which the Vooruit in Ghent (1880) provided the model. By the early twentieth century, it 'integrated production, consumption, politics, social service, and recreation'.[49] As Hendrik Defoort has shown, the Belgian path towards cooperation had been subject to transnational influences, with the efforts of the Rochdale Pioneers being debated among Belgian activists.[50] Key figures of the cooperatives movement maintained links to socialist internationalism: Théophile Massart of the cooperative Le Progrès in Jolimont (1885) had been active in the International Workingmen's Association, and Edouard Anseele of the Vooruit represented Belgium within the International Socialist Bureau alongside Vandervelde. Demonstrating the overlapping nature of different transnational networks, both Malssart and Anseele were involved in the freethought movement that has been discussed in chapter 3.[51] The Belgian cooperatives exemplify the multifaceted world of Belgian socialism: in Brussels, the Art Nouveau architect Victor Horta built the Maison du Peuple (1895–99) which hosted both a consumer cooperative and the BWP headquarters. Its opening allowed the BWP to broadcast its achievements to both a national and an international audience.[52] The building's construction was predated by the launch of an 'arts section', with frequent lectures by artists and academics. For this reason, the historian Paul Aron has suggested a convergence between 'literary and social practices', and stressed the relationship between the BWP's expansion and the new cultural movements of the fin de siècle.[53]

The prominence of cooperatives within the Belgian labour movement had a wider significance as Belgian cooperatives served as models beyond the country's borders.[54] The BWP actively promoted these achievements internationally: for instance, the 1891 congress of the Second International included an excursion to Ghent to demonstrate the 'small universe' created by the Ghent socialists. Anseele welcomed delegates such as August Bebel, Wihelm Liebknecht, Jules Guesde, Hjalmar Branting and Victor Adler to 'one of the cradles of international socialism'.[55] Thus, the trip was an opportunity to stage local or national achievements for an international audience. For instance, in the name of the French delegation Emmanuel Chauvière – a former Blanquist and Communard who had been born in Ghent to French parents – expressed 'the sympathies of the French socialists for the superb Belgian socialist movement'.[56] Belgian activists also participated in the International Cooperative Alliance, founded in London in 1895, with Anseele regularly attending its congresses. The international association represented itself as 'neutral' in ideological and religious matters, in marked contrast to the Belgian cooperatives which reflected the country's political and social divisions.[57]

The scale of socialism and cooperation in Belgium tends to overshadow the anarchist movement, which nonetheless had its followers and was a transnational movement in its own right. The international terrorist wave of the fin de siècle also affected Belgium, with explosions in Ghent in 1892 and 1894, as well as the assassination attempt of an Italian anarchist, Gennaro Rubino, on Leopold II.[58] At the organisational level, Belgian activists attempted to build on anarchism's internationalist legacy: in 1907, the Groupement Communiste Libertaire in Belgium co-organised an International Anarchist Congress in Amsterdam and subsequently prepared a *Bulletin de l'Internationale Libertaire*. However, such efforts proved short-lived and lacked support from French anarcho-syndicalists.[59]

The boundaries between anarchists and other groups were sometimes fluid. With regard to the mid-nineteenth century, the 'intimate relationship of anarchism to radical federalist and international republicanism' is worth noting.[60] Furthermore, in fin-de-siècle France and Belgium, many symbolists and neo-impressionists 'shared the… ideal, the social utopia of the anarchists'.[61] Several people around the poet Emile Verhaeren – who himself was prominently involved in the arts section of the Maison du Peuple – maintained links to anarchism. Furthermore, as discussed in chapter 3, the solidarity campaign for Francisco Ferrer showed how anarchists could cooperate with campaigners of other political persuasions. For instance, the historian Jan Moulaert has noted the anarchist links of the freethinker and progressive Georges Lorand, who played such a key role in the Ferrer campaign.[62]

Intersections between anarchism and other political currents became evident when the Free University of Brussels suspended a course by the French geographer and anarchist Élisée Reclus in December 1892. Hector Denis resigned as the university's rector in protest against this decision, and Emile Vandervelde later recalled 'the exaltation with which our young enthusiasm solidarised with Reclus'.[63] In 1894, the affair triggered the creation of the New University of Brussels (Université Nouvelle), with Reclus and his brother Elie among its lecturing staff. This institution was labelled 'the anarchist university' by some contemporaries and, despite its relatively short existence, has been described as 'one of the most durable educational ventures of the libertarian movement'.[64] A key Belgian protagonist of Ferrer's Ligue Internationale pour l'Éducation Rationelle de l'Enfance, Paul Gille, was associated with the New University. Yet the institution also attracted academics and activists whose background was distant from anarchism. Henri La Fontaine, for instance, lectured on international law; later on, Paul Otlet taught 'mondialism' at a university section that survived the war, the Institut des Hautes Études.

As the involvement of La Fontaine and Otlet suggests, the New University had clear international features. It attracted foreign students and scholars such as the French educator Paul Robin and Enrico Ferri, a disciple of Cesare Lombroso.[65] Inaugurating the new academic year in 1905, Guillaume De Greef – sociologist, BWP member and university founder – asserted that due to its non-dogmatic nature and its location in Brussels, the New University responded to a world which had reached its 'international' or 'global' stage.[66] His lecture – entitled *L'ère de la mondialité* – was indicative of internationalist narratives, proclaiming that 'The era of nationalities is closed, that of internationality and even of globality (*mondialité*) is open'.[67] In contrast with other contemporaries, he was ready to evoke 'cosmopolitanism': he proposed a 'new cosmopolitanism' which, unlike its individualistic eighteenth-century incarnation, was concerned with building adequate institutions.[68]

Beyond socialist politics

Activism on social issues was not confined to the left. In Belgium, a Federation of Catholic Workers' Organisations united various groups as early as 1868, although this initiative was linked to paternalistic models of society. From the 1890s, social Catholicism developed a strong presence in Belgium under the impetus of *Rerum Novarum*, as discussed in chapter 3. As with the cooperative movement, Ghent was a significant site: as Strikwerda has noted, the city hosted 'the first strong Christian Democratic movement in Belgium', benefiting from its links to 'independent associations of workers'.[69] Reflecting the increasing prominence of Christian trade unionism from the turn of the century, Belgian activists participated in the first international congress of Christian trade unions in 1908. After the Great War, Belgians helped establish an International Federation of Christian Trade Unions. In 1919, two competing meetings for the establishment of an International Confederation were held – one with participants from the Entente and one with representatives from the Central Powers. In 1920, a united organisation was established, with Belgian affiliates representing the highest number of members after Germany, Italy and Hungary.[70]

Ideological divisions between left and right did not preclude collaboration on social questions. In 1926, the social-Catholic politician Cyrille Van Overbergh wrote to Vandervelde on his sixtieth birthday, acknowledging their shared commitment to improving workers' lives.[71] Van Overbergh's statement came at a time when the Catholic Party and the BWP had collaborated in government. However, in limited fashion – and particularly in international settings – Catholic reformers and socialists already cooperated before the war. Child welfare was one example: international efforts on this issue were linked to the initiative of the Catholic politician Jules Lejeune, who had been Minister of Justice from 1887 to 1894. Through international congresses in Antwerp in 1890, 1894 and 1898, Belgium became ' "the international capital" of the patronage and protection of children'.[72] Looking back on the pre-war efforts, Vandervelde praised Lejeune's work for children.[73]

Similar cross-connections were evident in Belgian attempts to effect local change and tackle the problems caused by urbanisation. Such ambitions became manifest with the foundation of the International Union of Local Authorities during the Ghent world's fair of 1913. According to Pierre-Yves Saunier, it can be viewed as part of 'an Urban Internationale'.[74] The organisation was partly driven by socialist ideals, as reflected in the prominent role of Emile Vinck, a BWP senator from Ghent. Under his influence, a BWP committee tackled municipal questions from 1897, and his party also raised the issue at the international socialist congress of 1900.[75] Thus, while constituting part of a wider network on urban affairs, the International Union of Local Authorities stood within the specific context of municipal socialism. As Oscar Gaspari has argued, 'political/utopian reasons based on ideals of universal brotherhood and cooperation…permeated the entire history of the organisation', setting it apart 'from other organisations in the municipal movement'.[76] Nonetheless, the International Union presented itself as non-partisan; instead, it evoked the principles of 'urban science' and the politics of expertise. During the interwar years, as Stefan Couperus has argued, it became 'the main institutionalised platform for interchange of and debates about the alleged essence of local government'.[77]

The work of the lawyer and sociologist Louis Varlez illustrates the ideological cross-connections as well as the interplay between local, national and transnational activism.[78] Stemming from a progressive liberal, rather than socialist or Christian democratic background, he chaired the unemployment fund of Ghent from 1901. The local arrangements became known as the 'Ghent model': they included municipal subsidies for voluntary insurances that were administered by the trade unions. These measures, with their 'distinctly nonpartisan structure', had been introduced by a coalition of socialists, progressive liberals and Christian democrats.[79] Due to his local expertise, Varlez became the secretary of the Association Internationale pour la Lutte contre le Chômage (International Association for the Struggle against Unemployment). Having been founded in Paris in 1910, it held its first official congress one year later. Hosted by the city of Ghent, where the association also established its seat, the event featured the socialist Anseele among its speakers. The municipality allocated a subsidy of 7,000 francs for the new association and later enabled the association to organise a congress within the framework of the 1913 world's fair.[80]

In 1912, a committee meeting of the association commented on its good relations with other international initiatives for social assurance and workers' protection.[81] Indeed, the Ghent-based undertaking was but one of several international initiatives that worked on social issues in this period. In 1897, international congresses in Zurich (with labour activists) and in Brussels (organised by academics) set the path for the foundation of the International Association for Labour Legislation in Basel in 1901, a direct precursor of the ILO.[82] The ILO itself provided a distinct forum for transnational exchange through its tripartite structure, comprising the representatives of governments, trade unions and employers. Its director Albert Thomas had been a central figure in French reformist socialism before the war, and the historian Christophe Prochasson has even spoken of the 'Albert Thomas network'.[83] Vandervelde also contributed to this organisation. Meanwhile, Louis Varlez took up a post in the new organisation. After the war, he had briefly worked as an intermediary between the League of Nations secretariat and the ILO. Upon his transfer to the ILO, League secretary Eric Drummond expressed his 'very keen sense of the high value of your work' and, while regretting the departure from the secretariat, was 'glad… to think that we shall continue to be working for essentially the same high object'.[84] Within the ILO, Varlez headed the section on unemployment and migration, organising international migration conferences in Rome (1924) and Havana (1928), but also maintaining links with non-governmental organisations.[85] Meanwhile, bodies such as the International Federation of Trade Unions cooperated with the ILO from the start, albeit with varying results.[86]

Feminism and socialism

What was the relationship between socialist internationalism and feminism – another cause in which social and political change featured prominently? In his influential work *Die Frau und der Sozialismus*, the German socialist

August Bebel likened the conditions of women and workers, asserting that both had been suppressed throughout history.[87] Yet socialist attitudes varied. At the international socialist congress of 1891, Vandervelde argued that a woman's place was the domestic sphere – a view that was opposed by Wilhelm Liebknecht and the Dutch activist Wilhelmina Drucker. The BWP leader later suggested that his conversion to the cause of women's rights was linked to his experiences in 1891: 'I had found my road to Damascus'.[88] In 1907, female socialists such as Clara Zetkin, Louise Zietz and Alexandra Kollontai came together at an International Conference of Socialist Women, held in conjunction with the Stuttgart Congress of the Second International. This event established a new structure, the International Bureau of Socialist Women, which has been interpreted as the 'product of debates surrounding gender, class and unequal international development'.[89]

Freethinkers – whose constituency, as has been shown, overlapped with socialism – also addressed women's rights. Feminists such as the Belgian Isabelle Gatti de Gamond, the German Ida Altmann and the English Annie Besant participated in their international congresses. Observing an international women's congress in Berlin in 1896, the German freethought periodical concluded that the era of emancipated women being 'a laughing matter' had finally been overcome.[90] The BWP senator and president of the International Freethought Federation, Hector Denis, served as honorary president of the International Feminist Congress which the Belgian League of Women's Rights organised in 1912.[91] The case of Denis illustrates the direct involvement of male activists in Belgian feminism. Another prominent case was the lawyer Louis Frank, whose views on Belgian internationalism have been discussed in chapter 1.

Both at the Belgian and the international level, the socialist engagement with the women's movement was ambivalent. As the historian Marilyn Boxer has argued, 'bourgeois feminism' was a construct used for polemical purposes rather than a reflection of clear demarcation lines.[92] With regard to the Belgian case, some scholars have stressed the separate nature of socialist, bourgeois-liberal and Catholic feminisms, yet more recently, Julie Carlier has presented a convincing case for an 'entangled history' of Belgian feminism.[93] This entanglement had two dimensions: the connection between activists from different ideological backgrounds, and the linkages that they developed across national borders. As Carlier has demonstrated, Belgian feminism was shaped by, but also contributed to, developments abroad. One of the leading Belgian activists, Marie Popelin, had gained international prominence in her quest to qualify as a lawyer, inspiring French activists to challenge professional limitations in a similar manner. Their subsequent correspondence influenced the foundation of the Belgian League of Women's Rights (1892) along the lines of an existing French organisation.[94] The second instance of transnational entanglement was the connection between Dutch activists such as Wilhelmina Drucker and Belgians such as Emilie Claeys.[95] Drucker had lectured in Brussels in the wake of the Second International's 1891 congress. These contacts resulted in the formation of a Dutch–Flemish organisation, but also Belgian participation in the socialist Union pour la Solidarité des Femmes.[96] A third transnational connection traced by Carlier was the case of Christian feminism, as exemplified by the association Le Féminisme Chrétien en Belgique (1902), inspired by an existing organisation in France. According to Carlier, its activism undermines the 'presumed anti-thesis between feminism and Catholicism'.[97]

Hence, the history of Belgian feminism was clearly part of a wider international story. According to the historian Bonnie Anderson, the 'first international women's movement' emerged between the 1830s and 1860s around a core group of twenty women. None of them were Belgian, although the periodical *The Voice of Women* carried reports from the kingdom.[98] After these early efforts, an international umbrella organisation for female activists only followed in 1888: the International Council of Women (ICW). Popelin served as one of its vice-presidents and in 1905 co-founded a National Council of Belgian Women, which affiliated to the ICW.[99] By 1914, councils from 23 countries were associated with the international organisation.[100] Both the ICW and the National Council presented themselves as politically neutral and not as explicitly feminist. The composition of these bodies was largely middle class, while the ICW's president, Lady Aberdeen, had an aristocratic background. One of her successors (in 1936) was a Belgian noblewoman, Baroness Marthe Boël.

It would be simplistic to interpret Popelin's main organisation, the Belgian League of Women's Rights, as a mere example of 'bourgeois' feminism. Léonie La Fontaine, a key figure in the Belgian League and a co-founder of the Central Office of Female Documentation, maintained links to the socialist camp – not least through her brother Henri, who also supported feminist causes. Similarly, Gatti de Gamond increasingly moved towards socialism while remaining involved in the Belgian League and interacting with liberals in Masonic and freethought circles. When Belgian feminists organised international congresses in Brussels in 1897 and 1917, they raised a number of social concerns. According to Carlier, they were exemplary of the 'radical European feminist tradition which focused on women's equality to men in the labour market'.[101]

What about the other dividing line within both the socialist movement and the women's movement, namely women's suffrage? The issue of whether to focus on the right to vote was a divisive matter even among female activists. In 1904, the ICW created a Standing Committee on Suffrage – which was, as Leila Rupp has stressed, 'a highly controversial move'.[102] Its creation responded to the foundation of the International Woman Suffrage Alliance in the same year. Meanwhile, socialists disagreed on the issue: to European socialist leaders such as Keir Hardie, Domela Nieuwenhuis and Vandervelde, the right to vote should apply to both sexes. In 1907, resolutions at the International Conference of Socialist Women and the International's Stuttgart Congress portrayed women's suffrage as an integral part of the struggle for universal suffrage. Yet some socialists and liberals feared that female suffrage would deliver votes to conservative parties because of the perceived influence of priests over female votes.[103] In response, the German socialist and feminist Ida Altmann suggested to bring women closer to the secularist movement, asking freethinkers to use literature, artistic events and childcare to this end.[104] Education was a priority in this respect: to anticlerical activists in Belgium, it was evident that girls' education was required 'to struggle effectively against the Catholics'.[105]

After the First World War, Belgium was one of the few countries – alongside France, Bulgaria, Yugoslavia and Switzerland – where women could not vote in national elections. It has been argued that the BWP only gave half-hearted support to women's suffrage since the municipal elections of 1920 (where Belgian women were allowed to vote) revealed that 'socialist women lacked a constituency'.[106] Nonetheless, it was the BWP that sent the first women to parliament, even before the active right to vote was granted: Marie Spaak to the Senate in 1921; Lucie Dejardin and Isabelle Blume to the Chamber of Representatives in 1929 and 1936 respectively. Moreover, Denise De Weerdt has suggested that one of the major strengths of left-wing feminism in interwar Belgium resided in mutualist women's associations.[107] Fittingly, in their contributions to the international socialist women's conference of 1928, the Belgian delegates Isabelle Blume and Alice Pels both focused on social issues such as the rights of unwed mothers and financial support after childbirth.[108]

Socialism, feminism and the First World War

In spite of the fundamental rupture within the Second International in 1914, alternative forms of socialist cooperation continued during the war. In 1915, such efforts were exemplified by two encounters on neutral soil: the Zimmerwald conference in Switzerland and a meeting of Dutch and Scandinavian socialists in Copenhagen.[109] Huysmans persisted in promoting socialist cooperation and, in 1917, initiated an international conference in Stockholm with the Swedish socialist Hjalmar Branting. Huysmans's conciliatory stance caused controversy within his own party.[110] Bertrand later hinted at such misgivings, claiming that 'a curious book could be written about the wartime actions' of the Second International's secretariat, which Huysmans led from The Hague.[111]

Vandervelde and de Brouckère declined to participate in the Stockholm congress.[112] As their reaction highlighted, the experience of war and occupation made it difficult for them to cooperate with their German and Austrian comrades. In 1917, Vandervelde refused Victor Adler's invitation to a private meeting, even though the Austrian socialist leader and his Belgian counterpart had been known as 'the socialist Siamese twins'.[113] Expressing the views of the Zimmerwald Left, Lenin denounced Vandervelde's wartime stance as 'social Chauvinism'. The Belgian socialist, however, declined 'lessons in internationalism' from the 'pilgrims of Zimmerwald and Kienthal' or from German 'majority socialists' who backed their government.[114] He argued that the support for 'national defence' did not mean that Belgian socialists had abandoned internationalism.[115] In the final stages of the war, Vandervelde and de Brouckère reiterated the view that the German 'majority socialists' needed to admit their errors before an international congress could involve them. At the same time, they acknowledged that Austrian social democrats had made progress on this issue and expressed their 'deepest sympathy for the effort, as courageous as it is ungrateful and difficult, of the Independent Socialists of Germany'.[116]

These circumstances prevented Brussels from resuming its role as the centre for socialist internationalism. When attempting to re-build the Second International in 1918, the British Labour politician Arthur Henderson described Brussels as the 'most appropriate' site for a conference, but proposed to examine whether the Germans would support this choice.[117] Vandervelde pledged personal reasons when declining to host the conference: he referred to his work as cabinet minister, his likely participation in the Paris Peace Conference and the task of re-building his party: 'I am literally overworked'.[118] He also pointed out that Brussels was 'almost completely cut off from communication with the outside world – for lack of trains'. In the end, Vandervelde did indeed participate in the Paris Peace Conference where his role was somewhat ambiguous. The historian Sally Marks has even suggested that Vandervelde 'blamed everything socialists disliked on [the Belgian foreign minister] Hymans and carefully built a paper record consonant with his role in international socialism, but in his private actions (and later as Foreign Minister) he was a Belgian nationalist'.[119] Yet during the war, the German socialist Karl Kautsky had praised Vandervelde for having expressed himself 'very correctly', viewing the Belgian's stance on potential peace terms as remarkable 'given the fact that Belgium in particular was hit by enemy invasion which it had not provoked through any declaration of war'. To Kautsky, the socialist International had not been killed by the war, but merely proven that it was 'not an effective tool in times of war'.[120] Indeed, the BWP favoured a 'peace of justice' with conciliatory points regarding Germany.[121]

As had been the case for socialists, the First World War triggered internal divisions in the women's movement. In Britain, the anti-war leaders of the

National Union of Women's Suffrage Societies, for instance, had to realise that their arguments regarding the interrelation between women's rights and 'durable peace' were not shared by most of their members.[122] The strength of national sentiment in light of the war experience is illustrated by the case of the Belgian Federation for Women's Suffrage. In November 1914, the Dutch activist Aletta Jacobs invited the organisation to a peace meeting with feminists from the warring nations. Yet the letter only reached its recipient in January 1919. Having initially overlooked this delay of more than four years, the Belgian feminist and liberal Jane Brigode responded that no resumption of contacts was possible before Germany 'recognising its guilt, proclaims its remorse'.[123] After realising the original date of the invite, Brigode protested 'perhaps even more strongly against an invitation that was addressed to us at the moment that we suffered the odious German yoke'.[124] Jacobs expressed her dismay at this 'explosion of patriotism': upon reading the letter, her 'eyes [had] filled with tears'. She felt 'very sorry that women of high intellectual development, embittered by much sorrow, have lost their just view upon the interests of humanity'.[125]

Jacobs had indeed managed to organise an international congress at The Hague in 1915. At this event, the arrival of a small Belgian delegation created 'a moment of intense feeling': 'in token of respect', the audience rose to its feet and 'cheered heartily'.[126] The congress launched the International Committee of Women for Permanent Peace which was later transformed into the Women's International League for Peace and Freedom (WILPF). To some of its protagonists, for instance the American Jane Addams, WILPF's promotion of pacifism and feminism was intertwined with their commitment to social reform.[127] From 1921, WILPF was also represented in Belgium. In Brussels, its efforts were led by Leonie La Fontaine, who had previously been involved in the Union Internationale des Femmes pour la Paix alongside Marie Popelin.[128] A second Belgian WILPF group was based in Liège and led by the socialist feminist Lucie Dejardin. Looking back on the early years of WILPF in Belgium, one activist noted that La Fontaine's circle comprised 'about 15 elderly "bourgeoises"', while the Liège branch had 'about 25 working-class women, who never appeared quite at their ease, because they suspected "bourgeois" influence' and because WILPF was not officially backed by the BWP.[129] Such matters changed when the feminist Marcelle Leroy, 'revolutionised the Bruxelles group' and attracted a wider following in 1932.

There were limits to the spirit of dialogue promoted by WILPF, as became clear in 1927. That year, the organisation's international secretariat in Geneva proposed an appeal of Flemish nationalists who had been condemned for their war-time collaboration with Germany. Both the Brussels and the Liège branches objected to such an intervention in national affairs.[130] The WILPF secretariat regretted this stance: 'What we are concerned with here at

Headquarters is the softening of racial asperities'.[131] Even within an organisation such as WILPF – which collaborated with radical pacifists and social activists – there were evident limits to transnational action, especially when it came to matters that were perceived as 'national' ones.

Socialist internationalism in interwar Europe

The war years clearly affected the Belgian role in international socialism. In 1919, Vandervelde resigned as president of the International Socialist Bureau because party discipline prevented him from attending the Bern conference in which German social democrats participated.[132] In 1920, German and Belgian socialists met at an international socialist conference in Geneva, yet in 1923 the events surrounding the French and Belgian invasion of the Ruhr revealed the ongoing challenges for transnational exchange. The Austrian socialist Friedrich Adler praised Vandervelde's rejection of the occupation. Warning against a 'relapse into war ideologies', Adler attacked the 'nationalist' stance of Belgian socialists who remained hostile to Germany, for instance Jules Destrée and Louis Piérard.[133] To Adler's dismay, they had even opposed the final passage of Vandervelde's resolution which, in its denunciation of violence, did 'not contain anything that a socialist could not sign as a matter of course'. Adopting a line that was shared by socialists elsewhere, Vandervelde called upon the League of Nations to arbitrate.[134]

With the Ruhr crisis still ongoing, the Hamburg congress of May 1923 brought together two remnants of pre-war internationalism: on the one hand, the remainder of the Second International, whose efforts were coordinated from London; on the other hand, the International Working Union of Socialist Parties in Vienna, also known as the Two-and-a Half International. The result of this merger, the Labour and Socialist International (LSI), marked the reconstruction of socialist internationalism, but with less pronounced Belgian involvement: Friedrich Adler, rather than Huysmans, was the secretary, and British Labour politicians such as Ramsay MacDonald and Arthur Henderson took a prominent role. The organisation's offices were initially based in London and then Zurich. The latter location did not meet with universal acclaim: the Dutch social democrats commented that the secretariat was 'rather eccentrically located in Zurich' and proposed to move to 'the rather central city of Brussels instead'.[135] However, it was only in 1935 that the International returned to Brussels. Vandervelde, de Brouckère and Huysmans all contributed to the work of the organisation, and in 1927, a BWP party official, Joseph Van Roosbroeck, became LSI treasurer.

There was another challenge for socialist internationalism between the wars: socialist parties were increasingly represented in national governments, sometimes gaining ministerial positions or even higher office. Examples included the social democrats' participation in most governments of the Weimar Republic as well as Friedrich Ebert's presidency from 1919 to 1925; the short-lived coalition between Austrian social democrats and the Christian Social Party (1918–20); the Czech Socialist Party's representation in most Czechoslovak governments from 1919; the British Labour governments of 1924 and 1929; the French 'Cartel des Gauches' (1924–26; 1932–34) and 'Front Populaire' (1936–38); the republican-socialist government in the Second Spanish Republic (1931–33); and the 'Frente Popular' (1936–39). In a marked shift from the policies of the Second International, socialist parties formed coalitions with non-socialist ones. Such changes had implications for socialist internationalism. For instance, in 1925, upon forming a coalition with Christian democrats led by Prosper Poullet, Vandervelde passed on his seat on the LSI bureau to Brouckère and only resumed his international activities after the government's collapse. Furthermore, when Vandervelde became president of the LSI in 1929, it was a consequence of the appointment of its previous president, Arthur Henderson, as Foreign Secretary in Ramsay MacDonald's cabinet.

As a partial reflection of coalition-building at home, LSI congresses increasingly dealt with international relations rather than domestic matters. G. D. H. Cole noted this development with regard to the 1928 LSI congress, whose

> long report…hardly reads like the report of a body devoted essentially to the cause of Socialism. A very large part of it deals with issues, such as the policy and structure of the League of Nations, Disarmament, and Fascism, which, however important for Socialists, have little to do with the direct line of advance towards a Socialist society.[136]

The 1928 meeting was the first time since 1891 that socialists gathered in Belgium for an international congress. Having been scheduled to take place in England, the event was moved to mainland Europe for financial reasons. With Switzerland, Austria and Belgium all offering to act as hosts, the British representatives expressed a preference for Brussels.[137] The congress occurred at a time when the BWP had considerable support, as reflected by a membership of nearly 600,000.[138] This strength enabled the party to heed Adler's wish 'that our next Congress should demonstrate close contact with the masses'.[139] At the start of the congress, the BWP organised a demonstration in Brussels, followed a few days later by another 'great mass demonstration' that was combined with the jubilee celebrations of the Liège cooperative.[140]

The latter example also underlines the ongoing prominence of the cooperative movement. Indeed, four years before the Brussels congress, the city of Ghent hosted an international cooperative congress.[141] The gathering was framed by a wider event, the International Co-operative and Social Welfare Exhibition which, under Anseele's chairmanship, opened its gates in June, attracting 325,000 visitors over three months. In line with the 'neutral' character of the

International Cooperative Alliance, the event made no distinction on religious or political grounds. As a result, the organisers obtained a royal decree for a raffle, helping them to raise funds for both the exhibition and for a university chair in cooperative studies. Effectively, the exhibition was a showcase for the Vooruit. The president of the Belgian section of the exhibition was Victor Serwy who, back in 1900, had been the first – albeit unsuccessful – secretary of the Second International.[142]

While Vandervelde returned to the presidency of the International, a new generation came to the fore within the BWP. The party's defining figure of the 1930s, Hendrik de Man, had been involved in a variety of transnational exchanges. As a student in Ghent, he was active in a student association with individuals who later became protagonists of scientific internationalism (Georges Sarton) and interwar Europeanism (Irenée van der Ghinst).[143] He had undertaken parts of his studies in Germany and served as the secretary of the International Socialist Youth League, founded in 1907. In the 1920s, de Man gained prominence as a social theorist with his research at the Frankfurt Academy of Work, but also 'sought to become a trans-Atlantic intellectual broker'.[144] De Man described his stance as 'ecclectic internationalism' rather than 'cosmopolitanism', and alleged that he had only felt patriotism 'by loving Belgium as a microcosm of Europe'.[145] Yet today, he is not remembered for international activism but for two other reasons: his Plan de Travail in 1935 and – beyond the scope of this study – his collaboration with Nazi Germany in 1940. The 'labour plan' was meant to form a Belgian response to the world economic crisis and has been described as 'the most coherent neo-socialist project of the decade for the management of capitalism'.[146] It attracted particular interest among Dutch socialists and became the subject of international conferences.[147] Clearly, despite the plan's focus on the Belgian context, de Man's ideas also had a transnational potential. In other respects, however, both de Man and another rising BWP politician, Paul-Henri Spaak, were less attached to the principles of socialist internationalism. In 1936, they favoured non-intervention in the Spanish Civil War, in contrast to Vandervelde – who resigned as minister over this question – and de Brouckère. As Janet Polasky has argued, by 1936, 'Spaak and de Man had convinced the majority of Belgian Socialism to support their nationalist strategy and abandon the archaic internationalism of the old guard'.[148]

The communist challenge

During the interwar years, socialist internationalism faced competition from the Communist International which had been founded in March 1919. With the exception of the Russian and Dutch communists, whose parties had preceded the Comintern, communist parties were created as national Comintern affiliates.[149] In Belgium, a united communist party was slow to develop. In 1920, it was still uncertain whether one left-wing group, the Amis de l'Exploité, would affiliate.[150] The Belgian Communist Party remained very small, with around 500–700 members throughout the 1920s. The extent of Soviet control over other communist parties is still a subject of heated scholarly dispute.[151] In the Belgian case, however, the rise of Stalin impacted severely on the party: in 1928, the majority of its membership sided with Trotsky's supporters, resulting in the departure of two-thirds of its members and one of its two parliamentary representatives. According to the historian José Gotovitch, it temporarily became 'a party of foreigners'.[152] The Belgian communists' fortunes only changed in the early 1930s when, in the face of social and political crisis, its membership grew first to 2,600 (in 1935) and then 8,500 (1936).[153]

The conflict-ridden relationship between the LSI and the Comintern is well-known. Prior to the foundation of the LSI in 1923, activists such as Friedrich Adler had hoped for a merger between the socialist and communist movements. These efforts came to nothing – and when the Comintern adopted its 'class against class' strategy in 1928, the leeway for cooperation was reduced even further. According to Huysmans, the change in the Soviet leadership also affected the LSI: 'Lenin's premature death was a veritable catastrophe for us. His successor was an entirely different personality.'[154] In its United Front period (1922–27), the Comintern still evoked left-wing alliances, as exemplified by organisations such as the Workers' International Relief and International Red Aid. The LSI denounced these bodies as part of 'the "united front" swindle',[155] and the BWP deplored their 'disruptive manoeuvres' in Belgium.[156] In 1924, Belgian trade unionists declared that communists could not ascend to positions of responsibility, based on a resolution by Corneel Mertens, the activist who was also involved in the International Federation of Trade Unions.[157] Three years later, the BWP prohibited its members from joining Comintern front organisations.[158]

Workers' International Relief had been founded to deal with the famine in Russia and then extended its realm of action to other social and humanitarian causes. Although its success in Belgium remained limited, its membership in 1932 (2,400) outstripped that of the Communist Party.[159] International Red Aid attracted more extensive support in Belgium. It was supposed to provide assistance to left-wing activists around the world, taking a prominent role in the solidarity campaign for Sacco and Vanzetti. When the Belgian section of this organisation held its first congress in 1926, it had around 5,000 individual members and 15,000 affiliated members through the adhesion of other organisations.[160] Yet International Red Aid soon lost many of its Belgian supporters after the BWP had ruled out joint memberships. Furthermore, in 1927–28, the secretary of the Belgian section, Charles Plisnier – a novelist and founding member of the Belgian Communist Party – raised the issue of political persecution in the Soviet Union. In response, the Comintern disbanded the Belgian committee, later replacing it with a more submissive leadership.

Shortly before being removed from International Red Aid, Plisnier and his committee helped organise the International Congress against Imperialism and Colonial Oppression, held in Brussels in 1927.[161] Similar to Workers' International Relief and International Red Aid, the driving force behind the event was the German communist Willi Münzenberg. In line with the 'united front' strategy, it brought together a wide array of participants and created a new organisation, the League Against Imperialism. The range of participants extended beyond communist parties. Participants from Belgium included the BWP members Albert Marteaux and Paul-Henri Spaak; from Britain the ILP leader James Maxton, the future Labour Party leader George Lansbury and the philosopher Bertrand Russell; from Germany, Albert Einstein; and from France, the pacifist and feminist Gabrielle Duchêne as well as the leader of the Ligue des Droits de l'Homme, Victor Basch.[162] The congress was noteworthy for the involvement of anti-colonial activists, for instance Jawaharlal Nehru from India, J. T. Gumede from South Africa and Mohammed Atta from Indonesia. The Belgian press covered this event and paid specific attention to its debates on the Congo.[163] Yet by 1928, many non-communists abandoned their involvement when the 'front' character of the undertaking had become clear.

There was a striking connection between the Brussels congress of 1927, and the LSI congress in the Belgian capital one year later: the LSI placed the 'colonial question' on the agenda of its 1928 event. However, its pronouncements on the anti-colonial cause included various qualifications. The congress expressed 'warmest sympathy for the peoples who are waging the fight against imperialist and colonial oppression', but suggested that socialists should rather 'rally the working-class elements of these nations under the banner of international socialism'.[164] Such attitudes allowed the LSI to limit its criticism of national colonial policies. Furthermore, while the American, British, Danish, Dutch, French and Italian affiliates of the LSI produced reports, the published proceedings do not feature any Belgian contribution on the situation in the Congo.[165]

Even when attacking particular aspects of colonial policy, the LSI reinforced notions of civilisational hierarchies. The delegates called for the 'emancipation of those colonial races who now fulfil the basic conditions of modern independent civilisation and claim in their behalf complete liberation from the foreign yoke, or, if they so desire, the same political status and complete equality of rights with the citizens of the sovereign power'.[166] At the same time, however, the congress juxtaposed 'Colonies with a Higher Form of Civilisation' with 'Colonies with Primitive Culture'. The limited willingness to question existing assumptions was reflected in the demand to extend the principle of trusteeship 'to cover all tropical and sub-tropical Africa and similar colonies of primitive culture elsewhere'.[167] That said, Vandervelde did endorse nationalisms that had developed in response to oppression – but he confined his endorsement to 'nationalisms that carry on their side the germs of democracy and socialism'.[168]

The rise of fascism triggered efforts at both the national and the international level. In 1925, the Executive of the LSI unveiled a memorial to Giacomo Matteotti at the Maison du Peuple. The funds for this monument had been collected through the LSI's May Day Appeal of 1925 'to pay honour to the memory of its great martyr'.[169] In this period, socialists launched various efforts on behalf of the victims of fascism and dictatorship, exemplified by its Matteotti Fund which, in some respects, was a counterpart to the Comintern's International Red Aid.[170] At the LSI's 1928 congress, de Brouckère warned against the fascist threat, but also mentioned the fate of political prisoners in the Soviet Union.[171] Meanwhile, the International Federation of Christian Trade Unions, headed by the Belgian Christian Democrat Henri Pauwels, 'conducted a tireless crusade against fascism'.[172]

Given the events in Nazi Germany, such efforts took on particular urgency from 1933. The Matteotti Fund organised aid efforts for German refugees, although the scale of its Belgian activities remained relatively limited.[173] In the debates on Belgian refugee policy, the BWP and the Matteotti Fund argued that political asylum should extend to German communists. In this context, the stance of Camille Huysmans – by then mayor of Antwerp – has been described as a 'radical rejection of immigration controls': he also opposed restrictions that the Belgian state had imposed on exiles' participation in the labour market.[174] Meanwhile, in light of international developments, the Comintern abandoned 'class against class' and adopted the Popular Front policy in 1934. Despite the prominence of Moscow in this decision, some scholars have stressed a degree of agency of individual Comintern members.[175] Early on, in October 1934, the French communists Maurice Thorez and Marcel Cachin met with Adler and Vandervelde to explore the potential for cooperation, albeit without tangible results.[176]

Conclusion

We cannot consider socialist internationalism in isolation. The Belgian case shows how, both within their national and international settings, the efforts of socialists overlapped with other issues: social reform, feminism, freethought and, as will be discussed in chapter 5, pacifism. Indeed, the main institutions of socialists, feminists and pacifists – the Second International, the International Council of Women and the International Peace Bureau – were all founded between 1888 and 1891. Furthermore, socialists, progressive liberals and Christian democrats collaborated on specific issues, particularly when it came to social reform and the international organisations that promoted it. This is not to say that the relationship between different kinds of internationalism was always peaceful. The polemical use of the concept of 'bourgeois feminism' was a case in point, as was the desire of some women's or peace groups to maintain respectability. Furthermore, the relationship between socialist and communist internationalism was marked by conflict, despite their shared roots in the pre-1914 period.

The leaders of the BWP were closely integrated into the international world of socialism and made important contribution to its development. Yet the First World War had a significant impact on the Belgians' capacity to act as mediators. As a result, the centre of gravity moved away from Brussels, although figures such as Vandervelde, Huysmans and de Brouckère continued to be prominent figures in the LSI. In his closing speech at the international socialist congress of 1928, Vandervelde presented an analogy that described both the role of his peers and his country. To him, the Second International and the LSI stood on different banks of the same river. Those who, like himself and his compatriots Bertrand, Anseele and Huysmans, had been involved in both Internationals served as 'a bridge between the two banks'. Vandervelde reiterated the role of Belgium as a meeting place and mediator: 'in the same way that Belgium is the hyphen between all the peoples of Western Europe, coincidence has ensured that the Belgian veterans are all alive'.[177]

Notes

1 Victor Hugo and Alexandre Dumas, 'Ils ont une grande aptitude pour les spéculations et apportent en général dans leur relations beaucoup de droiture et de loyauté', *Guide du touriste en Belgique* as cited in Paul Aron (ed.), *La Belgique artistique et littéraire: une anthologie de langue française 1848–1914* (Brussels, 1997), p. 33.

2 John Bartier, 'Belgium in 1848', in Françoi Fejtö (ed.), *The Opening of an Era, 1848* (London, 1948), pp. 160–6; Georges-Henri Dunont, *Le Miracle belge de 1848* (Brussels, 2002).

3 David McLellan, *Karl Marx: A Biography* (4th edn., Basingstoke, 2006), pp. 129–76.

4 Sabine Freitag (ed.), *Exiles from European Revolution: Refugees in Mid-Victorian England* (New York, 2003).

5 Louis Bertrand, *Souvenirs d'un meneur socialiste*, vol. 1 (Brussels, 1927), p. 81.

6 Moulaert, *Rood en zwart*, pp. 66–9; Caestecker, *Alien Policy*, p. 31.

7 Jean Stengers, *Emigration et immigration en Belgique au XIXe et au XXe siècles* (Brussels, 1978), pp. 73–4.

8 The enduring nature of this discourse is exemplified by René Maurice, *La Fugue à Bruxelles: proscrits, exilés, réfugiés et autres voyageurs. Capitale de la liberté* (Paris, 2003).

9 Leaflet of the International Workingmen's Association 'The Belgian Massacres: To the Workmen of Europe and the United States' (May 1869), reprinted in Jan Dhondt (ed.), *Geschiedenis van de Socialistische Arbeidersbeweging in België* (Antwerp, 1960), p. 282.
10 Strikwerda, 'If all of Europe were Belgium', p. 512.
11 Gita Deneckere, *Sir het volk mort: sociaal protest in België 1831–1918* (Antwerp, 1997).
12 Magaly Rodríguez García, 'Early views on internationalism: Marxist socialists vs. liberals', *RBPH–BTFG*, 84 (2006), 1070.
13 James Joll, *The Second International* (2nd edn., London, 1974), p. 187; Georges Haupt, *Programm und Wirklichkeit: Die internationale Sozialdemokratie vor 1915* (Neuwied, 1970), p. 175.
14 Christine Lattek, 'The beginnings of socialist internationalism in the 1840s: the "Democratic Friends of All Nations" in London', in Frits van Holthoon and Marcel van der Linden (eds), *Internationalism in the Labour Movement, 1830–1940* (Leiden, 1988), p. 282.
15 Marcel van der Linden, *Workers of the World: Essays Toward a Global Labour History* (Leiden, 2008), p. 270.
16 Els Witte, 'The triumph of liberalism (1848–1884)', in Craeybeckx *et al.*, *Political History of Belgium*, p. 57. Cf. D.E. Devreese, 'An inquiry into the causes and nature of organization: some observations on the International Working Men's Association, 1864–1872 /1876', in van Holthoon and van der Linden, *Internationalism in the Labour Movement*, pp. 286–8.
17 MS AMSAB, Hins (205): Hins to Stepney Cowell, 21 January 1870.
18 Moulaert, *Rood en zwart*, pp. 31–4.
19 Bertrand, *Souvenirs*, vol. 1, pp. 144–5.
20 Guy Vanschoenbeek, *Novecento in Gent: de wortels van de sociaal-democratie en Vlaanderen* (Antwerp, 1995), pp. 17–18.
21 Polasky, *Democratic Socialism of Emile Vandervelde*, p. 25. Cf. Andre Mommen, *De Belgische Wirklidenpartij: ontstaan en entwekkeling van het reformistisch socialisme (1830–1914)* (Ghent, 1980).
22 *Ibid.*, pp. 259–64.
23 Geoff Eley, *Forging Democracy: The History of the Left in Europe, 1850–2000* (Oxford, 2000), pp. 66–74.
24 Moira Donald, 'Workers of the world unite? Exploring the enigma of the Second International', in Geyer and Paulmann, *The Mechanics of Internationalism*, p. 188.
25 Secrétariat Belge, *Congrès International Ouvrier Socialiste tenu à Bruxelles du 16 au 23 août* (new edn. introduced by Michel Winock, Geneva, 1977 [1893]), p. 37.
26 *Ibid.*, p. 62.
27 *Ibid.*, p. 46.
28 Haupt, *Programm und Wirklichkeit*, p. 32.
29 *Ibid.*, p. 3.
30 Georges Haupt (ed.), *Correspondance entre Lénine et Camille Huysmans 1905–1914* (Paris, 1963), p. 12.

31 Susan Milner, *The Dilemmas of Internationalism: French Syndicalism and the International Labour Movement, 1900–1914* (New York, 1990), pp. 87 and 91.
32 Geert Van Goethem, *The Amsterdam International: The World of the International Federation of Trade Unions (IFTU), 1913–1945* (Aldershot, 2006), p. 146.
33 Joll, *Second International*, p. 159
34 G. D. H. Cole, *The Second International, 1889–1914* (London, 1956) [*A History of Socialist Thought*, vol. III], p. 643. Cf. Polasky, *Democratic Socialism of Emile Vandervelde*, p. 91.
35 Conseil général du Parti Ouvrier Belge (ed.), *75 années de domination bourgeoise 1830–1905: Essais de Camille Huysmans, Louis de Brouckère et Louis Bertrand* (Ghent, 1905).
36 Janssens, *De belgische natie viert*, p. 188.
37 Marten Van Ginderachter, *Het rode vaderland: de vergeten geschiedenis van de communautaire spanningen in het Belgisch socialisme voor WO I* (Brussels, 2005).
38 *Ibid.*, p. 141.
39 Milner, *The Dilemmas of Internationalism*, p. 230.
40 Carl Levy, 'Anarchism, internationalism and nationalism in Europe, 1860–1939', *Australian Journal of Politics and History*, 50 (2004), 331.
41 van der Linden, *Workers of the World*, p. 270.
42 Secrétariat Belge, *Congrès International Ouvrier Socialiste*, pp. 64–5.
43 Vandervelde served as rapporteur for the relevant committee at the Stuttgart congress: Polasky, *Democratic Socialism of Emile Vandervelde*, p. 114.
44 Kevin Callahan, 'The international socialist peace movement on the eve of World War I revisited: the campaign of "War against War!" and the Basle International Socialist Congress in 1912', *Peace and Change*, 29 (2004), 168.
45 Nicholas Stargardt, *The German Idea of Militarism. Radical and Socialist Critics, 1866–1914* (Cambridge, 1994), p. 155.
46 Joll, *Second International*, p. 116; Christophe Prochasson, *Les Intellectuels, le socialisme et la guerre 1900–1938* (Paris, 1993), e.g. pp. 114–17.
47 Bertrand, *Souvenirs*, vol.II, p. 224.
48 *Ibid.*, p. 226.
49 Margaret Kohn, *Radical Space: Building the House of the People* (Ithaca, NY, 2003), p. 99. Cf. Peter Scholliers, 'The social-democratic world of consumption: the path-breaking case of the Ghent cooperative Vooruit prior to 1914', *International Labor and Working-Class History*, 55 (1999), 79–91.
50 Hendrik Defoort, *Werklieden, bemint uw profijt! De Belgische sociaaldemocratie en Europa* (Ghent, 2006), pp. 39–44. Cf. Vanschoenbeek, *Novecento in Gent*, p. 71.
51 For instance, Anseele attended the international freethought congress in Antwerp (1885).
52 Defoort, *Werklieden*, p. 417.
53 Aron, *Les Écrivains belges et le socialisme (1880–1913)*, pp. 8 and 170.
54 While having traced also its limits, Defoort has concluded that the international appeal of the Belgian model of socialism existed: Defoort, *Werklieden*, p. 485. Cf. Carl Strikwerda, '"Alternative visions" and working-class culture: the political economy of consumer cooperation in Belgium, 1860–1980', in Ellen Furlough and Carl Strikwerda (eds), *Consumers against Capitalism?*

Consumer Cooperation in Europe, North America, and Japan, 1840–1990 (Oxford, 1999), pp. 67–91.

55 Secrétariat Belge, *Congrès International Ouvrier Socialiste*, pp. 131–2.

56 *Ibid.*, p. 132. Cf. Defoort, *Werklieden*, pp. 313–16.

57 Johnston Birchal, *The International Co-Operative Movement* (Manchester, 1997), p. 58.

58 On the Ghent explosions, see Moulaert, *Rood en zwart*, p. 108.

59 *Ibid.*, pp. 242–50.

60 Levy, 'Anarchism, internationalism and nationalism', p. 333.

61 David Gullentops and Hans Vandevoorde, 'Anarchiste affiniteiten: Artiesten en intellectuelen rond Emile Verhaeren', in David Gullentops and Hans Vandevoorde (eds), *Anarchisten rond Emile Verhaeren* (Brussels, 2005), p. 8.

62 Moulaert uses the word 'crypto-anarchist' in this context: Moulaert, *Rood en zwart*, p. 67.

63 Vandervelde, *Souvenirs*, p. 36. On Reclus's significance, see Moulaert, *Rood en zwart*, pp. 179–89.

64 Nelly Wilson, *Bernard-Lazare: Antisemitism and the Problems of Jewish Identity in Late Nineteenth-Century France* (Cambridge, 1978), pp. 62–3.

65 Andrée Despy-Meyer, 'Un laboratoire des idées: l'Université nouvelle de Bruxelles (1894–1919)', in Kurgan-van Hentenryk, *Laboratoires et réseaux*, pp. 51–4.

66 Guillaume De Greef, *L'Ère de la mondialité: éloge d'Elie Reclus*. (Brussels, 1906), p. 16.

67 *Ibid.*, p. 3.

68 *Ibid.*, p. 14.

69 Strikwerda, *A House Divided*, p. 230.

70 Pasture, *Histoire du syndicalisme chrétien internationale*, pp. 64–83; Michael Schneider, *Die christlichen Gewerkschaften 1894–1933* (Bonn, 1982), pp. 483–6.

71 MS IEV, Emile Vandervelde, EV/IV/618: Overbergh to Vandervelde, 25 January 1926.

72 Ginette Kurgan-van Hentenryk 'Conclusions' in Ginette Kurgan-van Hentenryk (ed.), *Un Pays si tranquille: La violence en Belgique aux XIXe siècle* (Brussels, 1999), p. 245.

73 MS IEV, Emile Vandervelde, EV/II/64: 'Allocation au congrès de Médicine légale à l'Université de Bruxelles, le mercredi 17 juillet 1935'.

74 Pierre-Yves Saunier, 'Sketches from the Urban Internationale: voluntary societies, international organizations and US foundations at the city's bedside, 1900–1960', *International Journal for Urban and Regional Research*, 25 (2001), 380–403.

75 Patrizia Dogliani, 'European municipalism in the first half of the twentieth century: the socialist network', *Contemporary European History*, 11 (2002), 577–8.

76 Oscar Gaspari, 'Cities against states? Hopes, dreams and shortcomings of the European municipal movement, 1900–1960', *Contemporary European History*, 11 (2002), 598.

77 Stefan Couperus, 'In between "vague theory" and "sound practical lines": transnational municipalism in interwar Europe', in Laqua, *Internationalism Reconfigured*, p. 70.

78 Jasmien Van Daele, *Van Gent tot Genève: Louis Varlez. Een biografie* (Ghent, 2002).
79 Strikwerda, *A House Divided*, p. 260.
80 MS AMSAB, Louis Varlez (654): 'Agenda de la Séance du Comité', no. 5.3.
81 *Ibid.*
82 Madeleine Herren, *Internationale Sozialpolitik vor dem ersten Weltkrieg: Die Anfänge europäischer Kooperation aus der Sicht Frankreichs* (Berlin, 1993).
83 Prochasson, *Les Intellectuels, le socialisme et la guerre*, pp. 122–9.
84 Letter Eric Drummond to Louis Varlez, 21 March 1920, *Ibid.*
85 Van Daele, *Van Gent tot Genève*, pp. 162–200.
86 Lex Heerma van Voss, 'The International Federation of Trade Unions and the attempt to maintain the eight-hour working day (1919–1929)', in van Holthoon and van der Linden, *Internationalism in the Labour Movement*, pp. 518–41.
87 August Bebel, *Die Frau und der Sozialismus* (Zurich, 1879). In her discussion of the Belgian case, Penn Hilden has stressed the contribution of working women to the labour movement: Patricia Penn Hilden, *Women, Work, and Politics: Belgium 1830–1914* (Oxford, 1993).
88 Secrétariat Belge, *Congrès International Ouvrier Socialiste*, pp. 84–5; Vandervelde, *Souvenirs*, p. 143. Cf. Polasky, *Democratic Socialism of Emile Vandervelde*, p. 88.
89 Zimmermann, *GrenzÜberschreitungen*, p. 159.
90 Martha Asmus, 'Die bürgerliche und proletarische Frauenbewegung', in *Der Freidenker*, 5 (1896), 17–19 and 22–3.
91 UAI *La Vie Internationale*, 1 (1912), 131.
92 Marilyn Boxer, 'Rethinking the socialist construction and international career of the concept of "bourgeois feminism"', *American Historical Review*, 111 (2007), 131–58.
93 Denise De Weerdt, *En de vrouwen? Vrouw, vrouwenbeweging en feminisme en België 1830–1960* (Ghent, 1980); Julie Carlier, 'Moving Beyond Boundaries: An Entangled History of Feminism in Belgium 1890–1914 (PhD thesis, Ghent, 2010).
94 *Ibid.*, pp. 58–72.
95 Mieke Arts and Myriam Everard, 'Forgotten intersections: Wilhelmina Drucker, early feminism and the Dutch-Belgian connection', *RBPH–BTFG*, 77 (1999), 440–71.
96 Carlier, 'Moving Beyond Boundaries', p. 91.
97 *Ibid.*, p. 229.
98 Bonnie Anderson, *Joyous Greetings: The First International Women's Movement 1830–1860* (Oxford, 2000), p. 158.
99 Eliane Gubin, Valérie Piette and Catherine Jacques, 'Les féminismes belges et français de 1880 à 1914: une approche comparée', *Le Mouvement Social*, 178 (1997), 36–68.
100 Leila Rupp, 'The making of international women's organizations', in Geyer and Paulmann, *The Mechanics of Internationalism*, p. 211.
101 Carlier, 'Moving Beyond Boundaries', p. 121.
102 Leila Rupp, *Worlds of Women: The Making of an International Women's Movement* (Princeton, NJ, 1997), p. 22.
103 On the ambiguous relationship between French freethought and the women's movement, see Lalouette, *La Libre Pensée en France*, pp. 96–8; on the British case, see Royle, *Radicals, Secularists and Republicans*, pp. 246–50.

104 Altmann, 'Der internationale Freidenker-Kongress in Paris vom 17., 18. u. 19. September 1900. Vorbericht', *Der Freidenker*, 8 (1900), 153–4.
105 With reference to Eliane Gubin's work: Kurgan-van Hentenryk, 'Introduction', in Kurgan-van Hentenryk, *Laboratoires et réseaux*, p. 12.
106 Denise De Weerdt, 'Bread and roses: pragmatic women in the Belgium [sic] Workers' Party', in Helmut Gruber and Pamela Graves (eds), *Women and Socialism, Socialism and Women: Europe Between the Two World Wars* (New York, 1998), p. 240.
107 *Ibid.*, 241.
108 *Report of the Third Women's International Conference of the Labour and Socialist International* (London, 1928), pp. 10 and 34–5.
109 David Kirby, 'Zimmerwald and the origins of the Third International' in Tim Rees and Andrew Thorpe (eds), *International Communism and the Communist International 1919–1943* (Manchester, 1998), pp. 15–30; R. Craig Nation, *War on War: Lenin, the Zimmerwald Left, and the Origins of Communist Internationalism* (Durham, NC, 1989).
110 Mieke Claeys-Van Haegendoren, *25 jaar Belgisch Socliasme: evolutie van der verhouding van de Belgische Werkliedenpartij tot de parlementaire deomcratie in Belgïe van 1914 tot 1940* (Antwerp, 1967), pp. 77–90.
111 Bertrand, *Souvenirs*, vol. II, p. 230.
112 Polasky, *Democratic Socialism of Emile Vandervelde*, pp. 144–5.
113 *Ibid.,* pp. 98 and 229.
114 Vandervelde, *Souvenirs*, p. 200.
115 *Ibid.*, p. 97 and 281.
116 MS LSI 2.2: Vandervelde and de Brouckère to Henderson, 19 August 1918.
117 MS LSI 2.2: Henderson to Vandervelde, 18 November 1918.
118 MS LSI 2.2: Vandervelde to Henderson, 13 December 1918.
119 Sally Marks, *Paul Hymans: Makers of the Modern World. The Peace Conferences of 1919–23 and Their Aftermath* (London, 2010), pp. 52–3.
120 Karl Kautsky, *Die Internationalität und der Krieg* (Berlin, 1915), pp. 36–7.
121 MS LSI 5.4: 'Belgian Socialists and the Peace Terms' (Reuters), 5 June 1919.
122 Beryl Haslam, *From Suffrage to Internationalism: The Political Evolution of Three British Feminists, 1908–1939* (New York, 1999), p. xx.
123 MS WILPF, reel 56: Jane Brigode to Aletta Jacobs, 22 January 1919. Jacobs's invitation had been sent on 24 November 1914.
124 *Ibid.,* Brigode to Jacobs, 24 January 1919.
125 *Ibid.,* Jacobs to Brigode, 13 February 1919. On this episode and its wider context, see Annika Wilmers, *Pazifismus in der internationalen Frauenbewegung (1914–1920): Handlungsspielräume, politische Konzeptionen und gesellscahftliche Auseinandersetzungen* (Essen, 2008), pp. 181–3.
126 Women's Peace Party, *Report of the International Congress of Women. The Hague, The Netherlands. April 28th to May 1st, 1915* (Chicago, 1915), p. 5. On Belgian feminists' ambivalent position regarding the congress, see Wilmers, *Pazifismus*, e.g. pp. 40–6 and 106–8.
127 Linda Schott, *Reconstructing Women's Thoughts: The Women's International League for Peace and Freedom Before World War II* (Stanford, CA, 1997).

128 Gubin *et al.*, 'Les féminismes belges', p. 59.
129 MS WILPF, reel 57: Esther Chalmers to Gertrud Baer, 22 February 1937.
130 MS WILPF, reel 56: letters by Léonie La Fontaine, 9 November 1927, and Esther Chalmers, December 1927 (undated).
131 MS WILPF, reel 56: letter to Liège branch, 21 December 1927.
132 Polasky, *Democratic Socialism of Emile Vandervelde*, p. 193.
133 Friedrich Adler, *Die Besetzung des Ruhrgebiets und die Internationale: Nach einer Rede, gehalten am 14. Februar 1923 in the Wiener Konferenz der sozialdemokratischen Vertrauensmänner* (Vienna, 1923), p. 3.
134 Polasky, *Democratic Socialism of Emile Vandervelde*, p. 199.
135 MS LSI 15.4: Motion of the Dutch Social Democratic Party.
136 G. D. H. Cole, *Communism and Social Democracy, 1914–1931* (London, 1958), p. 697.
137 MS LSI 15.2: letter exchange between Adler and Henderson, 13 September, 2 October and 10 October 1927.
138 *The Congress of the Labour and Socialist International, Brussels, 5th to 11th August 1928: Reports and Proceedings*, vol. 1: *Reports of the Secretariat of the Labour and Socialist International*, section IV (London, 1928), p. 17.
139 MS LSI 15.2: Adler to Van Roosbroeck, 5 October 1927.
140 MS LSI 15.2: *International Information published for press use by the Secretariat of the Labour and Socialist International*, 5, 6 (28 February 1928).
141 Mary Hilson, 'A Consumers' International? The International Cooperative Alliance and cooperative internationalism: a Nordic perspective', *International Review of Social History*, 56 (2011), 203–33.
142 MS AMSAB, 'Internationale Tentoonstelling voor Cooperatie en Sociale Werken' (231): letter of 18 January 1924.
143 Christophe Verbruggen and Lewis Pyenson, 'History and the history of science in the work of Hendrik de Man', *BTNG–RBHC*, 41 (2011), 490.
144 *Ibid.*, 496.
145 *Ibid.*, 493.
146 Donald Sassoon, *One Hundred Years of Socialism: The West European Left in the Twentieth Century* (rev. edn., London, 2010), p. 67.
147 Bernard Rulof, 'Selling social democracy in the Netherlands: activism and its sources of inspiration during the 1930s', *Contemporary European History*, 18 (2009), 475–97; Gerd-Rainer Horn, 'From "radical" to "realistic": Hendrik de Man and the International Plan Conferences at Pontigny and Geneva, 1934–1937', *Contemporary European History*, 10 (2001), 239–65; Dirk Pels, 'Hendrik de Man and the ideology of Planism', *International Review of Social History*, 32 (1987), 206–29.
148 Polasky, *Democratic Socialism of Emile Vandervelde*, p. 222.
149 Gerrit Voerman, 'From Lenin's comrades in arms to "Dutch donkeys": the Communist Party in the Netherlands and the Comintern in the 1920s', in Rees and Thorpe, *International Communism and the Commmunist International*, p. 127.
150 Marcel Libman, 'Les Origines et la fondation du Parti Communiste de Belgique' *C.R.I.S.P., Courrier Hebdomadaire*, 12 avril 1963, p. 6; *Programme de l'Action Socialiste-Révolutionnaire en Belgique présenté au IIIe Congrès des 'Amis de l'Exploité'* (Brussels, 1921).

151 Andreas Wirsching, 'The impact of "Bolshevization" and "Stalinzation" on French and German Communism: a comparative view', in Norman La Porte *et al.* (eds), *Bolshevism, Stalinism and the Comintern: Perspectives on Stalinization, 1917–59* (Basingstoke, 2008), pp. 89–104.
152 José Gotovitch, *Du communisme et des communistes en Belgique: approches critiques* (Brussels, 2012), p. 64.
153 *Ibid.*, p. 64.
154 Camille Huysmans, 'Preface', in Haupt, *Correspondance*, p. 10.
155 *Reports of the Secretariat of the Labour and Socialist International*, section II, p. 45.
156 *Ibid.*, section IV, p. 18.
157 Gotovitch, *Du communisme et des communistes*, p. 45.
158 José Gotovitch, *Du rouge au tricolore: les communistes belges de 1939 à 1944. Un aspect de l'histoire de la Résistance en Belgique* (Brussels, 1992), p. 15.
159 *Ibid.*, p. 61.
160 *Ibid.*, p. 63.
161 MS UIA: 'Annuaire': 'Invitation au Congrès international contre l'oppression colonial et l'impérialisme'.
162 On Duchêne, see Emanuelle Carle, 'Women, anti-fascism and peace in interwar France: Gabrielle Duchêne's itinerary', *French History*, 18 (2004), 291–314.
163 'Le Congrès anticolonial et le Congo', *L'Indépendence Belge* (17 March 1927, 24 March 1927, 14 April 1927).
164 *Reports of the Secretariat of the LSI*, vol. 1, part II, p. 47.
165 *The Colonial Problem: Material submitted to the IIIrd Congress of the Labour and Socialist International* (Brussels, 1928).
166 'The Resolutions of the Congress of the Labour and Socialist International, 5th–11th August 1925', *Bulletin of the Labour and Socialist International* (September 1928), p. 11.
167 *Ibid.*, pp. 12–13.
168 *Third Congress of the Labour and Socialist International, Brussels, 5th to 11th August 1928. Reports and Proceedings*, vol. 3: *Proceedings of the Congress*, part VI (London, 1928), p. 20.
169 *Reports of the Secretariat*, part I, p. 19.
170 Cf. the contributions by Claudia Natoli and Bruno Groppo in José Gotovitch and Anne Morelli (eds), *Les Solidarités internationales: histoire et perspectives* (Brussels, 2003).
171 *Proceedings of the Congress*, part VI, pp. 127–32.
172 Patrick Pasture, 'The temptations of nationalism: regionalist orientations in the Belgian Christian labour movement', in Patrick Pasture and Johan Verberckmoes (eds), *Working-Class Internationalism and the Appeal of National Identity: Historical Debates and Current Perspectives on Western Europe* (Oxford, 1998), p. 119.
173 Frank Caestecker, 'Het reel bestaande socialisme in West-Eurpoa en de vlucht uit Nazi-Duitsland, 1933–1934: en oefening in private international solidariteit', *BEG–CHTP*, 15 (2005), 115–19.
174 *Ibid.*, 113.

175 Guillaume Bourgeois, 'French Communism and the Communist International', in Rees and Thorpe, *International Communism and the Communist International*, p. 97. Cf. Julian Jackson, *The Popular Front in France: Defending Democracy, 1934–1938* (Cambridge, 1988), pp. 17–51.

176 Gotovitch, *Du communisme et des communistes*, p. 78.

177 *Proceedings of the Congress*, part VI, p. 170.

5

Peace

Belgians had a vested interest in a world order based on the international rule of law, given their country's location between France and Germany. Belgian independence had bred antagonisms and border disputes with the Netherlands that lasted well into the 1920s. To avoid international rivalry over Belgium, the country's independence was tied to perpetual neutrality – a formula adopted at Aix-la-Chapelle in 1831 and cemented in 1839 through the Treaty of London. This 'imposed neutrality' was soon integrated into the country's political discourse; before the First World War, domestic debates on an abandonment of neutrality remained temporary episodes.[1] Neutrality meant that the kingdom's existence was tied to a concept in international law. In the 1860s, Emile Banning viewed the kingdom's 'neutralisation' as the making of a European vocation.[2] Three decades later, Edouard Descamps published a detailed study in which he portrayed neutrality as one aspect of 'our modern international constitution', which was influenced by the country's location and its 'international physiognomy'.[3]

The Belgian case reveals the interaction between different visions of international order, transnational activism and diplomacy. In Belgium, the seemingly pragmatic efforts of officials and scholars overlapped with the campaigns of peace activists. This chapter therefore approaches the engagement with questions of peace and international organisation at different levels and traces them across the First World War. It shows how support for the aims of peace groups cut across the political spectrum, based on the understanding that internationalism and national interest were compatible.

International law

In its early guises, international law was linked with the creation and regulation of post-war order, as exemplified by the Peace of Westphalia (1648), the Treaty of Utrecht (1713) and the Congress of Vienna (1814–15). However, even prior to the nineteenth century, diplomatic measures were complemented by ambitious intellectual projects such as the Abbé de Saint-Pierre's *Plan for*

Perpetual Peace in Europe of 1713 and Immanuel Kant's treatise *On Perpetual Peace* of 1795.[4] Whereas Kant's approach has often been described as 'cosmopolitan', Pierre Laberge has claimed that 'Kant would have understood the term "international society" in an internationalist sense; his "law of nations" deals with the rules of international society as a society of states'.[5] Interpreted in this way, Kant's vision was not dissimilar from the views espoused by scholars and activists a century later. As Sandi Cooper has observed, 'legal internationalists' in the nineteenth century rarely talked 'about the establishment of a single international government to substitute for or embrace all the national sovereign states'.[6]

The acceptance of national sovereignty did not, however, signify an embrace of the status quo. Whereas European diplomacy between the post-Napoleonic era and the Great War was dominated by a pentarchy of 'great powers', internationalists tended to denounce the concept of an 'aristocracy of states', formulating alternative visions of world order around a core belief in the equalising and pacifying impact of international law. By the mid-nineteenth century, many agreed that durable peace could be achieved by the legal anchoring of international norms. In 1873, these views received an institutional home at the Institute of International Law in Ghent and at the Association for the Reform and Codification of the Law of Nations in Brussels. The Ghent institute was an important forum for legal scholars; its prominent founders included the Italian politician Pasquale Mancini, the Heidelberg-based academic Jean-Gaspar Bluntschli, the US lawyer David Dudley Field and the Argentinian author Charles Calvo. The Belgian members – notably Gustave Rolin-Jaequemyns, Emile de Laveleye, Edouard Descamps, Ernest Nys and, later, Charles De Visscher – were renowned figures in their field; Rolin-Jaequemyns also founded the influential *Revue de Droit international et de Legislation comparée*.[7] Martti Koskenniemi views the history of the institute and its *Revue* as 'narratives of (relative) failure' since their further-ranging aspirations were soon replaced by a focus on technical questions.[8] However, members of the Institute of International Law continued to inform wider debates on peace and arbitration. In 1904, the organisation was awarded the Nobel Peace Prize. Its then president, the Norwegian prime minister George Francis Hagerup, described its activities as 'the basis necessary for all pacifistic work'.[9] At the same time, he distanced himself from 'utopian' schemes, asserting 'that the truly pacifistic movement has no more dangerous enemies than those who believe that they can anticipate natural developments and who try to persuade people to tackle the lofty summit of universal peace by a sort of "flight of Icarus" which would inevitably end … as sadly as did Icarus himself'.[10]

International law also held a more prosaic promise: the potential to address the challenges of global interdependence. Alongside general rules for international life, it could create new institutional structures: so-called 'public international unions' or 'public administrative unions'.[11] As a French observer put it in 1910, 'the nations have agreed to do together what they would do less well if they were isolated, or even to do things together which they would not be able to do alone'.[12] Health and medicine were spheres in which these efforts flourished early on, as reflected in the establishment of a Supreme Health Council at Constantinople in 1838 and the Sanitary Conventions of 1892 and 1903. From 1907, the International Office of Public Hygiene provided 'a remarkably effective instrument for its limited purposes'.[13] The struggle against epidemics and for the improvement of sanitary conditions depended on knowledge exchange and political action. Even at events that were not diplomatic conferences, officials often mingled with reformers and experts. This interplay was evident at several international congresses in Belgium, for instance on the prophylaxis of syphilis and venereal diseases (1899 and 1902) and on hygiene and demography (1909).[14]

Transnational cooperation was particularly pertinent in the fields of transport, communication and in economic affairs. The cross-border functioning of railways, telegraphs and postal services required collaborative efforts by experts and governmental agencies and necessitated the introduction of international standards. Between the 1860s and the 1890s, international conferences created the International Telegraphic Bureau, the Universal Postal Union and the International Union of Railway Freight Transportation, all based in Switzerland. The linkages between this form of internationalism and economic life were obvious: the Metre Convention and the International Bureau of Weights and Measures (1875–76), for example, were designed to facilitate international trade.[15] In many cases, such organisations continued their work during the Great War and, as Madeleine Herren has pointed out, even received subsidies from occupied Belgium.[16] Transnational economic links also formed the backdrop to conventions on patent rights (1883) and the protection of literary works (1886), and to the foundation of bureaus that collected and disseminated information on these agreements.[17]

Belgium hosted a variety of international congresses and offices. Intergovernmental institutions included the Sugar Union (1902), the Bureau on the Formulae of Potent Drugs (1920), the International Union for the Publication of Customs Tariffs (1890) and, as discussed in chapter 2, the Special Bureau Against the Slave Trade. The country was also the site for negotiations regarding the maritime trade and maritime law.[18] The case of the Sugar Union illustrates the long path towards the creation of international bureaus: from the 1860s, governments had sought to address the problem of export bounties for beet sugar. In a global economy with decreasing tariff barriers, these subsidies increased government expenditure, precipitated a slump in global sugar prices and damaged plantation economies in the Caribbean. At a diplomatic conference in Paris in 1863, France, Britain,

Belgium and Holland pledged themselves to prohibit sugar bounties. Further conferences followed in the 1870s, but no agreement was ratified and some countries – notably Germany – did not participate.[19] At subsequent meetings in London (1887), Vienna (1895) and Brussels (1896), delegates were under pressure from business groups and free-trade advocates.[20] Yet it was only in 1902 that a conference in Brussels agreed on an international convention, suppressing all direct and indirect bonuses on beet sugar. This document 'seems to have been the first international agreement on the sale of a primary commodity'.[21] The convention also established an office to supervise the international sugar economy and investigate whether illegal bonuses continued. Sugar bounties were to incur punitive duties, thus offsetting the advantages gained through them. In a contemporary analysis of 'public international unions', Paul Reinsch described the Brussels-based body as 'the only international organ which has a right, through its determinations and decisions, to cause a direct modification of the laws existing in the individual treaty states, within the dispositions of the convention'.[22] However, Britain soon decided to withdraw from the agreement, which by 1908 'had lost almost all its significance',[23] even though a re-negotiated version came into force in 1913. As such examples show, international law could indeed create new patterns of cooperation – yet the structures that it established were sometimes transient.

Pacifism

The term 'pacifism' was a neologism coined in 1901. Having made one of its earliest appearances in the newspaper *L'Indépendance Belge*, it did not denote a complete rejection of military conflict and often centred on a strengthening of international norms.[24] It is in this broader sense that the term is used in this chapter, although Martin Ceadel has suggested 'pacificism' as a more appropriate label for stances that accepted military conflict in some circumstances.[25] Underlining the centrality of international law in this context, the leading pacifist organisation in France was named 'La Paix par le Droit' from 1899. It briefly had a small Belgian sister organisation, the 'Ligue pour la Paix par le Droit'.[26] In the Netherlands, the largest peace society adopted the same leitmotif when adopting the name 'Vrede door Recht'. In viewing international law as prophylaxis or cure, the peace activists of the Belle Époque embraced an instrument that governments had already employed for other areas of international life.

The cause of peace was inherently transnational, yet peace activists were slow to establish international structures. In London, the World Anti-Slavery Convention of 1843 was directly followed by an international peace congress. Further contacts led to a series of peace congresses that started in Brussels in 1848, at the time of Europe's revolutionary upheavals. Supported by the liberal government of Charles Rogier and organised by the American activist Elihu Burritt, the Brussels gathering primarily drew Belgian, British and American delegates. The event's focus on free trade reflected the influence of the British radical Richard Cobden, who was a participant.[27] Indeed, a Belgian free trade association with international activities of its own had existed since 1847.[28] The 1848 Brussels congress was followed by a Parisian event in 1849. Supported by Cobden, Giuseppe Mazzini and the Archbishop of Paris, it attracted 700 British, 200 French, 21 Belgian and 20 American participants as well as 30 individuals from other countries.[29] It was on this occasion that Victor Hugo launched his famous call for a 'United States of Europe'. After further events in Frankfurt (1850) and London (1851), this initiative lost momentum, linked to the demise of revolutionary movements and the rise of international tensions that culminated in the Crimean War.

Sustained efforts to place international pacifism on an institutional footing resumed in the late 1860s. In 1867 Charles Lemonnier founded the Ligue Internationale de la Paix et de la Liberté as the first 'international' peace organisation; its Geneva congress has been described as 'the largest peace congress of the nineteenth century'.[30] In the same year, the French economist Frédéric Passy launched the Ligue Internationale et Permanente de la Paix. His attempt to build a broad coalition was rejected by protagonists of the First International, including César De Paepe, who deemed separate peace associations unnecessary.[31] Meanwhile, the Brussels-based International Social Science Association (Association Internationale pour le Progrès des Sciences Sociales) treated the causes of social reform and peace as interrelated.[32] In the 1880s, a British activist, Hogson Pratt, founded another body with an international remit: the International Arbitration and Peace Association. While the German resonance for his efforts remained limited,[33] Belgian support proved more extensive. In 1881, Brussels hosted its international congress, described by the historian Sandi Cooper as 'a serious and thoughtful affair'.[34] In 1889, activists created the Belgian Arbitration and Peace Society (BAPS, Société Belge de l'Arbitrage et de la Paix) as a branch of Pratt's society. Led by Emile de Laveleye, it became the most significant Belgian peace association. Another key member, the liberal deputy Auguste Couvreur, had previously been involved in the International Social Science Association, which had disintegrated around two decades earlier.

In the BAPS founding year, another event – namely a congress in Paris – stimulated closer transnational ties between pacifists. Held in changing cities, the Universal Peace Congresses became major occasions for the peace movement; from 1891, they were coordinated by the International Peace Bureau (IPB) in Bern. While national affiliates paid subscription fees, the bureau also supported them, as reflected in subsidies for the BAPS in 1906 and 1912.[35] The IPB's centrality for transnational peace activism was acknowledged with the Nobel Peace Prize of 1910 – and indeed, several of its members gained this accolade themselves. The Belgians de Laveleye and La Fontaine were involved in the IPB from the start, with the latter serving as its president from 1907 to 1943. In 1913, he gained a Nobel Prize for his work on the IPB – although the public response to his award was relatively limited and mostly focused on the financial implications.[36]

How did Belgium fit into the international picture? Nadine Lubelski-Bernard, whose unpublished doctoral thesis remains the most detailed study of Belgian pre-1914 peace activism, has concluded that the country 'never spearheaded the pacifist movement in Europe'.[37] It is also clear that Belgian peace organisations did not constitute mass organisations. The average membership of the BAPS between 1889 and 1900 is likely to have been around 450. Even if one adds up the members of different peace organisations, the overall number on the eve of the First World War barely exceeded 3,000.[38] Weakness in numbers was not a Belgian peculiarity: few European peace societies were mass organisations. Yet in terms of access to political authorities and the media, Belgian pacifism was rather strong. Whereas pacifists in countries such as Germany were divided into socialist and 'bourgeois' camps, the links between Belgium's progressive liberals, socialists and reform-minded Catholics facilitated cooperation on peace matters.[39] In its early years, the BAPS included socialists such as Edouard Anseele, Emile Vandervelde and Hector Denis, as well as progressive liberals such as Auguste Houzeau de Lehaie and Georges Lorand. Among Catholics, representation – while more limited – manifested itself in the involvement of Edouard Descamps. The Sixth Universal Peace Congress, which took place in Antwerp in 1894, exemplified the numerous connections of Belgian peace activists. Organised by La Fontaine, the congress patrons included individuals such as the industrialist Ernest Solvay, the Senator Levi Montifiore, the former Catholic Minister of Justice Jules Lejeune, the liberal politician Paul Janson and the mayor of Brussels Charles Buls.[40] The city of Antwerp provided free use of the conference venue and organised a reception at the town hall. More than a decade later, many supporters of this congress were still involved in pacifist activity: for instance, when the BAPS organised an event at the Hôtel Ravenstein in May 1907, Houzeau de Lehaie, Lejeune and La Fontaine all contributed.[41]

If one goes beyond mere membership numbers, the strengths of Belgian pacifism become more apparent. For instance, in 1895–96, three French pacifists – Gaston Moch, Charles Richet and Emile Arnaud – invested in *L'Indépendance Belge*, with the industrialist Ernest Solvay also taking a stake.[42] The aim was to turn the newspaper into a pacifist publication. When the Universal Peace Congress at Monaco discussed the creation of a 'great pacifist daily' in 1902, the newspaper's editor wrote to the IPB, stressing that 'the daily pacifist newspaper exists, it prospers and is distributed over the entire world in its three editions: daily, international and overseas; this newspaper is *L'Indépendance Belge* which for many years has supported the peace movement and has always been a supporter of international arbitration'.[43] As evidence, the author cited the newspaper's pacifist contributors, but also the fact that it had been the sole European newspaper to send a correspondent to the Monaco congress and cover its debates: 'Our columns are always open for all communications of general interest with regard to pacifist groups, their work and their efforts'. However, this period in the newspaper's history was characterised by financial losses and attacks from French nationalists.[44]

Both in Belgium and internationally, organised freethought provided an alternative vehicle for the dissemination of pacifist ideas. In 1909, Raphaël Rens, a Belgian activist in the International Freethought Federation, praised freethought as arguably 'the most solid column of pacifism'.[45] Yakov Novikov – whose work on *War and Its Alleged Benefits* had a profound impact on European pacifism – attended the 1904 congress in Rome.[46] In 1912, the international freethought congress in Munich described pacifist activities as a 'civilisational necessity' and urged freethinkers to strengthen their efforts in this field.[47] Several national groups took up these demands: for instance, in 1913, French freethinkers placed pacifism on the agenda of their national congress.[48] In December that year, the Libre Pensée de Bruxelles convened a special assembly at which it echoed the Munich resolution: it linked pacifism to the anticlerical cause, claiming 'that the churches have never done anything to prevent wars, that on the contrary, the belligerents of all Nations endeavour to implore their God for the success of their armies, and that it is precisely the reactionary and clerical parties that depend on militarism'.[49] Several months earlier, the organisation's then president, Guillaume De Greef, had expressed his optimism about the decreasing likelihood of war and the prospects for freethought: 'The Nation-State has become international, an international society is developing and the thinking of the latter can only be scientific and positive.'[50]

The pronouncements by Rens, De Greef and the Libre Pensée de Bruxelles suggest that pacifism was part of the reformist setting in which progressive liberals and moderate socialists interacted. Indeed, alongside his pacifist efforts, La Fontaine remained a member of the Libre Pensée de Bruxelles and took a key role in the Masonic lodge Les Amis Philanthropes. Another group often linked to freethought – secular school teachers – also engaged in peace campaigning. Charles Rossignol, for instance, was both a BAPS activist and leader of a Tournai-based international organisation of primary-school teachers. Indeed, an International Congress of Primary Education in 1905 had expressed the wish that primary-school teachers would become 'ardent propagandists of peace and fraternity'.[51] At a local level, schools could engage in pacifist propaganda, as illustrated by reports about the 'peace events' organised in 1908 and 1909 by a primary school in the West Flemish city of Roeselare.[52]

Feminism connected with peace activism, too. As part of an international organisation led by French activists, the Alliance Belge des Femmes pour la Paix par l'Éducation was founded in Antwerp in 1906, claiming nearly 1,000 members by 1914.[53] The organisation's driving force was Marie Rosseels, who also contributed to feminist pacifism at the international level. Domestically, as the historian Julie Carlier has noted, the organisation was 'firmly embedded in the same social reformist circles in which feminists moved'.[54] For instance, the honorary president of the Alliance, Florence-Ethel de Laveleye, daughter-in-law of Emile, regarded 'pacifism, temperance, and feminism… [as] connected causes'.[55] Belgian activists were involved in international endeavours, for instance a petition campaign which, however, had 'little success' and was ultimately interrupted by the war.[56] It is worth noting the interplay between pacifism, feminism and women's activism in this context. Leonie La Fontaine, for instance, headed the peace section of the National Council of Belgian Women, but also spoke at BAPS events and, in cooperation with her brother Henri, founded a Central Office of Female Documentation in 1909.[57] Meanwhile, the Alliance Belge des Femmes pour la Paix par l'Éducation held events with peace activists such as Emile Arnaud and Albert Marinus.[58]

Just as feminism was not a prerogative of the secular left, pacifism was not confined to the overlapping circles of freethinkers, progressive liberals and socialists. Contrary to the claims of the Libre Pensée de Bruxelles, many Belgian Catholics were sympathetic to the pacifist cause. The Catholic cabinet that succeeded the liberals in 1884 was led by politicians whom the historian Ernst Kossmann described as 'violent antimilitarists'.[59] Charles Woeste – leader of the Catholic Party's conservative wing – expressed such views even vis-à-vis politicians with whom he had little ideological common ground. In 1899, he congratulated Houzeau de Lehaeie and La Fontaine for 'their brave efforts for the cause of peace between civilised nations'. He incited them to go even further: 'if at least the progress of armaments was stopped and if one decided seriously to organise international arbitration, a great step would have been taken towards the realisation of the dearest wish of all friends of humanity.'[60] In the subsequent decade, the growth of Catholic lay activism both nationally and internationally was reflected in the creation of the International League of Catholic Pacifists. These international developments inspired a Belgian association. Founded in 1911, the Ligue des Catholiques Belges pour la Paix adhered to the IPB and claimed around 1,600 members soon after its foundation.[61] These are small numbers compared with the large-scale organisations that Catholic activists had established in other areas. However, the organisation was supported by leading politicians such as Auguste Beernaert, Gérard Cooreman and Henry Carton de Wiart and thus connected to the political and associational worlds of Catholic Belgium.

From 1911, Belgian pacifists sought to coordinate their action across different organisations. With support from the likes of Charles Rossignol and Albert Marinus, La Fontaine organised a national peace congress in 1913. Houzeau de Lehaie acted as president, whereas Marie Rosseels, the socialist Emile Royer and Georges Rutten – whom chapter 3 has introduced as a key figure in political Catholicism – were vice-presidents.[62] Lubelski-Bernard has stressed the way in which the event transcended traditional party lines: 'In this small country where the political passions are so great, liberals, Catholics and socialists have silenced their disagreements for two days so as to study together the problems posed for the maintenance of peace'.[63] The event resulted in the foundation of a Permanent Delegation of Peace Societies.

Arbitration

The promotion of international law intersected with wider pacifist propaganda in one major way: the idea that arbitration could help to avert or resolve conflicts. In 1888, Randal Cremer and Frédéric Passy initiated the Inter-Parliamentary Conferences, bringing together parliamentarians who shared many of the peace movement's concerns, but focused on the most respectable area, namely international legal mechanisms. The Inter-Parliamentary Union (IPU), which organised these events, has therefore been viewed as an 'intermediary between pacifists and diplomats'.[64] Inter-Parliamentary Conference and Universal Peace Congresses often took place in the same city and in quick succession, allowing delegates to attend both events. These gatherings furthered plans for arbitration mechanisms: in 1893, the Universal Peace Congress in Chicago set up a committee to elaborate the statute for a Permanent Court of Arbitration.[65] The same year, a meeting of the IPU bureau in Brussels prepared a draft treaty for international arbitration, presented by Houzeau de Lehaie. The text also formed the basis of a memorandum that Edouard Descamps addressed to the European powers.[66]

In Belgium, arbitration attracted broad political support: by 1914, 80 per cent of Belgian deputies had joined the IPU.[67] Between 1911 and 1914, the IPU bureau operated from Brussels, partly because its Danish secretary-general Christian Lange appreciated the city's 'international atmosphere'.[68] Prior to this move, Brussels had hosted the Inter-Parliamentary Conferences of 1897, 1905 and 1910. Furthermore, from 1899 until his death in 1912, Auguste Beernaert served as IPU president, a commitment that was rewarded with the Nobel Peace Prize of 1909. As a former prime minister (1884–94), Beenaert provided the supporters of arbitration with a voice in the highest echelons of

Belgian politics. While in government, he had shown his ability for compromise, for instance during debates on the introduction of universal male suffrage in 1893. His contemporary Henri Pirenne described him as 'a man who would have been seated at the centre, if there had still been a centre in the Belgian chambers'.[69] This legacy meant that in his subsequent campaign for arbitration, Beernaert could collaborate with other political groups. There was significant overlap between the membership and demands of the Inter-Parliamentary Union and the BAPS: as Lubelski-Bernard has argued, the society 'maintained one aspect of its programme, arbitration, and abandoned the other, disarmament'.[70] Its demands thus remained in line with the views promoted by the Inter-Parliamentary Union.

Pacifists responded enthusiastically when the first Hague Peace Conference in 1899 brought together the representatives of twenty-six governments to discuss arbitration and rules for the conduct of war. Leo Tolstoy praised the initiative and likened the abolition of war to the abolition of slavery. The leading German freethought periodical published his essay on this subject, exemplifying the alliances constituted by this cause.[71] Authorities in Massachusetts and Ohio asked schools to commemorate 18 May, the day on which the conference had been opened.[72] In Belgium, the BAPS launched a 'Peace Crusade' and asked mayors to back this undertaking.[73] The Dutch city experienced an influx of diplomats and legal experts, but also activists such as William Stead and Bertha von Suttner. Many stalwarts of legal internationalism and the Inter-Parliamentary Conferences were associated with this diplomatic event: for instance, the Belgian legal expert Edouard Rolin-Jaequemyns acted as *rapporteur* to the Conference's Second Commission, and Beernaert headed his country's delegation. At The Hague, Beernaert went so far as to ignore his government's instructions, favouring compulsory arbitration in contrast to the official Belgian position; as a result, he was stripped of his powers.[74]

The Hague Conference established a Permanent Court of Arbitration, issued declarations on the use of weaponry, extended the Geneva Convention of 1864 and passed a convention prohibiting the launch of projectiles and explosives from balloons. The successor event – held at The Hague in 1907 – broadened some of the rules adopted in 1899, yet failed to halt the arms race or render arbitration compulsory. As with its predecessor, important impulses had come from the Inter-Parliamentary Union, whose 1905 conference in Brussels had prepared a model treaty.[75] At their 1907 congress, freethinkers criticised the Second Hague Peace Conference for seeking to modernise warfare rather than outlawing it – echoing a critique that was widespread among pacifists.[76] Nonetheless, the French internationalist Léon Bourgeois viewed the event as the birth of a *société des nations* and pointed at successful applications of the rules adopted at The Hague.[77] Even in the midst of war, the British radical J. A. Hobson remained confident that the two conferences would 'rank in history as genuine and important contributions to constructive internationalism'.[78]

War

Among some segments of Belgian society, the embrace of a neutral foreign policy went hand in hand with hostility to the military: socialists viewed the army as a reactionary institution while Flemish activists resented the dominance of the French language in the military.[79] Furthermore, as late as 1912, the Catholic Party still ran on an antimilitarist platform. In the face of mounting international tensions, the Catholic prime minister Charles de Brocqueville increased the military budget and abolished exemptions granted under the old conscription law of 1902. However, these measures came too late to make for effective defence in 1914.[80]

To many internationalists, the German attack on Belgium represented an assault on internationalism: after all, it was the internationally enshrined principle of neutrality on whose grounds de Broqueville's government rejected the German note of August 1914. Many pacifists and feminists from Britain, the Dominions and Italy supported the war effort against the Central Powers because of the violation of Belgian neutrality.[81] Seen from this angle, Belgium itself became an internationalist cause: according to the Brussels-born French politician Paul Deschanel, the country had turned into 'the pledge of International Righteousness'.[82] After the war, Deschanel co-edited a newspaper issue on behalf of the French Associations against Enemy Propaganda, praising the moral accomplishments and moral fortitude of 'Loyal and Courageous Belgium'.[83] In Russia, a pamphlet on *The Belgian Victim* (1914) as well as the 'extraordinary stop-motion film' *Lily of Belgium* depicted the German invaders in drastic terms, and Emile Verhaeren's poem *La Belgique sanglante* (1915) appeared in translation.[84] As Sophie de Schaepdrijver has put it, the country's name 'became shorthand for the moral issues of the war'.[85]

Sympathy for 'brave little Belgium' was not a purely spontaneous act. In Britain, Belgium became 'the essential instrument of English propaganda'.[86] This dimension was evident during Lord Bryce's enquiry into claims about German war crimes and the widely translated publication of his report in 1915.[87] Germany launched a propagandistic counter-offensive: funded by the German authorities, *The Continental Times* – a newspaper which, prior to the war, had catered for British and American expatriates – ran items such as 'The Myth of the Destruction of Louvain Exploded!' or 'Americans Acknowledge German Civility'.[88] The public efforts from different sides were exemplified by the German White Book of 1915, with its accusations against Belgian *francs-tireurs* and the subsequent Belgian *Livre Gris* of 1916.[89]

As the historians John Horne and Alan Kramer have shown, the wartime events in Belgium remained a contentious issue during the interwar years. For pacifists such as Georges Demartial in France and Arthur Ponsonby in Britain, the dismissal of atrocity reports as 'myths' implied a general condemnation of war policies and a push for conciliatory attitudes towards Germany.[90]

Wartime propaganda took on a special meaning in America. Michaël Amara has stressed Belgium's role in the 'slow crumbling of American isolationism' as solidarity with Belgium provoked 'the first cracks in American neutrality'.[91] Belgian officials and politicians were busy rallying support for their country: in 1914, for instance, Vandervelde, Hymans and Carton de Wiart travelled to the USA, targeting different audiences linked to their respective political backgrounds.[92] The historian Alan Kramer has argued that such missions provided a forum to denounce 'crimes against humanity', especially because of the perception that the USA was 'the leading force in the development of international law'.[93] Similarly, in 1918, with a view to Belgian ambitions regarding the post-war order, the Belgian government sent Major Brassel to address the Luxembourg diaspora, and Pierre Daye – later a journalist and Rexist – to represent the country's colonial interests.[94] Meanwhile, the Catholic politician and diplomat Louis de Sadeleer worked with the American newspapers to encourage American aid. From 1917, his efforts were complemented by an – admittedly under-resourced – Belgian Official Information Service.[95]

The plight of the Belgians triggered manifold aid efforts, most famously the attempt to combat the war-induced famine in Belgium. Herbert Hoover's Commission for Relief in Belgium (CRB) provided food assistance to the Belgian population from October 1914 and maintained committees in most US states. During the war years, it collected donations worth one billion US dollars, a sum greater than the annual federal budget.[96] Hoover's efforts combined with those of the Comité National de Secours et d'Alimentation, which involved the Belgian businessmen Ernest Solvay and Emile Francqui as well as the Catholic politicians Léon Delacroix and Henri Jaspar. Michael Barnett has interpreted the CRB as a form of humanitarianism that stands in a line with earlier initiatives such as the International Committee of the Red Cross. At the same time, he argues that the CRB 'offered a glimpse of the future': it 'was a private international organization that nevertheless had many of the functions associated with the state, as it could conclude agreements with states, and states conferred on it political neutrality and operational independence'.[97] Efforts to secure American support took different forms: Lalla Vandervelde recounted her frustrations when addressing wealthy Americans on behalf of the Belgian Relief Committee: 'It was maddening to have to speak about the horrors of the War to the clicking of knitting needles.'[98] After moving to London in 1915, she established a fund seeking

'British Gifts for Belgian Soldiers'. To promote this charity, she performed recitals of Emile Cammaerts's patriotic poem *Carillon*, accompanied by Edward Elgar, who had set the piece to music.[99]

Relief efforts for the people in Belgium were complemented by, and sometimes competed with, fundraising for Belgian war refugees, whose overall number amounted to over 600,000. Displays of solidarity were particularly prominent in Britain, which hosted around one third of these exiles. Private initiative stepped in when government support proved insufficient, with around 2,000 committees working to support the refugees. As one study has suggested, 'The Belgians were arriving and were being welcomed enthusiastically by the British people'.[100] The main charity – the Belgian Refugees Committee – was headed by Flora Lugard (née Shaw), a prominent newspaper correspondent on colonial issues, who had also reported from the Brussels Anti-Slavery Conference of 1889–90. Her husband Frederick was a major figure in the history of British colonialism, for instance as Governor-General of Nigeria and later as a significant contributor to debates about mandates and trusteeship.[101] After the war, he also served on the League of Nations' Temporary Slavery Committee alongside its Belgian chair Albrecht Gohr. Flora Lugard's activism was not the only striking intersection between colonial matters and Belgian refugee relief: Herbert Samuel who, as President of the Local Government Board, organised state-led aid for the refugees, had previously supported the Congo reformers.[102] Furthermore, when an activist of the American Red Cross organised the transfer of relief funds, he contacted Vandervelde since he recalled the socialist's defence of the American missionaries Morrison and Sheppard in the Congo.[103]

Acts of charity for the Belgians were not always a matter of disinterested humanitarianism. As Peter Gatrell has pointed out, refugee relief fed into the 'appropriation of the refugee for the national cause'. Furthermore, among the wider population, hospitality slowly gave way to accusations against 'Belgian job-stealers' or 'won't-fight Belgians'.[104] Having suffered financial problems from the start, the Belgian Refugees Committee soon faced additional funding shortfalls.[105] Meanwhile, Belgian exiles also organised on their own behalf, founding committees such as Belgica (Union des Réfugiés Belges) and the Comité Officiel Belge pour l'Angleterre. Furthermore, as Belgian minister to Great Britain, Hymans initiated the celebrations of Belgian Independence Day in London on 21 July 1916, which included a *Te Deum* at Westminster Cathedral. A special festive evening took place in Albert Hall, with Prime Minister Herbert Asquith among the speakers.[106] In 1917, such celebrations were repeated in Queen's Hall with a speech by Asquith's successor, David Lloyd George.

What were the war's implications for Belgian attitudes to internationalism? The German attack on Belgium had revealed the fragility of international norms. As a result, an abandonment of neutrality enjoyed increasingly widespread support.[107] According to Hymans – subsequently Minister of Foreign Affairs – it was 'the search for more solid conditions of territorial security that inspired our effort for the revision of the 1839 treaties whose basis, the guaranteed and obligatory neutrality, had been torn apart by the war'.[108] Some politicians continued to defend the principle of neutrality, provided it was tied to specific guarantees.[109] Nonetheless, the secret Franco-Belgian Military Accord of 1920 marked a clear end to neutrality.[110] This shift became evident when Belgium joined France in occupying the Ruhr in 1923, partly linked to a desire to protect the city of Antwerp against the economic impact of French actions.[111] The willingness to enter into bilateral alliances was also reflected in the creation of the Belgium–Luxembourg Economic Union in 1921 as well as unsuccessful negotiations on an alliance with Britain in 1922.[112] Yet even with the abandonment of neutrality, Belgium remained interested in the effective workings of the new international order.

The League of Nations

In its lifetime, the League of Nations was subject to widely varying assessments. To some internationalists, it promised a new era in international relations, perhaps even the 'embryo of World Federal Government'.[113] In contrast, E. H. Carr challenged the expectations pinned to the League of Nations in his famous critique of interwar 'idealism'. As he argued, the League cemented an unequal status quo and was therefore unable to cope with states that had an interest in overturning the international order.[114] From the outset, the League had to cope with intrinsic obstacles: American and Soviet non-involvement, the initial exclusion of the former Central Powers and the veto rights of permanent Council members. The League's insufficiencies reflected the challenges of reconstruction after a war of unprecedented scope. According to his biographer James Barros, the problem with the approach of the League's Secretary-General Eric Drummond was his 'faith in the ability of rational discussion to resolve conflict, a by-product of the nineteenth-century belief in the inevitability of progress, which was soon shattered at the conference tables of Geneva by the power competition of the Great Powers, and the irrational forces of ideology and nationalism unleashed by the First World War'.[115] Accordingly, Zara Steiner has described the League as 'an experiment in internationalism at a time when the counterclaims of nationalism were running powerfully in the opposite direction'.[116]

Despite these challenges, the League deepened pre-war mechanisms of internationalism: from 1922, the League-affiliated Permanent Court of International Justice at The Hague complemented the Permanent Court of Arbitration. Furthermore, the League successfully mediated in the conflict between Greece and Bulgaria, administered the international territories of the Saar region and Gdansk, and established a High Commission of Refugees. Notwithstanding its manifold limitations, the League's Mandates system has been subject to positive reappraisal.[117] Similarly, it has been argued that the League's Health Organisation represented a shift in the management of public health and the ambition to 'reduce or eradicate many diseases and socio-economic causes of human illness'.[118] Another innovation was conceptual: articles 10 and 16 of the League charter introduced the principle of 'collective security' in international law, and the Kellogg–Briand Pact of 1928 strove to 'outlaw war'. Even with the absence of sanctioning mechanisms, such efforts went beyond the pre-war patterns of inter-state relations. Taken together, these novel institutions and mechanisms explain why the League of Nations can be interpreted as 'a radical departure from past international practice'.[119] In other respects, however, the League continued pre-war patterns of cooperation that referred back to the 'Concert of Europe' of the nineteenth century.[120] Furthermore, as specified in article 24 of the League Covenant, the new organisation coordinated tasks that had been associated with the public international unions of the pre-war years. Parts of the League system originated in earlier initiatives: the ILO built upon pre-war efforts for international labour legislation, while the origins of the League's Economic and Financial Organisation can be traced back to inter-allied cooperation during the war years.[121]

The relationship between Belgium and the League was somewhat ambivalent: during and after the First World War, many observers expected the future League to be based in Brussels.[122] The socialist Louis de Brouckère presented a common argument when he emphasised Belgian suffering in the war and claimed that the 'physical and moral position of Brussels has made it for many years the principal centre for global action'.[123] At the Paris Peace Conference, the Belgian delegate Paul Hymans adopted this cause. However, according to the historian Sally Marks, he 'irritated and bored almost everybody by his persistent pleading for Brussels as the site of the League of Nations, a quest doomed to failure from the outset'.[124] To both its supporters and detractors, the city would have been 'a League more anti-German in its orientation'.[125] Despite American pressure for Geneva, in October 1919, Paul Otlet was still optimistic that 'the initial choice of Geneva has not stopped the movement towards Brussels. The choice of that city before the war had already constituted a sort of plebiscite, a popular vote.'[126] The disappointment felt by the likes of Otlet has already been discussed in chapter 1. An altogether different response was provided by the Belgian author Albert Renard who argued in 1922 that Belgian 'glory' did not have to rely on hosting the League.[127]

Despite their disappointments, Belgian activists and diplomats were closely involved in the League's activities. Having acted as the '*de facto* leader of the small states' during the Paris Peace Conference,[128] Hymans became the first president of the League of Nations Assembly in November 1920 and performed this role again in 1932–33. Until 1927, the country also sat on the League Council. Emile Vandervelde and the Ghent liberal Louis Varlez made important contributions to the ILO.[129] In the management of international economic and financial cooperation, the Brussels Conference of 1921 set the precedent for the Genoa Conference (1922) and the International Economic Conference in Geneva (1927). As discussed in chapter 6, La Fontaine and Otlet provided a key impulse for the League's work for intellectual cooperation. However, as Maarten Van Alstein has pointed out, the internationalist enthusiasm of some activists contrasted with the 'sceptical reaction of most Belgian policymakers and diplomats to the League of Nations'.[130] Such attitudes do not necessarily indicate hostility to internationalism as such, but reveal concerns about the capacity of arbitration and collective security to act as adequate safeguards for Belgium.

Belgian internationalists formed part of an international movement to support the Geneva institutions and their underyling principles through League of Nations societies. In a letter to La Fontaine, David Davies – one of the movement's leading British exponents – proclaimed that popular backing for the League could 'only be gained by the educational work of voluntary associations', and viewed League of Nations societies as key agents in this quest.[131] Around one year later, in a letter to Davies, La Fontaine expressed his confidence about the popularity of this cause: 'We represent in fact the public opinion of the world and this opinion should be aroused as frequently as possible.'[132] La Fontaine's views echoed those of Robert Cecil, the driving force behind the League of Nations Union, a veritable mass organisation in interwar Britain: to Lord Cecil, effective international mechanisms depended on 'organised and concentrated international public opinion'.[133] Compared to their British counterpart, French and German associations had more limited memberships, but constituted a meeting ground for leading internationalists: experts on international law such as the Germans Hans Wehberg and Walther Schücking and early theorists of international relations were active in these associations.[134]

League advocacy drew upon transnational links. In a wartime letter to Léon Bourgeois, La Fontaine expressed his hope that France might 'express what the peoples think' and take decisive steps towards a new international organisation.[135] With Bourgeois's support, La Fontaine and the Association Belge pour la Société des Nations organised a congress in Brussels which took place in December 1919 with League supporters from over 14 countries.[136] Alongside liberal internationalists such as Bourgeois and Davies, the event attracted leading pacifists, from the Frenchmen Emile Arnaud and Jules Prudhommeaux to the Swiss IPB secretary Henri Golay.[137] As with pre-war internationalism, the Belgian participants covered a broad spectrum – with delegates including Carton de Wiart, Cooreman, Descamps, Rolin-Jacquemyns, Solvay and the mayor of Brussels, Adolphe Max. Belgian involvement was partly linked to the ongoing desire to see Brussels host the League of Nations, as a letter from La Fontaine made clear:

> It is…very important that the members of the conference, which will take place next week, are persuaded that the different authorities truly desire to see the League of Nations establish its permanent centre in Belgium. I think that a reception at the Hôtel de Ville augmented by a diplomatic speech from the mayor would be most useful.[138]

The Brussels conference established a new association, the International Federation of League of Nations Societies which soon established its headquarters in Brussels, held regular congresses in different European cities and 'regarded itself as an "avant-garde" of the League'.[139] La Fontaine served as its treasurer, yet the federation's driving force was the French peace leader Théodore Ruyssen. Its presidency rotated, with the British academic Willoughby Dickinson taking this role in 1925, the Swiss colonel Roger Dollfus in 1926 and the Polish diplomat Bronislaw Dembinski in 1928. The organisation's accounts indicate the relative strength of the different national League of Nations groups: in 1925, for instance, Britain contributed around 54,500 francs, followed by France with nearly 19,000 and Japan with nearly 10,500, Italy with under 6,000, and Turkey with just over 1,000. The USA, Greece, Netherlands, Romania, Switzerland and Haiti each contributed 1,000 francs.[140]

The Association Belge pour la Société des Nations had limited success. In a letter to the French pacifist Jules Prudhommeaux, La Fontaine blamed its president, Edouard Descamps, for this situation: 'Like you, I regret that the Association Belge pour la Société des Nations has not yet formulated its misgivings against the Pact of Paris, but I have in vain insisted with its president that he initiate a meeting to this effect.'[141] In 1921, La Fontaine reiterated his disappointment in a letter to Davies: 'we have not to reckon very much on the activity of our president. I have insisted many times in order that appeal should be made to the public at large but without any success.'[142] Such misgivings suggest tensions between two Belgians whose history of collaboration dated back to the 1890s. After Descamps's failed candidacy for the panel of judges of the Permanent Court of International Justice, La Fontaine suggested to the Ministry of Foreign Affairs that the outcome was attributable to 'the personality of the defeated candidate'.[143] Descamps had presided over the committee that laid the groundwork for the new court, yet his stint was marked by disagreements with other members. The French ambassador in Brussels later noted that the candidate 'had many personal enemies', and the Dutch Minister of Foreign Affairs allegedly described him as 'now quite gaga'.[144] Indeed, the historian Christian Birebent has suggested that Descamps's personality was also a reason why British League activists were initially lukewarm about proposals to base the International Federation of League of Nations Societies in Brussels.[145]

In 1922, the efforts of Henri Rolin placed Belgian League advocacy on a sounder footing. Rolin – nephew of Gustave Rolin-Jacquemyns – continued his family's distinguished tradition of legal scholarship. From a liberal background and employment with Hymans, he ventured towards the BWP and worked for Vandervelde in the 1920s. Driven by Rolin's efforts, the Union Belge pour la Société des Nations held its founding event at the Union Coloniale in Brussels in December 1922.[146] The meeting brought together an illustrious cast: Hymans, Destrée and Michel Levie spoke on behalf of the main political parties. The event also attracted La Fontaine and the Catholic politicians Jaspar, Poullet and Carton de Wiart; international guests came from Britain and France, including André Weiss, the Vice President of the Permanent Court of International Justice. Sending his wishes on behalf of the League secretariat, Eric Drummond praised Hymans for his role 'so useful and so brilliant' at the League of Nations Council and suggested that Hymans's involvement would provide a 'certain guarantee for prosperity and fruitful action'.[147] The opening event received press coverage from the Catholic *Le XXe Siècle* to the socialist *Le Peuple*.[148] The latter, however, noted the 'moderately full' hall and saw this as evidence that the number of Belgians 'interested in the great international questions is extremely limited'. Fifteen years later, a feminist peace activist observed similar reservations: 'once you move out of very left-wing circles, you can't get any real "peace consciousness" here – though of course everybody asserts that they are pacifists!' Yet she also noted the durability of Rolin's efforts when commenting that the Union Belge pour la Société des Nations seemed 'to be doing quite well in a quiet way'.[149]

Indeed, the Union Belge continued to promote internationalist ideas in the early 1930s. For instance, it organised a 'week of propaganda' for the League of Nations (1930) and marked the anniversary of the Hague Peace Conference of 1899 by launching a 'day of goodwill' (1932).[150] In 1930, Rolin affirmed his country's lasting interest in international mechanisms: 'Particularly sensitive to the repercussions of any European crisis, undermined by four years of war… Belgium has to seek [a way towards] the juridical consolidation of peace in the world, a security which, for a long time, it had hoped to find in the too precarious regime of guaranteed neutrality.'[151] That year, Belgium became party to the Oslo Agreement alongside Sweden, Norway, Denmark, the Netherlands, Luxemburg and Finland. The treaty brought together neutral states with a view to both economic cooperation and the promotion of collective security.[152] Belgium's willingness to enter into such alliances did not necessarily contradict a self-perception in which neutrality still featured. Tellingly, Hymans asserted that his country had merely rejected 'conventional' neutrality: 'If necessary, Belgium will know to defend itself and, faithful to its past, its traditions, its loyal interests, it will fulfil all its international obligations.'[153]

In 1936, Leopold III's announcement of a 'policy of independence' seemed to mark a step away from League internationalism, echoing both the discourse of Belgian neutrality and the Dutch 'zelfstandigheitspolitiek'.[154] Some observers argued that this 'policy of independence' was compatible with a commitment to the League of Nations: 'In refusing certain forms of obedience and special solidarities, Belgium – far beyond renouncing the obligations of the [League] Covenant – declares, on the contrary, to recognise only one international solidarity and only one authority above it: the League of Nations.'[155] Yet in practice, Belgian policy had shifted. In 1938, Rolin, disappointed with the government's inactivity over the Spanish Civil War, looked back to his country's earlier role in defending international law during the Italy–Corfu crisis of 1923: 'M. Hymans rose up, the first among the small powers, the first to speak a clear language amidst general emotion . . . He said . . . that for Belgium, a consideration above all others was the respect for the Covenant and the need for the integrity of small states.'[156]

Rebuilding the peace movement

The First World War caused severe rifts among pacifists. On 31 July 1914, La Fontaine organised an IPB meeting in Brussels. Attended by over 100 delegates, it attracted notable peace leaders such as Emile Arnaud from France, Ludwig Quidde from Germany and Edwin Mead from the USA. Stressing the peoples' desire for peace, delegates agreed to ask US president Woodrow Wilson to mediate between Austria-Hungary and Serbia.[157] Yet already before the war, many activists had been at pains to affirm their national credentials.[158]

Soon, national antagonisms divided the IPB, with La Fontaine being reluctant to meet his Austrian and German counter-parts after the attack on Belgium. When the bureau came together in January 1915, he declared that 'As much as I am . . . an internationalist, I am also . . . Belgian' and criticised the stance of his counterparts from the Central Powers.[159] Meanwhile, as leader of the German Peace Society, Quidde opposed the notion of unilateral war guilt. He therefore rejected the IPB's request to acknowledge his country's culpability and condemn the violation of Belgian neutrality.[160] Another prominent German activist, Hans Wehberg, also disagreed with the 'war guilt' thesis, although he denounced German actions in Belgium as a 'monstrous crime'.[161] Only a few German pacifists – notably Georg Friedrich Nicolai and Friedrich Wilhelm Foerster – blamed their country. For this reason, the first post-war Universal Peace Congress (1921) took place without German or Austrian involvement;

this only changed with the Berlin congress of 1924. Ruptures also became evident in the IPU, whose seat had moved from Brussels to Christiana during the war: in 1921, Belgian and French parliamentarians refused to participate in the Inter-Parliamentary Conference at Stockholm because of the presence of German delegates.[162] Meanwhile, within the International Federation of League of Nations Societies, Belgian delegates initially objected to the admission of organisations from the former Central Powers, albeit unsuccessfully.[163]

The war experience did not mean that pacifists abandoned their narratives about the advent of international unity. For instance, La Fontaine's *Magnissima Charta* reiterated the conviction that over fifty years, the development towards 'concerted international adminstration' had 'strongly intensified international life'.[164] He called for increasing awareness of this process and for institutions 'which can easily adapt themselves to circumstances and contribute to their own improvement'.[165] Within the IPU, La Fontaine was one of several activists who hoped to transform this association into a world parliament as part of the League system.[166] Such statements indicate the hopes vested in the new international structures. Yet the peace movement's situation remained perilous, also financially. The Carnegie Endowment for International Peace had ended its subsidies for the IPB, linked to a shift towards funding more 'respectable' activities.[167] In 1924, the IPB moved to Geneva, hoping to benefit from proximity to the League.[168] During subsequent debates about the bureau's reorganisation, its Swiss IPB secretary Golay was fearful of an American takeover: 'We must not allow the Geneva Bureau to fall into the hands of the Americans, as admirable… and generous as they may sometimes be'.[169] Such statements testify to the insecurities at the heart of the bureau.

The IPB's situation was complicated by major ideological divisions within the interwar peace movement. 'Organisational' pacifists remained wedded to traditional concepts such as arbitration and the strengthening of international institutions. From the 1920s, they were increasingly challenged by activists who rejected violence unconditionally and promoted 'integral' approaches such as strikes and conscientious objection.[170] These currents maintained international structures of their own, for instance the War Resisters' International (1921) and the Joint Peace Council (1930). Even beyond this rift, a range of new actors emerged, from the Women's International League for Peace and Freedom (WILPF) to religiously inspired associations such as the International Fellowship of Reconciliation.[171] Another body, the World Alliance for Promoting Friendship Through the Churches, had existed since 1914. Although it struggled with war-related divisions and primarily attracted members of Protestant denominations, it provided a forum for debates on peace, religion and the League of Nations.[172] Given the dominant role of Catholicism in Belgium's religious life, its national constituency remained small. Nonetheless, Belgians – mainly pastors – participated in its congresses, in a Regional Conference with French and British activists in Lille (1924), and in a meeting on 'Church and Peace' in Brussels (1936).[173]

Meanwhile, Catholics developed various pacifist activities, exemplified by the international congresses of the French Christian democrat Marc Sangnier.[174] Catholic clergymen and lay activists had initially feared socialist and Masonic influence within the League of Nations and were disappointed by the moves of the Italian and British governments to exclude the Vatican. Belgian Catholics played a role in the subsequent rapprochement, for instance through the Union International d'Études Sociales. With Cardinal Mercier's support, this organisation argued that 'the basic idea of the League stood in the Christian tradition'.[175] Furthermore, in 1926, the Brussels meeting of the International Secretariat of Parties of Christian Inspiration affirmed the League's importance in a resolution on 'the organisation of peace'.[176] Similarly, in the 1930s, a report by the Catholic Union of International Studies described the League as 'an important stage on the way towards an organic international status; the world has got beyond the period of anarchy and is entering on a period of organisation'.[177]

Faced with the fragmentation of interwar pacifism, the IPB created an International Committee for the Coordination of Pacifist Forces in 1927. The new body included representatives of the IPB, WILPF, freemasonry and the World Alliance for Promoting Friendship Through the Churches. Yet it attracted little support from integral pacifists. In practical terms, the IPB focused on supporting the League of Nations and organising its Universal Peace Congresses.[178] The 1931 congress took place in Brussels – the first such event in Belgium since the Antwerp congress of 1894. The main Belgian parties were strongly represented on the event's *comité d'honeur*, which included socialists such as Destrée and de Brouckère; Catholics such as Descamps, Carton de Wiart, Poullet and Rutten; and liberals such as Hymans and Janson. Economic recovery was one of two major topics. For instance, the French pacifist Lucien Le Foyer – former *député* and author of a study on the Belgian minimum wage – asked for joint European action to combat the Great Depression.[179]

The second theme at Brussels was disarmament.[180] The congress thus connected with the transnational disarmament campaign of the 1920s and the run-up to the World Disarmament Conference of 1932. In Belgium, support for this campaign ranged from Flemish veterans to WILPF, whose international secretary lectured in Brussels on 'women's expectations of the Disarmament Conference'.[181] Furthermore, Henri Rolin played an active role in the disarmament debates of the International Federation of League of Nations Societies, another participant in the wider movement.[182] However, this broader alliance around disarmament did not indicate a political consensus. Although the LSI maintained a committee on this issue, Friedrich Adler advised Vandervelde against supporting the Brussels peace congress: he feared 'misunderstandings if the LSI president figures on the *comité d'honeur* of this essentially bourgeois congress, whose demands will certainly be more feeble than ours'.[183] Vandervelde's name did appear on the official list, yet the incident illustrates the persistent tension between socialist antimilitarism and the peace movement. Such suspicions could go both ways: when the International Federation of Trade Unions organised an anti-war demonstration in Liège in 1924, liberals and Catholics did not back the event: 'Politics go very deep in Belgium', as one observer noted.[184]

A further factor can be added to such suspicions and tensions: communism. Affiliates of the Comintern remained critical of 'bourgeois pacifism', although they held a variety of stances on issues such as military service.[185] In 1932–33, the Amsterdam–Pleyel movement was a key example of how communists adopted the language of peace. Headed by the French authors Henri Barbusse and Romain Rolland, the initiative was viewed as a communist front.[186] In Belgium, it did indeed receive backing from the Communist Party, yet also attracted the support of Marcelle Leroy, who had been the secretary of the Belgian WILPF section since 1929. As a result of the Amsterdam congress, Leroy helped organise a Women's Congress Against War and Fascism together with Belgian socialists such as Isabelle Blume and Alice Pels, and also joined the international committee that resulted from this initiative.[187] Furthermore, in December 1934, an International Student Congress against War and Fascism took place in Brussels, following on from a World Youth Congress in Paris the previous year.

How did the transformations in interwar pacifism manifest themselves in Belgium? By the 1930s, radical stances had gained in prominence. In a survey of the peace movement, Bart de Ligt, a pacifist and Christian anarchist from the Netherlands, noted the growth of conscientious objection in Belgium, partly due to Dutch and English influences.[188] He also commented on the particular appeal of antimilitarist stances in Flanders. The Flemish movement's hostility to the Belgian army was linked to the legacy of the Frontbeweging and its campaign against Francophone dominance of the military. As de Ligt noted, the periodical of the Flemish veterans organisation, the Verbond der Vlaamsche Oudstrijders (later Verbond V.O.S.), regularly featured 'antimilitarist propaganda'.[189] In a letter to the American activist Jane Addams, a member of the Verbond claimed that his organisation, with its 80,000 members, was 'fighting every-day militarism in this country'.[190] The Verbond's campaign against the Franco-Belgian military accord exemplified potential intersections between nationalism and antimilitarism.[191] Furthermore, in November 1934, the Verbond V.O.S. organised a meeting to discuss measures against the arms industry. It involved representatives from very different groups including the War Resisters' International, the Vlaamsche Jongeren Vredesactie (Young Flemish Peace Action, partner organisation of a Dutch group) as well as youth groups of communists, Trotskyites and Flemish Catholics (Katholieke Vlaamse Vredes Actie).[192] Meanwhile, another organisation with 'integral stances', the Union Jeune Europe from Geneva, attracted followers among Francophone Belgians.[193]

Belgian groups such as the Verbond V.O.S. and the Katholieke Jongeren Vredesaktie also signed up to the principles of the Ligue Internationale des Combattants pour la Paix, which called for universal disarmament and the abolition of military service.[194] The French activist and former Congo reformer Félicien Challaye had founded this organisation as an alliance of integral pacifists in 1936. The Ligue Internationale listed prominent Belgian figures such as the writer and former communist Charles Plisnier, the Flemish activist Franz Daels and the artist Frans Masereel among its supporters, although there is limited evidence of their actual involvement.[195] The divide between the old and the new pacifism became clear in a letter from La Fontaine to Challaye: the Belgian peace leader affirmed his intention to maintain 'contact with all groups and initiatives' for peace. However, his own position focused on the need for global order and, implicitly, made the case for an international peace force.[196] Such views clearly differed from stances based around an individual commitment to non-violence and a rejection of military institutions.

Internationalism and Europeanism

Alongside League advocacy and pacifism, another internationalist current gained prominence in the 1920s: Europeanism. While much internationalism had been Eurocentric from its earliest manifestations, one variety viewed peace as a distinctly European task. Victor Hugo's call for a 'United States of Europe' in 1849 and the periodical *Les Etats-Unis d'Europe*, published by the International League for Peace and Freedom from 1868, were cases in point.[197] The pacifist William Stead, editor of the *Pall Mall Gazette*, expressed similar ideas at the turn of the century.[198] In the wake of the Great War, calls for closer European integration gathered momentum, from intellectuals to trade unions.[199] For some, such as the French prime minister Edouard Herriot, Europeanism was primarily an economic project.[200] However, the political and economic strands of Europeanism were not contradictory: Aristide Briand's call for a United States of Europe (1929–30) initially emphasised the economic dimensions, while the 1930 French memorandum on European integration featured detailed political proposals.[201]

Richard Coudenhove-Kalergi's Pan-European Union was the most well-known group of interwar Europeanism. Through a European federation (which notably excluded Russia and Britain), the Pan-Europeanists sought to counter notions of European decline.[202] At the same time, *Paneuropa* formed part of an effort to promote a world federation based on regional unions. According to Coudenhove-Kalergi, the League of Nations 'might become the final world authority, while the settlement of local conflicts and issues would be left to the more limited national groups'.[203] Nicholas Murray Butler, president of the Carnegie Endowment for International Peace, alleged that Pan-Europe could join earlier forces that 'knit[ted] together in closer bounds widely separated portions of the earth's surface', namely 'the Roman Empire, the British Commonwealth of Nations and the United States of America'.[204] Aristide Briand used the League of Nations Assembly as a forum for his call for a 'United States of Europe'. In contrast, Alfred Zimmern – a key figure in the League's efforts for intellectual cooperation – feared that Pan-Europeanism might emerge as a competitor to League internationalism.[205] Similarly, while the Universal Peace Congresses gave increasing prominence to this topic, the Peace Congress at Berlin in 1924 revealed internationalist concerns about Pan-Europe. As La Fontaine reported, the congress favoured a 'universal tariff union' instead.[206] The International Federation of League of Nations Societies also debated the issue: some activists feared that European regionalism might challenge the existing institutions, whereas others saw it as a chance to decentralise the League.[207]

In Belgium, Europeanism inspired a great range of associations and periodicals. The historian Geneviève Duchenne has considered the Belgian Pan-European Committee as the 'primus inter pares' in this context.[208] Founded in December 1926, it remained a small association, with barely 200 members by 1927. However, its membership included significant political figures such as the former prime minister Aloys Van de Vyvere, the socialist Jules Destrée, the Catholic Frans van Cauwelaert and the liberal Paul-Emile Janson.[209] Although it focused on one region in the world – namely Europe – its activism could be conceived as a form of internationalism. Duchenne has captured this compatibility when describing Destrée's stance as a 'European internationalism'.[210]

The overlapping nature of national, international and European persuasions was exemplified by Irenée Van der Ghinst, a key figure in the Belgian section of Paneuropa and the Institut d'Economie Européenne (founded in 1932 to promote economic integration). Prior to the war, Van der Ghinst had been a student activist alongside Georges Sarton, and also maintained links with Belgian socialists.[211] At the first Pan-European Congress in 1926, Van der Ghinst stressed that the League should not 'remain uninterested in the constitution of Pan-Europe' and expressed his wish that the League be 'reassured [that] the Pan-European Movement would be neither a competitor nor an adversary, but a good collaborator which specialises within a European context'.[212] While combining Europeanism and League advocacy, he embraced the discourse of Belgium as an international crossroads. In an article for the periodical *Le Flambeau*, he presented Belgium as a potential force for European integration:

> Our sort would be more enviable if our country presided over the union of our neighbours rather than serving as the combat area…Furthermore, the small peoples have no reason to mistrust us as they could mistrust a powerful State. We are the guarantors of their rights because to protect theirs means to protect ours.[213]

The historian Luisa Passerini has highlighted both the diffuse nature and emotional resonance of European visions in the interwar years.[214] While many internationalists were concerned with the rise of fascism, the trajectories of some Europeanists show the diversity of political agendas associated with the promotion of European integration. In 1936, the Belgian journalist Pierre Daye – a member of the Union Jeune Europe, the Institut d'Économie Européenne and the Union Belge pour la Société de Nations – stood for the Rexist party. He later embraced visions of a New European Order and collaborated with the German occupiers.[215] Raymond de Becker, a prominent figure in Catholic Action and Belgian Europeanism, promoted similar stances. Indeed, in the 1930s, the Union Jeune Europe supported a rapprochement with the Third Reich. In this context, the historian John Hellman has argued that 'Nazi operatives were using avant-garde Europeanist idealism and Christian-socialist dialogue to infiltrate both the Belgians and their Catholic sympathizers in France'.[216] During the Second World War, activists of the Verbond V.O.S. – which had participated in a range of peace campaigns – collaborated with the Germans and provided members of the Vlaamse Wacht, an auxiliary force in occupied Belgium.[217] Such examples show that pacifism and Europeanism were not inherently progressive: a commitment to 'peace' or 'Europe' could take activists in very different directions. Norman Ingram has traced similar ambiguities with regard to the stances adopted by French pacifists after 1940.[218]

Conclusion

By the 1930s, internationalists faced fragmentation and a volatile international situation. These challenges became evident when, in 1935, peace societies met in Brussels and discussed the situation in Abyssinia.[219] One year later, in September 1936, the Belgian capital hosted a large-scale World Peace Congress, as part of the 'International Peace Campaign' launched by Lord Robert Cecil and Pierre Cot.[220] The event brought together a broad alliance, with participants such as the former French prime minister Edouard Herriot, the widow of Fridtjof Nansen, representatives of different League of Nations associations, the exiled German peace leader Ludwig Quidde, international associations such as the World Union of Freethinkers, as well as representatives of the ILO and the League of Nations Secretariat. The Belgian cohort counted 1,100 delegates who represented 211 different organisations. One of its members – Louis de Brouckère, then president of the LSI – stressed the international obstacles as well as the 'anxiety and distrust' encountered by pacifists.[221] By this point, the challenges for an order based on international law and the League of Nations had become evident. The League's lack of sanctioning mechanisms against those who violated international law were reflected in its failure to prevent or punish the Japanese invasion of

Manchuria (1931), Italy's occupation of Abyssinia (1935–36) and Germany's re-militarisation of the Rhineland (1936). While the delegates were gathering in Brussels, many movements were divided over their response to the Spanish Civil War. Seen in this context, the Brussels event of 1936 was the last great assertion of an internationalism whose roots went back to the pre-war years.

Throughout the period under consideration, Belgian activists were prominently involved in a variety of pacifist or 'pacificist' organisations and hosted many of their events. Indeed, many Belgian efforts were connected to transnational stimuli: the impulse for the creation of the BAPS came from Britain; Catholic and women's peace activism in Belgium were inspired by French examples; Europeanists cooperated with Coudenhove-Kalergi in Vienna; and League advocacy gravitated towards the Geneva institutions. This is not to say that Belgians were more 'peace-minded' than people from other countries. Indeed, some Belgians continued to hold designs on Dutch Limburg and Luxembourg and sought to promote their annexation as part of the interwar order, expressing their disappointment when territorial gains were confined to Eupen-Malmedy and Moresnet. And as in other countries, pacifism and League advocacy did not translate into durable mass movements and often struggled to find broad public support. Nonetheless, the picture that emerges is that of a country in which – partly due to its precarious position – politicians and campaigners from different political camps could agree on the need for robust international norms and organisations. Pacifism depended upon networking, and well-networked the Belgian internationalists certainly were.

Notes

1 Horst Lademacher, *Die belgische Neutralität als Problem der europäischen Politik 1830–1914* (Bonn, 1971), pp. 294–8.

2 Horst Lademacher, 'Belgien als Objekt und Subjekt europäischer Außenpolitik: Historische Fallstudie zu den politischen Determinanten und Möglichkeiten eines kleinen europäischen Landes', *BTNG–RBHC*, 35 (2004), 466. Cf. Emile Banning, *La Belgique au point de vue militaire et européen*, ed. Ernest Godart (Brussels, 1887).

3 Edouard Descamps, *La Neutralité de la Belgique au point de vue historique, diplomatique, juridique et politique: Étude sur la constitution des états pacifiques à titre permanent* (Brussels, 1902), p. 26.

4 Charles Castel de Saint Pierre, *A Project of Perpetual Peace* (transl.; London, 1927 [1713]); Immanuel Kant, *Zum ewigen Frieden: Ein philosophischer Entwurf. Mit Einleitung und Anmerkungen*, ed. Heiner Klemme (Hamburg, 1992 [1795]). For discussions of (perpetual) peace before Kant, see Jean-Christoph Merle, 'Zur Geschichte des Friedensbegriffs vor Kant: Ein Überblick', *ibid.*, pp. 31–42.

5 Pierre Laberge, 'Kant on justice and the law of nations', in David Mapel and Terry Nardin (eds), *International Society: Diverse Ethical Perspectives* (Princeton, NJ, 1998); For the debate on the meaning of 'federation' in Kant's treatise, see Otfried Höffe, 'Völkerbund oder Weltrepublik?', in Höffe (ed.), *Immanuel Kant: Zum ewigen Frieden* (2nd edn., Berlin, 1992), pp. 109–32.

6 Sandi E. Cooper, 'Introduction' in Cooper (ed.), *Arbitration: Two Views* (New York, 1971), p. 7.

7 On Charles De Visscher, the Institute's secretary-general from 1925 to 1937: Joe Verhoeven, 'Charles De Visscher: living and thinking international law', *European Journal of International Law*, 11 (2000), 887–904.

8 Koskennieni, *The Gentle Civilizer of Nations*, pp. 88–9.

9 Haberman, *Nobel Lectures*, p. 66.

10 *Ibid.*, p. 67.

11 For contemporary discussions, see Reinsch, *Public International Unions*, and René Lavollée, 'Les Unions internationales', *Revue d'histoire diplomatique*, 1 (1887), 331–62.

12 Lestrade, *La Vie internationale*, p. 6.

13 Neville Goodman, *International Health Organizations and Their Work* (Edinburgh, 1972), p. 93.

14 Anne Rasmussen, 'L'hygiène en congrès (1852–1912): circulation et configurations internationales', in Patrice Bourdelais (ed.), *Les Hygiénistes: enjeux, modèles et pratiques, XVIIIe–XX siècles* (Berlin, 2001), pp. 213–39.

15 Martin Geyer, 'One language for the world: the metric system, international coinage, gold standard, and the rise of internationalism, 1850–1900', in Geyer and Paulmann, *The Mechanics of Internationalism*, pp. 55–92.

16 Herren, 'Modernisierung, Außenpolitik und Integration', p. 18.

17 Isabella Löhr, *Die Globalisierung des geistiger Eigentumsrechte: Neue Strukturen internationaler Zusammenarbeit 1886–1952* (Göttingen, 2010).

18 Herren, *Hintertüren zur Macht*, pp. 128–36.

19 Philip Chalmin, 'The important trends in sugar diplomacy before 1914', in Bill Albert and Adrian Grave (eds), *Crisis and Change in the International Sugar Economy 1860–1914* (Norwich, 1984), pp. 8–19.

20 Free-traders objected to punitive tariffs which a convention would impose against violating countries. See George Matthisson, *The Sugar Convention from a Confectioner's Stand-point* (London, 1889) and idem, *The Sugar Convention: Its Costs and Consequences* (London, 1905).

21 Chalmin, 'Important trends in sugar diplomacy', p. 9.

22 Reinsch, *Public International Unions*, p. 51.

23 Chalmin, 'Important trends in sugar diplomacy', p. 14.

24 Karl Holl, 'Pazifismus', *Geschichtliche Grundbegriffe*, iv. 771–3.

25 Martin Ceadel, *Thinking About Peace and War* (Oxford, 1987), p. 5; Ceadel, *Pacifism in Britain 1914–1945: The Defining of a Faith* (Oxford, 1980), p. 3.

26 Nadine Lubelski-Bernard, 'Les Mouvements et les idéologies pacifistes en Belgique 1830–1914' (PhD thesis, Université Libre de Bruxelles, 1977), pp. 410–12.

27 David Nichols, 'Richard Cobden and the international peace congress movement 1848–1853', *Journal of British Studies*, 30 (1994), 351–76. On Cobden's

peace activism, see Martin Ceadel, *The Origins of War Prevention: The British Peace Movement and International Relations, 1730–1854* (Oxford, 1996), pp. 414–69.

28 Frederick [Friedrich] Engels, 'The Free Trade Congress in Brussels', *Northern Echo* (9 October 1847).

29 Lyons, *Internationalism in Europe*, p. 315.

30 David Cortright, *Peace: A History of Movements and Ideas* (Cambridge, 2008), p. 37.

31 Cooper, *Patriotic Pacifism*, p. 40.

32 Lubelski-Bernard, 'Les mouvements', pp. 350–1; Christian Müller, 'Designing the model European – liberal and republican concepts of citizenship in Europe in the 1860s: the Association Internationale pour le Progrès des Sciences Sociales', *History of European Ideas*, 37 (2011), 223–31.

33 Karl Holl, *Pazifismus in Deutschland* (Frankfurt, 1988), p. 40.

34 Cooper, *Patriotic Pacifism*, p. 54.

35 MS IPB 241/17: Ducommun to La Fontaine, 5 July 1906; MS IPB 247/25: Ducommon to La Fontaine, 27 December 1906; Lubelski-Bernard, 'Les mouvements', p. 397.

36 Lubelski-Bernard, 'The Institute of International Law, Auguste Beernaert and Henri La Fontaine' in Holl and Kjelling, *The Nobel Peace Prize and the Laureates*, pp. 109–33.

37 Lubelski-Bernard, 'Les mouvements', p. 315.

38 *Ibid.*, pp. 377 and 465.

39 On Germany, see Roger Chickering, *Imperial Germany and a World Without War: The Peace Movement and German Society* (Princeton, NJ, 1975).

40 La Fontaine, *Bulletin Officiel du VIme Congrès International de la Paix*, p. 2.

41 'Pour l'Arbitrage et la Paix', *La Dernière Heure* (*c.* 19 May 1907).

42 MS IPB 131/10: Arnaud to IPB, 7 November 1895. Cf. Stengers, 'La Belgique, un foyer de Dreyfusisme', p. 286.

43 MS IPB 163/4: 'Propagande en Belgique': undated letter, *c.* 1902.

44 Verdiana Grossi, *Le Pacifisme européen: 1889–1914* (Brussels, 1994), pp. 198–9.

45 Rens, 'Rapport au Bureau International par le Secrétaire du Bureau Permanent', p. 7.

46 *Congrès de Rome*, p. lxxx.

47 Hins, *La Libre Pensée internationale en 1912* (Brussels, 1913), p. 11.

48 Hins, *La Libre Pensée internationale en 1913* (Brussels, 1914), p. 72.

49 Libre Pensée de Bruxelles, *Rapport présenté par le Comité de la Libre Pensée de Bruxelles à l'Assemblée générale* (Brussels, 1913), p. 10.

50 De Greef, *L'Internationalisation de la pensée*, pp. 23–4.

51 Charles Rossignol, 'Pour la Paix', *Journal des Instituteurs* (23 January 1908).

52 MS IPB/129/10: Letters from École laique/Ecole libre pour Garçons, Roulers, 24 February 1908 and 22 February 1909.

53 Lubelski-Bernard, 'Les mouvements', p. 414.

54 Carlier, 'Moving beyond boundaries', p. 453.

55 *Ibid.*
56 Lubelski-Bernard, 'Les mouvements', pp. 398–400.
57 See e.g. 'Pour l'Arbitrage et la Paix', *La Dernière Heure* (*c.* 19 May 1907); Carlier, 'Moving beyond boundaries', p. 451.
58 MS IPB 129/2 and IPB/129/10: letters by Marie Rosseels, 26 February 1908 and 19 March 1909.
59 Kossmann, *The Low Countries*, p. 368.
60 Lubelski-Bernard, 'Les mouvements', p. 396.
61 *Ibid.*, p. 441.
62 *Ibid.*, pp. 447–8.
63 *Ibid.*, p. 450.
64 Ralph Uhlig, *Die Interparlamentarische Union 1889–1914: Friedenssicherungsbemühungen im Zeitalter des Imperialismus* (Stuttgart, 1988), p. 2.
65 La Fontaine, *Bulletin officiel du VIme Congrès International de la Paix*, pp. 161–2.
66 Uhlig, *Interparlamentarische Union*, pp. 201–2. Cf. Descamps, 'Essai sur l'organisation de l'arbitrage international: mémoire aux Puissances', reproduced in Cooper, *Arbitration: Two Views*.
67 Nadine Lubelski-Bernard, 'Les débats de l'Union interparlementaire et la Belgique (1884–1914)', in Jacques Bariéty and Antoine Fleury (eds), *Mouvements et initiatives de paix dans la politique internationale* (Bern, 1987), p. 86.
68 Uhlig, *Interparlamentarische Union*, p. 419.
69 Pirenne, *Histoire de Belgique*, vii, p. 115. Carton de Wiart viewed Beernaert as representative of his era in Belgian politics: Henry Carton de Wiart, *Beernaert et son temps* (Brussels, 1945), p. 2.
70 Lubelski-Bernard, 'Les mouvements', p. 395.
71 'Leo Tolstoi über das Friedensmanifest des Czaren', *Der Freidenker*, 7 (1899), 26.
72 Lucia Ames Mead, *Patriotism and the New Internationalism* (Boston, MA, 1906), p. ii.
73 Lubelski-Bernard, 'Les mouvements', p. 396.
74 Charles Woeste, *Mémoires pour servir à l'histoire contemporaine de la Belgique*, vol. 2 (Brussels, 1937), pp. 322–3.
75 Uhlig, *Interparlamentarische Union*, pp. 357–71.
76 Hins, *Le Congrès de Prague*, p. 39.
77 Bourgeois, *Pour la Société des Nations*, p. 287.
78 John A. Hobson, *A League of Nations* (London, 1915), p. 3.
79 Bitsch, *La Belgique entre la France et l'Allemagne*, pp. 397–8.
80 David Stevenson, 'Battlefield or barrier? Rearmament and military planning in Belgium, 1902–1914', *International History Review*, 29 (2007), 473–507. On the objectives of the Belgian military reforms of 1912–13, see Bitsch, *La Belgique entre la France et l'Allemagne*, pp. 470–5.
81 Laity, *The British Peace Movement*, pp. 216–29; Judith Smart, '"Poor little Belgium" and Australian popular support for war, 1914–1915', *War and Society*, 12 (1994), 27–46; Sandi Cooper, 'The guns of August and the doves of Italy: intervention and internationalism', *Peace and Change*, 7 (1981), 29–43.
82 Henry Carton de Wiart, *The Way of Honour* (London, 1918), p. 2.

83 'La Belgique loyale et courageuse', *Toute la France debout pour la Victoire du Droit* (15 March 1919).
84 Richard Stites, 'Days and nights in wartime Russia: cultural life, 1914–1917', in Aviel Roshwald and Richard Stites (eds), *European Culture in the Great War* (Cambridge, 1999), pp. 20–1.
85 Sophie de Schaepdrijver, 'Occupation, propaganda and the idea of Belgium', in *ibid.*, p. 268.
86 Amara, 'La propagande belge', p. 175.
87 Trevor Wilson, 'Lord Bryce's investigation into alleged German atrocities in Belgium', *Journal of Contemporary History*, 14 (1979), 369–83.
88 *The Continental Times* (18 September 1914, 30 October 1914). Cf. Gary Messinger, *British Propaganda and the State in the First World War* (Manchester, 1992), p. 17.
89 Horne and Kramer, *German Atrocities*, pp. 227–61.
90 *Ibid.*, pp. 366–75. See Arthur Ponsonby, *Falsehood in Wartime: Containing an Assortment of Lies Circulated Throughout the Nations during the Great War* (London, 1928).
91 Amara, 'La propagande belge', p. 221.
92 See e.g. *The Case of Belgium in the Present War* (s.l., 1914).
93 Kramer, *Dynamic of Destruction*, p. 24.
94 Amara, 'La propaganda belge', p. 199.
95 *Ibid.*, 182–4 and 193–7 respectively.
96 Sophie de Schaepdrijver, *De Groote Oorlog: het Konikrijk België tijdens de Eerste Wereldorlog* (Antwerp, 1997), p. 110
97 Barnett, *Empire of Humanity*, p. 87.
98 Vandervelde, *Monarchs and Millionaires*, p. 70.
99 *Ibid.*, 115.
100 Peter Cahalan, *Belgian Refugee Relief in England during the Great War* (New York, 1982), p. 71; cf. Michaël Amara, *Des Belges à l'épreuve de l'Exil: les réfugies de la Première Guerre mondiale. France, Grance-Bretagne, Pays-Bas* (Brussels, 2008); Tony Kushner, 'Local heroes: Belgian refugees in Britain during the First World War', *Immigrants and Minorities*, 18 (1999), 1–28.
101 Frederick Lugard, *The Dual Mandate in Tropical Africa* (London, 1922).
102 Peter Gatrell, 'Refugees and forced migrants during the First World War', *Immigrants and Minorities*, 26 (2008), 91.
103 Vandervelde, *Souvenirs*, pp. 211–12.
104 Amara, *Des Belges à l'épreuve de l'Exil*, pp. 355–61; Cahalan, *Belgian Refugee Relief*, p. 259.
105 *Ibid.*, 407.
106 Paul Hymans, *Mémoires*, vol. 1 (Brussels, 1958), pp. 144–7.
107 Michael Palo, 'The question of neutrality and Belgium's security dilemma during the First World War: the search for a politically acceptable Solution', *BTNG–RBHC*, 29 (2000), 227–304.
108 Hymans, *Mémoires*, vol. 2, p. 551. See also his explanations on neutrality, *ibid.*, vol. 1, 281–97.

109 Edmond Carton de Wiart, 'La neutralité garantie: ses inconvenients et ses avantages. Notes revisée. 15 March 1918' as featured in Lademacher, *Die belgische Neutralität*, pp. 493–504. See also MS Mundaneum doc. 234.4 (493): Otlet, 'La politique belge et l'avenir de la neutralité'.

110 Helmreich, *Belgium and Europe*, pp. 229–41; Rik Coolsaet, *La Politique extérieure de la Belgique: au cœur de l'Europe, le poids d'une petite puissance* (Brussels, 2002), pp. 349 and 355.

111 Lademacher, 'Belgien als Objekt und Subjekt', p. 484.

112 Sally Marks, 'Ménage à trois? The negotiations for an Anglo-French-Belgian Alliance in 1922', *International History Review*, 4 (1982), 524–52.

113 Salvador de Madariaga, *The World's Design* (London, 1938), p. xvi.

114 E.H. Carr, *The Twenty Years' Crisis, 1919–1939: An Introduction to the Study of International Relations* (London, 1939).

115 James Barros, *Office Without Power: Secretary-General Sir Eric Drummond 1919–1933* (Oxford, 1979), pp. 43–4.

116 Steiner, *The Lights That Failed*, p. 349.

117 Susan Pedersen, 'Metaphors of the schoolroom: women working the Mandates system of the League of Nations', *History Workshop Journal*, 66 (2008), 88–207; Pedersen, 'The meaning of the Mandates system'; Callahan, *Mandates and Empire*; Callahan, *A Sacred Trust*.

118 Martin David Dubin, 'The League of Nations Health Organisation', in Paul Weindling (ed.), *International Health Organisations and Movements, 1918–1939* (Cambridge, 1995), p. 73.

119 Steiner, *The Lights That Failed*, p. 40.

120 David Armstrong, *The Rise of the International Organisation: A Short History* (London, 1982), p. 5.

121 Jasmin Van Daele, 'Engineering social peace: networks, ideas, and the founding of the International Labour Organization', *International Review of Social History*, 50 (2005), 435–66; Yann Decorzant, 'Internationalism in the Economic and Financial Organisation of the League of Nations', in Laqua, *Internationalism Reconfigured*, esp. pp. 116–18.

122 'Brussels may be the League seat', *New York Times* (12 January 1920).

123 Louis de Brouckère, 'Bruxelles, siège de la Société des Nations', *Le Mouvement Communal* (15 March 1919).

124 Marks, *Innocent Abroad*, p. 110.

125 Barros, *Office Without Power*, p. 82.

126 Otlet, 'La Belgique, siège de la Société des Nations', *Bulletin d'Informations de Presse* (5 October 1919).

127 Albert Renard, *La Paix par la pacification* (Brussels, 1922), p. 11.

128 Sally Marks, 'The small states at Geneva', *World Affairs*, 157 (1995), 191.

129 On Vandervelde's role in the preparations for the ILO, see Vandervelde, *Souvenirs*, pp. 287–92.

130 Maarten Van Alstein, 'No more war? Belgian reception of the League of Nations and arbitration after the First World War', *Diplomacy and Statecraft*, 18 (2007), 138.

131 MS IFLNS: David Davies to La Fontaine, 22 April 1920.

132 *Ibid.*, La Fontaine to Davies Davies, 21 May 1921.

133 Robert Cecil, *World Opinion and the League of Nations* (London, 1918), p. 11. On the British association, see Helen McCarthy, *The British People and the League of Nations: Democracy, Citizenship and Internationalism, c. 1918–45* (Manchester, 2011).

134 Christian Birebent, *Militants de la Paix et de la SDN: les mouvements de soutien à la Société des nations en France et au Royaume-Uni 1918–1925* (Paris, 2008); Jean-Michel Guieu, *Le Rameau et le glaive: les militants français pour la Société des Nations* (Paris, 2008); Jost Dülffer, 'Vom Internationalismus zum Expansionismus: Die Deutsche Liga für Völkerbund', in Wolfgang Elz and Sönke Neitzel (eds), *Internationale Beziehungen im 19. und 20. Jahrhundert: Festschrift für Winfried Baumgart zum 65. Geburtstag* (Paderborn, 2003), pp. 251–66.

135 MS IFLNS: La Fontaine to Léon Bourgeois, 15 September 1918.

136 Birebent, *Militants de la Paix*, pp. 67–9.

137 MS IFLNS: 'Textes des Propositions et des Vœux présentés par les Sociétés ayant adhéré à la Conférence (Bruxelles, 1919)'.

138 *Ibid.*, La Fontaine, 24 November 1919.

139 Anne-Isabelle Richard, 'Competition and complementarity: civil society networks and the question of decentralizing the League of Nations', *Journal of Global History*, 7 (2012), 246.

140 MS HLF 213: 'Situation active au 31 décembre 1925: Constitution du Fonds de Garantie. Versements par pays'.

141 MS IFLNS: La Fontaine to Jules Prudhommeaux, 2 November 1919.

142 *Ibid.*, La Fontaine to Davies Davies, 21 May 192.

143 *Ibid.*, Letter to La Fontaine, 27 September 1921.

144 Ole Spiermann, '"Who attempts too much does nothing well": the 1920s Advisory Committee of Jurists and the Statute of the Permanent Court of International Law', *British Yearbook of International Law*, 73 (2002), 256.

145 Birebent, *Militants de la Paix*, pp. 317–18.

146 MS LON, 24718/24718 ('Ligue belge pour la Société des Nations'): Henri Rolin to Eric Drummond, 15 November 1922. I thank Frank Beyersdorf for providing me with copies of this file.

147 *Ibid.*, Eric Drummond to Henri Rolin, 24 November 1922.

148 'Pour appuyer la S.D.N.', *Le XXe Siècle* (3 December 1922); 'Union belge pour la Société des Nations', *L'Etoile Belge* (2 December 1922); 'Le rôle et l'histoire de la S.D.N.: L'Union belge pour la Société des Nations', *L'Indépendance Belge* (3 December 1922); 'À l'Union Belge pour la S.D.N.', *Le Soir* (3 December 1922); 'L'Union belge pour la Société des Nations s'est crée vendredi, à Bruxelles', *Le Peuple* (3 December 1922).

149 MS WILPF, reel 57: Esther Chalmers to Gertrud Baer, 22 February 1937.

150 Christophe Bechet, 'La révision pacifiste des manuels scolaires: les enjeux de la mémoire de la guerre 14–18 dans l'enseignement belge de l'Entre-deux-guerres', *CHTP–BEG*, 20 (2008), 60–1.

151 Henri Rolin, *La Belgique à la Société des Nations* (Brussels, 1930), p. 12.
152 Ger van Roon, *Small States in Years of Depression: The Oslo Alliance, 1930–1940* (Maastricht, 1989).
153 Hymans, *Mémoires*, vol. 2, 579–80, citing a speech of 4 March 1931.
154 Johan den Hertog, 'Zelfstandigheidspolitiek: de achtergrond van een cruciale term in het buitenlands beleid van Nederland 1900–1940', *Bijdragen en mededelingen betreffende de geschiedenis der Nederlanden*, 124 (2009), 163–85.
155 E. Boyet, 'La Belgique neutre et loyale', *Der Völkerbund* (15 November 1936), 120.
156 Rolin, *Notre politique extérieure, conduit-elle à la paix?* (Brussels, 1938), p. 21.
157 'Contre la guerre: les pacifistes internationaux manifestent à Bruxelles', *La Dernière Heure* (1 August 1914).
158 See Grossi's comments on the 'patriotic attitude' of French and Italian activists: Grossi, *Le Pacifisme européen*, pp. 41–2.
159 Cooper, *Patriotic Pacifism*, p. 196. Cf. Grossi, *Le Pacifisme européen*, p. 387.
160 Helmut Mauermann, *Das Internationale Friedensbüro 1892–1950* (Stuttgart, 1990), p. 182–3.
161 *Ibid.*, p. 185.
162 Ralph Uhlig, 'Internationalismus in den zwanziger Jahren: die Interparlamentarische Union', *Historische Mitteilungen*, 4 (1991), 92.
163 Birebent, *Militants de la Paix*, p. 322.
164 La Fontaine, *The Great Solution*, p. 75.
165 *Ibid.*, p. 6.
166 Martin Albers, 'Between the crisis of democracy and world parliament: the development of the Inter-Parliamentary Union in the 1920s', *Journal of Global History*, 7 (2012), 199.
167 Katharina Rietzler, 'American internationalists in Europe: the Carnegie endowment for international peace in the early twentieth century' (MA thesis, UCL, 2005).
168 Mauermann, *Das Internationale Friedensbüro*, p. 194.
169 Letter *Golay to* Ruyssen, 26 March 1927 in 'Appel de M. Lafontaine (20 April 1927)', *MS IPB* 330/3.
170 Ingram, *The Politics of Dissent*, p. 121; Ceadel, *Semi-Detached Idealists*, pp. 239–376; Reinhold Lütgemeier-Davin, *Pazifismus zwischen Kooperation und Konfrontation: Das Deutsche Friedenskartell in der Weimarer Republik* (Cologne, 1982).
171 Peter Farurugia, 'The conviction of things not seen: religious pacifism in France, 1919–1945', in Brock and Socknat, *Challenge to Mars*, pp. 101–16.
172 Daniel Gorman, 'Ecumenical internationalism: Willoughby Dickinson, the League of Nations and the World Alliance for Promoting International Friendship through the Churches', *Journal of Contemporary History*, 45 (2010), 51–73; Harmjan Dam, *Der Weltbund für Freundschaftsarbeit der Kirchen 1914–1948: Eine ökumenische Friedensorganisation* (Frankfurt, 2001).
173 *Ibid.*, 179–82 and 418–22. On the 1936 event, see *Der Völkerbund: Mitteilungen der Schweizer Vereinigung für den Völkerbund* (15 November 1936), 116–18.

174 Géaroid Barry, *The Disarmament of Hatred: Marc Sangnier, French Catholicism and the Legacy of the First World War* (Basingstoke, 2012).
175 Heribert Köck, *Die völkerrechtliche Stellung des Heiligen Stuhls. Dargestellt an seinen Beziehungen zu Staaten und internationalen Organisationen* (Berlin, 1975), p. 630. See chapter 3: this body should not be confused with the Union Catholique d'Études Sociales et Économiques in Fribourg.
176 Müller, 'Anticipated exile of Christian democrats', p. 257.
177 Marcel Prelot, 'Organisation and activity of the League of Nations', in Stephen Brown (ed.), *International Relations from a Catholic Standpoint* (Dublin, 1932), p. 132.
178 Enrica Costa Bona, 'Le Bureau international de la paix et la Société des Nations', in Marta Petricioli and Donatella Cherubini (eds), *Pour la paix en Europe: institutions et société civile dans l'entre-deux-guerres* (Brussels, 2007), 19–39.
179 Jean-Michel Guieu, 'Les Congrès universels de la paix et la question de l'unité européenne, 1921–1939', in *ibid.*, pp. 399–400.
180 Enrica Costa Bona, *Il Bureau International del Paix nelle relazioni internationali (1919–1939)* (Milan, 2010), pp. 142–4.
181 MS WILPF, reel 56: flyer, 7 October 1931.
182 Thomas Davies, *The Possibilities of Transnational Activism: The Campaign for Disarmament Between the World Wars* (Leiden, 2007), p. 93. On the campaign, see also Andrew Webster, 'The transnational dream: politicians, diplomats and soldiers in the League of Nations' pursuit of international disarmament, 1920–1938', *Contemporary European History*, 14 (2005), 493–518.
183 MS HLF 031: Friedrich Adler to Emile Vandervelde, 2 June 1931.
184 MS WILPF, reel 56: letter by Esther Chalmers, 24 November 1924.
185 Kevin Morgan, 'Militarism and anti-militarism: socialists, communists and conscription in France and Britain 1900–1940', *Past and Present*, 202 (2009), 207–44.
186 See e.g. Barry, *The Disarmament of Hatred*, pp. 191–2.
187 Gotovitch, *Du communisme et des communistes*, pp. 403–4.
188 Bart de Ligt, *La Paix créatrice: histoire des principes et des tactiques de l'action directe contre la guerre*, vol. 2 (Paris, 1934), pp. 443–7. Cf. Herman Noordegraaf, 'The Anarchopacifism of Bart de Ligt', in Peter Brock and Thomas Socknat (eds), *Challenge to Mars: Essays on Pacifism from 1918 to 1945* (Toronto, 1999), pp. 89–100.
189 de Ligt, *La Paix créatrice*, vol. 2, 445.
190 MS WILPF, reel 57: G.O. Sanders to Jane Addams, 13 December 1931.
191 Bruno De Wever, *Greep naar de macht: Vlaams-nationalisme en Nieuwe Orde. Het VNV 1933–1945* (Tielt, 1994), p. 192.
192 MS HLF 148: 'Verbond V.O.S., Vergadering van 18 October 1934'.
193 Geneviève Duchenne, 'Les nouvelles relèves en Belgique francophone (1926–1936): une source pour l'européisme ?' in Olivier Dard and Etienne Deschamps (eds), *Les relèves en Europe d'un après-guerre à l'autre: racines, réseaux, projets et postérités* (Brussels, 2005), pp. 331–54.
194 'Rassemblement International contre la Guerre et le Militarisme', *Le Barrage*, 22 October 1936.

195 MS HLF 148: Challaye to La Fontaine, 22 August 1936. The organisation's letterhead actually misspelt Masereel's name.

196 *Ibid.*, La Fontaine to Challeye, 7 April 1937.

197 Marta Petricioli, Donatella Cherubini and Alessandra Anteghini (eds), *Les Etats-Unis d'Europe: un projet pacifiste* (Bern, 2004).

198 Maurice Agulhon, 'Victor Hugo et l'Europe: les Etats-Unis d'Europe', in Gilles Pécout (ed.), *Penser les frontières de l'Europe du XIXe au XXIe siècle* (Paris, 2003), pp. 41–52; William Stead, *The United States of Europe on the Eve of the Parliament of Peace* (Toronto, 1899).

199 Carl Pegg, *Evolution of the European Idea, 1914–1932* (Chapel Hill, NC, 1983), pp. 8–13; Patrick Pasture, 'The interwar origins of international labour's European commitment (1919–1934)', *Contemporary European History*, 10 (2001), 221–37.

200 Edouard Herriot, *Europe* (Paris, 1930).

201 Richard, 'Competition and complementarity', 242.

202 For a famous example of the 'decline' discourse, see Oswald Spengler, *Der Untergang des Abendlandes. Umrisse einer Morphologie der Weltgeschichte*, 2 vols (Munich, 1920–1922).

203 Richard Coudenhove-Kalergi, *Pan-Europe* (New York, 1926), p. 99.

204 Nicholas Murray Butler, 'Introduction', in Coudenhove-Kalergi, *Pan-Europe*, p. viii.

205 Alfred Zimmern, 'Europe and the world community' in Geneva Institute of International Relations, *The Problems of Peace. 6th Series* (London, 1932), pp. 122–33.

206 Jean-Michel Guieu, 'Les Congrès universels de la paix et la question de l'unité européenne, 1921–1939', in Petricioli and Cherubini, *Pour la paix en Europe*, pp. 392–5.

207 Richard, 'Competition and complementarity', pp. 247 and 251–4.

208 Duchenne, *Esquisses d'une Europe nouvelle*, p. 203.

209 Duchenne, 'L'idée d'Europe en Belgique dans l'entre-deux-guerres (1919–1939), in Duchenne, Michel Dumoulin and Arthe Van Laer (eds), *La Belgique, les petits États et la construction européenne* (Brussels, 2003), pp. 46–7.

210 Duchenne, 'La pensée européenne du socialiste Jules Destrée: un internationalisme européen (1906–1936)', *Annales d'Études européennes de l'Université catholique de Louvain*, 5 (2001), 21–45.

211 Christophe Verbruggen, 'Het egonetwerk van Reiner Leven en George Sarton als toegang tot transnationaal intellectueel engagement', *BTNG–RBHC*, 38 (2008), 87–129.

212 Irénée Van der Ghinst, 'Le Congrès paneuropéen', *Le Peuple* (11 October 1926).

213 Van der Ghinst, 'Paneurope', *Le Flambeau*, 10 (1927), 223–30, as cited in Duchenne, *Visions et projets belges pour l'Europe*, pp. 60–5.

214 Luisa Passerini, *Europe in Love, Love in Europe: Imagination and Politics in Britain Between the Wars* (London, 1999).

215 Duchenne, *Esquisses d'une Europe nouvelle*, pp. 35–6.

216 John Hellman, *The Communitarian Third Way: Alexandre Marc and Ordre Nouveau, 1930–2000* (Montreal, 2002), p. 134.

217 De Wever, *Greep naar de macht*, pp. 415–19.

218 Norman Ingram, '"Nous allons vers les monastères": French pacifism and the crisis of the Second World War', in Martin Alexander and Kenneth Mouré (eds), *Crisis and Renewal in Twentieth Century France* (Oxford, 2002), pp. 132–51.

219 Costa Bona, *Il Bureau* international de la Paix, pp. 159 –62.

220 *World Peace Congress*. Brussels. 3, 4, 5, 6 September 1936 (Paris, 1936). See Ceadel, *Semi-Detached Idealists*, pp. 348–58.

221 *World Peace Congress*, p. 187.

6

Universalism

Internationalism was sustained by ideas about civilisation, international relations and society. It was, however, also a cultural phenomenon in which politics, science and visions of modernity intersected. This aspect is illustrated by two figures who have featured at various parts of this study and whose joint efforts warrant detailed examination: Henri La Fontaine and Paul Otlet. The basic outline of their activism is well known, yet any account of internationalism in Belgium needs to consider their role at the nexus of different transnational projects. The multifaceted nature of their internationalism makes it possible to interpret it as a form of universalism.[1] By the 1890s, La Fontaine was closely involved in several interrelated movements, including pacifism, feminism, freemasonry, freethought and socialism. Meanwhile, Otlet's intertwined commitment to bibliography and internationalism has been the subject of several publications and even a film.[2] He has been described as the author of 'the first treatise on documentation',[3] and the *New York Times* has lauded his 'remarkable foresight into the possibilities of electronic media'.[4]

Universalism was inherent in the shared projects of La Fontaine and Otlet, notably the International Institute of Bibliography (IIB, 1895), the Union of International Associations (UIA, 1907/1910), the *Palais Mondial* in Brussels (1919) and their campaign for the construction of a world capital city (*Cité Mondiale*). To the two Belgians, these undertakings formed part of a comprehensive endeavour. If, for purposes of clarity, this chapter sometimes divides them into separate parts, it does not deny their shared conceptual underpinnings. Existing accounts tend to accentuate the visionary nature of these schemes. However, as this chapter argues, their endeavours reflected widespread concerns in the age of internationalism. With their optimism about scientific progress and its ability to organise the world, their ideas can be located within the wider context of European modernism.[5] For this reason, it is apposite to begin with the wider cultural and scientific contexts of Belle Époque Belgium.

Science, art and transnational exchange in Belgium

Belgium's role as a key site for international congresses has been acknowledged in Anne Rasmussen's major study on pre-1914 scientific internationalism.[6] The country's economic prosperity contributed to its involvement in scholarly networks, as exemplified by the role of the industrialist Ernest Solvay. While his wealth derived from the production of soda carbonate, Solvay had an interest in social theory, expressed in his *Principes d'orientation sociale*.[7] He championed the progressive liberalism of Paul Janson and was a senator from 1892 to 1894 and from 1897 to 1900. Solvay funded a variety of institutes that were based in the Parc Léopold of Brussels, including institutions for Physiology (1891), Hygiene, Bacteriology and Therapy (1894), the Social Sciences (1902), Physics (1912) and Chemistry (1913). These centres for Belgian scientific life also hosted international conferences such as the 'Conseils Solvay'.[8] Solvay contributed financially to the foundation of La Fontaine and Otlet's IIB, in line with his role as 'a kind of Belgian Carnegie'.[9]

The growth of scientific institutions coincided with significant developments in Belgian culture. In his memoirs, the Austrian writer Stefan Zweig mentioned Belgium's 'artistic upturn' at the fin de siècle, estimating that, to some extent, the intensity of its cultural life had overtaken that of France.[10] This process had begun in the 1880s, when 'for the first time, Belgium was to become a literary centre in its own right'.[11] From 1881, the periodical *La Jeune Belgique* offered a voice for 'Art for Art's Sake'. In its early days, the periodical's associates also included key figures in symbolist literature, notably Emile Verhaeren, Maurice Maeterlinck and Georges Rodenbach.[12] Verhaeren, Rodenbach and the painter Fernand Khnopff subsequently joined the naturalist writer Camille Lemonnier and the realist sculptor Constantin Meunier in the rival circle surrounding *L'Art Moderne* and *La Société Nouvelle*. These two periodicals attacked the *La Jeune Belgique* for its remoteness from everyday concerns, promoting the vision of 'social art' instead.[13] La Fontaine and Otlet had toyed with literary efforts during their youth. Moreover, they were personally connected to the driving force behind *L'Art Moderne* and *La Société Nouvelle*: both had started careers in the legal profession by working for Edmond Picard, whose cultural impact has been discussed in chapter 1.

In spite of their contrasting views, both *La Jeune Belgique* and *L'Art Moderne* drew heavily on Wagnerism when it came to music.[14] Wagnerism was an international movement which displayed universal ambitions with its conception of the *Gesamtkunstwerk*. As a young man, La Fontaine had attended the very first Wagner *Festspiele* in Bayreuth (1876) alongside individuals who became key figures in Belgium's cultural life, including the author Octave Maus, the critic Maurice Kufferath and the conductor Joseph

Dupont.[15] La Fontaine later served as treasurer of the Belgian Wagner committee which organised further trips to Bayreuth.[16] In 1885, he even translated sections of Wagner operas into French verse; they were recited at an evening hosted by Constantin Meunier.[17] La Fontaine's Wagnerian enthusiasm was not unique. For instance, in 1891, the arts section of the Maison du Peuple in Brussels launched its lecture programme with a presentation by Kufferath on Wagner. Fittingly, Emile Verhaeren explicitly referred to Wagner when describing the Section's aim as 'initiating workers to modern aesthetic movements'.[18] The variety of Wagner's supporters highlights the observation 'that the movement behaved very much like a chameleon, and a particularly crafty one at that, in its ability to insinuate itself into so many different cultural and political scenes'.[19]

The cultural vigour of fin-de-siècle Belgium extended to the visual arts. In 1883, Octave Maus established the artistic circle Les XX, with James Ensor and Fernand Khnopff among its members. Reflecting an internationalism that has been described as 'unique in its genre', the circle invited artists from abroad, organised exhibitions of non-Belgian painters and fostered links with the British Arts and Crafts movement.[20] Art Nouveau, which gathered momentum from the 1890s, was intrinsically connected with the concepts promoted by Wagnerians and Les XX, especially in championing the 'unity of all the arts'.[21] The art historian Jeremy Howard has stressed the 'cosmopolitan nature of Belgian Art Nouveau' in this context.[22] With architects and artists such as Paul Hankar, Victor Horta and Henry Van de Velde, Brussels was a centre for this international artistic movement in which both local peculiarities and European trends converged. Even though La Fontaine and Otlet were not artists in their own right, they operated within the cultural setting of fin-de-siècle Brussels. For instance, in 1894, Otlet commissioned the Art Nouveau architect Octave Van Rysselberghe to build and Van de Velde to furnish his city house. Octave Maus praised Otlet for supporting the new movement and 'braving the jeers and criticism' of traditionalists.[23]

Scientific internationalism and bibliography

Scholarly exchange was a key feature of La Fontaine and Otlet's joint efforts. They engaged with Brussels-based sociology and its institutions, for instance the Société d'Etudes Sociales et Politiques, whose members included Emile Vandervelde, Hector Denis, Guillaume De Greef and Jules Destrée.[24] This society built upon the earlier efforts of the International Social Science Association, whose relationship with the peace movement has been mentioned in chapter 5. La Fontaine and Otlet were also among the early associates of Solvay's Institute of Social Sciences (1894), once again alongside Vandervelde and De Greef.[25] In the meantime, an International Institute of Sociology had been founded in Paris (1893). Although La Fontaine and Otlet only joined it at a later stage, its case is important for understanding the wider phenomenon of internationalism: the institution involved key figures from Belgian sociology and, as Peter Wagner has argued, its history challenges narratives about the primacy of national traditions in the social sciences.[26]

The sociological context contributed to La Fontaine and Otlet's foundation of the International Institute of Bibliography in 1895: they had gathered expertise in this area by compiling surveys of sociological literature. The new body drew on the repertoire of scientific internationalism, from conferences to periodicals. It also promoted the Universal Decimal Classification (UDC) as an international standard for bibliographies and libraries, based on a translated and expanded version of Melvil Dewey's Decimal Classification. Alongside the promotion of the UDC, whose first complete edition appeared in 1905, the IIB compiled a Universal Bibliographical Repertory – a card catalogue aimed to capture 'the totality of human knowledge' by gathering information on every book published in the world.[27] By 1912, it comprised around 11.7 million cards.[28] As an international information service, the IIB received over a thousand bibliographic queries per annum before the First World War.[29]

The circumstances of the IIB's foundation demonstrate the fluid boundaries between non-governmental and governmental internationalism. Otlet and La Fontaine hoped that the Belgian government would convene an official conference and provide diplomatic assistance for the creation of a public international union.[30] In line with this aim, a quasi-governmental twin organisation, the International Office of Bibliography, was set up alongside the IIB. Franz Schollaert, then Minister for Education, had recommended such patronage in a letter to Leopold II, stating that this step would help the government to 'establish in our country an institution that could become... a principal organ for the intellectual life of the peoples'.[31] Although the International Office was run by Otlet and La Fontaine, its first president was another prominent internationalist: Edouard Descamps. In 1907, Solvay succeeded him in this position.

Looking back upon the turbulent relationship between the Belgian government and the IIB in 1933, Otlet explained the motivations behind the creation of two separate entities: the Office had been established as there was no legal statute that covered an international institution such as the IIB. Otlet himself stressed that, although based at the International Office of Bibliography, the Universal Bibliographic Repertory was never understood as a purely Belgian matter but conceived as 'international, global'.[32] Nonetheless, its founders were happy to accept the financial rewards of this relationship. The Belgian government supported the bibliographic endeavours, starting with an annual subsidy of 10,000 Belgian Francs, rising further until its suspension in 1927.[33]

La Fontaine and Otlet's bibliographic efforts seem to exemplify internationalism as a tool for scholarly and professional cooperation. After the foundation of the American Library Association (1876), similar organisations emerged in countries such as Britain (1877), Germany (1900) and France (1906). Bibliography was linked to the promotion of unified cataloguing rules in the mid-nineteenth century, yet key contributions to bibliographic practices were also made by outsiders without a background in librarianship.[34] The efforts of the IIB's founders were a case in point: despite the voluntary nature of their bibliographic work, Otlet and La Fontaine participated in congresses of editors, archivists and librarians.[35] They also collaborated or competed with projects such as the *International Catalogue of Scientific Literature*, launched by the Royal Society of London.[36]

As Anne Rasmussen has shown, Otlet and La Fontaine constituted one of several *milieux organisatrices* of the pre-war years.[37] Yet the IIB's bibliographic internationalism proved resilient beyond the Great War. In this context, the IIB's internationalisation in the 1920s is particularly instructive. The body had been centred on Brussels, with corresponding institutions in Paris and Zurich. After the war, new hubs developed in London around the British Society for International Bibliography, and at The Hague around the Netherlands Institute for Documentation and Filing. The changing host cities and increasing frequency of their congresses testify to these shifts. The Cologne congress in 1929, for instance, featured delegates from affiliates in Germany, Belgium, France, Great Britain, Holland, Switzerland and Czechoslovakia as well as by representatives of various international associations.[38] The Paris congress of 1937, organised within the framework of the International Exposition of Arts and Technology in Modern Life, marked the culmination of this process. Run by an international committee rather than the institute itself, it attracted 350 participants from 48 countries with representatives from 40 governments and 50 international associations.[39] Underlining the Institute's decentralised character, the organisation was renamed 'International Federation for Documentation' at the event.

The IIB's interwar growth revealed the tensions between transnational aspirations and practices. The Belgian founders were increasingly concerned about their loss of control: in 1932, Otlet alleged that expansion had led to 'problems', proposing that conference be held biannually, with Brussels as the site every six years.[40] At the time, he expressed his fear of German dominance of the organisation,[41] and complained that 'The Dutch…constantly demonstrate their mistrust of the IIB's founders'.[42] Arguments focused on the institute's priorities: its non-Belgian members were primarily interested in the promotion and elaboration of the UDC, and less keen on the Universal Bibliographical Repository. To Otlet and La Fontaine, the IIB was a holistic project, based on the ideas of its founders and their 'organic, continuous development'.[43] During the institute's 1932 congress in Frankfurt, matters nearly reached a breaking point. The Belgian founders protested against the neglect of their catalogue and described it as 'barely comprehensible to negate or push aside... a "child" whose birth one has assisted and whom one has ceaselessly encouraged; a grown child, strong and robust, which certainly has ruined neither the family nor the friends of the family and who has never conducted himself badly'.[44] The conflicts led La Fontaine and Otlet to consider founding a separate association.[45] Although these tensions were ultimately resolved, they revealed the conflict caused by the shift away from a Brussels-centred endeavour. Internationalisation could meet with suspicions, even among internationalists.

From bibliographic internationalism to international order

The IIB's history beyond the Great War illustrates various obstacles to transnational collaboration – some of them scholarly, some national, and others personal. Seen in its wider context, the case of the IIB also illustrates how 'scientific internationalism' was not exclusively concerned with scholarship, but potentially underpinned by universalist aspirations. Bibliography sought to answer a central challenge of modernity: the creation of order in an age when 'all that was solid melted into air'.[46] The UDC and the Universal Bibliographic Repertory were conceived as tools for the creation of order, combating 'anarchy' in the realm of bibliography.[47] As Rayward has pointed out, these schemes were launched at a time when people questioned 'the effectiveness of the now long-established organisational arrangements for managing public knowledge'.[48] Significantly, the conception of these new institutions was international rather than national. The founders of the IIB were not alone in developing such schemes: initiatives such as Wilhelm Ostwald's *Die Brücke* before the First World War, or H. G. Wells's 'world brain' and Otto Neurath's *International Encyclopedia of Unified Science* during the interwar years were driven by related concepts and motivations.[49]

The epistemic project of Otlet and La Fontaine revolved around organisation and classification. By breaking down 'universal knowledge' into its individual components, the UDC and the Universal Bibliographical Repertory formed part of an encyclopaedic tradition.[50] Early on, the IIB expanded its collections beyond written sources, highlighted by a photo collection that included over 81,000 items in 1912.[51] The Belgian efforts had conceptual resemblances with world's fairs which created their own classifications with universal ambitions.[52] Indeed, another project of La Fontaine and Otlet, namely their 'international museum', originated in an exhibition that coincided with the Brussels *exposition universelle* of 1910.[53] One observer described this museum as a 'vast encyclopaedic book whose pages, instead of being bound together, are spread out on the walls and whose images are replaced by large schematic tables, or comparative objects in display cases'.[54]

As Nader Vossaughian has pointed out, Otto Neurath offers a useful point of comparison: his aforementioned encyclopaedia was complemented by projects on museums, pictorial representation and town planning.[55] Such observations underline the modernist dimension of La Fontaine and Otlet's efforts.

Given their encyclopaedic approach, it should barely surprise us that La Fontaine and Otlet did not confine their collaboration to the field of bibliography. As highlighted by chapter 5, a concern with international order was intrinsic to La Fontaine's pacifist endeavours from the 1880s. Meanwhile, in conceptual terms, Otlet's interest in classification ranged beyond science and literature. This broader conception was testified by his increasing use of the term 'documentation' – rather than bibliography – after 1903.[56] The stimulus to create an institution for their further-reaching ambitions arrived with the Congress of Global Economic Expansion in Mons in 1905. In response to one of its resolutions, La Fontaine, Otlet and the Catholic civil servant Cyrille Van Overbergh founded the Central Office of International Institutions which, three years later, turned into the UIA. These bodies were conceived as clearing houses for all kinds of international organisations.

Internationalism as science

The idea that internationalism could and should be documented was central to two publications launched by the Central Office/UIA: the first was the *Annuaire de la Vie Internationale*, a yearbook published in 1909 and 1911 together with the Austro-German pacifist Alfred Fried; the second was the periodical *La Vie Internationale*, co-founded with Van Overbergh in 1912. Even before his association with the Brussels activists, Fried had collected and disseminated information on peace societies, international congresses and arbitration.[57] Fried's commitment was informed by his ideas about 'scientific pacifism', which asserted that the study of international processes would reveal the world's increasing interdependence. His theories exemplified the teleological aspects of internationalist thought. The German legal scholar Hans Wehberg – who later succeeded Fried as editor of the periodical *Die Friedenswarte* – expressed comparable views in an article for *La Vie Internationale*. Discussing 'Le Pacifisme comme Science', Wehberg argued that the different manifestations of internationalism merited serious study because they were 'good omens for a peaceful future'.[58] In other words, documentation in the field of internationalism was linked to particular expectations of historical change and an attempt to educate the public about this alleged process.

La Fontaine and Otlet adopted a similar discourse. One example is Otlet's 1907 essay on 'La Loi d'Ampliation et l'Internationalisme', first published in a sociological periodical that Van Overbergh edited. In an earlier issue of the journal, the historian Hubert Van Houtte had outlined the features of this 'law': 'In the present period, the concentration becomes increasingly intense..., the new groupings take the form of a union – sometimes economic, sometimes political – but they nonetheless determine a form of internationalism which gradually replaces the nationalism that has blossomed in modern times'.[59] Otlet argued that development of internationalism validated Van Houtte's theory.[60] He suggested that five international forces contributed towards this process: the international law community, the Inter-Parliamentary Conferences, socialists, pacifists and – with particular significance for Otlet – international associations. Otlet and La Fontaine reiterated such notions when outlining the UIA's agenda in 1914:

> The organisation of the world is due to a vast and continuous movement which, remote in origin, has, of late years, acquired an immense impetus. It tends to stimulate more cooperation among similar groups in all countries, insures a greater acquisition of knowledge and of technical expertise throughout the world, promotes the unification of methods and international agreements on all subjects wherever possible and desirable.[61]

As chapter 1 has shown, La Fontaine and Otlet accorded a special role to their own country in their representations of an onward march towards global integration. Otlet argued that the 'very idea of congresses truly matured and was perfected in Belgium', which had 'founded and inaugurated the work of international congresses for the world'.[62] To him, a study of international congresses revealed both the general growth of international life and the specific 'international spirit' of their own country, which was located 'at the crossroads of three great nations, each of which personify a great civilising spirit'.[63]

In interpreting internationalism as a historical process, Otlet and La Fontaine stressed the significance of international associations. For the first issue of the *Annuaire de la Vie Nationale*, Otlet wrote an essay of over 130 pages which sought to represent and classify such organisations in their different guises.[64] Other sections of the publication listed a great variety of associations and their activities. From this, it was only a small step to bring them together not only on paper, but also at an actual event. The first such occasion, the 'world congress of international associations', was held in Brussels in 1910, attracting delegates from 132 international organisations and 13 governments.[65] It took place within the framework of the world's fair, as did its successor event, the 1913 congress in Ghent. Rayward has described the latter's scale as 'such a success as to make the whole internationalist program of the UIA not only possible but on the point of fulfilment'.[66] While the scheduled 1915 congress in San Francesco was cancelled, further events were held after the First World War, yet by the seventh and final congress in 1927, their scale had diminished.

The linkages with the world's fairs facilitated the UIA's collaboration with Belgian elites. As Madeleine Herren has shown, the Belgian government's support for La Fontaine and Otlet's efforts reflected a policy of official support for internationalist ventures.[67] The 1910 congress was chaired by Auguste Beernaert and featured prominent Catholic politicians such as Henry Carton de Wiart and Gérard Cooreman on its organising committee. The event's Belgian focus and its international ambitions were noted abroad. Having been invited by the Belgian government, the French Minister of Foreign Affairs advised against his government's participation. He expressed his concern about certain 'particularities of the programme and reports published by the congress organisers, which seem to reflect tendencies that are hardly compatible with the essential independence of each international institution'.[68] In a post-congress report, the French ambassador argued that the congress had indeed been linked to efforts that aimed to make Brussels 'the capital of international institutions and the centre where the increasingly numerous manifestations of international life converge'.[69] However, because of the 'vast and rather vague' nature of the event's objectives, fears of centralisation were unfounded: 'the sheer scale of the indetermination regarding action… seems to allow all associations to compete without suffering a reduction in their own sphere. What the congress primarily seems to seek is to unite and not to dominate.'[70] Such an assessment was evidently compatible with ideas about Belgium as a meeting ground, rather than a place that would overrule efforts in other countries.

The UIA did not confine itself to seeking support from the Belgian government. For the publication of the *Annuaire*, Fried had acquired funds from the Institute of Peace, an institution founded by Prince Albert I of Monaco. The launch of *La Vie Internationale* was made possible by an annual subsidy of 15,000 US dollars from the Carnegie Endowment for International Peace.[71] The journal was but one of several projects supported by the American foundation, which also awarded annual support of 24,000 US dollars to the IPB.[72] Indeed, both Fried and La Fontaine served on the Advisory Council for the Endowment's European Centre in Paris. Nicholas Murray Butler, President of Columbia University and a leading figure in the Endowment, initially suggested moving the IPB to Brussels so that it could merge with the UIA.[73] Although European pacifists did not back this idea, the UIA cultivated its links with Butler, for instance translating one of his articles for *La Vie Internationale*.[74] After the outbreak of the First World War, the Belgians lost their Carnegie grant. Having protested about this treatment during the war, La Fontaine renewed his pleas in 1922: 'Eight years have passed since the Carnegie Endowment for International Peace decided to stop support…We have remained silent for three years hoping a for a spontaneous recognition that the Union had not demented and [had] not want[ed] to look like beggars.'[75] One year later, La Fontaine complained to the Belgian ambassador in Washington about the 'massive deception' he had experienced.[76]

The souring of this relationship did not mean that the Carnegie Endowment withdrew from Belgium in all respects. For instance, Butler personally raised funds for the reconstruction of Louvain library.[77] Furthermore, in 1921, the foundation launched an enquiry into the contents of Belgian school textbooks as part of a wider project.[78] The cessation of Carnegie support for the UIA and the IPB was, however, indicative of a grant-giving policy which increasingly focused on other activities, for instance the 'scientific study' of international relations.[79] Despite their own claims to represent a 'scientific' approach to internationalism, the apparent idealism of the UIA's founders did not fit this agenda.

Mondialism

Beyond the attempt to document international life, the UIA maintained a greater ambition: namely to represent the needs of international associations. During the war, Otlet argued that they should become constituent parts of the new order, for instance as consultative councils for public international unions.[80] He even proposed an international bicameral system, with the lower chamber representing national parliaments and the upper house comprising delegates of international associations.[81] The focus on the associational dimension of internationalism was reflected in demands for a legal statute for international organisations. In October 1919, this campaign resulted in a new Belgian law. Passed at a point when Belgium had lost its campaign to host the League of Nations, the Belgian legislation was an attempt to affirm the country's ongoing significance for international encounters. It promised legal recognition for international associations that had their seat in Belgium and that involved at least one Belgian in the running of the organisation.

In the 1920s and 1930s, the collaboration between La Fontaine and Otlet increasingly focused on two projects that have already been mentioned in chapter 1: the *Palais Mondial* and the *Cité Mondiale*. The intellectual roots of both schemes dated back to the pre-war years, when the UIA had argued for the creation of an 'intellectual centre' to support international efforts.[82] Based on state-owned premises in a wing of the Palais du Cinquantenaire, the *Palais Mondial* hosted the IIB, the UIA and several other organisations. La Fontaine and Otlet's 'international museum' had already been based in this location since 1910 and thus preceded the larger institution; its collections expanded after the war. Conceptually and practically, the *Palais Mondial* united different strands of La Fontaine and Otlet's work for organisation and documentation: it hosted the Universal Bibliographic Repertory and an international library as well as the permanent exhibitions on books and the periodical press.

The palace also provided the setting for the so-called 'international fortnights' that took place four times between 1920 and 1927.[83] On the first such occasion, the French pacifist Jeanne Mélin combined her participation with a speaker tour and meetings, including one with La Fontaine's sister Léonie. In doing so, she inspired the foundation of a Belgian WILPF section.[84] In addition to its own initiatives, the *Palais Mondial* hosted events from other organisations, for instance the Pan-African Congress of 1921 and the Universal Peace Congress of 1931. These activities were part of a wider effort to forge alliances and put the Brussels institution at the heart of different internationalisms. For instance, when the Belgians launched a series of 'international university' sessions in 1920, they sought support from the League of Nations and the Belgian government, but also partnerships with the International Olympic Committee, the Universities Bureau of the British Empire, the Office of French Universities and a Barcelona-based Ibero-American Association.[85] This particular educational project was conceived as the nucleus of a more permanent institution, but competed with several other schemes for resources and patronage.[86] The competitive dimension became evident when the question of an international university was placed on the agenda of the League of Nations: Otlet insisted upon the 'anterior rights' of his organisation. In a letter to Geneva, he asserted that 'public opinion would hardly accept it if, instead of helping an institution such as ours, the League of Nations initiated, several years after its creation, a new establishment with the same aim'.[87] Seen in their wider context, these efforts reveal the ambition to gain official recognition and make the *Palais Mondial* the central site for a variety of international efforts.

In the mid-1920s, with the survival of their *Palais Mondial* temporarily under threat, La Fontaine and Otlet considered a move to Geneva. They envisaged 'splendid results' by combining the work of the existing libraries of international organisations with their own projects, from the IIB to their 'international museum': this, they argued, would be the making of a 'Universal Documentation Centre'.[88] Such language expressed the conceptual resemblances to their other major project in the interwar years: the campaign for a *Cité Mondiale* – a 'world capital' that was to serve as a centre for international life. The inspiration for this project stemmed from the Belgians' 1911 encounter with the 'World Communication Centre', a scheme developed by the sculptor Hendrik Christian Andersen and the architect Ernest Hébrard. Built on extra-territorialised soil, the *Cité Mondiale* was to host the headquarters of international associations, a permanent world exhibition and scientific institutions.[89] The project stimulated the imagination of several architects, the most famous being Le Corbusier who elaborated drafts for a *Cité Mondiale* in Geneva in 1928–29.[90]

The vision for a *Cité Mondiale* suggested a partial shift in Otlet's thought. Back in 1907, when the Dutch internationalist Pieter Eijkman proposed to transform The Hague into a 'world capital', Otlet deemed such a construct unnecessary. According to the Belgian bibliographer, several world cities – including Brussels as a site for international associations – had emerged naturally.[91] Was this merely a way of defending Brussels over a potential rival? The allegation that Belgium had been chosen 'spontaneously' was indeed a frequent feature of Otlet's writings.[92] However, Louis Frank, who promoted the idea of creating a 'federal district of the world' in Belgium, also believed Otlet to be opposed to this concept. As late as 1913, Frank referred to Otlet's opposition to centralising attempts and his emphasis on the collaboration of different groups or clusters.[93] Elements of this earlier perspective were still in evidence during the 1930s, as Otlet proposed a so-called *Mundaneum* for every city with international significance, with a central *Mundaneum* coordinating this network from the *Cité Mondiale*.[94]

While his access to Belgian and international authorities declined in the 1930s, Otlet's rhetoric on the *Cité Mondiale* became ever-more emphatic:

> Summary of the total, symbol of all symbols... classification of classifications, documentation of documentations, home of homes, university of universities. It will be like the 101st wonder of the world, a monument to all the material and intellectual glories of the Universe; sacred inspiration of great ideas and noble activities; treasure made by duplication of the sum of all creative works, brought here as a contribution to science and to the universal organisation.[95]

Faced with such statements, it is tempting to dismiss his schemes as utopias – yet a utopian streak was intrinsic to many internationalist ventures. Furthermore, the *Cité Mondiale* reflected the intertwined currents of urban planning and reform: the early twentieth century was characterised by a wide range of efforts to reshape the urban space, from the garden town movement to urbanist visions engendered by the Russian Revolution.[96] In his study of capital city planning, the architectural historian Wolfgang Sonne has considered the precursor of the *Cité Mondiale* – the 'World Centre of Communication' – alongside schemes for the capital cities of Washington, Greater Berlin, Canberra and New Delhi. According to Sonne, the World Centre of Communication 'was the glittering high point of French urbanism in the twentieth century, a hybrid of technological advancement and traditional design philosophy'.[97]

Social reform, sociology and city planning were closely entwined and often driven by transnational exchanges.[98] Underlining such connections, La Fontaine and Otlet were in contact with Patrick Geddes, the Scottish reformer, town planner and scholar whose interests were similarly broad-ranging.[99] World exhibitions emerged as points where such strands converged: on these occasions, urban reformers and philanthropists presented their visions of the future.[100] The Ghent exhibition of 1913 was a case in point, as Otlet and La

Fontaine helped to found the International Union of Local Authorities. They thus provided a link between two currents that underpinned the organisation, namely 'utopian aspirations towards universal co-operation and science'.[101] In similar fashion, Patrizia Dogliani has argued that at Ghent, three different trends of municipalism intersected, namely aims for an 'inter-class alliance', 'networks of exchange and opposition' and 'utopianism'.[102] The municipal movement was also related to internationalising efforts in administrative science: three years before the Ghent meeting, a *congrès international des sciences administratives* had taken place during the Brussels world's fair. Again, these activities were backed by La Fontaine and Otlet. Spanish exhibits on local administration were subsequently passed on to the Belgian internationalists for their international museum work.[103] Juan Conde de Torre-Vélez, a Spanish member of administrative networks, supported the work of the UIA and participated in its events.[104]

In 1930, Otlet reaffirmed the connection between social reform and his 'world capital', arguing that the latter might foster new models of social organisation.[105] One year later, at an event organised by Belgian urban reformers, Otlet introduced a new concept, the *Urbaneum*, to tackle urban problems.[106] Meanwhile, La Fontaine remained supportive of various reformist ventures, reflected in his political activities as a socialist senator, his support for the ILO and his interest in projects such as the National Unit Plan in Cincinnati, which aimed to transform the social infrastructure of a local quarter.[107] The UIA's collaboration with Le Corbusier was another example of such shared concerns, as the architect was renowned for his engagement with urban and social questions. However, rather than appearing as exceptional, a project such as the *Cité Mondiale* can also be interpreted as a particular form of internationalism in which different impulses converged: internationalism as universalism.

To Otlet, international plans did not preclude national ones, as evidenced by his *Plan Belgique* of 1935. However, he stressed that national action should be conceived within the framework of further-reaching integration, envisaging an 'Interplan… Plan of Plans… Universal and Global Plan'.[108] His starting point was the perception of a 'great movement for standardisation and organisation', exemplified by Schacht's economic plan in Nazi Germany, the Soviet Union's Five-Year Plans, the National Recovery Act in the USA, the scientific organisation of labour in France, as well as the de Man and Van Zeeland plans in Belgium.[109] This indiscriminate listing suggested a problematic conception of centralised power. Otlet acknowledged that 'organisation' or 'the concentration of forces' could be attained in two ways: either 'dictatorship aided by bureaucracy, secret police, censorship, with all the internal and external risks that are inherent to this regime: the Soviet, Mussolini, Hitler types' or 'free associations…based on persuasion, negotiation and clear demonstration of the common good'.[110] He stressed that only democratic work would render a plan truly sustainable. Nonetheless, his comments reveal a clear tension: on the one hand, the focus on independent actors which the UIA had previously sought to represent; on the other hand, the implicit top-down nature of seeking change on a grand scale.

Intellectual cooperation

Although the campaign for the *Cité Mondiale* attracted little official support, the interwar work of the UIA was not without consequence. In 1920, the UAI's World Congress of International Associations presented the draft convention for an intergovernmental organisation for intellectual work. The conceptualisation of this body as a 'vast collective brain' echoed the encyclopaedic aspects that featured so prominently in La Fontaine and Otlet's work.[111] However, the UIA's campaign also exemplified two key dimensions of the 'internationalisation of the intellectual field'.[112] The first aspect was the support for a broadly defined constituency of 'intellectual workers'. Such efforts built upon pre-1914 traditions. As early as 1858, a congress in Brussels had pushed for the international recognition of intellectual property rights, and in 1886 the Bern Convention for the Protection of Literary Works of 1886 became a landmark document on these issues.[113] After the war, the precarious situation of many intellectuals lent particular urgency to efforts that can be described as 'intellectual trade-unionism'.[114] The UIA's efforts formed part of this development, as did the International Confederation of Intellectual Workers, in which Otlet was also active. The second aspect was the connection between intellectual endeavour and international order. Even though science and the arts evoked universal values, the events of 1914 had revealed the competing appeal of nationalism among intellectuals.[115] After the war, the International Research Council and the International Union of the Academies, both based in Brussels, implemented a 'scientific boycott' of the Central Powers, causing German counter-measures.[116] Seen from this angle, the UIA's campaign for a new organisation was congruent with the ambition to build cultural and scientific bridges.

At the first League of Nations Assembly in November 1920, Paul Hymans took up the UIA's proposals. La Fontaine subsequently acted as rapporteur of the League committee which considered the foundation of an intellectual branch of the League.[117] These efforts ultimately produced the International Committee on Intellectual Cooperation (ICIC) in 1922 and the International Institute of Intellectual Cooperation (IIIC) in 1926. Both bodies operated under the auspices of the League of Nations and later constituted – with several other entities – the League's Organisation for Intellectual Cooperation. In an essay on the ICIC, Otlet portrayed the UIA as its direct precursor.[118]

Studies of the League's work for intellectual cooperation have acknowledged the formative role of La Fontaine and Otlet, yet they have also shown that their influence on the League remained limited.[119] To their dismay, neither Otlet nor La Fontaine was appointed to the ICIC.[120] While not officially based on national delegates, national considerations affected the selection process of ICIC members. Nonetheless, the ICIC's initial twelve members included figures of international renown, for instance Marie Curie, Albert Einstein, Gilbert Murray and, as chair, Henri Bergson. The body and its sub-committees covered areas that were connected to La Fontaine and Otlet's initiatives: bibliography, support for international congresses, museum projects and education for peace. The League developed its own efforts for the documentation of international life, issuing a quarterly bulletin on the work of international organisations (1922–39) as well as a *Handbook of International Associations* in 1921.

For La Fontaine and Otlet, such developments were a double-edged sword, as the Belgians aspired to official backing for their own projects. When the League founded its IIIC, its location was Paris rather than Brussels, thanks to a grant from the French government. The institute boasted features – notably an international statute – that the Belgians had desired for their *Palais Mondial*. Nonetheless, the UIA engaged with the League's work for intellectual cooperation. It did, for instance, secure a subsidy from the IIIC to collect and publish the resolutions of international associations.[121] Furthermore, the UIA continued to engage with the new institutions: when Bergson resigned from the ICIC, the UIA reminded the League of Nations secretariat of their demand that international associations should have an 'organic link' with the League, for instance through a regular intellectual cooperation conference.[122] In 1927, the UIA reiterated its call for a procedure through which international associations could present their demands.[123] In this respect, the UIA's activism formed part of the pre-history of modern NGOs, including the quest for recognition within the international system. Indeed, at the international level it was only with the Economic and Social Council of the United Nations in 1948 that such demands bore fruition.[124]

Belgium and the League's work for intellectual cooperation

Unlike La Fontaine and Otlet, other Belgians held official roles within the League bodies for intellectual cooperation. The socialist Jules Destrée was an ICIC member from the start – arguably a less than obvious choice. For instance, his post-war stance on Germany and on border revisions has been described as one of 'demonstrative nationalism'.[125] Regarding cultural matters, Henry Carton de Wiart later commented on Destrée's 'fundamentally aristocratic taste and an invincible tendency towards dilettantism'.[126] In the Belle Époque,

Destrée had initially been close to *La Jeune Belgique* and subsequently to the rival circle around Picard. As Louis Piérard later observed, Destrée's renown was initially confined to Belgium, although this began to change when he went on foreign missions during the war.[127] From 1919 to 1921, he served as the Belgian Minister for Science and Arts, which suggests that his appointment to the ICIC was linked to political considerations, rather than his transnational appeal.

Once he had joined the International Committee, Destrée energetically launched himself into a range of League efforts. For instance, he successfully proposed that the International Committee should maintain a separate entity on Arts and Letters.[128] Furthermore, he helped prepare the revision of the Bern Convention for the Protection of Literary Works.[129] Alongside his active role on the ICIC, he was involved in several of its subsidiary bodies: he presided over the Permanent Committee of Arts and Letters and over the International Committee of Museums; and he was a member of expert committees on intellectual property rights and on the 'education of youth in the aims of the League of Nations'. Despite his commitment to intellectual cooperation, Destrée's conception of the international sphere remained rooted in national concepts. For instance, in 1930, he planned a series of talks on national art to promote 'the rapprochement of elites and the mutual comprehension of peoples' and the 'educational role of museums' – yet this series was based on experts presenting their country's artistic traditions to foreign audiences.[130]

Destrée also chaired the Belgian Committee for Intellectual Cooperation. Such national committees were conceived as go-betweens between the League bodies and national scholarly and artistic circles. By 1923, eleven commissions existed; the same year, the Belgian Committee held its inaugural meeting at the *Palais Mondial*.[131] Otlet was not involved, but La Fontaine was a member, albeit with a limited role. Even beyond Destrée and La Fontaine, the twelve-person committee comprised prominent figures, for instance Hymans, Pirenne and the industrialist Emile Francqui (who headed the Belgian University Foundation, created with funds from the wartime relief efforts). As Destrée acknowledged, the committee members were 'all considerable and very busy personalities', which meant that they could only meet sporadically and had to conduct much of their business by correspondence.[132] Destrée's somewhat irate response to a request for information from Geneva – 'Me, I'm here all alone to do everything' – suggests that this was hardly the most fruitful way of working.[133] In 1930, the committee member and bibliographer Eugène Bacha noted that 'busy members often send their excuses'; he unsuccessfully proposed a mechanism that would have allowed members to nominate substitutes.[134] Following a visit to Brussels in 1935, an IIIC official suggested another solution: namely to designate the present members as patrons and to create a working committee with Belgians who were actively involved in the League efforts for intellectual cooperation.[135]

Despite these practical obstacles, the Belgian committee produced or sponsored various publications, including a catalogue of Belgian museums, a national yearbook of art and an index of Belgian periodicals.[136] Beyond its scholarly and artistic work, the committee supported an explicitly internationalist agenda. Having examined a League draft to 'educate youth in the aims and activities of the League of Nations', the committee approvingly cited the Belgian initiatives of 1926: headmasters, teachers and school inspectors had been asked to expand teaching on the League, for instance by instructing pupils about its 'pacific mission'. Such efforts extended to higher education: at the University of Liège, medical students learned about League efforts for public health; pre-university students at the Free University of Brussels heard a lecture from Hymans; and the University of Louvain invited a Swiss ICIC member, the Catholic conservative Gonzague de Reynold, for a guest lecture.[137] The committee also engaged with the League's efforts for textbook reform – a sensitive topic as Belgian history books covered the German wartime actions.[138] The diversity of these activities highlights how seemingly apolitical work on science and the arts could go together with the promotion of international reconciliation and the League of Nations.

In 1936, the Belgian Committee for Intellectual Cooperation experienced a rupture. Destrée passed away in January that year, the latest of several members: Ursmer Berlière, a well-known Benedictine historian and librarian, had died in 1932, followed by Francqui and Pirenne in 1935. When it came to potential successors for Destrée, the committee's secretary suggested François Bovesse, Minister of Public Education and the Arts. He described the politician as 'a remarkably cultivated man, a great admirer of the arts and letters' who would work for 'the intellectual cooperation of the nations'.[139] After Bovesse declined the invitation, the Flemish intellectual Auguste Vermeylen was praised as a 'very happy' choice.[140] Vermeylen had previously been a committee member and liaised with the IIIC on behalf of the Belgian state. He had risen to prominence as founder of the literary periodical *Van Nu en Straks* (1893) and was well known for his promotion of Flemish language and culture. As mentioned in chapter 1, this view was not detrimental to internationalism, captured by his famous dictum of the need to 'be Flemish to become European'.[141] By the interwar years, Vermeylen taught at Ghent University, becoming its rector after its transformation into a purely Dutch-speaking institution in 1930.

Vermeylen's background offered a delicate contrast to other members on the Belgian Committee for Intellectual Cooperation: Pirenne had resigned his chair at Ghent in protest at the end of the institution's bilingualism. Meanwhile, Vermeylen's predecessor Destrée was a founding figure of the Walloon movement, reflected in another famous dictum: 'Sire, there are no Belgians', from his open letter to King Albert I in 1912. For Destrée as for Vermeylen, regional and international attachments were compatible: Destrée viewed Wallonia in its European context and thus combined 'notions such as regionalism, socialism, idealism and internationalism'.[142] Strikingly, Destrée's proposed successor Bovesse was another prominent figure in the Walloon movement. Such constellations extended to other areas of intellectual cooperation: as president of the Belgian PEN Club (1928–30), Vermeylen succeeded Louis Piérard, who combined socialism with an attachment to Wallonia. Unlike the Belgian Committee for Intellectual Cooperation, the Belgian PEN split into French- and Dutch-speaking sections in 1930–31.[143]

The Belgian Committee for Intellectual Cooperation was merely one interface for official Belgian engagement with the League bodies. In 1929, Vermeylen as well as the IIIC staff had assumed that a Belgian subsidy for the Paris institute, worth 75,000 French francs, would be renewed annually.[144] This, however, was not the case: the only other instances of Belgian funding for the IIIC were 20,000 francs in 1928 and 1932, with France being the principal donor.[145] Meanwhile, several Belgians took official functions within the League structures for intellectual cooperation. A document from 1933 listed ten Belgians who were officially involved in the League work for intellectual cooperation. One such figure, Albert Marinus, had worked with La Fontaine in the BAPS and the UIA before 1914, but increasingly shifted his activism to the promotion of folklore and 'popular arts' after the war. Under the aegis of the IIIC, the city of Prague hosted the First World Congress of Popular Arts in 1928, which established the Commission Internationale des Arts et Traditions Populaires (CIAP), a body in which Marinus took a leading role. Linked to his commitment, the Second International Congress of Popular Arts took place in Antwerp, Liège and Brussels in 1930. Within the IIIC which, as Renoliet has pointed out, was dominated by French officials, there was one Belgian staff member: Charles Mercier, a Belgian academic who had taught in the USA and is likely to have benefited from being the nephew of Cardinal Mercier.[146] Belgian involvement in intellectual cooperation had many faces – with La Fontaine and Otlet being but two of them.

Bibliography and the League of Nations

The UIA had little influence over the practical work of the League bodies of intellectual cooperation. Nonetheless, in the more limited sphere of bibliography, La Fontaine and Otlet maintained relations with the League, albeit in somewhat fractious manner. Various parts of the League system addressed bibliographic matters, and after its creation in 1926, the IIIC maintained a Section for Scientific Relations in which bibliography and documentation played a key role.[147] This wider context explains why League cooperation with the IIB was perhaps more likely than with the UIA. Indeed, in November 1924, the League of Nations Assembly approved a convention with the IIB. The agreement allowed for League patronage; in return, the Brussels-based institute agreed to prepare the *Index Bibliographicus*, a printed catalogue of works dealing with bibliography and intellectual cooperation.[148] The League Assembly accorded a subsidy of 1,000 Swiss francs for this publication. Having faced several delays with its completion, the IIB came under increasing pressure to complete the *Index*.[149] Eventually, a volume was published, but with a foreword in which Otlet and La Fontaine distanced themselves from the project.[150] Subsequent League enquiries – for instance among historians and literary scholars – revealed that the consulted experts 'were all unfavourable' to the idea of a re-edition.[151] When the IIIC ultimately decided to prepare a second edition in 1931, the task was no longer entrusted to the IIB, but to the Prussian State Library in Berlin.

Owing to the conflicts surrounding the *Index*, the convention with the League of Nations was never fully implemented. Indeed, as early as 1926, several librarians and bibliographers were critical about the Belgian bibliographers. Barrau Dihigo, a bibliographer and librarian at the Sorbonne, clearly stated his opposition to any cooperation with the IIB directors.[152] De Vos van Steenwijk, the head of the IIIC's Section for Scientific Relations, acknowledged Otlet's and La Fontaine's bitterness. In 1926, he concluded that, for personal reasons, collaboration was 'currently impossible'.[153] Indeed, British and Dutch representatives of the IIB stressed that La Fontaine and Otlet had lost influence within the organisation to ensure further League support. Writing to De Vos van Steenwijk in 1929, for instance, the Dutch IIB member Donker Duyvis claimed that the 'most important work is done in England, Germany and the Netherlands at the present time. The personality of M. Otlet has not much importance in the practical work [of the IIB].'[154]

One factor that made collaboration difficult had less to do with personality and more with outlook: for La Fontaine and especially Otlet, the different ventures – UDC, Universal Bibliographic Repertory, *Palais Mondial* and *Cité Mondiale* – had become inseparable because of their all-embracing definition of internationalism. The League personnel remained wary about the wide-ranging aspirations of the initiators of the *Palais Mondial*: as one official stated, 'I am not at all sure that MM. Otlet and Fontaine will consent to stop their other activities and deal only in the future with bibliographical work'.[155] This echoed earlier concerns voiced by the head librarian of the Swiss National Library, who had referred to the 'difficulties resulting from the character – very respectable for that matter – of the current directors, their inability to limit themselves, their intransigence…I know their utopian tendencies are ill-suited to inspire confidence in those who hold the purse strings'.[156] Otlet, on his part, attacked the timidity of the League of Nations, reproaching it for having been 'too slow to... accomplish the integration of the world, too hesitant, too limited'.[157] Such comments suggest an evident tension between the pragmatic outlook of League officials and the universalist aspirations of the Belgian activists.

Furthermore, other organisations competed with the IIB for the IIIC's support. The French chemical engineer and bibliographer Jean Gérard, for instance, promoted the idea of an 'International Union of Documentation'.[158] Gérard had cooperated with the IIB in the past: the International Union of Pure and Applied Chemistry, of which Gérard was a member, participated in IIB congresses, and Otlet had spoken at the international chemistry conference in 1919.[159] In 1931, Gérard co-founded the Union Française des Organismes de Documentation which worked towards a documentation network in France and fostered links between different documentation centres.[160] Reacting to Gérard's initiative, Otlet argued that the IIB had promoted ideas for an international network of documentation offices for a long time.[161] Nonetheless, it was in response to Gérard's suggestions that the IIIC issued a guide to documentation centres and conducted a questionnaire survey on such institutions.[162] Many bibliographers and librarians welcomed this initiative as a step towards more active IIIC involvement in the coordination of documentation.[163] Gérard's experience suggests that other individuals found it easier to cooperate with the IIIC when they confined themselves to specific areas.

Conclusion

The case of the IIB and UIA illustrates the inbuilt tensions of internationalism: on the one hand, such projects reflected universal ambitions, combining an encyclopaedic streak, confidence in planning and a concern for order at different levels. On the other hand, the success of their schemes depended on backing from either national or international authorities. This dependence evidently bore a great potential for frustration. In a report to the IIB conference of 1932, Otlet summarised four kinds of international agreements into which his institute had tried to enter, beginning with a draft intergovernmental statute for the *Palais Mondial*.[164] However, beyond the initial impetus for the creation of League mechanisms for intellectual cooperation as well as a few limited and somewhat ill-fated projects, collaboration barely took off.

Given these limitations, what were the alternatives? From the foundation of the Office of International Bibliography, La Fontaine and Otlet had sought backing from the Belgian government. Initially, this approach worked: the UIA's roots in the Mons congress of 1905 suggest that their early activity went with the grain of Belgian internationalism, and the success in obtaining premises in the Palais du Cinquantenaire shows that cooperation continued beyond the Great War. However, this relationship soured when, because of the government's plans for a trade fair, they were forced to vacate parts of the building in 1924.[165] The episode clearly affected the relationship with the government. One year later, La Fontaine and Otlet described the history of the relations with the Belgian government as 'one of hesitation, then indifference and finally hostility'.[166] At the time, they sought an intergovernmental status as an alternative to dependence on the Belgian government – yet, given their ambivalent rapport with the League of Nations, this strategy had little likelihood of success.[167] After the temporary expulsion, the Palais operated under difficult financial circumstances and endured further debates about its future. Otlet claimed that its ultimate closure in 1934 was attributable to a fundamental issue, namely their 'desire to realise an international project and not a national Belgian one'.[168] Nonetheless, as chapter 1 has shown, he continued to evoke national arguments when they promised recognition for his ventures.

Boyd Rayward has suggested that Otlet sensed a 'double betrayal', namely 'that of the Belgian Government at the time of expulsion [from the Palais du Cinquantenaire] in 1923–1924, and that of the League of Nations at that same important moment when the Committee and the Institute of Intellectual Co-operation had been created according to the circumstances of that time'.[169] Nonetheless, he continued to pin his hopes on official backing. As Madeleine Herren has shown, this led to an unlikely scenario: after the German occupation of Belgium in 1940, Otlet sought to convince the German authorities to provide funds in order to revive the UIA – although the Germans instead chose to take over the organisation and end Otlet's role in it.[170] The *Kongress-Zentrale* itself had been founded in 1934 to counter what National Socialist authorities had perceived as a Franco-Belgian dominance of internationalist ventures. In their memorandum, the Nazi authorities described Brussels as 'the second capital of France',[171] and the First World Congress of International Associations as 'effectively a final (military) review' before the First World War.[172] Strikingly, some of this assessment regarding the alleged French 'dominance' seems to have been based on pre-1914 data from the UIA – which arguably tended to hold more complete information on congresses held in France and Belgium. From a very different angle, then, this episode reminds us of the ideas discussed in chapter 1: the complex rapport between internationalism and questions of nationhood.

Notes

1 Cf. Wouter Van Acker, 'Universalism as Utopia: a historical study of the schemes and schemas of Paul Otlet (1868–1944)' (PhD thesis, Ghent, 2011).

2 The film was directed by Françoise Levie, who subsequently published a book with the same title, *L'Homme qui voulait classer le monde: Paul Otlet*

et le Mundaneum (Brussels, 2006). Cf. Rayward's pioneering *Universe of Information* and two volumes compiled under the auspices of the Mundaneum, *Cent ans de l'Office international de bibliographie, 1895–1995: les prémisses du Mundaneum* (Mons, 1995) and *Paul Otlet, fondateur du Mundaneum (1868–1944): architecte du savoir, artisan de paix* (Brussels, 2010).

3 Georges Van Slype, 'La genèse d'une science de l'information et d'une documentologie', in *Cent ans de l'OIB*, p. 174. The work in question is Paul Otlet's *Traité de Documentation: le livre sur le livre. Théorie et pratique* (Brussels, 1934).

4 Alex Wright, 'The web that time forgot', *New York Times* (17 June 2008). Cf. Boyd Rayward, 'Visions of Xanadu: Paul Otlet (1868–1944) and hypertext', *Journal of the American Society for Information Science*, 45 (1994), 235–50; Charles van den Heuvel, Boyd Rayward and Pieter Uyttenhove, 'L'Architecture du savoir: une recherche sur le Mundaneum et les précurseurs européens de l'Internet', *Transnational Associations*, 1–2 (2003), 16–23.

5 Body Rayward, 'Introduction', in Rayward (ed.), *European Modernism and the Information Society: Informing the Present, Understanding the Past* (Aldershot, 2008), pp. 1–25.

6 Rasmussen, 'L'Internationale scientifique', pp. 75–7. Cf. Georges Speeckaert, *Le Premier siècle de la coopération internationale 1815–1914: l'apport de la Belgique* (Brussels, 1980), p. 6.

7 Jean-François Crombois, 'Energétisme et productivisme: la pensée morale, sociale et politique d'Ernest Solvay' in Andrée Despy-Meyer and Didier Devriese (eds), *Solvay et son temps* (Brussels, 1997), pp. 209–20.

8 Andrée Despy-Meyer and Valérie Montens, 'Le mécénat des frères Ernest et Alfred Solvay', in *ibid.*, pp. 238–9; Liliane Viré, 'La "Cité scientifique" du Parc Léopold à Bruxelles. 1890–1920', *Cahiers Bruxellois*, xix (1974), 86–180.

9 Boyd Rayward, 'The origins of information science and the International Institute of Bibliography/International Federation for Information and Documentation (FID)', in Trudi Bellardo Hahn and Michael Buckland (eds), *Historical Studies in Information Science* (Medford, NJ, 1998), p. 24.

10 Stefan Zweig, *Die Welt von gestern: Erinnerungen eines Europäers* (Frankfurt, 1955 [1944]), p. 145.

11 Claire Morgan, 'Invention and reinvention: word, image and modernity in James Ensor', in Aubert *et al.*, *La Belgique entre deux siècles*, p. 115.

12 Patrick McGuinness (ed.), *Symbolism, Decadence and the Fin de Siècle: French and European Perspectives* (Exeter, 2000); McGuinness, *Maurice Maeterlinck and the Making of Modern Theatre* (Oxford, 2000).

13 Aron, *Les Écrivains belges et le socialisme*, pp. 25–42.

14 Jean-Louis Jam and Gérard Loubinoux, 'Les productions francophones des opéras de Wagner à la Monnaie', in Manuel Couvreur (ed.), *La Monnaie Wagnérienne* (Brussels, 1998), p. 296.

15 Karel Wauters, *Wagner en Vlaanderen 1844–1914* (Ghent, 1983), p. 144.

16 MS HLF 130: leaflet 'Association Universelle Richard Wagner. Comité Belge' and 'Sechstes, vollständiges, Verzeichnis der Vertretungen des Allgemeinen R. Wagner-Vereines. März 1894'.

17 La Fontaine, *Richard Wagner: La Walkyrie. Premier Acte. Essai de traduction rythmée* (Brussels, 1885); La Fontaine, *Richard Wagner: Le Crépuscule des Dieux. Prologue. Seconde scène. Essai de traduction rythmée* (Brussels, 1885).
18 Emile Verhaeren, 'Une section d'art nouvelle', *La Nation* (1 November 1891) in Aron, *Les Écrivains belges et le socialisme*, p. 263.
19 David Clay Large and William Weber, 'Conclusion' in Large and Weber (eds), *Wagnerism in European Culture and Politics* (Ithaca, NY, 1984), p. 278.
20 Nathalie Aubert *et al.*, 'Introduction', in Aubert *et al.*, *La Belgique entre deux siècles*, p. 14. See also Anne Leonard, 'Internationalist in spite of themselves: Britain and Belgium at the fin de siècle', in Grace Brockington, *Internationalism and the Arts in Britain and Europe at the Fin de Siècle* (Oxford, 2009), pp. 225–46; Aron, *La Belgique artistique et littéraire*, p. 341; Jane Block, *Les XX and Belgian Avant-Gardism 1868–1894* (Ann Arbor, MI, 1984).
21 Gabriel Weisberg and Elizabeth Menon, *Art Nouveau: A Research Guide for Design Reform in France, Belgium, England, and the United States* (New York, 1998), pp. ix ff. Cf. Michel Winock, *La Belle Époque: la France de 1900 à 1914* (Paris, 2002), pp. 349–55.
22 Jeremy Howard, *Art Nouveau: International and National Styles in Europe* (Manchester, 1996), p. 32.
23 Octave Maus, 'Il ne suffit pas, pour un architecte, d'avoir des idées novatrices: il faut trouver l'occasion de les appliquer', *Architecture Moderne* (1900), cited in Aron, *La Belgique artistique et littéraire*, p. 328.
24 On this environment, see Jean-François Crombois, *L'Univers de sociologie en Belgique de 1900 à 1940* (Brussels, 1994), Paul Aron, 'La vie intellectuelle en Belgique à la fin du XIXe siècle' and Jean-François Crombois, 'Bibliographie, sociologie et coopération internationale: de l'Institut International de Bibliographie à l'Institut de Sociologie Solvay', both in *Cent ans de l'OIB*, pp. 17–32 and 215–38; Kurgan-van Hentenryk, *Laboratoires et réseaux*.
25 Van Acker, 'Universalism as Utopia', pp. 208–10.
26 Peter Wagner, 'Varieties of interpretations of modernity: on national traditions in sociology and the other social sciences', in Charle *et al.*, *Transnational Intellectual Networks*, p. 43. Cf. Johan Heibron, Nicolas Guilhot and Laurent Jeanpierre, 'L'internationalisation des sciences sociales: les leçons d'une histoire transnationale', in Sapiro, *L'Espace intellectuel*, pp. 319–46; Van Acker, 'Universalism as Utopia', pp. 207–9.
27 La Fontaine and Paul Otlet, *Sur la création d'un répertoire bibliographique universel: Conférence bibliographique internationale* (Brussels, 1895), p. 6.
28 MS FID 1, 'Les institutions et leurs activités': IID (1931–1936): Otlet, 'Sur la Crise de l'IIB. Le vrai rapport annuel', p. 12 (note no. 2946, 29 July 1932).
29 Louis Masure, *Rapport sur la situation et les travaux pour l'année 1912* (Brussels, 1913), p. 93.
30 MS FID 1, 'Les institutions et leur activitiés': IIB (1905–1930): 'Communication de l'Institut international de Bibliographie en séance de l'Office international de Bibliographie du mardi 24 mars 1925, doc. 727 (24 March 1925).
31 MS HLF 140: 'Rapport au Roi présenté par M. le Ministre de l'Instruction publique'.

32 MS FID 1, 'Les institutions et leurs activités', IID (1931–1936): Otlet, 'XIIème Conférence internationale – Bruxelles, 18 juillet 1933: rapport du secrétariat général', p. 8.

33 Rayward, *Universe of Information*, p. 50. See also MS IIIC, DVIII. 13a ('Institut de Documentation'): letter from the Administration for Higher Education and Science, Belgian Foreign Affairs Ministry to Dupieurreux, (IIIC), 28 October 1927.

34 David Batty and Toni Carbo Bearman, 'Knowledge and practice in library and information sciences', in Fritz Machlup and Una Mansfield (eds), *The Study of Information: Interdisciplinary Messages* (New York, 1983), p. 366.

35 Paul Otlet and Ernest Vandeveld, *La Réforme des bibliographies nationales et leur utilisation pour la Bibliographie Universelle: rapport présenté au Ve Congrès international des Editeurs* (Milan, 1906) (Brussels 1906); Commission permanente des Congrès internationaux des Archivistes et des Bibliothécaires, *Congrès de Bruxelles 1910. Vœux émis par les Sections et ratifiés par l'Assemblée générale du 31 Août* (Brussels, 1912).

36 Eckhardt Fuchs, 'The International Catalogue of Scientific Literature as a mode of intellectual transfer: promises and pitfalls of international scientific co-operation before 1914', in Charle *et al.*, *Transnational Intellectual Networks*, pp. 165–93; Daniel Laqua 'Transnational endeavours and the "totality of knowledge": Paul Otlet and Henri La Fontaine as "integral Internationalists" in fin-de-siècle Europe', in Brockington, *Internationalism and the Arts*, pp. 253–7.

37 Rasmussen, 'L'Internationale scientifique', p. 388.

38 'N° 810: Conférence internationale de Bibliographie 1929' in *IIB Bulletin*, 37 (18 October 1929).

39 MS FID 1, 'Les institutions et leur activités': IIB (1905–1930): Otlet, 'Après le congrès mondial de la documentation universelle'. See also MS BSIB, box 1, folder 1: 'Congrès Mondial de la Documentation Universelle. Paris, 16–21 août 1937. Cf. W. Boyd Rayward, 'The International Exposition and the World Documentation Congress of 1937', *Library Quarterly*, 53 (1983), 254–68.

40 MS FID 1, 'Les institutions et leurs activités', IID (1931–1936): Otlet, 'Rapport annuel présenté à la XIème conférence internationale – Francfort', note no. 3073, 9 June 1933.

41 Otlet, 'Après le congrès mondial de la documentation universelle'.

42 Otlet, 'Sur la Crise de l'IIB. Le vrai rapport annuel'.

43 Otlet, 'Rapport annuel présenté à la XIème conférence internationale', p. 3.

44 Otlet 'XIIème Conférence internationale – Bruxelles, 18 juillet 1933', p. 5.

45 MS HLF 140: 'Société auxiliaire de l'Office international de Bibliographie et de Documentation. Association sans but lucratif'.

46 This famous Karl Marx quotation provides the title of Marshal Berman's study *All That Is Solid Melts Into Air: The Experience of Modernity* (London, 1983).

47 La Fontaine and Otlet, *Sur la création d'un répertoire bibliographique universel*, p. 10.

48 Boyd Rayward, 'The historical development of information infrastructures and the dissemination of knowledge: a personal reflection', *Bulletin of the American Society for Information Science and Technology*, 31 (2005), 21.

49 Rayward, 'The march of the modern and the reconstitution of the world's knowledge apparatus: H.G. Wells, Encyclopedism and the World Brain', in Rayward, *European Modernism and the Information Society*, pp. 223–40; Giuliano Gresleri, 'Convergences et divergences: de Le Corbusier à Otto Neurath', *Transnational Associations*, 1–2 (2003), 72–81; Van Acker, 'Universalism as Utopia', pp. 248–61.

50 Erik Van Binsbergen, 'Le Livre Universel: classification et connaissance universelle à l'âge classique', in *Cent ans de l'OIB*, pp. 137–43.

51 Masure, *Rapport sur la situation et les travaux*, p. 17.

52 Anne Rasmussen, 'Les classifications d'Exposition Universelle', in Schroeder-Gudehus and Rasmussen, *Les Fastes du progrès*, p. 21.

53 Van Acker, 'Universalism as Utopia', pp. 278–84.

54 M. Bourdelain, 'Visite au Musée International du Cinquantenaire', *L'Essor Intellectuel*, 2 (1912), 42.

55 Nader Vossoughian, 'The language of the world museum: Otto Neurath, Paul Otlet, Le Corbusier', *Transnational Associations*, 1/2 (2003), 82–93; cf. Hadwig Kräutler, '"Scientific world conceptions" and museum planning', *Encyclopedia and Utopia*, pp. 191–200; Andreas Faludi, 'Otto Neurath and planning theory', in *ibid.*, pp. 201–32.

56 Boyd Rayward, *International Organisation and Dissemination of Knowledge: Selected Essays of Paul Otlet* (Amsterdam, 1990), p. 3; Van Slype, 'La genèse d'une science de l'information et d'une documentologie', *Cent ans de l'OIB*, pp. 162–4. From 1931 to 1937, the IIB was called International Institute of Documentation.

57 He had prepared the *Annuaire* on a smaller scale since 1905. See also Fried, *Das internationale Leben der Gegenwart.*

58 Hans Wehberg, 'Le pacifisme comme science', *La Vie Internationale*, 1 (1912), 213–14.

59 Hubert Van Houtte, 'Une loi d'ampliation: essai sur l'évolution politique, économique, morale et intellectuelle de l'Europe moderne', *Le Mouvement Sociologique International*, 8 (1907), 86.

60 Otlet, *La Loi d'ampliation*, p. 33.

61 Otlet and La Fontaine, 'The Union of International Associations: a world centre', in Rayward, *International Organisation and Dissemination of Knowledge*, p. 112.

62 Otlet, 'La Belgique et le Mouvement International', *La Vie Internationale*, 1 (1912), 123.

63 *Ibid.*, pp. 134–6.

64 Otlet, 'L'organisation internationale et les associations internationales', *Annuaire de la Vie Internationale (1909)*, pp. 29–166.

65 Georges Patrick Speeckaert, 'A glance at sixty years of activity (1910–1970) of the Union of International Associations', in UIA, *Union of International Associations 1910–1970: Past, Present Future* (Brussels, 1970), pp. 126–8.

66 Rayward, *Universe of Information*, p. 194.

67 Herren, *Hintertüren zur Macht*, e.g. pp. 150 and 186–7.

68 Archives Nationales de la France, Paris, fonds 'Police Générales: Congrès divers en France et à l'étranger' (F7/12525): le Ministre des Affaires Etrangères

au Monsieur le Président du Conseil, 30 April 1910. I thank Maike Thier for providing copies of this exchange.

69 *Ibid.*, Jean-Baptiste Beau to Stéphen Pichon, 10 June 1910.

70 *Ibid.*, p. 6.

71 MS HLF 218: 'Faits relatifs au développement de l'Union des Associations Internationales', 5 May 1912.

72 Rietzler, 'American internationalists in Europe', p. 26.

73 *Ibid.*, p. 28. Cf. Cooper, *Patriotic Pacifism*, p. 82.

74 Nicholas Murray Butler, 'L'Exposition Panama-Pacifique et la Paix universelle', *La Vie Internationale*, 1 (1912), pp. 300–1 (first published in the *American Review of Reviews*).

75 Rare Books and Manuscript Library, Columbia University, Carnegie Endowment for International Peace Records, part III: Division of Intercourse and Education, vol. 179: 'L'Office Central, Brussels, 1915–1922': La Fontaine to Butler, 19 July 1922. I thank Pierre-Yves Saunier for sharing his notes on this exchange.

76 MS HLF 139: La Fontaine to the Belgian ambassador to the USA, 5 March 1923.

77 Schivelbusch, *Ruine im Krieg der Geister*, pp. 126–35.

78 Bechet, 'La révision pacifiste des manuels scolaires', 67.

79 Katharina Rietzler, 'Experts for peace: structures and motivations of philanthropic internationalism in the interwar years', in Laqua, *Internationalism Reconfigured*, pp. 45–64

80 Otlet, *La Fin de la Guerre*, p. 14.

81 *Ibid.*, p. 5.

82 Office Central des Associations Internationales, *L'Union des Associations Internationales: constitution du Centre International. Congrès Mondial. Office Central. Musée International. Documentation Universelle* (Brussels, 1912).

83 Rayward, *Universe of Information*, pp. 226–8.

84 MS WILPF, reel 56: 'Rapport sur le voyage de Mlle Jeanne Melin en Belgique', undated.

85 MS Bxl. Royaume, fonds Jules Destrée (T205), II.Enseignement supérieure, 16: 'Université Internationale. 1ère session – Bruxelles: 5–20 septembre 1920'.

86 UAI, *L'Université internationale: notice et programme* (Brussels, 1920); Otlet, *Sur la création d'une Université internationale*. On the wider context of such schemes, see Laqua, 'Transnational intellectual cooperation', pp. 239–41.

87 MS LON, 13/30886/28370, 'Université Internationale' (R1056): letter by Otlet, 7 September 1923.

88 MS FID 1, 'Les institutions et leurs activités', IIB (1905–1930): 'La Société des Nations et l'Institut international de Bibliographie', doc. 692 (25 January 1925).

89 Otlet, 'Considérations finales' in Anna Nilsson, *ABC du mouvement pour la paix: dates et faits* (Brussels, 1933), p. 78.

90 UAI, *Cité Mondiale à Genève: World Civic Center. Mundaneum avec des plans de Le Corbusier et Pierre Jeanneret* (Brussels, 1929).

91 'La Haye, Capitale des Etats-Unis du Monde', *Courrier de la Conférence* (11 August 1907); Paul Otlet, 'Bruxelles: la capitale du monde', *Courrier de la Conférence* (13 October 1907); Pieter Eijkman, *Over Internationalisme* (The

Hague, 1908). Otlet's arguments are noted in De Groof, 'Promoting Brussels as a political world capital', pp. 101–3.

92 Otlet, 'La Belgique et le Mouvement International', p. 135.

93 Louis Frank, *La Paix et le District Fédéral du Monde: l'avenir de la Belgique au point de vue international* (Paris, 1913), pp. 13–14.

94 Otlet, *Plan Belgique*, p. 136

95 *Ibid.*, p. 453

96 Anthony Sutcliffe, *Towards the Planned City: Germany, Britain, the United States and France 1780–1914* (Oxford, 1981); Richard Stites, *Revolutionary Dreams: Utopian Vision and Experimental Life in the Russian Revolution* (Oxford, 1998), pp. 190–204.

97 Wolfgang Sonne, *Representing the State: Capital City Planning in the Early Twentieth Century* (Munich, 2003), p. 285.

98 Daniel Rodgers, *Atlantic Crossings: Social Politics in a Progressive Age* (Cambridge, MA, 1998).

99 Rayward, *Universe of Information*, e.g. pp. 184, 264–5 and 296–7.

100 Helen Meller, 'Philanthropy and public enterprise: international exhibitions and the modern town-planning movement 1889–1913', *Planning Perspectives*, 10 (1995), 295–310.

101 Gaspari, 'Cities against States?', 603.

102 Dogliani, 'European municipalism', 484.

103 Stefan Fisch, 'Origins and history of the International Institute of Administrative Sciences: from its beginnings to its reconstruction after World War II (1944/47)', in Fabio Rugge and Michael Duggett (eds), *IIAS/IISA Administration and Service 1930–2005* (Amsterdam, 2005), p. 36.

104 Comte de Torre-Vélez, *Vers le Monde Nouveau* (Brussels, 1921).

105 Otlet, *L'Exposition Universelle de 1930*, p. 1.

106 Otlet, 'L'Urbaneum – Bruxelles, Cité Mondiale. Bruxelles, Grande Ville. Bruxelles, Capitale de la Belgique', p. 122. Van Acker explains the ideas behind this project in 'Universalism as Utopia', pp. 474–81.

107 MS HLF 139: 'National Social Unit Organization (USA, 1917–1920)'.

108 *Ibid.*, p. ii.

109 Otlet, *Plan Belgique*, pp. 12–13.

110 *Ibid.*, pp. 160–1.

111 UAI, *Organisation internationale du travail intellectuel* (Brussels, 1921), pp. 8 and 11–19.

112 Sapiro, 'Introduction', in Sapiro, *L'Espace intellectuel*, p. 19.

113 Löhr, *Globalisierung geistiger Eigentumsrechte*, p. 68; Verbruggen, *Schrijverschap in het Belgische belle époque*, pp. 44–8.

114 Christophe Verbruggen, '"Intellectual workers" and their search for a place within the ILO in the interwar years', in Jasmien Van Daele *et al.* (eds), *ILO Histories: Essays on the International Labour Organization and Its Impact on the World during the Twentieth Century* (Bern, 2010), pp. 272–92. Cf. Laqua, 'Transnational intellectual cooperation', pp. 241–6; Sapiro, 'L'internationalisation des champs intellectuels dans l'entre-deux-guerres: facteurs professionnels et politiques', in Sapiro, *L'Espace intellectuel*, pp. 112–22.

115 Jürgen von Ungern-Sternberg, *Der Aufruf "An die Kulturwelt!": Das Manifest der 93 und die Anfänge der Kulturpropaganda im Ersten Weltkrieg* (Stuttgart, 1996); Christophe Prochasson and Anne Rasmussen, *Au nom de la patrie: les intellectuels et la première guerre mondiale (1910–1919)* (Paris, 1996).

116 Brigitte Schroeder-Gudehus, 'Challenge to transnational loyalties: international scientific organizations after the First World War', *Science Studies*, 3 (1973), 93–118.

117 IIIC, *L'Institut international de Coopération intellectuelle 1925–1946* (Paris, 1946), p. 13.

118 Otlet, *Introduction aux travaux de la Commission de Coopération intellectuelle de la Société des Nations* (Brussels, 1922), p. 2.

119 Renoliet, *L'UNESCO oublié*, pp. 11–17. Cf. Riemens, *De passie voor vrede*, pp. 215–17.

120 'L'union est écartée', in UAI, *La Société des Nations et l'Union des Associations Internationales* (Brussels 1923), pp. 7–8.

121 UAI, *Code des vœux internationaux: codification générale des vœux et résolutions des organismes internationaux* (Brussels, 1910–1923).

122 MS LON, 13C/46945/34468, 'Collaboration de l'Union des Associations internationales (Bruxelles) avec la Commission international de Coopération intellectuelle': UIA to Drummond, 6 October 1925.

123 MS IPB 331/2: UIA, 'À la Société des Nations et aux gouvernements qui en font partie', forwarded by Paul Otlet, 27 August 1927.

124 Pierre-Yves Saunier, 'NGOs', in Iriye and Saunier, *Palgrave Dictionary*, pp. 573–80.

125 Bechet, 'La révision pacifiste des manuels scolaires', 53.

126 Henry Carton de Wiart, *Beernaert et son temps*, p. 109.

127 Piérard, *Regards sur la Belgique*, p. 309.

128 MS LON, A.24.1925.XII: ICIC, 'Sixth Plenary Session. Report of the Committee submitted to the Council and the Assembly'.

129 Löhr, *Globalisierung geistiger Eigentumsrechte*, pp. 191–8, 206–10 and 219–22.

130 MS IIIC, A.III.23 ('Commission nationale belge de Coopération intellectuelle'): Destrée to Luchaire, 13 February 1929.

131 Renoliet, *L'UNESCO oubliée*, p. 32.

132 MS IIIC, A.III.23: Destrée to Luchaire, 24 November 1926.

133 *Ibid.*, Destrée to Prezzolini, 18 February 1927, *Ibid.*

134 *Ibid.*, 'Commission national belge: réunion du dimanche, 30 janvier 1930 à la Fondation Universitaire'.

135 *Ibid.*, Daniel Secrétan to Léon Bersou, May/June 1936.

136 *Ibid.*, Dupierreux to Secretary of the Education Commission of the League of Nations Union, 10 December 1926; also minutes of National Committee, 6 January 1927.

137 *Ibid.*, Rapport de la Commission nationale belge, *c.* January 1927.

138 Bechet, 'La révision pacifiste des manuels scolaires', 82–7.

139 MS IIIC, A.III.23: Bersou to Montenach, 25 January 1936.

140 *Ibid.*, Bersou to Montenach, 7 February 1936.

141 Auguste Vermeylen, 'Vlaamsche en Europeesche Beweging', *Van nu en Straks*, 4 (1900), 299–310.
142 Duchenne, 'La pensée européenne du socialiste Jules Destrée', 21.
143 Christophe Verbruggen, 'Hoe literair internationalisme organisieren? De "vervlochten" geschiedenis van de Belgische PEN-club (1922–1931), *Nederlandse Letterkunde*, 16 (2011), 152–81.
144 MS IIIC, A.I.88 ('Relations avec le gouvernement de la Belgique'): letter by Vermeylen of 14 March 1931.
145 Renoliet, *L'UNESCO oubliée*, p. 208.
146 MS IIIC, A.IV.28 ('Personnel'): dossier Charles Mercier (96). On the composition of the IIIC's staff, see Renoliet, *L'UNESCO oubliée*, pp. 187–9.
147 IIIC, *Institut international de Coopération Intellectuelle, 1925–1946* (Paris, 1946), p. 28.
148 Convention entre l'IIB et la Société des Nations', *IIB Bulletin*, July 1924. See also MS FID 1, 'Les institutions et leur activités', IIB. (1905–1930): 'La Société des Nations et l'Institut international de Bibliographie', correspondence with Eric Drummond, 7 November 1924 (reproduced 2 January 1925 in doc. 692).
149 MS IIIC, D.VIII.13a ('Institut de Documentation'): correspondence between De Vos van Steenwijk, Oprescu and Luchaire, 6 February to 16 March 1926.
150 CICI, *Index Bibliographicus: répertoire internationale des sources de bibliographie courante* (Geneva, 1925).
151 MS LON, 5B /4987/4987 'International Bureaux, Intellectual Cooperation. Index Bibliographicus': report from the Sub-Committee on Science and Bibliography to the IICI, 'Projet de publication d'une second edition de l'Index Bibliographicus', 12 June 1928.
152 MS IIIC, DVIII.13a: handwritten note, De Vos van Steenwijk, 11 March 1926. The dispute is also discussed in Rayward, *Universe of Information*, pp. 291–4.
153 MS IIIC, DVIII.13a: Draft letter of De Vos van Steenwijk to Dawson Johnson, 14 April 1926.
154 *Ibid.*, Donker Duyvis to De Vos van Steenwijk, 17 January 1929.
155 *Ibid.*, George Oprescu to Gilbert Murray, 29 August 1928.
156 *Ibid.*, Marcel Godet, Swiss National Library to Alfred Zimmern, 2 February 1926.
157 Otlet, 'Considérations finales', p. 77.
158 MS IIIC, DVIII, 13a (Institut de Documentation): Jean Gérard to IIIC, 11 February 1932.
159 Otlet, *L'Organisation de la Documentation Internationale et le rôle des associations de chimie* (Paris, 1919).
160 Sylvie Fayet-Scribe, *Histoire de la documentation en France: culture, science et technologie d'information, 1895–1937* (Paris, 2000).
161 'Rapport annuel présenté à la XIème Conférence internationale – Francfort août 1932', p. 4.
162 XIIème Conférence internationale – Bruxelles, 18 juillet 1933: rapport du secrétariat général'. See MS BSIB 1.5: 'The World Conference on Universal Documentation. Confidential (Bradford, 1936). Also MS BSIB 2.7: 'Union Internationale de la Chimie Pure et Appliquée'.

163 MS BSIB 2.8: Frederic Nathan, 'Memorandum on International Abstracting and Classifying of Scientific and Technical Literature', May 1930.

164 Otlet, 'Rapport annuel présenté à la XIème conférence internationale – Francfort, août 1932, p. 4.

165 MS FID Correspondances, 'Correspondance IIB (1905–1930)': Ministry of Science and Arts (section for Higher Education and Sciences) to OIB, 5 March 1925.

166 MS FID 1, 'Les institutions et leurs activités', IIB (1905–1930): La Fontaine and Otlet, 'Communication de l'Institut international de Bibliographie en séance de l'Office international de Bibliographie du mardi 24 mars 1925', doc. 727.

167 MS IIIC, D.VIII, 13a (Institut de Documentation): UAI to Luchaire, 4 June 1924.

168 MS FID 1, 'Les institutions et leurs activités', IID (1931–1936): Otlet, 'L'Affaire du Palais Mondial', doc. 7480, 15 June 1934.

169 Rayward, *Universe of Information*, p. 328

170 Madeleine Herren, '"Outwardly ... an innocuous conference authority": National Socialism and the logistics of international information management', *German History*, 20 (2002), 67–92.

171 MS BA, Reichskanzlei: Auswärtige Angelegenheiten 11, 'Internationale Kongresse' (RA431/559): 'Reichsminister für Volksaufklärung und Propaganda an sämtliche Reichsministerien. Betr: Einrichtung einer wissenschaftlichen Kongresszentrale', 22 December 1934.

172 *Ibid.*, p. 2.

Conclusion: Internationalism and the Belgian crossroads

Internationalism was an amorphous phenomenon that could be placed at the disposal of conflicting forces and ideologies. Belgian intellectuals portrayed their country as the 'crossroads of Europe' and used internationalism as a source of national prestige. Meanwhile, supporters of King Leopold depicted expansion in Central Africa as an international 'philanthropic' cause. World exhibitions were emblematic of this kind of internationalism, marked by representations of national progress and imperial propaganda, trailing international congresses in their wake. Yet internationalism was also evoked by activists who opposed such discourses: to them, it was a tool that helped them question national sovereignty or challenge colonial rule. In light of this inherent malleability, are we actually faced with a coherent phenomenon at all? As this monograph has suggested, internationalism was shaped by impulses that sometimes overlapped or converged, and at other times pushed in opposing directions.

The Belgian case illustrates the ambivalent yet often symbiotic relationship between internationalism, nationhood and empire. Even internationalists who were far from ardent imperialists were involved in the Mons Congress of Global Economic Expansion of 1905, which was tied up with efforts to justify Belgian actions in the Congo. Furthermore, the Belgian setting reveals the intersecting nature of various forms of internationalism. The activists, academics and politicians that feature in this monograph were involved in multiple campaigns and associations. They shared an interest in interconnected causes, from social justice and women's rights to peace and arbitration. This is not to say that their outlook on these matters was identical. However, the effort to promote an issue across national borders helped activists to affirm both the progressive nature of their specific undertaking and of internationalism more generally – even if the essence of such 'progress' was defined differently by different actors.

This aspect is particularly interesting if one bears in mind that Belgian activists disagreed with each other in domestic debates, for instance on church–state relations, the social question and women's suffrage. At the international level, activists from opposing ideological camps could still collaborate on specific projects, from international bibliographies to support for the League of Nations. Why could internationalism occasionally transcend the political, cultural and social divisions that existed in Belgium? One potential explanation is tied to the very nature of Belgium's 'small-nation internationalism'. Connected to the country's geographical position, its multilingual nature and government support for internationalist ventures, Belgian activists could engage in transnational endeavours and simultaneously affirm their national credentials.

Despite occasional broader alliances, many activists resembled each other through their links to liberalism and socialism, and their educational or professional backgrounds. The socialists Vandervelde, Destrée and La Fontaine, the progressive Lorand and the liberal Hymans had all studied in Brussels and subsequently trained as lawyers. Freethought and freemasony provided further common ground for many activists. This evidently prompts the question of the relationship between internationalism and religion. Rather than covering religious cross-border movements in a broad array of guises, our discussion of Catholic internationalism has concentrated on its secular varieties, for it was here that the links to other varieties of internationalism were most pronounced. Belgian Catholics such as Beernaert and Descamps cooperated with their liberal and socialist peers to promote arbitration and the extension of international law. Furthermore, from the 1890s, the development of new forms of political Catholicism meant that a younger generation of Catholic activists shared certain interests and experiences with their liberal or socialist peers.

The case of Henry Carton de Wiart – later a Catholic minister and, briefly, prime minister – is instructive, as it illustrates the 'similarity in the social milieu of Socialist and Christian Democratic leaders in Brussels'.[1] With a university education in law and early employment by Edmond Picard, he shared formative experiences with Vandervelde, La Fontaine and Otlet. Like them, he maintained links to artistic and cultural circles, seeing himself as a writer as well as a politician.[2] In 1892 – four years before being elected to parliament – Carton de Wiart even demonstrated alongside progressive liberals and socialists for the introduction of universal suffrage.[3] He was supportive of causes such as child welfare and feminism and coordinated the international congresses during the 1910 world's fair in Brussels. After the First World War, Carton de Wiart was a delegate to the League of Nations Assembly (1928–35), participated in the ILO's International Labour Conferences and served as president of the IPU.

Belgian internationalism bore a close relation to the national and international development of sociology. Several protagonists of this monograph had a pronounced interest in the social sciences, for instance De Greef, Denis, La Fontaine, Otlet and Vandervelde. Just as sociology was conceived as a science of society, some activists believed that internationalism could become a science of international life. The connection between sociology and internationalism extended to the Catholic world: the University of Louvain supported the development of Christian sociology, and the Christian democrat Cyrille Van Overbergh served as president of the Société Belge de Sociologie. He also edited the association's journal, which adopted an explicitly international remit in 1907. On that occasion, his editorial comments specifically referred to the desirability of ethnographic studies and the discussions at the Mons congress of 1905.[4] Van Overbergh had been personally involved in the Mons event, as he served as Director-General in the Administration of Higher Education, Arts and Science at the time.[5] Yet his international activities ranged beyond sociological networks and governmental work: with La Fontaine and Otlet, Van Overbergh co-founded the periodical *La Vie Internationale* and later participated in the Paris Peace Conference, where his brief included international labour law.

In discussing the age of internationalism, this study has focused on one particular generation of activists: people who were born in the 1850s and 1860s and who started to make their mark in national culture and politics in the 1880s and 1890s. In the decade before the First World War, they engaged in a range of international activities, either linked to their government's interest in strengthening the country's international role or to the European heyday of the international socialist and pacifist movements. The celebration of scientific progress, the staging of Belgium's 'civilising mission' and pacifist narratives about the movement towards a global community suggest that internationalism embraced modernity. These modern features are further underlined by secularists' confidence about the ultimate triumph of rationalism and by the Catholic response to modernity, which involved the creation of international organisations and events.

The First World War produced ruptures at various levels, as evidenced by the consequences for socialists and pacifists. While these movements had portrayed themselves as transnational, they struggled to uphold and develop such links in the face of military conflict. Despite their respective roles in the Second International and the IPB, La Fontaine and Vandervelde found it difficult to overcome national antagonisms. Nonetheless, it is fruitful to transcend chronologies that treat 1914 as a terminus. After the war, many protagonists rebuilt the ties that had been ruptured. They also engaged with the new institutions, either by taking an active role in the League of Nations or by seeking to lobby it. The examples discussed in this monograph show that the interwar years were a period of organisation-building and lively debates on global order. Internationalism, then, did not simply disappear. Indeed, in spite of many obstacles, the number of international associations continued to grow: Boli and Thomas have counted around 200 active groupings in 1900, but 800 in 1930 – based on data compiled by the Belgian internationalists of the UIA.[6] The persistence of internationalism in the face of many setbacks became evident in 1935 when over 200 international congresses where scheduled within the framework of the Brussels world's fair.[7] These events covered industry, commerce, culture, science and sports, but also a congress of the International Federation of League of Nations Societies. The Brussels exhibition contained echoes of Belle Époque optimism. A British guide praised the 'decision... to organise, in the midst of the world-wide trade depression, an International Exhibition on so ambitious a scale as that which is now drawing visitors from all over the world to Brussels, ...[as] a notable proof of faith and confidence in the future peace and prosperity of the world'.[8]

Although the pre-1914 generation of internationalists rescued and translated their commitment into the new structures of the interwar years, they operated in a challenging environment. Suspicions between activists persisted beyond 1918 despite the reconstruction of movements and organisations. And while the League of Nations gave institutional shape to pre-war ideas, the Comintern challenged both the liberal and socialist guises of internationalism. By the 1930s, the global economic crisis and the rise of fascist or ultranationalist movements created further challenges for internationalists. Furthermore, at the personal level, key figures of the pre-1914 era found it difficult to adapt to changing circumstances. Otlet's 'mondialism', for instance, became ever-more grandiose as his resonance among national and international authorities declined. Meanwhile, his friend La Fontaine barely managed to engage with the new antimilitarist currents. This picture looks different if one considers the representatives of a younger generation of internationalists, who forged alliances of their own. For instance, through their leading roles in WILPF, Lucie Dejardin and Marcelle Leroy combined an involvement in the new pacifist currents with a commitment to women's rights. Dejardin's role in the socialist movement ultimately led to her landmark election as the first female member of the Belgian Chamber of Representatives in 1929. For Leroy, participation in the World Congress against War and Fascism resulted in her contribution to the Comintern-backed 'Amsterdam-Pleyel' movement.

While the First World War changed the context for transnational activism, it also affected Belgium's role within it. After the German attack of 1914, activists in different countries declared their solidarity with 'poor little Belgium' and launched relief efforts for its population. Yet the experience of invasion and occupation also triggered Belgium's abandonment of neutrality. In the subsequent decades, effective security arrangements took on a greater meaning – and it was not necessarily within international congresses or institutions that people expected security to reside in. Furthermore, domestically, the country experienced a range of tensions, from instable governments, economic crisis, Rexism and radical Flemish nationalism. If Belgian intellectuals had presented their own country as an 'international nation', political life also showed the challenges of coexistence.

This is not to say that the history of Belgian internationalism is a history of failure. For instance, although the country did not succeed in gaining the headquarters of the League of Nations, the likes of Hymans, Rolin and Destrée supported its work in a variety of ways. Furthermore, the efforts that have been discussed in this study lasted for a considerable time: they were more than merely a 'Belgian moment' in the history of internationalism. And while this account ends in the early 1930s, internationalism continued to display its ability to shift shape according to political circumstances and power relations. In the post-1945 era, the foundation of the UN, bloc formation and Western European integration all evoked internationalist concepts or engaged with international organisations. These developments also fed into narratives about 'international Belgium', as underscored by the establishment of the European institutions and the NATO headquarters in Brussels. In 1967, a book entitled *The World's Meeting Place* accompanied the Belgian contribution to the International Exhibition in Montreal. Aiming to provide 'a faithful portrait of a small country which has become a great European centre', it lauded Belgians as model international citizens:

> Geography lays down some laws no nation is allowed to elude. Those laws? A hearty welcome, a touch of fair-play, a great deal of mutual understanding. Otherwise? The Belgian cross-roads would come to a dead-lock… Grown into the first European citizen, the Belgian has no more the right or the envy to lose his time in vain family squabbles.[9]

Even though contemporary Belgium has been subject to tensions that seem to go beyond 'family squabbles', there are still attempts to draw lines of continuity between the role of Brussels as a 'capital of Europe' and earlier internationalist schemes.[10] This does not mean that such continuities always exist – yet it certainly illustrates the persistent representation of Belgium as an 'international nation'.

Notes

1 Strikwerda, *A House Divided*, p. 246.
2 Henk De Smaele, 'Henry Carton de Wiart (1869–1905): Christen-democratisch politicus en literator', *Trajecta*, 4 (1995), 22–41.
3 Deneckere, *Les Turbulences de la Belle Époque*, pp. 77–8.
4 'Aux Lecteurs', *Le Mouvement Sociologique International*, 8 (1907), 2.
5 Cyrille Van Overbergh, *National Biografisch Woordenboek*, vol. 8 (Brussels, 1990), 607–18. The context of Van Overbergh's interrelated projects is discussed in Herren, *Hintertüren zur Macht*, pp. 172–80.
6 Bolia and Thomas, 'INGOs and the organization of world culture', pp. 13–14.

7 *Bulletin officiel*, 26 (3 May 1935), p. 368; *Exposition universelle et internationale de Bruxelles 1935. Programme des Fêtes et Congrès. Avril-Octobre 1935.*

8 *Grande Bretagne à Bruxelles (Guide to the Pavillon of the British Government at the International Exhibition, Brussels. April–October 1935)*, pp. 1–2.

9 Jacques Van Offelen and Jo Gerard, *Belgium: The World's Meeting Place* (Brussels, 1967), p. 91. The authors were, respectively, Minister for Economic Affairs and a journalist.

10 See e.g. the exhibition at the Royal Archives of Belgium, held in 2010: the catalogue is Roel De Groof and Geertrui Elaut, *Brussels in Europe – Europe in Brussels: From Federal World District to Capital of Europe, 1900–2010* (Brussels, 2010).

Select bibliography

Archival sources

Amsab-Instituut voor sociale geschiedenis, Ghent

Eugène Hins papers [abbreviated MS AMSAB]

Archives du Ministère des Affaires Étrangères, Brussels

Correspondance et Documents. Afrique: États Indépendant du Congo: 'Conférence des Spiritueux de 1899', 'Conférence des Spiritueux de 1906', 'Conférence des Spiritueux de 1912'

Correspondance et Documents. Afrique: 'Esclavage'

Correspondance et Documents. Afrique: État Indépendant du Congo, 'Incident Stokes'

[all abbreviated MS Bxl. FO]

Archives du Royaume, Brussels

Fonds Enseignement

Fonds Jules Destrée

Fonds Schollaert/Helleputte

[all abbreviated MS Bxl. Royaume]

Bodleian Library of Commonwealth and African Studies, Rhodes House, Oxford

Papers of the Anti-Slavery Society [abbreviated MS Brit. Emp.]

Bundesarchiv, Berlin

Reichskolonialamt: Akten betreffend Sklavenfrage in Afrika. Allgemeines

Reichskolonialamt: Sklavensachen 5, 9, 11

Reichskanzlei: Auswärtige Angelegenheiten. Internationale Kongresse

[all abbreviated MS BA]

Groupe d'Études Histoire de l'Europe Contemporaine, Université Catholic de Louvain

Série A.XVI: Papiers Irénée Van der Ghinst [abbreviated MSS GEHEC]

Institut de Recherche et d'Etude de la Libre Pensée, Paris

Fonds L. Lacassagne 1
Fonds IC/1
[abbreviated MS IRELP]

Institut Emile Vandervelde, Brussels

Archives Rationalistes
Archives Léon Furnémont
Archives Louis Bertrand
Emile Vandervelde
[all abbreviated MS IEV]

International Institute of Social History, Amsterdam

World Union of Freethinkers [abbreviated MS IFF]
Archief Hector Denis
Archief César de Paepe

Labour History Archive and Study Centre, People's History Museum, Manchester

Labour Party Archives: Labour and Socialist International [abbreviated MS LSI]

League of Nations Archives, United Nations Library, Geneva

Archives of the League of Nations [abbreviated MS LON]
Archives of the International Peace Bureau [abbreviated MS IPB]

LSE Archives, London School of Economics and Political Science, London

E. D. Morel papers [abbreviated MS Morel]

Mundaneum, Mons

Archives Henri La Fontaine [abbreviated MS HLF]
Fonds 'Ami du Palais Mondial' [abbreviated MS APM]
Fonds 'Fédération internationale de documentation' [abbreviated MS FID]
Fonds 'Musée international'
Fonds 'Expositions universelles'

School of Arts and Social Sciences, Northumbria University, Newcastle upon Tyne

Microfilm records of the Women's International League for Peace and Freedom [abbreviated MS WILPF]

Science Museum Library, Imperial College, London

Archives of the British Society for International Bibliography [abbreviated MS BSIB]

UNESCO Archives, Paris

Archives de l'Institut international de Coopération Intellectuelle (1925–46) [abbreviated MS IIIC]

Union of International Associations, Brussels

Archives La Fontaine [abbreviated MS UIA]
Fonds 'Union internationale des Associations pour la SDN, 1920–1923' [abbreviated MS IFLNS]

Printed primary sources

Adler, Friedrich, *Die Besetzung des Ruhrgebiets und die Internationale: Nach einer Rede, gehalten am 14. Februar 1923 in the Wiener Konferenz der sozialdemokratischen Vertrauensmänner* (Vienna, 1923).

Angell, Norman, *The Great Illusion: A Study of the Relation of Military Power in Nations to Their Economic and Social Advantage* (London, 1910).

——, *The Foundations of International Polity* (London, 1914).

Anon., *La Conférence anti-esclavagiste et les droits d'entrée dans l'État du Congo: par un négociant hollandais* (Rotterdam, 1890).

——, *La Conférence de Bruxelles et les Pays-Bas: par un ami de la vérite* (Anvers, 1890).

——, *Francisco Ferrer, sa vie – Ses œuvres* (Iseghem, 1909).

——, *La Vérité sur Francisco Ferrer et les événements de Barcelone* (Brussels, 1909).

Anspach, Lucien, *Le Péril clérical et l'affaire Dreyfus* (Brussels, 1899).

Banning, Emile, *L'Afrique et la Conférence géographique de Bruxelles* (Brussels, 1877).

——, *La Belgique au point de vue militaire et européen*, ed. Ernest Godart (Brussels, 1887).

——, *La Conférence de Bruxelles: son origine et ses actes. Communication faite à l'Académie Royale dans la séance du 13 octobre 1890* (Brussels, 1890).

——, *Réflexions morales et politiques* (Brussels, 1899).

——, *Mémoires politiques et diplomatiques: comment fut fondé le Congo Belge* (Paris, 1927).

Bebel, August, *Die Frau und der Sozialismus* (Zurich, 1879).

Bertrand, Louis, *Le Scandale congolais* (Brussels, 1908).

——, *Souvenirs d'un meneur socialiste* (Brussels, 1927).

Bibliothèque de La Pensée, *Le Congrès de Bruxelles et la Manifestation Ferrer 20–24 août 1910* (Brussels, 1910).

Bloch, Jan, *Is War Now Impossible? Being an Abridgment of 'The Future of War in Its Technical, Economic and Political Relations'* (London, 1899).

Bolce, Harold, *The New Internationalism* (New York, 1907).
Bots, Marcel (ed.), *Lettres adressées à Emile de Laveleye* (Ghent, 1992).
Bourgeois, Léon, *Pour la Société des Nations* (Paris, 1910).
Brown, Stephen (ed.), *International Relations from a Catholic Standpoint* (Dublin, 1932).
Bureau International contre la Traite, *Documents relatifs à la répression de la traite des esclaves publiés en exécution des articles 81 et suivants de l'Acte Général de Bruxelles* (Brussels, 1892–1914).
Cammaerts, Emile, *The Treasure House of Belgium: Her Land and People. Her Art and Literature* (London, 1924).
Carr, E. H., *The Twenty Years' Crisis, 1919–1939: An Introduction to the Study of International Relations* (London, 1939).
Carton de Wiart, Henry, *The Way of Honour* (London, 1918).
——, *Souvenirs littéraires* (Brussels, 1938).
——, *Beernaert et son temps* (Brussels, 1945).
Cattier, Félicien, *Étude sur la Situation de l'Etat indépendant du Congo* (Brussels, 1906).
Cecil, Robert, *World Opinion and the League of Nations* (London, 1918).
Cercle de l'Expansion Belge, *L'Expansion Belge*, vols. 1–7 (Brussels, 1908–14).
Chapelier, Emile, *La Libre-Pensée prolétarienne contre la Libre Pensée bourgeoise* (Brussels, 1929).
Christ-Socin, Hermann, *Les Missions évangéliques et l'État du Congo: l'affaire Morrison-Sheppard* (Saint-Blaise, 1909).
Colin, Paul, *Belgique: Carrefour de l'occident* (Paris, 1933).
Combes de Lestrade, Gaëtan, *La Vie internationale* (Paris, 1911).
Conan Doyle, Arthur, *The Crime of the Congo* (London, 1909).
Congo Reform Association, *Témoignage devant la Commission d'Enquête au Congo: évènements qui se sont déroulés au Congo depuis le retour de la Commission* (Liverpool, 1905).
Conseil général du Parti Ouvrier Belge (ed.), *75 années de domination bourgeoise 1830–1905: Essais de Camille Huysmans, Louis de Brouckère et Louis Bertrand* (Ghent, 1905).
Cooper, Sandi (ed.), *Arbitration: Two Views* (New York, 1971).
Coudenhove-Kalergi, Richard, *Pan-Europe* (New York, 1926).
d'Ursel, Hippolyte (ed.), *La Campagne antiesclavagiste belge racontée par les lettres de Jacques de Dixmude* (Brussels, 1929).
De Greef, Guillaume, *L'Ère de la mondialité: éloge d'Elie Reclus. Université Nouvelle. Discours prononcé le 31 octobre, à la séance de rentrée par M. le recteur Guillaume De Greef* (Brussels, 1906).
——, *L'Internationalisation de la pensée: Congrès international de la Libre Pensée à Lisbonne (Octobre 1913). Discours du président* (Brussels: Bibliothèque de *La Pensée*, 1913).
de Ligt, Barthélemy, *La Paix créatrice: histoire des principes et des tactiques de l'action directe contre la guerre* (Paris, 1934).
de Man, Hendrik, *Nationalisme en socialisme* (Brussels, 1931).
Delmer, Louis, *L'Esclave: drame antiesclavagiste et national. Pièce en quatre actes* (Brussels and Paris, 1890).

Descamps, Edouard, *La Part de la Belgique dans le mouvement Africain* (Louvain, 1889).
——, *Africa: drame en cinq actes* (Paris, 1893).
——, *La Neutralité de la Belgique au point de vue historique, diplomatique, juridique et politique: Etude sur la constitution des états pacifiques à titre permanent* (Brussels, 1902).
——, *New Africa: An Essay on Government Civilization in New Countries and on the Foundation, Organization and Administration of the Congo Free State* (London, 1903).
Dumont-Wilden, Louis, *La Belgique illustrée* (Paris, 1911).
Eppstein, John, *A Catholic Looks at the League* (Oxford, 1937).
Fédération des Sociétés Rationalistes de la Belgique, *Compte-rendu du VIII Congrès Rationaliste, Bruxelles, le 28 et 29 mars 1880* (Brussels, 1880).
Fédération Internationale de la Libre Pensée, *Congrès de Paris: 3, 4, 5, 6, 7 septembre 1905 au Palais du Trocadéro* (Paris, 1905).
——, *Congrès de Rome: XX Septembre 1904. Compte-Rendu Officiel* (Ghent, 1905).
——, *Almanach-annuaire illustré de la Libre-Pensée Internationale* (Brussels, 1908).
——, *Annuaire illustré de la Libre Pensée Internationale 1909* (Brussels, 1909).
Fédération Nationale des Sociétés de Libres-Penseurs, *Guide illustré dédié aux Libres-Penseurs qui assisteront au Congrès International et Universel de Bruxelles* (Brussels, 1910).
Frank, Louis, *Les Belges et la paix* (Brussels, 1905).
——, *La Paix et le District Fédéral du Monde: l'avenir de la Belgique au point de vue international* (Paris, 1913).
Fried, Alfred H, *Das internationale Leben der Gegenwart* (Leipzig, 1908).
——, *Handbuch der Friedensbewegung* (Berlin, 1911).
——, *Europäische Wiederherstellung* (Zürich, 1915).
Fris, Victor, *La Vieille Flandre: Exposition Universelle et Internationale de Gand 1913* (Brussels, 1913).
Gatti de Gamond, Isabelle, *Education – Féminisme*, ed. Hector Denis and Eugène Hins (Brussels, 1907).
Geddes, Patrick, *Two Steps in Civics: 'Cities and Town Planning Exhibition' and the 'International Congress of Cities', Ghent International Exhibition, 1913* (Liverpool, 1913).
Griffis, William Elliot, *Belgium: The Land of Art: Its History, Legends, Industry and Modern Expansion* (London, 1912).
Haberman, Frederick (ed.), *Nobel Lectures, Peace 1901–1925* (new edn., Singapore, 1999).
Haupt, Georges (ed.), *Correspondance entre Lénine et Camille Huysmans 1905–1914* (Paris, 1963).
Herriot, Edouard, *Europe* (Paris, 1930).
Hins, Eugène, *Le Congrès de Prague: 8 au 12 septembre 1907* (Brussels, 1908).
——, *La Libre Pensée internationale en 1910* (Brussels, 1911).
——, *La Libre Pensée internationale en 1911* (Brussels, 1912).

——, *La Libre Pensée internationale en 1912* (Brussels, 1913).
——, *La Libre Pensée internationale en 1913* (Brussels, 1914).
Hobson, John A., *A League of Nations* (London, 1915).
Hocart, James, *Le Congrès de la Libre-Pensée à Rome* (Brussels, 1905).
Homans, J., 'La Philosophie au Congrès Scientifique International des Catholiques', *Revue neo-scholastique*, 3 (1896), 84–91.
Hymans, Paul, *Mémoires* (Brussels, 1958).
IIB, *Bulletin* (Brussels, 1926–30).
IIIC, *Institut international de Coopération Intellectuelle, 1925–1946* (Paris, 1946).
Kautsky, Karl, *Die Internationalität und der Krieg* (Berlin, 1915).
La Fontaine, Henri, *The Great Solution: Magnissima Charta* (Boston, MA, 1916).
La Fontaine, Henri (ed.), *Bulletin officiel du VIme Congrès International de la Paix, tenu à Anvers (Belgique) du 29 août au 1 septembre 1894* (Antwerp, 1895).
La Fontaine, Henri and Paul Otlet, *Sur la création d'un répertoire bibliographique universel: Conférence bibliographique internationale* (Brussels, 1895).
Lavigerie, Charles, *L'esclavage africain: conférence sur l'esclavage dans le Haut Congo, faite à Sainte-Gudule de Bruxelles* (Brussels, 1888).
Lavollée, René, 'Les Unions internationales', *Revue d'histoire diplomatique*, 1 (1887), 331–62.
Lindemann, Walter and Anna, *Die proletarische Freidenker-Bewegung: Geschichte, Theorie, Praxis* (Leipzig, 1926).
LSI, *The Colonial Problem: Material submitted to the IIIrd Congress of the Labour and Socialist International* (Brussels, 1928).
——, *The Congress of the Labour and Socialist International, Brussels, 5th to 11th August 1928. Reports and Proceedings*, 3 vols (London, 1928).
Mercier, Désiré-Joseph, *La 'Libre Pensée' athée et la moralité publique: lettre pastorale pour le carême de 1912* (Brussels, 1912).
Morel, E. D., *The Congo Slave State: A Protest against the New African Slavery; and an Appeal to the Public of Great Britain, of the United States, and of the Continent of Europe* (Liverpool, 1903).
Muir, Ramsay, *Nationalism and Internationalism: The Culmination of Modern History* (London, 1916).
Mulle, Marie, *L'Éducation Rationaliste: telle qu'elle est donnée à l'Orphelinat de Forest (Bruxelles). Rapport présenté au Congrès de Lisbonne* (Brussels, 1913).
Nilsson, Anna, *ABC du mouvement pour la paix: dates et faits* (Brussels, 1933).
Novicow, Jaques, *Die Föderation Europas: Autorisierte Übersetzung von A.H. Fried* (Berlin, 1901).
Novikov, Yakov Aleksandrovich [= Novicow, Jacques], *War and Its Alleged Benefits: With an Introduction by Norman Angell* (London, 1912).
Œuvre Francisco Ferrer, *Le Cardinal Mercier et l'Affaire Ferrer: un crime clérical* (Brussels, 1910).
Office Centrale des Institutions Internationales, *Annuaire de la Vie Internationale* (Brussels, 1909).
Otlet, Paul, *La Loi d'ampliation et l'internationalisme* (Brussels, 1908).
——, *La Fin de la guerre: traité de paix générale basé sur une Charte Mondiale déclarant les droits de l'humanité et organisant la confédération des états* (Brussels, 1914).

——, *Constitution mondiale de la Société des Nations: le nouveau droit des gens* (Geneva, 1917).

——, *L'Organisation de la Documentation Internationale et le rôle des associations de chimie* (Paris, 1919).

——, *Sur la création d'une Université internationale: rapport présenté à l'Union des Associations internationales* (Brussels, 1920).

——, *Introduction aux travaux de la Commission de Coopération intellectuelle de la Société des Nations* (Brussels, 1922).

——, *L'Exposition Universelle de 1930 en Belgique et l'établissement d'une Cité Mondiale* (Brussels, 1930).

——, 'L'Urbaneum – Bruxelles, Cité Mondiale. Bruxelles, Grande Ville. Bruxelles, Capitale de la Belgique', *La Cité*, 9 (1931), 121–9.

——, *Traité de Documentation: le livre sur le livre. Théorie et pratique* (Brussels, 1934).

Otlet, Paul and Ernest Vandeveld, *La Réforme des bibliographies nationales et leur utilisation pour la Bibliographie Universelle: rapport présenté au Ve Congrès international des Editeurs* (Milan and Brussels, 1906).

——, *Monde: essai d'universalisme* (Brussels, 1935).

——, *Plan Belgique: essai d'un plan national général, économique, social, culturel* (Brussels, 1935).

Picard, Edmond, *Synthèse de l'Antisémitisme* (Brussels, 1892).

——, *Essai d'une psychologie de la nation belge: suivi de l'idée du droit en Belgique* (Brussels, 1906).

——, *Nécessité et conditions de l'Expansion belge au dehors* (Brussels, 1906).

Piérard, Louis, *Wallons et Flamands* (Brussels, 1929).

——, *Regards sur la Belgique* (Grenoble, 1945).

Pirenne, Henri, *La Nation belge* (Brussels, 1900).

——, *Histoire de Belgique*, vol. 1: *Des origines au commencement du XIVe siècle* (5th edn., Brussels, 1929 [1900])

——, *Histoire de Belgique*, vol. 7: *De la révolution de 1830 à la guerre de 1914* (Brussels, 1932).

Ponsonby, Arthur, *Falsehood in Wartime: Containing an Assortment of Lies Circulated Throughout the Nations during the Great War* (London, 1928).

Quetelet, Adolphe, *Du Système social et des lois qui le régissent* (Paris, 1848).

Rappard, William, *International Relations as Viewed from Geneva* (New York, 1925).

——, 'Small states in the League of Nations', *Political Science Quarterly*, 49 (1934), 544–75.

——, *Collective Security in Swiss Experience 1291–1948* (London, 1948).

——, 'Woodrow Wilson, la Suisse et Genève', in Centre Européen de la Dotation Carnegie, *Centenaire Woodrow Wilson 1856–1956* (Geneva, 1956), pp. 29–74.

Rayward, W. Boyd (ed.), *International Organisation and Dissemination of Knowledge: Selected Essays of Paul Otlet* (Amsterdam, 1990).

Reinsch, Paul, *Public International Unions: Their Work and Organization. A Study in International Administrative Law* (Boston, MA, 1911).

Renard, Albert, *La Paix par la pacification* (Brussels, 1922).

Reynold, Gonzague de, *Grandeur de la Suisse* (Neuchâtel, 1940).
Roelandts, Léon [Maison d'Action Catholique], *Catholique ou Libre Penseur?* (Brussels, 1910).
Rolin, Henri, *La Belgique à la Société des Nations* (Brussels, 1930).
——, *Notre politique extérieure, conduit-elle à la paix?* (Brussels, 1938).
Sarton, George, *War and Civilization* (Brussels, 1919).
Société Antiesclavagiste de Belgique, *Le Mouvement Antiesclavagiste* [merged with *Le Mouvement des Missions catholiques en Congo* from 1903] (Brussels, 1888–1914).
Stead, William, *The United States of Europe on the Eve of the Parliament of Peace* (Toronto, 1899).
Strivay, Renaud, *Libre-Pensée universelle: documents généraux indispensables à tout esprit libre* (2nd edn., Liège, *c.* 1931).
Swanwick, Helena, *Collective Insecurity* (London, 1937).
Torre-Vélez, Comte de, *Vers le Monde Nouveau* (Brussels, 1921).
UAI, *L'Union des Associations Internationales: constitution du Centre International. Congrès Mondial. Office Central. Musée International. Documentation Universelle* (Brussels, 1912).
——, *La Vie Internationale*, vols. 1–3 (Brussels, 1912–14).
——, *L'Université internationale: notice et programme* (Brussels, 1920).
——, *Organisation internationale du travail intellectuel* (Brussels, 1921).
——, *La Société des Nations et l'Union des Associations Internationales* (Brussels 1923).
——, *Cité Mondiale à Genève: World Civic Center. Mundaneum avec des plans de Le Corbusier et Pierre Jeanneret* (Brussels, 1929).
Union Internationale des Associations pour la Société des Nations, *The League of Nations Societies and Their International Federation* (Brussels, 1926).
Van Houtte, Hubert, 'Une loi d'ampliation: essai sur l'évolution politique, économique, morale et intellectuelle dans l'Europe moderne', *Le Mouvement Sociologique International*, 8 (1907), 85–120.
Van Ortroy, Fernand, *Congrès colonial international de Bruxelles: extrait de la Revue des questions scientifiques, avril 1898* (Brussels, 1898).
Van Overbergh, Cyrille, *Le Mouvement scientifique en Belgique 1830–1905* (Brussels, 1905).
Vandervelde, Emile, *La Belgique envahie et le socialisme internationale* (Paris, 1917).
——, *Souvenirs d'un militant socialiste* (Paris, 1939).
Vandervelde, Lalla, *Monarchs and Millionaires* (New York, 1925).
Vaudon, Jean, *L'œuvre des congrès eucharistiques* (Paris, 1910).
Vermeylen, Auguste, 'Vlaamsche en Europeesche Beweging', *Van nu en Straks*, 4 (1900), 299–310.
Vertongen, Lucien, *Le Congrès de Lisbonne (4 au 8 Octobre 1913)* (Brussels, 1913).
Whitlock, Brand, *Belgium: A Personal Narrative* (New York, 1919).
Winandy, Armand, *La Répression de la traite et de l'esclavage* (Brussels, 1909).
Winock, Michel (ed.) *Congrès International Ouvrier Socialiste tenu à Bruxelles du 16 au 23 août* (new edn., Geneva, 1977 [1893]).

Woeste, Charles, *Mémoires pour servir à l'histoire contemporaine de la Belgique* (Brussels, 1937).

Women's Peace Party, *Report of the International Congress of Women. The Hague, The Netherlands. April 28th to May 1st, 1915* (Chicago, 1915).

Zimmern, Alfred, 'Europe and the world community' in Geneva Institute of International Relations, *The Problems of Peace. 6th Series* (London, 1932), pp. 122–33.

Zweig, Stefan, *Die Welt von gestern. Erinnerungen eines Europäers* (Frankfurt, 1955 [1944]).

Secondary sources

Albers, Martin, 'Between the crisis of democracy and world parliament: the development of the Inter-Parliamentary Union in the 1920s', *Journal of Global History*, 7 (2012), 189–209.

Amara, Michaël, 'La propagande belge et l'image de la Belgique aux Etats-Unis pendant la première guerre mondiale', *BTNG–RBHC*, 30 (2000), 173–226.

——, *Des Belges à l'épreuve de l'Exil: les réfugies de la Première Guerre mondiale. France, Grande-Bretagne, Pays-Bas* (Brussels, 2008).

Anderson, Bonnie, *Joyous Greetings: The First International Women's Movement 1830–1860* (Oxford, 2000).

Anghien, Antony, *Imperialism, Sovereignty and the Making of International Law* (Cambridge, 2004).

Armstrong, David, *The Rise of the International Organisation: A Short History* (London, 1982).

Arnal, Oscar, 'Towards a lay apostolate of the workers: three decades of conflict for the French Jeunessse Ouvrière Chrétienne', *Catholic Historical Review*, 73 (1987), 211–27.

Aron, Paul, *Les Écrivains belges et le socialisme (1880–1913)* (Brussels, 1985).

——, 'Le Symbolisme belge et la tentation de l'art social: une logique littéraire de l'engagement politique', *Les Lettres romanes*, 40 (1986), 307–17.

Aron, Paul (ed.), *La Belgique artistique et littéraire: une anthologie de langue française 1848–1914* (Brussels, 1997), p. 33.

Arts, Mieke and Myriam Everard, 'Forgotten intersections: Wilhelmina Drucker, early feminism and the Dutch-Belgian connection', *RBPH–BTFG*, 77 (1999), 440–71.

Ascherson, Neal, *The King Incorporated: Leopold the Second and the Congo* (new edn., Cambridge, 2001).

Aubert, Nathalie, Pierre-Philippe Fraiture and Patrick McGuiness (eds), *La Belgique entre deux siècles: laboratoire de la modernité, 1880–1914* (Bern, 2007).

Auerbach, Jeffrey, *The Great Exhibition of 1851: A Nation on Display* (New Haven, CT, 1999).

Bariéty, Jacques and Antoine Fleury (eds), *Mouvements et initiatives de paix dans la politique internationale* (Bern, 1987).

Barnett, Michael, *Empire of Humanity: A History of Humanitarianism* (Ithaca, NY, 2011).

Barros, James, *Office Without Power: Secretary-General Sir Eric Drummond 1919–1933* (Oxford, 1979).

Barry, Géaroid, *The Disarmament of Hatred: Marc Sangnier, French Catholicism and the Legacy of the First World War* (Basingstoke, 2012).

Barth, Boris and Jürgen Osterhammel (eds), *Zivilisierungsmissionen: Imperiale Weltverbesserung seit dem 18. Jahrhundert* (Konstanz, 2005).

Bartier, John, *Laïcité et franc-maçonnerie: études rassemblées et publiées par Guy Gambier* (Brussels, 1981).

Baubérot, Jean, *Histoire de la laïcité française* (Paris, 2000).

——, *Laïcité 1905–2005, entre passion et raison* (Paris, 2004).

Bayly, Christopher, *The Birth of the Modern World, 1780–1914: Global Connections and Comparison* (Oxford, 2004).

Bechet, Christophe, 'La révision pacifiste des manuels scolaires: les enjeux de la mémoire de la guerre 14–18 dans l'enseignement belge de l'Entre-deux-guerres', *CHTP–BEG*, 20 (2008), 49–101.

Beck, Ulrich and Edgar Grande, *Cosmopolitan Europe* (Cambridge, 2007).

Beretta, Francesco, 'Les Congrès scientifiques internationaux des catholiques (1888–1900) et la production d'orthodoxie dans l'espace intellectuel catholique', pp. 4–7 and 10–16, http://hal.inria.fr/docs/00/45/32/94/PDF/Beretta_Congres.pdf, first published in Claude Langlois and Christian Sorrel, *Le Catholicisme en congrès (XIXe – XXe siècles)* (Paris, 2009).

Beyen, Marnix and Benoit Majerus, 'Weak and strong nations in the Low Countries: national historiography and its "others" in Belgium, Luxembourg, and the Netherlands in the nineteenth and twentieth centuries', in Stefan Berger and Chris Lorentz (eds), *The Contested Nation: Ethnicity, Class, Religion and Gender in National Histories* (Basingstoke, 2009), pp. 283–310.

Birchal, Johnston, *The International Co-Operative Movement* (Manchester, 1997).

Birebent, Christian, *Militants de la paix et de la SDN: les mouvements de soutien à la Société des nations en France et au Royaume-Uni 1918–1925* (Paris, 2008).

Bitsch, Marie-Thérèse, *La Belgique entre la France et l'Allemagne 1905–1914* (Paris, 1994).

Block, Jane, *Les XX and Belgian Avant-Gardism 1868–1894* (Ann Arbor, MI, 1984).

Blocker, Jack, David Fahey and Ian Tyrell (eds), *Alcohol and Temperance in Modern History: An International Encyclopaedia*, 2 vols (Oxford, 2003).

Boli, John and George Thomas (eds), *Constructing World Culture: International Nongovernmental Organizations since 1875* (Stanford, CA, 1999).

Bookchin, Murray, *The Spanish Anarchists: The Heroic Years 1868–1936* (Edinburgh, 1998).

Borutta, Manuel, *Antikatholizismus: Deutschland und Italien im Zeitalter der europäischen Kulturkämpfe* (Göttingen, 2009).

Boxer, Marilyn, 'Rethinking the socialist construction and international career of the concept of "bourgeois feminism"', *American Historical Review*, 111 (2007), 131–58.

Boxer, Marilyn and Jean Quataert (eds), *Socialist Women: European Socialist Feminism in the Nineteenth and Twentieth Century* (New York, 1978).

Boyce, Robert, *The Great Interwar Crisis and the Collapse of Globalization* (Basingstoke, 2009).

Breuilly, John, *Nationalism and the State* (2nd edn., Manchester, 1993).

Brock, Peter and Thomas Socknat (eds), *Challenge to Mars: Essays on Pacifism from 1918 to 1945* (Toronto, 1999).

Busekist, Astrid von, *La Belgique: politique des langues et construction de l'état. De 1780 à nos jours* (Paris, 1998).

Caestecker, Frank, *Alien Policy in Belgium, 1840–1940: The Creation of Guest Workers, Refugees and Illegal Aliens* (New York, 2000).

——, 'Het reel bestaande socialisme in West-Eurpoa en de vlucht uit Nazi-Duitsland, 1933–1934: en oefening in private international solidariteit', *BEG–CHTP*, 15 (2005), 107–22.

Cahalan, Peter, *Belgian Refugee Relief in England during the Great War* (New York, 1982).

Callahan, Kevin, 'The international socialist peace movement on the eve of World War I revisited: the campaign of "War against War!" and the Basle International Socialist Congress in 1912', *Peace and Change*, 29 (2004), 147–76.

Callahan, Michael, *Mandates and Empire: The League of Nations and Africa, 1914–1931* (Portland, OR, 1999).

——, *A Sacred Trust: The League of Nations and Africa, 1929–1946* (Brighton, 2004).

Carle, Emanuelle, 'Women, anti-fascism and peace in interwar France: Gabrielle Duchêne's itinerary', *French History*, 18 (2004), 291–314.

Carlier, Julie, 'Moving beyond boundaries: an entangled history of feminism in Belgium 1890–1914' (PhD thesis, Ghent, 2010).

Ceadel, Martin, *Pacifism in Britain 1914–1945: The Defining of a Faith* (Oxford, 1980).

——, *Thinking About Peace and War* (Oxford, 1987).

——, *Semi-Detached Idealists: The British Peace Movement and International Relations, 1854–1945* (Oxford, 2000).

Charle, Christophe, Jürgen Schriewer and Peter Wagner (eds), *Transnational Intellectual Networks: Forms of Academic Knowledge and the Search for Cultural Identities* (Frankfurt, 2004).

Chickering, Roger, *Imperial Germany and a World Without War: The Peace Movement and German Society* (Princeton, NJ, 1975).

Claeys-Van Haegendoren, Mieke, *25 jaar Belgisch Socliasme: evolutie van der verhouding van de Belgische Werkliedenpartij tot de parlementaire deomcratie in Belgïe van 1914 tot 1940* (Antwerp, 1967).

Clark, Christopher and Wolfram Kaiser (eds), *Culture Wars: Secular-Catholic Conflict in Nineteenth-Century Europe* (Cambridge, 2003).

Clavin, Patricia, *The Failure of Economic Diplomacy: Britain, Germany, France and the United States, 1931–1936* (Basingstoke, 1996).

——, 'Defining transnationalism', *Contemporary European History*, 14 (2005), 421–39.

Cline, Catherine Ann, 'The church and the movement for Congo reform', *Church History*, 32 (1963), 46–56.

——, 'E.D. Morel and the crusade against the Foreign Office', *Journal of Modern History*, 39 (1967), 126–37.

Cole, G. D. H., *The Second International, 1889–1914* (London, 1956).

Conard, Sebastian and Dominc Sachsenmeier (eds), *Competing Visions of Global Order: Global Movements and Moments, 1880s–1930s* (Basingstoke, 2007).

Conway, Martin, 'Building the Christian city: Catholics and politics in interwar Francophone Belgium', *Past and Present*, 128 (1990), 117–51.

Conway, Martin and Tom Buchanan (eds), *Political Catholicism in Europe, 1918–1965* (Oxford, 1996).

Coolsaet, Rik, *La Politique extérieure de la Belgique: au cœur de l'Europe, le poids d'une petite puissance* (Brussels, 2002).

Cooper, Frederick, Thomas Holt and Rebecca Scott (eds), *Beyond Slavery: Explorations of Race, Labor, and Citizenship in Postemancipation Societies* (Chapel Hill, NC, 2000).

Cooper, Sandi, 'The guns of August and the doves of Italy: intervention and internationalism', *Peace and Change*, 7 (1981), 29–43.

——, *Patriotic Pacifism: Waging War on War in Europe, 1815–1914* (New York, 1991).

——, 'Pacifism, feminism and fascism in interwar France', *International History Review*, 19 (1997), 103–14.

Corduwener, Pepijn, 'Risee van de wereld of land van Grotius? De synthese tussen nationalisme en internationalisme in het Nederlandse fin de siècle', *Tijdschrift voor Geschiedenis*, 125 (2012), 205–15.

Cortright, David, *Peace: A History of Movements and Ideas* (Cambridge, 2008).

Costa Bona, Enrica, *Il Bureau International del Paix nelle relazioni internationali (1919–1939)* (Milan, 2010).

Couttenier, Maarten, *Congo tentoongesteld: een geschiedenis van de Belgische antropologie en het museum van Tervuren (1882–1925)* (Leuven, 2005).

Couvreur, Manuel (ed.), *La Monnaie Wagnérienne* (Brussels, 1998).

Craeybeckx, Jan, Alain Meynen and Els Witte (eds), *Political History of Belgium from 1830 Onwards* (Brussels, 2000).

Crawford, Elisabeth, *Nationalism and Internationalism in Science, 1880–1939: Four Studies of the Nobel Population* (Cambridge, 1992).

Crombois, Jean-François, *L'Univers de sociologie en Belgique de 1900 à 1940* (Brussels, 1994).

Cullinane, Michael Patrick, 'Transatlantic dimensions of the anti-imperialist movement, 1899–1909', *Journal of Transatlantic Studies*, 4 (2010), 301–14.

Curthoys, Ann and Marilyn Lake (eds), *Connected Worlds: History in Transnational Perspective* (Canberra, 2005).

Dam, Harmjan, *Der Weltbund für Freundschaftsarbeit der Kirchen 1914–1948: Eine ökumenische Friedensorganisation* (Frankfurt, 2001).

David, Thomas and Janick Marina Schaufelbuehl, 'Swiss conservatives and the struggle for the abolition of slavery at the end of the nineteenth century', *Itinerario*, 34 (2010), 87–103.

Davies, Thomas, *The Possibilities of Transnational Activism: The Campaign for Disarmament Between the World Wars* (Leiden, 2007).

de Bont, Raf, '"Foggy and contradictory": evolutionary theory in Belgium, 1859–1945', in Eve-Marie Engels and Thomas F. Glick (eds), *The Reception of Charles Darwin in Europe*, vol. 1 (London, 2008), pp. 188–98.

De Groof, Roel (ed.), *Brussels and Europe – Bruxelles et l'Europe* (Brussels, 2008).

De Groof, Roel and Geertrui Elaut, *Brussels in Europe – Europe in Brussels: From Federal World District to Capital of Europe, 1900–2010* (Brussels, 2010).

De Maeyer, Jan, *De rode baron: Arthur Verhaegen, 1847–1917* (Leuven, 1994).

De Schaepdrijver, Sophie, *Elites for the Capital: Foreign Migration to Mid-Nineteenth Century Brussels* (Amsterdam, 1990).

——, *De Groote Oorlog: het Konikrijk België tijdens de Eerste Wereldorlog* (Antwerp, 1997).

De Smaele, Henk, 'Henry Carton de Wiart (1869–1905): Christen-democratisch politicus en literator', *Trajecta*, 4 (1995), 22–41.

De Vroede, Maurice, 'Francisco Ferrer et la Ligue internationale pour l'éducation rationelle de l'enfance', *Paedagogica Historica*, 19 (1979), 278–95.

De Weerdt, Denise, *En de vrouwen? Vrouw, vrouwenbeweging en feminisme en België 1830–1960* (Ghent, 1980).

De Wever, Bruno, *Greep naar de macht: Vlaams-nationalisme en Nieuwe Orde. Het VNV 1933–1945* (Tielt, 1994).

Defoort, Hendrik, *Werklieden, bemint uw profijt! De Belgische sociaaldemocratie en Europa* (Ghent, 2006).

della Porta, Donatella and Sidney Tarrow (eds), *Transnational Protest and Global Activism* (Lanham, MD, 2005).

Den Hertog, Johan, 'Zelfstandigheidspolitiek: de achtergrond van een cruciale term in het buitenlands beleid van Nederland 1900–1940', *Bijdragen en mededelingen betreffende de geschiedenis der Nederlanden*, 124 (2009), 163–85.

Deneckere, Gita, *Sir het volk mort: sociaal protest in België 1831–1918* (Antwerp, 1997).

Despy-Meyer, Andrée and Didier Devriese (eds), *Solvay et son temps* (Brussels, 1997).

Despy-Meyer, Andrée and Hervé Hasquin (eds), *Libre Pensée et pensée libre: combats et débats. Hommage à André Uyttebrouck* (Brussels, 1996).

Deutsch, Karl, *Nationalism and Social Communication: An Enquiry into the Foundations of Nationality* (Cambridge, 1953).

Dhondt, Jan (ed.), *Geschiedenis van de Socialistische Arbeidersbeweging in België* (Antwerp, 1960).

Dogliani, Patrizia, 'European municipalism in the first half of the twentieth century: the socialist network', *Contemporary European History*, 11 (2002), 573–96.

Dowe, Dieter, David Higgins, Heinz-Gerhard Haupt and Jonathan Sperber (eds), *Europe in 1848: Revolution and Reform* (New York, 2001).

Drouin, Michel (ed.), *L'Affaire Dreyfus* (Paris, 1994).

Duchenne, Geneviève, 'La pensée européenne du socialiste Jules Destrée: un internationalisme européen (1906–1936)', *Annales d'Études européennes de l'Université catholique de Louvain*, 5 (2001), 21–45.

——, *Visions et projets belges pour l'Europe: de la Belle Époque aux Traités de Rome* (Brussels, 2001).

——, 'Les nouvelles relèves en Belgique francophone (1926–1936): une source pour l'européisme ?' in Olivier Dard and Etienne Deschamps (eds), *Les relèves en Europe d'un après-guerre à l'autre: racines, réseaux, projets et postérités* (Brussels, 2005), pp. 331–54.

——, *Esquisses d'une Europe nouvelle: l'européisme dans la Belgique de l'entre-deux-guerres (1919–1939)* (Brussels, 2008).

Dumoulin, Michel and Arthe Van Laer (eds), *La Belgique, les petits États et la construction européenne* (Brussels, 2003).

Dumoulin, Michel and Eddy Stols (eds), *La Belgique et l'étranger aux XIXe et XXe siècles* (Louvain-la-Neuve, 1987).

Dumoulin, Michel, Emmanuel Gerard, Mark Van den Wijngaert and Vincent Dujardin, *Nouvelle Histoire de Belgique, II: 1905–1950* (Brussels, 2006).

Eley, Geoff, *Forging Democracy: The History of the Left in Europe, 1850–2000* (Oxford, 2000).

Erdmann, Karl Dietrich, *Die Ökumene der Historiker: Geschichte der Internationalen Historikerkongresse und des Comité International des Sciences Historiques* (Göttingen, 1987).

Fayet-Scribe, Sylvie, *Histoire de la documentation en France: culture, science et technologie d'information, 1895–1937* (Paris, 2000).

Featherstone, David, *Solidarity: Hidden Histories and Geographies of Internationalism* (London, 2012).

Fischer, Karin and Susan Zimmermann (eds), *Internationalismen: Transformation weltweiter Ungleichheit im 19. und 20. Jahrhundert* (Vienna, 2008).

Fleckenstein, Gisela and Jochen Schmiedl (eds), *Ultramontanismus: Tendenzen der Forschung* (Paderborn, 2005).

Förster, Stig, Wolfgang Mommsen and Ronald Robinson (eds), *Bismarck, Europe and Africa: The Berlin Africa Conference and the Onset of Partition* (New York, 1988).

Freitag, Sabine (ed.), *Exiles from European Revolution: Refugees in Mid-Victorian England* (New York, 2003).

Fuchs, Eckhardt, *Weltausstellungen im 19. Jahrhundert* (Leipzig, 2000).

Furlong, Paul and David Curtis (eds), *The Church Faces the Modern World: Rerum Novarum and Its Impact* (Hull, 1994).

Furlough, Ellen and Carl Strikwerda (eds), *Consumers against Capitalism? Consumer Cooperation in Europe, North America, and Japan, 1840–1990* (Oxford, 1999).

Gaspari, Oscar, 'Cities against States? Hopes, dreams and shortcomings of the European municipal movement, 1900–1960', *Contemporary European History*, 11 (2002), 597–621.

Gatrell, Peter, 'Refugees and forced migrants during the First World War', *Immigrants and Minorities*, 26 (2008), 82–110.

Gellner, Ernest, *Nations and Nationalism* (Oxford, 1983).

Gerard, Emmanuel, *De katholieke partij in crisis: partijpolitiek leven in België 1918–1940* (Leuven, 1985).

Gerard, Emmanuel and Kaat Wils, 'Catholics and sociology in Leuven from Désiré Mercier to Jacques Leclerq: a process of appropriation', in Liliane Voyé and Jaak

Billiet (eds), *Sociology and Religions: An Ambiguous Relationship* (Leuven, 1999), pp. 38–56.

Gerard, Emmanuel and Paul Wynants (eds), *Histoire du mouvement ouvrier chrétien en Belgique*, 2 vols (Leuven, 1994).

Geyer, Martin and Johannes Paulmann (eds), *The Mechanics of Internationalism: Culture, Society, and Politics from the 1840s to the First World War* (Oxford, 2001).

Gotovitch, José, *Du rouge au tricolore: les communistes belges de 1939 à 1944. Un aspect de l'histoire de la Résistance en Belgique* (Brussels, 1992).

——, *Du communisme et des communistes en Belgique: approches critiques* (Brussels, 2012).

Gotovitch, José and Anne Morelli (eds), *Les Solidarités internationales: histoire et perspectives* (Brussels, 2003).

Grant, Kevin 'Christian critics of empire: missionaries, lantern lectures, and the Congo reform campaign in Britain', *Journal of Imperial and Commonwealth History*, 29 (2001), 27–58.

——, *A Civilised Savagery: Britain and the New Slaveries in Africa, 1884–1926* (New York, 2005).

Greenhalgh, Paul, *Ephemeral Vistas: The Expositions Universelles, Great Exhibitions and World's Fairs, 1851–1939* (Manchester, 1988).

Gresleri, Giuliano, 'Convergences et divergences: de Le Corbusier à Otto Neurath', *Transnational Associations*, 1–2 (2003), 72–81.

Grossi, Verdiana, *Le Pacifisme européen: 1889–1914* (Brussels, 1994).

Gruber, Helmut and Pamela Graves (eds), *Women and Socialism, Socialism and Women: Europe Between the Two World Wars* (New York, 1998).

Gubin, Eliane, Valérie Piette and Catherine Jacques, 'Les féminismes belges et français de 1880 à 1914: une approche comparée', *Le Mouvement Social*, 178 (1997), 36–68.

Guieu, Jean-Michael, *Le Rameau et le glaive: les militants français pour la Société des Nations* (Paris, 2008).

Gullentops, David and Hans Vandevoorde (eds), *Anarchisten rond Emile Verhaeren* (Brussels, 2005).

Haag, Henri, 'Le Cardinal Mercier devant la guerre et la paix', *Revue d'histoire ecclésiastique*, 79 (1984), 709–83.

Halliday, Fred, 'Three concepts of internationalism', *International Affairs*, 64 (1988), 187–98.

Harris, Ruth, *Dreyfus: Politics, Emotion, and the Scandal of the Century* (New York, 2010).

Haslam, Beryl, *From Suffrage to Internationalism: The Political Evolution of Three British Feminists, 1908–1939* (New York, 1999).

Hasquin, Hervé (ed.), *Histoire de la laïcité en Belgique* (Brussels, 1994).

Haupt, Georges, *Programm und Wirklichkeit: Die internationale Sozialdemokratie vor 1915* (Neuwied, 1970).

Heerma van Voss, Lex, Patrick Pasture and Jan De Maeyer (eds), *Between Cross and Class: Comparative Histories of Christian Labour in Europe 1840–2000* (Bern, 2005).

Hellemans, Staf, *Strijd om de moderniteit: sociale bewegingen en verzuiling in Europa sinds 1800* (Leuven 1990).

Hellman, John, *The Communitarian Third Way: Alexandre Marc and Ordre Nouveau, 1930–2000* (Montreal, 2002).

Helmreich, Jonathan, *Belgium and Europe: A Study in Small Power Diplomacy* (The Hague, 1976).

Herren, Madeleine, *Internationale Sozialpolitik vor dem ersten Weltkrieg: Die Anfänge europäischer Kooperation aus der Sicht Frankreichs* (Berlin, 1993).

——, 'Modernisierung, Außenpolitik und Integration im Jahrhundert des Internationalismus', *Historische Mitteilungen*, 7 (1994), 1–43.

——, *Hintertüren zur Macht: Internationalismus und mordenisierungsorientierte Außenpolitik in Belgien, der Schweiz und den USA, 1865–1914* (Munich, 2000).

——, '"Outwardly … an innocuous conference authority": National Socialism and the logistics of international information management', *German History*, 20 (2002), 67–92.

Hilson, Mary, 'A consumers' international? The international cooperative alliance and cooperative internationalism: a Nordic perspective', *International Review of Social History*, 56 (2011), 203–33.

Hochschild, Adam, *King Leopold's Ghost: A Story of Greed, Horror and Heroism in Colonial Africa* (New York, 1995).

Holl, Karl, *Pazifismus in Deutschland* (Frankfurt, 1988).

Holl, Karl and Anne C. Kjelling (eds), *The Nobel Peace Prize and the Laureates: The Meaning and Acceptance of the Nobel Peace Prize in the Prize Winners' Countries* (Frankfurt, 1994).

Horn, Gerd-Rainer, 'From "radical" to "realistic": Hendrik de Man and the International Plan Conferences at Pontigny and Geneva, 1934–1937', *Contemporary European History*, 10 (2001), 239–65.

Horne, John and Alan Kramer, *German Atrocities, 1914: A History of Denial* (New Haven, CT, 2005).

Howard, Jeremy, *Art Nouveau: International and National Styles in Europe* (Manchester, 1996).

Hroch, Miroslav, *Social Preconditions of National Revival in Europe: A Comparative Analysis of the Social Composition of Patriotic Groups Among the Smaller European Nations* (Cambridge, 1985).

Ingram, Norman *The Politics of Dissent: Pacifism in France, 1919–1939* (Oxford, 1991).

Iriye, Akira, *Cultural Internationalism and World Order* (Baltimore, 1997).

——, *Global Community: The Role of International Organizations in the Contemporary World* (Berkeley, CA, 2002).

Iriye, Akira and Pierre-Yves Saunier (eds), *Palgrave Dictionary of Transnational History: From the Mid-19th Century to the Present Day* (Basingstoke, 2009).

Janssens, Jeroen, *De belgische natie viert: de Belgische nationale feesten 1830–1914* (Louvain, 2001).

Jaumain, Serge and Wanda Balcers (eds), *Bruxelles 1910: de l'Exposition universelle à l'Université* (Brussels, 2010).

Jodock, Darrell (ed.), *Catholicism Contending with Modernity: Roman Catholic Modernism and Anti-Modernism in Historical Context* (Cambridge, 2000).

Joll, James, *The Second International* (2nd edn., London, 1974).

Kaiser, Jochen-Christoph, *Arbeiterbewegung und organisierte Religionskritik: Proletarische Freidenkerverbände im Kaiserreich und der Weimarer Republik* (Stuttgart, 1981).

Kaiser, Wolfang and Helmut Wohnout (eds), *Political Catholicism in Europe 1918–45* (London, 2004).

Keck, Margaret and Kathryn Sikkink, *Activists Beyond Borders: Advocacy Networks in International Politics* (Ithaca, NY, 1998).

Keohane, Robert and Joseph Nye, 'Transnational relations and world politics: an introduction', *International Organisation*, 25 (1971), 329–49.

——, *Power and Interdependence: World Politics in Transition* (Boston, MA, 1977).

Kinet, Ruth, '*Licht in die Finsternis*': *Kolonisation und Mission im Kongo, 1876–1908: Kolonialer Staat und nationale Mission zwischen Kooperation und Konfrontation* (Münster, 2005).

Knock, Thomas, *To End All Wars: Woodrow Wilson and the Quest for a New World Order* (Oxford, 1992).

Köck, Heribert, *Die völkerrechtliche Stellung des Heiligen Stuhls: Dargestellt an seinen Beziehungen zu Staaten und internationalen Organisationen* (Berlin, 1975).

Koll, Johannes (ed.), *Nationale Bewegungen in Belgien: Ein historischer Überblick* (Münster, 2005).

Körner, Axel, *Das Lied von einer anderen Welt: Kulturelle Praxis im deutschen und französischen Arbeitermilieu* (Frankfurt, 2007).

Körner, Axel (ed.), *1848: A European Revolution? International Ideas and National Memories of 1848* (Basingstoke, 2000).

Koskenniemi, Martti, *The Gentle Civilizer of Nations: The Rise and Fall of International Law 1870–1960* (Cambridge, 2002).

Kossmann, Ernst, *The Low Countries, 1780–1940* (Oxford, 1978).

Kramer, Alan, *Dynamic of Destruction: Culture and Mass Killing in the First World War* (Oxford, 2007).

Kurgan-van Hentenryk, Ginette (ed.), *Laboratoires et réseaux de diffusions des idées en Belgique (XIXe-XXe siècle)* (Brussels, 1994).

——, *Un pays si tranquille: la violence en Belgique aux XIXe siècle* (Brussels, 1999).

Kushner, Tony, 'Local heroes: Belgian refugees in Britain during the First World War', *Immigrants and Minorities*, 18 (1999), 1–28.

La Porte, Norman, Kevin Morgan and Matthew Worley (eds), *Bolshevism, Stalinism and the Comintern: Perspectives on Stalinization, 1917–59* (Basingstoke, 2008).

Lademacher, Horst, *Die belgische Neutralität als Problem der europäischen Politik 1830–1914* (Bonn, 1971).

——, 'Belgien als Objekt und Subjekt europäischer Außenpolitik: Historische Fallstudie zu den politischen Determinanten und Möglichkeiten eines kleinen europäischen Landes', *BTNG–RBHC*, 35 (2004), 457–502.

Laity, Paul, *The British Peace Movement, 1870–1914* (Oxford, 2001).
Lalouette, Jacqueline, *La Libre Pensée en France, 1848 à 1940* (Paris, 1997).
——, *La République anticléricale: XIXe – XXe siècles* (Paris, 2002).
——, *La Séparation des églises et de l'état: genèse et développement d'une idée, 1789–1905* (Paris, 2005).
Lamberts, Emiel, 'Les Semaines Sociales en Belgique', in Jean-Dominique Durand (ed.), *Les Semaines Sociales de France: cent ans d'engagement social des catholiques français, 1904–2004* (Paris, 2006), pp. 341–58.
Lamberts, Emiel (ed.), *The Black International 1870–1878: The Holy See and Militant Catholicism in Europe* (Brussels, 2002).
Lamberts, Emiel and Jacques Lory (eds), *1884: un tournant politique en Belgique/de machtswisseling van 1884 in België* (Brussels, 1986).
Laqua, Daniel, '"Laïque, démocratique et sociale"? Socialism and the Freethinkers' International', *Labour History Review*, 74 (2009), 257–73.
——, 'Internationalisme ou affirmation de la nation? La coopération intellectuelle transnationale dans l'entre-deux-guerres', *Critique Internationale*, 52 (2011), 51–67.
——, 'The tensions of internationalism: transnational anti-slavery in the 1880s and 1890s', *International History Review*, 33 (2011), 705–26.
——, 'Transnational intellectual cooperation, the League of Nations, and the problem of order', *Journal of Global History*, 6 (2011), 223–47.
Laqua, Daniel (ed.), *Internationalism Reconfigured: Transnational Ideas and Movements Between the World Wars* (London, 2011).
Large, David Clay and William Weber, *Wagnerism in European Culture and Politics* (Ithaca, NY, 1984).
Levie, Françoise, *L'homme qui voulait classer le monde: Paul Otlet et le Mundaneum* (Brussels, 2006).
Levy, Carl, 'Anarchism, internationalism and nationalism in Europe, 1860–1939', *Australian Journal of Politics and History*, 50 (2004), 330–42.
Liebman, Marcel, *Les Socialistes belges, 1885–1914: La révolte et l'organisation* (Brussels, 1979).
Lindley, Jeanne, *Seeking and Finding: The Life of Emile Cammaerts* (London, 1962).
Löhr, Isabella, *Die Globalisierung des geistiger Eigentumsrechte: Neue Strukturen internationaler Zusammenarbeit 1886–1952* (Göttingen, 2010).
Long, David and Peter Wilson (eds), *Thinkers of the Twenty Years' Crisis* (Oxford, 1995).
Louis, Wm. Roger, 'The Stokes affair and the origins of the anti-Congo campaign, 1895–1896', *RBPH–BTFG*, 43 (1965), 572–84.
——, *Ends of British Imperialism: The Scramble for Empire, Suez and Decolonization* (London, 2006).
Lubelski-Bernard, Nadine, 'Les Mouvements et les idéologies pacifistes en Belgique 1830 –1914' (PhD thesis, Université Libre de Bruxelles, 1977).
Lyons, F. S. L., *Internationalism in Europe 1815–1914* (Leiden, 1963).
MacKenzie, John (ed.), *European Empires and the People: Popular Responses to Imperialism in France, Britain, the Netherlands, Belgium, Germany and Italy* (Manchester, 2011).

Manela, Erez, *The Wilsonian Moment: Self-Determination and the International Origins of Anti-Colonial Nationalism* (Cambridge, MA, 2007).
Marchal, Jules, *E.D. Morel contre Léopold II: L'histoire du Congo 1900–1910* (Paris, 1996).
Marks, Sally, *Innocent Abroad: Belgium at the Paris Peace Conference in 1919* (Chapel Hill, NC, 1981).
——, 'Ménage à trois? The negotiations for an Anglo-French-Belgian Alliance in 1922', *International History Review*, 4 (1982), 524–52.
——, *Paul Hymans: Makers of the Modern World. The Peace Conferences of 1919–23 and Their Aftermath* (London, 2010).
Mattelart, Armand, *Networking the World, 1794–2000* (Minneapolis, 2000).
Mauermann, Helmut, *Das Internationale Friedensbüro 1892–1950* (Stuttgart, 1990).
Mayné, Marc, *Eugène Hins: une grande figure de la Première Internationale en Belgique* (Brussels, 1994).
Mazower, Mark, *No Enchanted Palace: The End of Empire and the Ideological Origins of the United Nations* (Princeton, NJ, 2009).
McCarthy, Helen, *The British People and the League of Nations: Democracy, Citizenship and Internationalism, c. 1918–45* (Manchester, 2011).
McGuinness, Patrick (ed.), *Symbolism, Decadence and the Fin de Siècle. French and European Perspectives* (Exeter, 2000).
McLeod, Hugh and Werner Ustorf (eds), *The Decline of Christendom in Western Europe, 1750–2000* (Cambridge, 2003).
Meller, Helen, 'Philanthropy and public enterprise: international exhibitions and the modern town-planning movement 1889–1913', *Planning Perspectives*, 10 (1995), 295–310.
Messinger, Gary, *British Propaganda and the State in the First World War* (Manchester, 1992).
Miers, Suzanne, *Britain and the Ending of the Slave Trade* (London, 1975).
——, 'Slavery and the slave trade as international issues 1890–1939', *Slavery and Abolition*, 19 (1998), 16–37.
——, *Slavery in the Twentieth Century: The Evolution of a Global Problem* (Lanham, MD, 2002).
Milner, Susan, *The Dilemmas of Internationalism: French Syndicalism and the International Labour Movement, 1900–1914* (New York, 1990).
Mommen, Andre, *De Belgische Wirklidenpartij: ontstaan en entwekkeling van het reformistisch socialisme (1830–1914)* (Ghent, 1980).
Morelli, Anne and Jacques Lemaire (eds), *Francisco Ferrer: cent ans après son exécution. Les avatars d'une image* (Brussels, 2010), pp. 199–222.
Morgan, Kevin, 'Militarism and anti-militarism: socialists, communists and conscription in France and Britain 1900–1940, *Past and Present*, 202 (2009), 207–44.
Moulaert, Jan, *Rood en zwart: de anarchistische beweging in België 1880–1914* (Leuven, 1995).
Mundaneum, *Cent ans de l'Office international de bibliographie, 1895–1995: les prémisses du Mundaneum* (Mons, 1995).
——, *Paul Otlet, fondateur du Mundaneum (1868–1944): architecte du savoir, artisan de paix* (Brussels, 2010).

Müller, Christian, 'Designing the model European – liberal and republican concepts of citizenship in Europe in the 1860s: the Association Internationale pour le Progrès des Sciences Sociales', *History of European Ideas*, 37 (2011), 223–31.

Nation, R. Craig, *War on War: Lenin, the Zimmerwald Left, and the Origins of Communist Internationalism* (Durham, NC, 1989).

Nichols, David, 'Richard Cobden and the international peace congress movement 1848–1853', *Journal of British Studies*, 30 (1994), 351–76.

Orzoff, Andrea, *Battle for the Castle: The Myth of Czechoslovakia in Europe, 1914–1948* (Oxford, 2009).

Osterhammel, Jürgen, 'Transnationale Gesellschaftsgeschichte: Erweiterung oder Alternative?', *Geschichte und Gesellschaft*, 27 (2001), 464–79.

——, *Die Verwandlung der Welt: Eine Geschichte des 19. Jahrhunderts* (Munich, 2008).

Pagden, Anthony (ed.), *The Idea of Europe: From Antiquity to the European Union* (Cambridge, 2002).

Palo, Michael, 'The question of neutrality and Belgium's security dilemma during the First World War: the search for a politically acceptable solution', *BTNG–RBHC*, 29 (2000), 227–304.

Papini, Roberto, *The Christian Democrat International* (Lanham, MA, 1997).

Park, T. Peter, 'The European reaction to the execution of Francisco Ferrer' (PhD dissertation, University of Virginia, 1970).

Pasture, Patrick, *Histoire du syndicalisme chrétien internationale: la difficile recherche d'une troisième voie* (Paris, 1999).

——, 'The interwar origins of international labour's European commitment (1919–1934)', *Contemporary European History*, 10 (2001), 221–37.

Pasture, Patrick and Johan Verberckmoes (eds), *Working-Class Internationalism and the Appeal of National Identity: Historical Debates and Current Perspectives on Western Europe* (Oxford, 1998).

Pavlakis, Dean, 'The development of British overseas humanitarianism and the Congo reform campaign', *Journal of Colonialism and Colonial History* 11 (2010) [online via *Project MUSE*, http://muse.jhu.edu]

Pécout, Gilles (ed.), *Penser les frontières de l'Europe du XIXe au XXIe siècle* (Paris, 2003).

Pedersen, Susan, 'The meaning of the Mandates system: an argument', *Geschichte und Gesellschaft*, 32 (2006), 560–82.

——, 'Back to the League of Nations', *American Historical Review*, 112 (2007), 1091–1115.

——, 'Metaphors of the schoolroom: women working the Mandates system of the League of Nations', *History Workshop Journal*, 66 (2008), 188–207.

Pegg, Carl, *Evolution of the European Idea, 1914–1932* (Chapel Hill, NC, 1983).

Pels, Dirk, 'Hendrik de Man and the ideology of Planism', *International Review of Social History*, 32 (1987), 206–29.

Peter, Ania, *William E. Rappard und der Völkerbund. Ein Schweizer Pionier der internationalen Verständigung* (Bern, 1973).

Petricioli, Marta and Donatella Cherubini (eds), *Pour la paix en Europe: institutions et société civile dans l'entre-deux-guerres* (Brussels, 2007).

Petricioli, Marta, Donatella Cherubini and Alessandra Anteghini (eds), *Les Etats-Unis d'Europe: un projet pacifiste* (Bern, 2004).
Phipps, William, *William Sheppard: Congo's African American Livingstone* (Louisville, KY, 2002).
Polasky, Janet, *The Democratic Socialism of Emile Vandervelde: Between Reform and Revolution* (Oxford, 1995).
Porter, Andrew, *Religion Versus Empire? British Protestant Missionaries and Overseas Expansion, 1700–1914* (Manchester, 2004).
——, 'Evangelical visions and colonial realities', *Journal of Imperial and Commonwealth History*, 38 (2010), 145–55.
Prochasson, Christophe, *Les Intellectuels, le socialisme et la guerre 1900–1938* (Paris, 1993).
Prochasson, Christophe and Anne Rasmussen, *Au nom de la patrie: les intellectuels et la première guerre mondiale (1910–1919)* (Paris, 1996).
Pyenson, Lewis and Christophe Verbruggen, 'Elements of the modernist creed in Henri Pirenne and George Sarton', *History of Science*, 49 (2011), 377–94.
Quaghebeur, Marc and Madéleine Rebérioux, 'Intellectuels en Belgique et en France: "Pilliers", citoyenneté, Etat', *Le Mouvement Social*, 178 (1997), 110– 2.
Quaghebeur, Marc and Nicole Savy (eds), *France – Belgique (1848–1914): affinités – ambiguities*, (Brussels, 1997).
Randeraad, Nico, 'The International Statistical Congress (1853–1876): knowledge transfers and their limits', *European History Quarterly*, 41 (2011), 50–65.
Ranieri, Lianne, *Léopold II, Urbaniste* (Brussels, 1972).
Rasmussen, Anne, 'L'Internationale scientifique (1890–1914)' (PhD thesis, EHESS, 1995).
——, 'L'hygiène en congrès (1852–1912): circulation et configurations internationales', in Patrice Bourdelais (ed.), *Les Hygiénistes: enjeux, modèles et pratiques, XVIIIe-XX siècles* (Berlin, 2001), pp. 213–39.
Rayward, W. Boyd, *The Universe of Information: The Work of Paul Otlet for Documentation and International Organisation* (Moscow, 1975).
——, 'The International Exposition and the World Documentation Congress of 1937', *Library Quarterly*, 53 (1983), 254–68.
——, 'Visions of Xanadu: Paul Otlet (1868–1944) and hypertext', *Journal of the American Society for Information Science*, 45 (1994), 235–50.
——, 'The origins of information science and the International Institute of Bibliography/International Federation for Information and Documentation (FID)', in Trudi Bellardo Hahn and Michael Buckland (eds), *Historical Studies in Information Science* (Medford, NJ, 1998), pp. 289–300.
Rayward, W. Boyd (ed.), *European Modernism and the Information Society: Informing the Present, Understanding the Past* (Aldershot, 2008).
Rees, Tim and Andrew Thorpe (eds), *International Communism and the Communist International 1919–1943* (Manchester, 1998).
Rémond, René, *L'Anticléricalisme en France: de 1815 à nos jours* (3rd edn., Paris, 1999).
Renault, François, *Lavigerie, l'esclavage africain et l'Europe, 1868–1892* (Paris, 1971).

Ribi, Amalia, 'Humanitarianism imperialism: the politics of anti-slavery activism in the interwar years' (DPhil thesis, Oxford, 2008).

Richard, Anne-Isabelle, 'Competition and complementarity: civil society networks and the question of decentralizing the League of Nations', *Journal of Global History*, 7 (2012), 233–56.

——, 'Huizinga, the Netherlands and the spirit of Europe, 1933–1945', in Mark Hewitson and Matthew d'Auria (eds), *Europe in Crisis: Intellectuals and the European Idea, 1917–1957* (New York, 2012), pp. 243–56.

Riemens, Michael, *De passie voor vrede: de evolutie van de internationale politieke cultuur in de jaren 1880–1940 en het recipiëren door Nederland* (Amsterdam, 2005).

Rietzler, Katharina, 'American internationalists in Europe: the Carnegie endowment for international peace in the early twentieth century' (MA thesis, UCL, 2005).

——, 'American foundations and the "scientific study" of international relations in Europe, 1910–1940' (PhD thesis, UCL, 2009).

Righart, Hans, *De katholieke zuil in Europa: het ontstaan van verzuiling onder katholieken in Oostenrijk, Zwisterland, België en Nederland* (Meppel, 1986).

Rodgers, Daniel, *Atlantic Crossings: Social Politics in a Progressive Age* (Cambridge, MA, 1998).

Rodríguez García, Magaly, 'Early views on internationalism: Marxist socialists vs. liberals', *RBPH–BTFG*, 84 (2006), 1049–73.

Romero Maura, Joaquín, 'Terrorism in Barcelona and its impact on Spanish politics, 1904–1909', *Past and Present*, 41 (1968), 130–84.

Rosart, Françoise and Thierry Scaillet, *Entre jeux et enjeux: mouvements de jeunesse catholiques en Belgique 1910–1940* (Louvain-la-Neuve, 2002).

Roshwald, Aviel and Richard Stites (eds), *European Culture in the Great War* (Cambridge, 1999).

Royle, Edward, *Radicals, Secularists and Republicans: Popular Freethought in Britain, 1866–1915* (Manchester, 1980).

Rulof, Bernard, 'Selling social democracy in the Netherlands: activism and its sources of inspiration during the 1930s', *Contemporary European History*, 18 (2009), 475–97.

Rupp, Leila, *Worlds of Women: The Making of an International Women's Movement* (Princeton, 1997).

Rydell, Robert and Nancy Gwinn (eds), *Fair Representations: World's Fairs and the Modern World* (Amsterdam, 1994).

Sapiro, Gisèle (ed.), *L'Espace intellectuel en Europe: de la formation des États-nations à la mondialisation, 19–20e siècle* (Paris, 2009).

Sassoon, Donald, *One Hundred Years of Socialism: The West European Left in the Twentieth Century* (rev. edn., London, 2010).

Saunier, Pierre-Yves, 'Sketches from the Urban Internationale: voluntary societies, international organizations and US foundations at the city's bedside, 1900–1960', *International Journal for Urban and Regional Research*, 25 (2001), 380–403.

Schivelbusch, Wolfgang, *Eine Ruine im Krieg der Geister: Die Bibliothek von Löwen, August 1914 bis Mai 1940* (Frankfurt, 1993).

Schneider, Michael, *Die christlichen Gewerkschaften 1894–1933* (Bonn, 1982).

Scholliers, Peter, 'The social-democratic world of consumption: the path-breaking case of the Ghent cooperative Vooruit prior to 1914', *International Labor and Working-Class History*, 55 (1999), 79–91.

——, 'An essay on the internationalisation and representation of Brussels, 1800–2000', in Els Witte and Ann Mares (eds), *19 Keer Brussels* (Brussels, 2001), pp. 497–515.

Schott, Linda, *Reconstructing Women's Thoughts: The Women's International League for Peace and Freedom Before World War II* (Stanford, CA, 1997).

Schroeder-Gudehus, Brigitte, 'Challenge to transnational loyalties: international scientific organizations after the First World War', *Science Studies*, 3 (1973), 93–118.

Schroeder-Gudehus, Brigitte and Anne Rasmussen, *Les Fastes du progrès: le guide des expositions universelles 1851–1992* (Paris, 1992).

Schwarzenbach, Alexis, *Portraits of the Nation: Stamps, Coins and Banknotes in Belgium and Switzerland, 1880–1945* (Bern, 1999).

Seibert, Julia, 'Travail Libre ou Travail Forcé? Die "Arbeiterfrage" im belgischen Kongo 1908–1930', *Journal of Modern European History*, 7 (2009), 93–108.

Sluga, Glenda, *The Nation, Psychology, and International Politics, 1870–1919* (Basingstoke, 2006).

Smart, Judith, '"Poor little Belgium" and Australian popular support for war, 1914–1915', *War and Society*, 12 (1994), 27–46.

Sonne, Wolfgang, *Representing the State: Capital City Planning in the Early Twentieth Century* (Munich, 2003).

Spear, Sheldon, 'Pacifist radicalism in the post-war British Labour Party: the case of E. D. Morel, 1919–1924', *International Review of Social History*, 23 (1978), 193–223.

Speeckaert, Georges, *Le Premier siècle de la coopération internationale 1815–1914: l'apport de la Belgique* (Brussels, 1980).

Spiermann, Ole, '"Who attempts too much does nothing well": the 1920s Advisory Committee of Jurists and the statute of the Permanent Court of International Law', *British Yearbook of International Law*, 73 (2002), 187–260.

Stanard, Matthew, *Selling the Congo: A History of European Pro-Empire Propaganda and the Making of Belgian Imperialism* (Lincoln, NE, 2012).

Stargardt, Nicholas, *The German Idea of Militarism: Radical and Socialist Critics, 1866–1914* (Cambridge, 1994).

Steiner, Zara, *The Lights That Failed: European International History, 1919–1933* (Oxford, 2004).

Stengers, Jean, *Emigration et immigration en Belgique au XIXe et au XXe siècles* (Brussels, 1978).

——, 'La Belgique, un foyer de dreyfusime', *RBPH–BTFG*, 82 (2004), 359–76.

——, *Congo: mythes et réalités* (Brussels, 2005).

Stengers, Jean (ed.), *Bruxelles: croissance d'une capitale* (Brussels, 1979).

Stengers, Jean and Eliane Gubin, *Le Grand Siècle de la nationalité belge: de 1830 à 1918* (Brussels, 2002).

Stengers, Jean and W. Roger Louis (eds), *E. D. Morel's History of the Congo Reform Movement* (Oxford, 1968).

Stevenson, David, 'Battlefield or barrier? Rearmament and military planning in Belgium, 1902–1914', *International History Review*, 29 (2007), 473–507.

Storm, Eric, *The Culture of Regionalism: Art, Architecture and International Exhibitions in France, Germany and Spain, 1890–1939* (Manchester, 2011).

Strikwerda, Carl, *A House Divided: Catholics, Socialists and Flemish Nationalists in Nineteenth-Century Belgium* (Lanham, MD, 1997).

——, 'If all of Europe were Belgium: lessons in politics and globalization from one country', *BTNG–RBHC*, 35 (2005), 503–22.

Sutcliffe, Anthony, *Towards the Planned City: Germany, Britain, the United States and France 1780–1914* (Oxford, 1981).

Sutton, Michael, *Nationalism, Positivism and Catholicism: The Politics of Charles Maurras and French Catholics, 1890–1914* (Cambridge, 1982).

Temperley, Howard (ed.), *After Slavery: Emancipation and Its Discontents* (London, 2000).

Thomas, Mary Elizabeth, 'Anglo-Belgian military relations and the Congo question, 1911–1913', *Journal of Modern History*, 25 (1953), 157–65.

Tiedau, Ulrich, 'De Duitse cultuurpolitiek in België tijdens de Eerste Wereldoorlog', *BEG–CHTP*, 11 (2003), 21–45.

Tollebeek, Jo, 'At the crossroads of nationalism: Huizinga, Pirenne and the Low Countries in Europe', *European Review of History*, 17 (2010), 187–215.

——, 'The hyphen of national culture: the paradox of national distinctiveness in Belgium and the Netherlands, 1860–1918', *European Review*, 18 (2010), 207–25.

Tyssens, Jeffrey, 'Les associations de libre pensée pendant l'entre-deux-guerres', in Centre d'Action Laïque, *1789–1989: 200 ans de Libre Pensée en Belgique* (Charleroi, 1989), pp. 43–7.

Tyssens, Jeffrey and Els Witte, *De vrijzinnige traditie en België: van getolereerde tegencultuur tot erkende levensbeschouwing* (2nd edn., Brussels, 1996).

Uhlig, Ralph, *Die Interparlamentarische Union 1889–1914: Friedenssicherungsbemühungen im Zeitalter des Imperialismus* (Stuttgart, 1988).

——, 'Internationalismus in den zwanziger Jahren: die Interparlamentarische Union', *Historische Mitteilungen*, 4 (1991), 89–100.

Ungern-Sternberg, Jürgen von, *Der Aufruf "An die Kulturwelt!": Das Manifest der 93 und die Anfänge der Kulturpropaganda im Ersten Weltkrieg* (Stuttgart, 1996).

Van Acker, Wouter, 'Universalism as Utopia: a historical study of the schemes and schemas of Paul Otlet (1868–1944)' (PhD thesis, Ghent, 2012).

Van Alstein, Maarten, 'No more war? Belgian reception of the League of Nations and arbitration after the First World War', *Diplomacy and Statecraft*, 18 (2007), 133–53.

Van Daele, Jasmien, *Van Gent tot Genève: Louis Varlez. Een biografie* (Ghent, 2002).

——, 'Engineering social peace: networks, ideas, and the founding of the International Labour Organization', *International Review of Social History*, 50 (2005), 435–66.

Van Daele, Jasmien, Magaly Rodriguez Garcia, Geert Van Goethem and Marcel van der Linden (eds), *ILO Histories: Essays on the International Labour Organization and Its Impact on the World during the Twentieth Century* (Bern, 2010).

Van den Dungen, Pierre, *Milieux des presse et journalistes en Belgique (1828–1914)* (Brussels, 2005).

van den Heuvel, Charles, Boyd Rayward and Pieter Uyttenhove, 'L'Architecture du savoir: une recherche sur le Mundaneum et les précurseurs européens de l'Internet', *Transnational Associations*, 1–2 (2003), 16–23.

van der Linden, Marcel, *Transnational Labour History: Explorations* (Aldershot, 2003).

——, *Workers of the World: Essays Toward a Global Labour History* (Leiden, 2008).

van Diepen, Remco, *Voor volkenbond en vrede: Nederland en het streven naar een nieuwe wereldorde 1919–1946* (Amsterdam, 1999).

Van Ginderachter, Maarten, *Het rode vaderland: de vergeten geschiedenis van de communautaire spanningen in het Belgisch socialisme voor WO I* (Brussels, 2005).

Van Goethem, Geert, *The Amsterdam International: The World of the International Federation of Trade Unions (IFTU), 1913–1945* (Aldershot, 2006).

Van Haegendorn, Mieke, *Van werken krijg je vuile handen: de belgische werkliedenpartij 1914–1940* (Louvain, 1989).

van Holthoon, Frits and Marcel van der Linden (eds), *Internationalism in the Labour Movement, 1830–1940* (Leiden, 1988).

Van Offelen, Jacques and Jo Gerard, *Belgium: The World's Meeting Place* (Brussels, 1967).

Van Oostveldt, Bram and Stijn Bussels, 'De Antwerpse wereldtentoonstelling van 1894 als ambigu spektakel van de moderniteit', *Tijdschrift voor Geschiedenis*, 125 (2012), 4–19.

van Roon, Ger, *Small States in Years of Depression: The Oslo Alliance, 1930–1940* (Maastricht, 1989).

van Ypersele Laurence, *Le Roi Albert, histoire d'un mythe* (Ottignies, 1995).

Vandersmissen, Jan, *Koningen van de Wereld: Leopold II en de aardijkskundige beweging* (Leuven, 2009).

——, 'The king's most eloquent campaigner: Emile de Laveleye, Leopold II and the creation of the Congo Free State', *BTNG–RBHC,* 41 (2011), 7–57.

Vangansbeke, Jeannick, '"Comrades in arms?" Het diplomatieke streekspsiel tussen België en het Britse "Empire" tijdens de Groote Oorlog', *BTNG–RBHC*, 38 (2008), 131–58.

Vangroenweghe, Daniel, *Rood rubber: Leopold II en zijn Kongo* (Brussels, 1985).

Vanschoenbeek, Guy, *Novecento in Gent: de wortels van de sociaal-democratie en Vlaanderen* (Antwerp, 1995).

Vanthemsche, Guy, 'De belgische socialisten en Congo 1895–1960', *Brood en Rozen*, 2 (1999), 31–65.

——, *La Belgique et le Congo: empreintes d'une colonie 1885–1980* (Brussels, 2007).

Vellut, Jean-Luc (ed.), *La Mémoire du Congo: le temps colonial* (Tervuren, 2005).

Verbruggen, Christophe, 'Het egonetwerk van Reiner Leven en George Sarton als toegang tot transnationaal intellectueel engagement', *BTNG–RBHC*, 38 (2008), 87–129.

——, *Schrijverschap in het Belgische belle époque: een sociaal-culturele geschiedenis* (Ghent, 2009).

——, 'Hoe literair internationalisme organisieren? De "vervlochten" geschiedenis van de Belgische PEN-club (1922–1931), *Nederlandse Letterkunde*, 16 (2011), 152–81.

Verbruggen, Christophe and Lewis Pyenson, 'History and the history of science in the work of Hendrik de Man', *BTNG–RBHC*, 41 (2011), 487–511.

Verhoeven, Joe, 'Charles De Visscher: living and thinking international law', *European Journal of International Law*, 11 (2000), 887–904.

Vertovec, Steven and Robin Cohen (eds), *Conceiving Cosmopolitanism: Theory, Context and Practice* (Oxford, 2003).

Verucci, Guido, *L'Italia laica prima e dopo l'unità 1848–1876: Anticlericalismo, libero pensiero e ateismo nelle società italiana* (Rome, 1981).

Viaene, Vincent, *Belgium and the Holy See from Gregory XVI to Pius X, 1831–1859: Catholic Revival, Society and Politics in 19th-Century Europe* (Brussels, 2001).

——, 'International history, religious history, Catholic history: perspectives for cross-fertilization (1830–1945)', *European History Quarterly*, 38 (2008), 578–607.

——, 'King Leopold's imperialism and the origins of the Belgian Colonial Party, 1860–1905', *Journal of Modern History*, 80 (2008), 741–90.

Viaene, Vincent (ed.), *The Papacy and the New World Order: Vatican Diplomacy, Catholic Opinion and International Politics at the Time of Leo XIII* (Brussels, 2005).

Viaene, Vincent, David Van Reybrouck and Bambi Ceuppens (eds), *Congo in België: Koloniale cultuur in de metropol* (Leuven, 2009).

Vijgen, Ingeborg, *Tussen mandaat en kolonie: Rwanda, Burundi en het Belgische bestuur in opdracht van de Volkenbond (1916–1932)* (Leuven, 2005).

Viré, Liliane, 'La "Cité scientifique" du Parc Léopold à Bruxelles. 1890–1920', *Cahiers Bruxellois*, xix (1974), 86–180.

Vos, Louis and Kas Deprez (eds), *Nationalism in Belgium: Shifting Identities, 1780–1945* (Basingstoke, 1995).

Vossoughian, Nader, 'The language of the world museum: Otto Neurath, Paul Otlet, Le Corbusier', *Transnational Associations*, 1/2 (2003), 82–93.

Voyé, Liliane, Karel Dobbelaere, Jean Rémy and Jaak Billiet (eds), *La Belgique et ses dieux: Eglises, mouvements, religieux et laïques* (Louvain-la-Neuve, 1985).

Watson, D. R., 'Jean Pelissier and the Office Central des Nationalités, 1912–1919', *English Historical Review*, 110 (1995), 1191–206.

Wauters, Karel, *Wagner en Vlaanderen 1844–1914* (Ghent, 1983).

Webster, Andrew, 'The transnational dream: politicians, diplomats and soldiers in the League of Nations' pursuit of international disarmament, 1920–1938', *Contemporary European History*, 14 (2005), 493–518.

Weindling, Paul (ed.), *International Health Organisations and Movements, 1918–1939* (Cambridge, 1995).

Wilmers, Annika, *Pazifismus in der internationalen Frauenbewegung (1914–1920): Handlungsspielräume, politische Konzeptionen und gesellscahftliche Auseinandersetzungen* (Essen, 2008).

Wils, Kaat, *De omweg van de wetenschap: Het positivisme en de Belgische en Nederlandsche intellectuelle cultuur, 1845–1914* (Amsterdam, 2005).

Wils, Lode, *Het Daenisme* (Leuven, 1969).

——, *Van Clovis tot Di Rupo: de lange weg van de naties in de Lage Landen* (Antwerp, 2005).

——, *Van de belgische naar de Vlaamse natie: een geschiedenis van de Vlaamse beweging* (Leuven, 2009).

Wilson, Trevor, 'Lord Bryce's investigation into alleged German atrocities in Belgium', *Journal of Contemporary History*, 14 (1979), 369–83.

Winock, Michel, *La Belle Époque: la France de 1900 à 1914* (Paris, 2002).

Winter, Jay, *Dreams of Peace and Freedom: Utopian Moments in the Twentieth Century* (New Haven, CT, 2006).

Witte, Els, Eliane Gubin, Jean-Pierre Nandrin and Gita Deneckere, *Nouvelle Histoire de Belgique, I: 1830–1905* (Brussels, 2005).

Wörner, Martin, *Vergnügung und Belehrung: Volkskultur auf den Weltausstellungen 1851–1900* (Münster, 1999).

Wynants, Maurits, *Des Ducs de Brabant aux villages Congolais: Tervuren et l'Exposition Coloniale de 1897* (Tervuren, 1997).

Zimmermann, Susan, *GrenzÜberschreitungen: Internationale Netzwerke, Organisationen, Bewegungen und die Politik der globalen Ungleichheit vom 17. bis zum 21. Jahrhundert* (Vienna, 2010).

Index